The European Union

The European Union

A Polity of States and Peoples

Walter van Gerven

STANFORD UNIVERSITY PRESS, CALIFORNIA 2005

Stanford University Press
Stanford, California
© 2005 by the Board of Trustees of the
Leland Stanford Junior University

Printed in the United States of America

Library of Congress Cataloging-in-Publication Data

Gerven, W. van (Walter)
    The European Union : A polity of states and peoples / Walter van Gerven.
    p. cm.
    Includes bibliographical references and index.
    ISBN 0-8047-5063-7 (cloth : alk. paper) — 0-8047-5064-5 (pbk. : alk. paper)
    1. Europe—Politics and government—21st century.   2. European Union.   I. Title.

D2009.G475   2005
341.242'2—dc22   2004026677

This book is printed on acid-free, archival-quality paper.

Original printing 2005

Last figure below indicates year of this printing:
14   13   12   11   10   09   08   07   06   05

Typeset at Stanford University Press in 10/13 Minion

Acknowledgments

I owe my thanks to many. Thanks in the first place to Gerhard Casper, President emeritus of Stanford University, and David Holloway, former director of the Stanford Institute for International Studies, as well as to Chip Blacker and Stephen Krasner, the current Director and Deputy Director of the Institute, for their hospitality during my stay at the Institute from January to June 2003, and again from January to March 2004, and for having introduced me to Stanford's intellectual community. Thanks also to Klas Bergman, Mary Ellen Horwath, Ingrid Deiwiks, Anne Marie Kodama, and Raphaël Fleishman for their help to make Frieda's stay and mine agreeable. The chance to work in one of the world's leading centers of excellence has given me the opportunity to discover some of the many parallels that exist between the United States and the European Union and that have not attracted enough attention of researchers on both sides of the Atlantic, or at least not the attention of legal experts.

My thanks go also to Piet Eeckhout, Director of the Centre of European Law at King's College, London, who invited me to give four lectures on European constitutionalism in December 2003, and who chaired the first lecture. Thanks also to Lord Slynn of Hadley, Lord Hope of Craighead, and Lord Justice Sedley, who kindly agreed to chair the three following lecture meetings. Their comments, and those of the participants, many of them colleagues from King's College, offered me a second look at my subject.

Much appreciation goes to those who helped me turn this manuscript into readable English: to Christopher Brown of King's College, London, and to Carrie Simons of Stanford University, who not only improved the style of the text but also drew my attention to points of substance that required revision; and to Kathleen Gutman of Leuven University, who helped me with last-minute changes. Thanks as well to Eugene Mazo of Stanford University, who drew my attention to literature I needed to read, and to Alan Isenberg and André Vanier, both of Stanford University, who gave me their support. I thank all of them for their friendship. My appreciation also extends to the students in the class on European Union law that I taught at Stanford Law School in 2003 and in the Stanford International Relations Program in 2004.

My thanks for help and advice are due to many friends and colleagues, especially Deirdre Curtin of Utrecht University, Takis Tridimas of Queen Mary College, London, Antoon Herpels, René Foqué, and Jan Wouters of Leuven University, and Christophe Crombez of Leuven and Stanford University. I am also particularly grateful to the members of the work group of the Center on Democracy, Development, and the Rule of Law, Stanford Institute for International Studies, Gerhard Casper, Helen Stacy, Erik Jensen, and Allen Weiner, who allowed me to participate in their Tuesday morning breakfast meetings.

I owe a particular debt to Richard Hart of Hart Publishing Oxford and Amanda Moran of Stanford University Press, who made it possible for the book to be published in both the United Kingdom and the United States. I also thank the anonymous reviewers who pointed to several shortcomings of the first manuscript and encouraged me to improve (and, in the process, expand) the book.

I am especially indebted to Linda Mees who took care of this manuscript, as she did numerous earlier manuscripts.

The book could not have been written without the enduring patience of Frieda, who suffered the many inconveniences that partners suffer when their spouses embark on a time-consuming project.

Contents

Preface

In May 1940, when I was five years old, I watched the first of the German soldiers arrive in my hometown of Sint-Niklaas, near Antwerp in Belgium. In
September 1944, I saw the last German soldier, pistol in hand and hatred on
his face, leave Sint-Niklaas the day before British, Canadian, and Polish troops
liberated it. These events deeply affected the men and women of my generation, and motivated them to change history.

In July 1957, I took my law degree at the University of Leuven. This was
five years after the creation of the European Coal and Steel Community. This
Community united six countries: France, Germany, Italy, and the three
Benelux countries, Belgium, the Netherlands, and Luxembourg, in an effort to
overcome the past and to build a new future. On March 25, 1957, just before I
completed my law studies, the same six countries signed the Treaty establishing the European Economic Community in Rome. The Community came
into existence on January 1, 1958. Since then, I have witnessed one of the most
remarkable historic events of the last few centuries: the emergence of a steadily
enlarging European Union of states and peoples. This Union currently has
twenty-five Member States and will soon expand to twenty-eight.

In the years since the Community was established I have had the privilege
of working with American colleagues, starting as a young associate in the newly created Brussels office of Clearly Gottlieb and serving as a teaching assistant
for Max Rheinstein at the University of Chicago from 1959 to 1960, and then as
his successor for one year in 1968–69. Max Rheinstein was one of the great
comparative lawyers who escaped the European continent to begin a new life
in the United States. He devoted his career to familiarizing American students
with European law, and European students with American law.

The development of a united Europe has shaped my professional life, both
as an academic and as a practicing lawyer in different positions—as a barrister,

as President of the Belgian Banking Commission, and as Advocate General at the European Court of Justice. Forty years of teaching have given me the opportunity to introduce many hundreds of students to European Community law. All these years Europe has been my motivation to carry on, and to share with as many people as possible the opportunity of gradually transforming the European subcontinent into a political unity, and giving it a new peaceful future and a new supranational identity.

When CBS reporter Dan Rather was interviewed by CNN's anchorman Aaron Brown during the war in Iraq, I heard him say that of course he wanted the United States to win that war, but that this did not prevent him from being objective. That is exactly how I feel about explaining to Americans, and Europeans, what Europe is about. Even though I deeply believe in the necessity of building a united Europe, I owe the readers of this book an objective account of Europe's successes and shortcomings. This is what I tried to do in the four public lectures that I delivered in the spring of 2003, as the Arthur and Mark Payne Distinguished Lecturer at the Institute of International Studies at Stanford University.

I am very grateful to the Payne family and to Stanford University for this great experience. More particularly, I am grateful to Gerhard Casper and to David Holloway for inviting me to give these lectures. The periods Frieda and I spent at Stanford in 2003 and 2004 were some of the most rewarding of our lives. Our stay in 2003 was also a most instructive period, as it took place during the war in Iraq when tensions developed between and within the Western countries even while a constitutional convention in Brussels was reflecting on the future of Europe. It was during this period that the United States of America and the European Union discovered how similar and how different they truly are. However real these differences may prove to be, we are nevertheless bound to work together for a better and safer world.

Walter van Gerven
Stanford, 2004

Abbreviations

All ER	All England Law Reports
Am.J.Comp.L.	*American Journal of Comparative Law*
Amsterdam Treaty	Treaty of Amsterdam amending the Treaty on European Union, signed on October 2, 1997, and entered into force on May 1, 1999
CFI	Court of First Instance
CFSP	Common Foreign and Security Policy
CMLRev.	*Common Market Law Review*
Colum.L.Rev.	*Columbia Law Review*
Cornell Int.l. L.J.	*Cornell International Law Journal*
Draft Constitution	Draft Treaty Establishing a Constitution for Europe submitted to the European Council meeting in Thessaloniki on June 20, 2003
EAEC	European Atomic Energy Community; also, when following number of treaty provision, Treaty Establishing the European Atomic Energy Community (Euratom), signed in Rome on March 25, 1957, and entered into force on January 1, 1958
EC	European Community; also, when following number of treaty provision, European Community Treaty (formerly EEC Treaty; see EEC)
ECB	European Central Bank
ECHR	European Convention for the Protection of Human Rights and Fundamental Freedoms signed in Rome on November 4, 1950, and entered into force on September 3, 1953

ECJ	European Court of Justice
ECLR	*European Competition Law Review*
ECSC	European Coal and Steel Community; also, when following number of treaty provision, Treaty Establishing the European Coal and Steel Community signed in Paris on April 18, 1951, entered into force on July 23, 1952, and expired on July 23, 2002
ECtHR	European Court of Human Rights
EEC	European Economic Community; also, when following number of treaty provision, Treaty Establishing the European Economic Community signed in Rome on March 25, 1957, and entered into force on January 1, 1958 (now EC Treaty, as renamed by the EU or Maastricht Treaty: see EC)
EHRR	European Human Rights Reports
EJML	*European Journal of Migration and Law*
ELJ	*European Law Journal*
ELRev.	*European Law Review*
EP	European Parliament
EPL	*European Public Law*
ESCB	European System of Central Banks
EU	European Union; also, when following number of treaty provision, European Union (or Maastricht) Treaty
European Convention	The European Convention on the Future of Europe convened by the European Council meeting in Laeken, Belgium, on December 14–15, 2001
Hast.L.J.	*Hastings Law Journal*
IGL	Intergovernmental Conference
JEPP	*Journal of European Public Policy*
JLS	*Journal of Law and Society*
JTDE	*Journal des Tribunaux. Droit européen*
Maastricht Treaty	Treaty of Maastricht, or European Union Treaty (see also EU), signed on February 7, 1992, and entered into force on November 1, 1993
MEP	Member of the European Parliament

MJ	*Maastricht Journal of European and Comparative Law*
MP	Member of Parliament
NGO	Non-governmental Organization
Nice Treaty	Treaty of Nice amending the EU, EC, EAEC, and ECSC Treaties, signed on February 26, 2001, and entered into force on February 1, 2003
NJB	*Nederlands Juristenblad*
NJW	*Neue Juristische Wochenschrift*
OJ	*Official Journal of the European Communities*
OMC	Open method of coordination
PJCC	Police and Judicial Cooperation in Criminal Matters
PL	Public Law
PM	prime minister
QMV	qualified majority voting
RDP	*Revue du Droit Public*
RFDA	*Revue Française du Droit Administratif*
SEA	Single European Act, signed on February 17, 1986, and entered into force on July 1, 1987
Stan.J.Int'l.L.	*Stanford Journal of International Law*
U.Ill.L.Rev.	*University of Illinois Law Review*

Introduction

The aim of this book is twofold. First, it attempts to explain the European Union (EU) as it currently exists, how the Union will be if the Treaty establishing a Constitution for Europe (now submitted for the ratification procedure) is adopted by the twenty-five Member States, and how it may evolve thereafter. Second, it aims to show how the distinctive features of a democratic polity that characterize the Member States can be gradually transplanted to the European Union. The book is written from a legal perspective, though I will make many references to political science and recent history. It attempts to explain to a general audience how the Union's complex structure operates. To make the book useful to a more specialized subset of the public as well, it contains a large number of notes with detailed information that point to additional reading on a variety of topics. Because I wrote the book with a diverse readership from both sides of the Atlantic in mind, and as it was actually written at both Stanford and Leuven, the book regularly compares the European and the American political scenes and draws on sources from both sides of the ocean.

The book is not about the EU's obvious successes: its establishment of a common internal or single market with economic freedoms, its external trade and competition policies, and its monetary union. In addition, the book will no more than occasionally deal with the Union's growth from the six original Member States to its most recent enlargement to twenty-five Member States, which took effect on May 1, 2004. It focuses instead on lesser-known aspects of the Union, including how "Europe" was gradually transformed from a technocratic organization into an ever-closer union of states and peoples with a growing democratic legitimacy. This process of democratic growth has been underway for more than half a century, from the European Community's modest beginnings in 1952 as the European Coal and Steel Community to the creation in 1992 of the European Union, which now encompasses all economic and many non-economic sectors and is steadily developing into a democratic political entity.

The proposition underlying the book is that the most appropriate way to turn the Union into a full-fledged "body politic"—a polity of states and peoples[1]—is to replicate, at Union level, the parliamentary form of government, which is familiar to all of the Member States in one way or another, rather than to invent a new doctrine of democratic legitimacy. That does *not* imply, however, that the Union should become a large nation-state. Even if the European peoples and governments did wish to go in that direction, which I doubt, the Union would be better off evolving into a "citizen-state" rather than a "nation-state," that is, into a political entity in which nationalistic feelings are left behind. These feelings, and the concept of the nation-state, have been associated with one of Europe's darkest eras. Consequently, calling the Union a citizen state (or, rather, a polity of states *and* citizens) reflects the Union's desire to adhere to a new political arrangement: a supranational community increasingly characterized by "a sense of common belonging among those who share civic institutions, with no exclusiveness towards any person or group willing to participate in them."[2]

The book is divided into seven chapters. The first is an introductory chapter in which I describe the EU's institutions and explore the Union's identity and values. In the second and the third chapters, two distinctive features of democratic government are examined: accountability of government and adherence to the rule of law. In chapter 4, I deal with the concept of good governance, which is the exercise of public power to pursue citizens' goals in accordance with proper procedures and with equal concern for citizens and residents. In chapter 5, I discuss civic responsibility, open government, and citizen

---

[1] The title of the book, *The European Union: A Polity of States and Peoples*, refers to the special character of the Union, which, from the outset, has been built on a succession of treaties concluded by the Member States and with the assent of the peoples of Europe—not only as a result of the ratification of these treaties in accordance with each Member State's constitutional requirements but also, increasingly, with the peoples' involvement in the Union's legislative process through their directly elected European representatives. See further chapter 1. For a discussion of this development within the context of the draft Treaty establishing a Constitution for Europe (dealt with in chapter 6), see Koen Lenaerts and Damien Gerard, "The Structure of the Union According to the Constitution for Europe: The Emperor Is Getting Dressed," 29 *ELRev.*, 2004, 289–322.

[2] See Neil MacCormick, *Questioning Sovereignty: Law, State, and Nation in the European Commonwealth* (Oxford: Oxford University Press, 1999), 170. See also J. H. H. Weiler, "Europe: The Case Against the Case for Statehood," 4 *ELJ*, 1998, 43–62, at 62. See further chapter 1, pp. 40–41.

participation. In chapter 6 the proposed Constitution for Europe is described and analyzed, and in chapter 7 the form of government Europe may wish to take in the future is examined. I conclude the book with a short epilogue indicating the most recent constitutional developments, that is, those that have occurred since the completion of this manuscript, and briefly describing the Union's relationship with its neighbors—a subject that I intended to discuss in an additional chapter 8, if space had permitted me to do so.

As mentioned, the proposition underlying this book is that it is advisable for the Union to become a full-fledged democratic political entity by the replication of the Member States' political systems at the EU level. Though this may seem a bold proposition, it is not really a controversial one. Indeed, it can hardly be disputed that a government that is accountable, open, and in compliance with the rule of law, as the Member States' democracies are (themes that will be discussed in chapters 2, 3, and 5), is the sort of government that would enhance the Union's democratic legitimacy. The same holds true for good governance and the goals that it implies: a commitment to ethics and the pursuit of efficiency, equal treatment, and affirmative action to reduce disparities, themes that will be examined in chapter 4. Obviously, the content of each of these instruments is uncertain, and I will attempt to define their content within the European Union. The most controversial point in that regard is whether, and to what extent, social policy is part of good governance. The point is not disputed among the EU Member States, all of which accept that a comprehensive social security system is closely associated with the concept of *Rechtsstaat,* or rule of law. It is, however, a controversial point in comparing the EU to the United States, where the pursuit of social welfare is not generally considered to be part of good governance.

The themes discussed in chapters 6 and 7, constitution making and form of government, relate, respectively, to the question of whether the legislative and institutional revisions embodied in the draft Constitution for Europe turn the Union into a more integrated and a more democratic political entity (chapter 6), and to the question—which was not discussed in the Convention preparing the draft—of which form of government the Union should take in the future (chapter 7). In both these respects, the underlying proposition is, again, that democratic legitimacy in the Union should be achieved in accordance with a system of checks and balances comparable to (albeit more complicated than) the one existing in the Member States, and that preference should be given to a parliamentary form of government (rather than a presidential one), which is the one adopted by most of the twenty-five Member States.

The book originated as a series of public lectures given at the Stanford Institute for International Studies in March and April of 2003 and at the Centre of European Law at King's College, London, in December 2003. Both series of lectures gave me the opportunity to better understand the implications of the Union's democratic legitimacy. However, the redrafting of the text of these lectures for publication expanded my subject matter. Whereas the focus was first on executive accountability, it gradually shifted toward democratic legitimacy as a whole. The drafting has not been an easy process, not the least because writing a book in a language other than the author's mother tongue remains a delicate undertaking, and it confronts the author with the reality that form and substance are very much related. Moreover, the subject of the book is not one I was familiar with when I started to prepare the lectures. Writing the book has therefore been as much a learning process for me as it might be for the readers.

One last point concerning terminology: As chapter 1 will discuss, the European Union (EU) currently consists of three pillars, the first of which encompasses primarily the European Community (EC). Hereinafter I will use the term European Community (EC) when I am referring specifically to matters regulated under the provisions of the EC Treaty, that is, the first pillar of the European Union, and I will use the term European Union (EU) when I refer to provisions in the EU Treaty regulating the Union as a whole (that is, the three pillars taken together) or regulating specific matters falling under the second or third pillars. The situation is even more confusing than it appears because some EU institutions, such as the EU Commission and the EU Council of Ministers, refer to themselves as EU institutions, while the two EU courts, the European Court of Justice and the Court of First Instance, still refer to themselves as EC or Community courts (as I will mostly do hereinafter).[3] Moreover, it is necessary to distinguish the two Community courts, which are located in Luxembourg, from the European Court of Human Rights (ECtHR), which is located in Strasbourg. The ECtHR belongs to a different European organization, called the Council of Europe, and is founded on the European Convention on Human Rights (ECHR). The ECtHR is responsible for most of the human rights case law discussed in the following chapters.

The book is up to date as of April 15, 2004. However, in the epilogue (and occasionally in the text, or in the footnotes) I refer to events that have taken place after that date. Moreover, the draft Constitution for Europe (described in chapter 6 and mentioned in other chapters as well) was amended by the June 18, 2004 IGC meeting in Brussels and, before being solemnly signed at

---

[3] The reason for this is that the Community courts have no, or only limited, jurisdiction in matters falling under the second and third pillars: see chapter 1, pp. 118–21.

the October 29, 2004 IGC meeting in Rome, was revised by linguists and law-yers. Part of the revision process was the renumbering of the articles, which was carried out as follows: the articles in the four parts of the final constitu-tional text, as signed in Rome and submitted for ratification to the Member States, are now numbered continuously and not, as in the initial version, starting from 1 again for each of the four parts.[4] However, the division into four parts is still reflected in the numbering by the use of roman numerals (I, II, III, and IV) alongside the arabic article numbers. To make it easy for the reader to find the renumbered (and sometimes reworded) articles in the final text, I give the new numbers in square brackets each time an article of the ini-tial version is mentioned in the text or the footnotes.

When the book is published, in early 2005, the draft Constitutional treaty will not yet have entered into force. Indeed, in the most optimistic scenario that will not happen before 2007, that is, provided that all twenty-five Member States have ratified the text in accordance with their constitutional require-ments, as foreseen in Article IV-8 of the initial version [now Article IV-447] of the draft.[5] Even after the draft Constitution does enter into effect (if ever), this book will remain of interest to those who wish to know how the European in-stitutional system has evolved over the last fifty years, and the directions it may take in the future, with or without constitutional text, in order to become a more perfect union in terms of democratic legitimacy.

[4] The final text of the proposed Treaty establishing a Constitution for Europe, as signed by the heads of state or government in their meeting at Rome on October 29, 2004, is contained in document CIG 87/1/04, REV 1, of October 13, 2004. The thirty-six protocols and annexes I and II annexed to the Treaty are contained in Addendum I, of the same date, to CIG 87/1/04, REV 1, and the forty-eight declarations annexed to the Treaty are contained in Addendum II, dated October 25, 2004, to CIG 87/1/04 REV 2. They can all be found at http://www.europa.eu.int/constitution/constitution_en.htm.

[5] On what might happen to the draft Constitution if it were not ratified by all Member States, and therefore would not enter into effect, see Bruno de Witte, "The Process of Ratification and the Crisis Options: A Legal Perspective," forthcoming (lec-ture held in The Hague at the Asser Colloquium on 13–16 October 2004).

CHAPTER ONE

The European Union's Institutions, Identity, and Values

I. THE EUROPEAN UNION IN A NUTSHELL

Explaining fifty years of European Union history is a daunting task. In this introductory chapter I will focus first on Union pillars, institutions, and competences, and on differences in integration (Section I); second on the nature of a European "body politic," and on the emergence of a European public space and public opinion (Section II); and third on European values (Section III). Toward the end of this chapter I will draw some conclusions (Section IV).

Three Pillars under One Roof

The European construction emerged in 1952 with six countries: France, Germany, Italy, and the three Benelux countries (Belgium, the Netherlands, and Luxembourg). Together, on April 18, 1951, in Paris, these nations concluded the treaty establishing the European Coal and Steel Community (ECSC) for a period of fifty years, which entered into force on July 23, 1952, and expired in July 2002. Six years later in Rome, on March 25, 1957, the treaty establishing the European Economic Community (EEC, now EC) and the treaty establishing the European Atomic Energy Community (EAEC) were both concluded for an unlimited period and entered into force on January 1, 1958. Together these treaties formed the three communities. By far the most important of these three was the European Economic Community, which created, progressively, a common market of goods, persons, services, and capital subject to free competition and with a common commercial policy, and which was applicable to all economic sectors (including agriculture and transport) not addressed by the other two treaties.

These communities were gradually enlarged, the two existing ones (EC and EAEC) currently comprising (as of May 1, 2004) twenty-five Member

States. Moreover, the European Economic Community (EEC) was broadened in scope, first by the Single European Act of February 1986, which improved the functioning of the common market and laid down a timetable for the achievement of the so-called "internal market"—defined in Article 14 (2) EC as "an area without internal frontiers in which the free movement of goods, persons, services and capital is ensured." Later, in the 1990s, further steps were taken to intensify European integration in the monetary and political fields. This evolution took forty years and led, on February 7, 1992, to the signing by the (then) twelve Member States of the Treaty on European Union (EU, or Maastricht, Treaty).[1] As a result of both the Single Act and the EU Treaty, a variety of new competencies were conferred upon the Community related to such diverse matters as social policy and employment, research and technological development, the environment, culture and education, public health and consumer protection, economic and social cohesion, and development cooperation. However, the most dramatic addition to the EC "portfolio" was the insertion of a chapter on monetary policy, leading in the final stage to a single European currency. The amendments to the EC Treaty provided an institutional framework and a timetable for turning that policy into a monetary union.[2]

The EU Treaty entered into force on November 1, 1993, after ratification by all of the existing Member States.[3] It renamed the European Economic Community the European Community (EC), thus dropping the word "economic" in order to indicate that many non-economic matters had become part of its architecture. As mentioned above, it added the concept of a monetary union

[1] The EU Treaty is also known as the Maastricht Treaty, after the town in the Netherlands where it was signed. Names of towns have been used to refer to European treaties that were signed there since before Maastricht. Thus the ECSC Treaty has long been called the Treaty of Paris and the EEC and EAEC Treaties have often been referred to as the Treaties of Rome. Reference is made below to the Treaties of Amsterdam and Nice.

[2] For a historical perspective, see D. Wyatt and A. Dashwood, *European Law* (London: Sweet and Maxwell, 2000), chapter 18.

[3] As a result of ratification by the (then) Member States, treaty amendments become part of the so-called *acquis communautaire*. New states that wish to gain access to the Union will need to accept the existing *acquis communautaire* as a condition of accession. Although the concept remains imprecise, it is generally understood to include full acceptance of the rights and obligations attaching to the Union and its institutional framework and comprises the obligation for the Member States to ensure effective application of the *acquis* through appropriate administrative and judicial structures. See Christine Delcourt, "The *Acquis Communautaire*: Has the Concept Had Its Day?" 38 *CMLRev.*, 2001, 829–70.

with the creation of a European System of Central Banks (ESCB) and the European Central Bank (ECB), both in charge of conducting the Union's monetary policy.[4] It also added two "annexes" to the main Community "building": the Common Foreign and Security Policy (CFSP) and the Justice and Home Affairs (JHA), the latter now, as a result of later changes, known as Police and Judicial Cooperation in Criminal Matters (PJCC). In notorious Community jargon, the main "building" housing the three initial communities—the EC (formerly the EEC), the EAEC, and (until 2002, when it expired) the ECSC—is now called the first pillar of the European Union. The two "annexes," the CFSP and PJCC, are known as the second and third pillars, respectively.

This strange terminology was developed in the negotiations between the Member States for easy reference: the three components of the entire European construction were compared with the three pillars of a Greek temple supporting a common roof. That common roof, consisting of the common provisions in Title I of the EU Treaty, and the three pillars were, together, called the European Union (EU). Of these three pillars, the first—and particularly the European Community part thereof[5]—is the most supranational in nature, the other two pillars remaining more intergovernmental,[6] and is therefore also the pillar where the democratic legitimacy of the European construction is most developed. Hereinafter, reference will frequently be made to the "Community institutions" when discussing first-pillar matters, whereas I will refer to the "Union institutions" when second- or third-pillar matters are at issue, or when I refer to the European construction as a whole. The aforementioned common provisions in Title I of the EU Treaty contain the objectives of the Union (Article 2) and set out the structure of the Union's single institutional framework with special reference to the European Council (Articles 3–5). They also enumerate the principles on which the Union is founded (Article 6) and the procedure to be followed if a Member State were found to act in serious breach of those principles (Article 7). All of these matters will be dealt with later.

European Union literature makes frequent reference to the Treaties of Maastricht (1992), Amsterdam (1997), and Nice (2000), named after the town in which they were signed, in the Member State holding the presidency of the

[4] See n. 18 below.
[5] In this work, I will only exceptionally refer to the two other Community Treaties (the ECSC and the EAEC Treaty).
[6] See below, pp. 12–14 and 22; also pp. 58ff.

Council at the time of signature.[7] These treaties, and other acts agreed on between the Member States, such as the 1986 Single European Act, have
amended the three initial (or founding) Community Treaties—the 1951 Treaty
of Paris (ECSC) and the two 1957 Treaties of Rome (EEC and EAEC)—which
together constitute the first pillar of the Union. The most drastic change was
introduced by the Treaty of Maastricht, which, as mentioned, established the
European Union (including the monetary union) and created the three-pillar
system, while the most conspicuous change was introduced by the Treaty of
Amsterdam, which renumbered the articles, titles, and sections of the Treaty
on European Union (EU) and the European Community (EC) Treaty, and
deleted lapsed provisions of those treaties and of the ECSC and EAEC Treaties.
As for the Nice Treaty, it confirmed in a protocol the transfer of all assets and
liabilities of the ECSC, expiring on July 23, 2002, to the European Community
and stated that, except as otherwise provided, the provisions of the EC Treaty
shall apply from then on to coal and steel.

The most important achievement of the Nice Treaty, however, was the
political agreement reached, after a notoriously fractious summit meeting, on
the institutional questions relevant to the upcoming (May 2004) enlargement:
voting in the Council; composition of the Commission; and allocation of seats
in the European Parliament. Some of the arrangements were introduced as
legal amendments in a protocol on enlargement; others were simply set out in
a declaration on enlargement and were to be made binding upon accession of
the new Member States. Also important from a legal standpoint was the
(modest) reform of the Union's judicial system.[8]

How do the three pillars operate in relation with third countries (namely
countries that are not members of the EU)? An illustration of the difference
between the first pillar and the second and third pillars is the European Community's common commercial policy, which belongs to the first pillar
(Articles 131–34 EC), as compared with the European Union's foreign and security policy, which belongs to the second pillar (Articles 11–28 EU), and the
European Union's cooperation in criminal matters, which belongs to the third
pillar (Articles 29–42 EU). As for the first, the Community institutions have
exclusive powers to shape the Community's trade relations with third countries. This means that, in discussions with the United States about, for instance, the import into Europe of genetically modified food products, the

---

[7] See n. 1 above.

[8] As a result of the reform, it is possible for the Council to create judicial panels to
hear and determine at first instance certain classes of action in specific areas; see n. 16
below.

European commissioner for trade (currently Pascal Lamy) will be directly in touch with the United States trade representative (currently Robert Zoellick). Representatives of the European Community therefore also sit at the World Trade Organization in Geneva—together with representatives of the Member States sitting in their national capacities for matters for which the Community has no exclusive competence.[9] However, when foreign policy matters falling under the second pillar are to be discussed between the United States and the Union, the U.S. president and secretary of state will deal directly with the political leaders of the Member States, particularly with those sitting on the UN Security Council, as recent events have made abundantly clear. That is so, even though the Union has the competence to define and implement a common foreign and security policy (Article 11 EU) and may conclude international agreements with one or more third states or with international organizations (Article 24 EU). However, any such action requires unanimity on the part of all of the Member States, each one therefore possessing the power of veto. The same applies with respect to police and judicial cooperation in criminal matters, more particularly in view of combating organized crime and terrorism (Article 38 EU). I will return to the differences between pillars when discussing the institutions and their competences.

Completely separate from the European Union (including the European Community), there is another supranational European organization, called the Council of Europe, of which forty-five European states are now members, including all of the twenty-five EU Member States, as well as Russia and Turkey. The organization, based in Strasbourg,[10] was founded in 1949.[11] It concerns itself with all political, economic and social matters of European interest, and thus has a wider field of activity than the European Union. However, it does not have any power to make laws, and it can only propose non-binding resolutions and draft conventions for ratification by the participating states. The organization has a Committee of Ministers and a Parliamentary Assembly

---

[9] See further P. Craig and G. de Búrca, *EU Law, Text, Cases and Materials*, 3d ed. (Oxford: Oxford University Press, 2003), 128.

[10] Strasbourg also occasionally houses the European Union's Parliament, whose main meeting place is, however, in Brussels, which also houses the Council and the Commission. The Community courts and the Court of Auditors have their seats in Luxembourg. The European Central Bank is located in Frankfurt.

[11] The organization was established as a result of the European Congress of the Hague (May 7–10, 1948) chaired by Winston Churchill, who on September 19, 1946, in Zürich, had pronounced the famous words, "If we are to form a United States of Europe . . . we must begin now." On this immediate postwar history, see N. Davies, *Europe: A History* (London: Pimlico, 1996), 1064–67.

with advisory powers that is made up of delegates from the national parliaments. The most prominent institution of the organization is the European Court of Human Rights (ECtHR). That court applies the provisions of the European Convention for the Protection of Human Rights and Fundamental Freedoms (ECHR) of November 4, 1950.[12] It supervises the contracting states' compliance with the provisions of the Convention and annexed protocols, and can render judgments against a state holding that it has violated a Convention right. Cases can be brought before the court by a contracting state, but also by a private party or non-governmental organization. The EU itself is not a member of the Council of Europe, and is not submitted to the jurisdiction of the ECtHR.[13] However, according to Article 6 (2) EU, the Union "shall respect fundamental rights as guaranteed by the European Convention . . . and as they result from the constitutional traditions common to the Member States."[14]

EU Institutions and Their Competences under the Three Pillars

a)   The first pillar

The European Community contains three institutions engaged in general policy making: the European Commission ("the Commission"), the Council of Ministers ("the Council"), and the European Parliament ("Parliament"). Members of the first are proposed by the Member States; members of the second are ministerial-level representatives of the Member States; and members of the third are, since 1979, elected by direct universal suffrage in all Member States.[15] Besides those three, there are three sets of specialized institutions. The first, representing the judicial branch, consists of the two Community courts, the European Court of Justice (ECJ) and the Court of First Instance (CFI), each of which ensures, within its jurisdiction, that Community law is properly interpreted and observed.[16] A second specialized institution is the Court of

[12] For a short description, see M. Dixon, *Textbook on International Law*, 4th ed. (London: Blackstone Press, 2000, reprinted 2002), 337–40.

[13] Although the Union is not submitted to the jurisdiction of the ECtHR, its Member States are submitted to that Court's jurisdiction, even when they act in their capacity as EU members. This can obviously lead to conflicts of jurisdiction between the ECtHR and the Community courts. See further chapter 3, n. 112.

[14] The EU adopted its own, and broader, Charter of Fundamental Rights in 2000: see chapter 3, p. 123.

[15] On the Commission see Articles 211–19 EC, on the Council see Articles 202–10 EC, and on the European Parliament see Articles 189–201 EC.

[16] On the organization of the ECJ and CFI, see Articles 220–25a EC, as amended by the Nice Treaty, and the (new) Protocol on the Statute of the Court of Justice attached to that treaty. See also chapter 3, n. 25. On the proceedings that can be initiated before these courts, see Articles 226–45 EC, and chapter 3, p. 110. According to Article 225a EC,

Auditors, which examines the accounts of all revenue and expenditure of the Community.[17] Third, the European Central Bank (ECB) directs the European System of Central Banks (ESCB), which has autonomous powers in the monetary sector.[18]

All of the aforementioned institutions were designed to play a role under the first, or Community, pillar of the European Union. They play a more limited role (or no role, in the case of the ECB) under the second and third pillars of the Union, with the exception of the Council of Ministers. That Council, as we will see later, constitutes the prime law-making institution under the second and the third pillars, that is, in matters of foreign policy and security, and of police and judicial cooperation. In addition to the three aforementioned institutions, there is the European Council, sitting on top of the Union as a whole, which brings together, in regular summit meetings at least twice a year, the heads of state or government of the Member States and the president of the Commission. They are assisted by the ministers for foreign affairs of the Member States and one additional member of the Commission.[19] The task of the European Council is to "provide the Union with the necessary impetus for its development and . . . [to] define the general political guidelines thereof."[20] It oversees the three pillars but focuses particularly on the second and third

---

it is possible for the Council, acting at the request of the ECJ, to add a third layer of Community courts, so-called "judicial panels," which would hear at first instance certain classes of action, e.g., cases brought by Community civil servants against the employer institution. See Bo Vesterdorp, "The Community Court System Ten Years from Now and Beyond: Challenges and Possibilities," *ELRev.*, 2003, 303–23, at 312–14; also J.-V. Louis, "La fonction juridictionnelle de Nice à Rome," *JTDE*, 2003, 257–63, at 259.

[17] See Articles 246–48 EC Treaty. See also chapter 4, p. 167.

[18] On the monetary policy, and the monetary bodies, of the Community, see Articles 105–15 EC Treaty; and nn. 88 and 89 below. It may suffice to mention here that the ECB has a Governing Council that comprises the members of the Executive Board of the ECB and the governors of the national central banks: Article 112 (1) EC. The Member States that do not participate in the euro-zone (before the May 2004 accession, only Denmark, Sweden, and the United Kingdom; n. 89 below) are not a member of this governing structure but do nevertheless participate, with respect to matters affecting them, in the General Council of the ECB. That Council is set up by Article 45 of the Protocol on the Statute of the European System of Central Banks and of the European Central Bank attached to the Maastricht Treaty. See further S. Douglas-Scott, *Constitutional Law of the European Union* (Harlow: Longman, 2002), 99–101; also K. Lenaerts and P. Van Nuffel, *Constitutional Law of the European Union*, ed. R. Bray (London: Sweet and Maxwell, 1999), 345–48, and, by the same authors, *Europees recht in hoofdlijnen*, 3d ed. (Antwerp: Maklu, 2003), 564.

[19] Article 4 EU, second para.

[20] Article 4 EU, first para.

pillars as they relate to common foreign and security policy, and police and judicial cooperation, respectively.

Those readers used to the neat separation of power enshrined in the American Constitution (which vests the legislative power in Congress, the executive power in the president, and the judicial power in one Supreme Court and lower courts) might think that such powers are as neatly separated in the European Union.[21] But on the continent where John Locke and Baron de Montesquieu once resided, their teachings were never followed quite as well: that certainly holds true for the European Union in general, and the European Community in particular. Except for the judicial power, which is, indeed, in separate and independent hands, the legislative power in the Community is shared, and delicately balanced, between the Commission, the Council, and Parliament whereas the executive power is shared, and less delicately balanced, between the Commission and the Council. In other words, checks and balances—for which the European Court of Justice has coined the term "institutional balance"[22]—do exist in the European Union, but the Union, or Community, hardly incorporates the doctrine of separation of power. I will return to that subject in chapter 2 when highlighting the role of the executive in democratic government, but I will mention a few points here (primarily in connection with the first pillar) for a better understanding of what follows.

The first point concerns the exercise of legislative power, legislative procedures, and legislative instruments. The way in which legislative power is shared in the Community can be summarized in three propositions. First, generally the Commission, and only the Commission, has the right of initiative.[23] In

---

[21] I would note, incidentally, that under the U.S. Constitution the principle of separation of power is not strictly observed. The most important illustration of this check on powers is the president's veto power, under art. I, sec. 7, cl. 2 and 3, of the Constitution, which provides that "Every Bill" and "Every Order, Resolution, or Vote to which the Concurrence of the Senate and House of Representatives may be necessary" must be presented to the president, to be approved or disapproved: if the latter, a special majority of two-thirds is needed in both Houses to have the act passed. For further discussion on this topic, see N. Redlich, J. Attanasio, and J. K. Goldstein, *Understanding Constitutional Law*, 2d ed. (New York: Lexis Nexis), 147–49, where it is noted, at 148, that this provides the president with substantial leverage in the legislative process.

[22] ECJ, Case C-70/88, *European Parliament v. Council*, [1990] ECR I-2041, para. 21, where it is stated that the institutional balance is based on "a system for distributing powers among the different Community institutions, assigning to each institution its own role in the institutional structure of the Community and the accomplishment of the tasks entrusted to the Community."

[23] That follows from the various legislative procedures under the first pillar. See,

other words, no legislative act can be legally enacted if the Commission has not proposed it. Second, the Council adopts and enacts legislation proposed by the Commission. At the outset, the Council could only act by consensus, but now, in an ever-growing number of instances, it adopts legislation by so-called "qualified majority." Qualified majority voting gives Member States a number of votes in (a certain) proportion to their population, and implies that a minority of Member States can be outvoted in the Council.[24] Third, Parliament, which at the outset had only consultative powers, now has decisional legislative powers that have increased with successive treaty amendments—and will be further increased if the draft Constitution (discussed in chapter 6)[25] is adopted.

The Community's legislative power is exercised in accordance with complicated legislative procedures. The most important of these procedures is the "co-decision" procedure established in Article 251 EC, under which the Council exercises its legislative power in concert with Parliament. The procedure implies that legislation proposed by the Commission can only be adopted if approved by a majority in Parliament *and* by a qualified majority in the Council.[26] Notwithstanding its complexity, the procedure has functioned miraculously well, so well, in fact, that in the draft Constitution (discussed in chapter 6) it is proposed that the co-decision procedure be the standard legislative procedure. Besides the co-decision procedure, there are other legislative procedures in which Parliament is less involved, or not involved at all[27]—a situa-

---

for instance, Article 251 (2) EC. There are exceptions explicitly mentioned in one or another treaty article; see, for instance, Article 144 EC.

[24] See Article 205 (2) and (3) EC, where qualified majority decision making and the weighting of votes of Member States in the Council are defined. For a detailed discussion, see chapter 6, pp. 281–84.

[25] See below, pp. 280–81. "Draft Constitution" is the term used hereinafter for the draft Treaty Establishing a Constitution for Europe. The draft was prepared by the so-called European Convention on the Future of Europe (convened by the European Council at its meeting in Laeken, Belgium, on December 14–15, 2001) and submitted to the European Council meeting in Thessaloniki on June 20, 2003. On all this, see chapter 6.

[26] Generally Parliament shall act by an absolute majority of the votes cast, save where otherwise provided in the treaty: see Article 198 EC. Under Article 251 EC, Parliament must sometimes act by an absolute majority of its component members: see, e.g., Article 251 (2) EC under (b) and (c), as opposed to Article 251 (5) EC, where a majority of the votes cast is prescribed. As for the Council, it shall generally act by a majority of its members, save as otherwise provided in the treaty: see Article 205 (1) EC. There are, however, many instances in which the Council acts by qualified majority, as under Article 251 (2), (3), and (5) EC.

[27] Craig and de Búrca, n. 9 above, distinguish six major types of procedure, Parliament being involved in three of them (pp. 139–50). See further chapter 6, p. 280.

tion that is considered to be the essence of the Community's so-called "democratic deficit."[28] For now, it may suffice to point out that the EC Treaty stipulates, in different articles, which one of the existing legislative procedures is to be used in any given policy area.

In the past the co-decision procedure has allowed for the passage of many binding legislative acts, mainly regulations and directives. Regulations and directives are the usual legislative instruments to produce binding Community law. The former are binding in their entirety and directly applicable in all Member States; the latter are binding upon the Member States as to the result to be achieved, leaving it to the Member States' authorities to choose the form and methods of implementation and which choice they must make within the period of time prescribed in the directive concerned.[29] Regulations and directives are not only enacted as a result of the co-decision procedure, but may also be the result of the other legislative procedures, and may even be passed by the Commission, acting alone in its executive capacity. In other words, currently, there is no hierarchy of norms in Community law (a matter that the draft Constitution would change).[30]

The preceding brings us to a second subject, which is the role of Parliament. As mentioned previously, that role is currently limited because of the necessity for Parliament to exercise its legislative power in concert with the Council. The reason why the Council—composed, as we have seen, of Member State ministers and therefore in their own state members of the executive branch—plays such a prominent role in the Community's legislative branch lies in the technocratic past of the Community. For much of the 1950s, '60s, and '70s, the Community as an institution had jurisdiction only over economic, and highly technical, matters, mainly in sectors such as coal and steel, agriculture, transport, and commercial policy. In these matters technical expertise was in greater demand than democratic accountability. This has changed over the years with the addition of spheres of competence that, like consumer and environmental protection and, even more so, culture and education, are of great concern to the average citizen. As a result, to enhance the legitimacy of the Community in those matters, but also in all others—that is, as the expression goes, to bring Europe "as closely as possible to the citizen"[31]—Parliament became directly

---

[28] On the different features of "democratic deficit," see Craig and de Búrca, n. 9 above, 167–75. Obviously, that deficit is even larger for the Union as a whole because of the prominent role of the Council, and the negligible role of Parliament, under the second and third pillar.

[29] See Article 249 EC.

[30] See below, p. 277.

[31] Article 1, second para., EU.

elected, and obtained co-decision power in many legislative matters as well as with regard to the approval and discharge of the Community's annual budget. Along with Parliament's power—subject to procedural and voting restrictions—to force the Commission "to resign as a body," which existed from the outset,[32] this has considerably reduced the Community's "democratic deficit."[33]

To be sure, this evolution in Parliament's powers has not come to an end. Parliament continues to insist on the need for the Union to increase its democratic legitimacy by relying more on Parliament's capacity to represent the people. As we will see in chapter 6, the adoption of the draft Constitution would constitute a further step in that direction.

The third point concerns the exercise of executive power in the Community. In the absence of a uniform system for implementation of Community legislation, each legislative act must determine its specific implementation procedure. Where it does not do so explicitly, it is up to the Member States to ensure implementation.[34] When the EC Treaty does entrust implementation to the Community itself, it sometimes grants *autonomous* power of implementation to the Commission.[35] If not—and if it is nevertheless felt that the matter of implementation cannot, for the sake of uniformity, be left entirely to the Member States—it must be decided in the legislative act concerned how it will be implemented at the Community level. In that case, the Council will frequently delegate implementation to the Commission, often, however, subject to certain requirements.[36] One typical requirement is that the Commission be assisted, in its preparatory work, by a committee composed of civil servants, or external experts, from the Member States. This technique—in Community jargon known as "comitology"—is used by the Council to restrict the discretionary power of the Commission and to boost its own influence and that of the Member States in the implementation of Community legislation.

The technique has, for a long time, been a bone of contention between the Council and the Parliament, which rightly claims that it diminishes Parlia-

---

[32] Article 201, second para., EC, which in the original EEC Treaty was Article 144.

[33] On "democratic deficit," see the reference in n. 28 above.

[34] Article 10, first para., EC.

[35] For instance, in Article 88 EC relating to state aid. The treaty may also designate another body, such as, in monetary matters, the European Central Bank. See Article 110 EC.

[36] Article 202 EC. According to that article, the Council may "in specific cases" reserve the implementing power to itself, in which case it must state in detail the grounds for its decision: ECJ, Case 16/88, *Commission v. Council*, [1989] ECR 3457, para. 10.

ment's role in exercising political control over the implementation process and enhances that of the Council. To address that criticism, and to enhance transparency of the procedure, but at the same time to preserve the Member States' involvement, the functioning of committees is now regulated by the Council Decision of 1999,[37] which provides for three forms of committees: advisory, management, and regulatory. In the latter two forms of committee the hands of the Commission are tied, especially in the case of a "regulatory committee" procedure. Under that procedure, if the Commission declines to follow the qualified majority opinion of the committee, it must submit a proposal to the Council as to the measures it intends to take and provide the Parliament with the same information, upon which the two institutions must follow a procedure that may eventually lead to the blocking of the Commission's proposal in the Council (where the Member States are represented).[38]

The fourth and last point relating to the institutions concerns the division of power at the vertical level, that is, between the Community and its Member States. The basic principle in this respect is that the Community and the Union possess only those sovereign powers that the Member States have agreed to attribute to them, expressly or implicitly (as recognized in case law of the Court of Justice), in the founding treaties. Increasingly so, such powers have accrued as a result of amending treaties approved by the Member States at successive intergovernmental conferences, such as those that resulted in the Maastricht and Amsterdam treaties.[39] However, few of these attributed powers are exclusive (as they are in the area of a common commercial policy toward third countries, as mentioned previously). By contrast, most attributed powers are shared with the Member States, which implies that the Member States may act as long as the Community has not exercised its own competence, thus preempting the Member States' concurrent power, or has ceased to exercise its competence. Moreover, in the case of non-exclusive powers, the Community

---

[37] Taken in accordance with Article 202 EC, which requires "rules laid down in advance." That occurred in the so-called "comitology" decision: Council Decision 1999/468 of July 28, 1999, laying down the procedures for the exercise of implementing powers conferred on the Commission, [1999] OJ L184/23.

[38] See Article 5 of Council Decision 1999/468. The technique of "comitology" is differently assessed by legal writers. Some see it as a form of neo-corporatism at the level of the Member States: see J. Weiler, U. Haltern, and F. Mayer, "European Democracy and Its Critique," in *The Crisis of Representation in Europe*, ed. Jack Hayward (London: Frank Cass, 1995), 32. Others view it as an example of deliberative democracy at work: see C. Joerges and J. Neyer, "From Intergovernmental Bargaining to Deliberative Political Processes: The Constitutionalisation of Comitology," 3 *ELJ*, 1997, 273–99.

[39] Text accompanying nn. 7 and 8 above.

institutions may only exercise their competence in accordance with the principle of subsidiarity. According to that principle, the Community may take action only when the objectives of the proposed action can be better achieved by it than by the Member States, because of the "scale or effects of the proposed action."[40]

Delineation of powers between the Community and the Member States is in itself a most sensitive and disputed matter, and much of the litigation brought by the Member States, or Community institutions, before the Court of Justice indeed concerns delineation of powers. The question is even more sensitive whenever the Community has acted, and therefore pre-empted concurrent powers of Member States, because Community law then takes precedence over national laws. This principle of the supremacy, or primacy, of Community law was not incorporated in the founding treaties but was read into them by the Court of Justice as early as 1964.[41] It operates often to the dislike of Member States' constitutional courts whenever matters that affect those courts' constitutional prerogatives are concerned. Over the years, this has led to temporary conflicts between the European Court of Justice and national courts such as the French Conseil d'Etat and the German and Italian constitutional courts.[42]

The division of power between the "federal" and the "state" level is even more complicated in the Community than it is in federal systems like those of the United States or Germany. The two levels are so inextricably intertwined in the European Community, at both the legislative and the executive levels, that the situation is hardly compatible with constitutional theory. In the legislative field, the most prominent illustration thereof is the Council of Ministers, which, as seen previously, is (the dominant) part of the Community's legislative branch (the other branch being the European Parliament). As mentioned, the Council is a body consisting of Member State ministers. Moreover, its composition is ever-changing, depending on the points on the agenda, the

---

[40] Article 5, second para., EC. On the division of power between the Community and the Member States, and the principle of subsidiarity, see Lenaerts and Van Nuffel, n. 18 above, 88–106.

[41] Case 6/64, *Costa v. ENEL*, [1964] ECR 585. The draft Constitution contains explicit recognition of the principle: see Article I-10 (1) and chapter 6, p. 269.

[42] For references to the relevant case law of the French Conseil d'Etat, the German Federal Constitutional Court and the Italian Constitutional Court, see Craig and de Bùrca, n. 9 above, 285–301. These authors speak of an evolving "co-operative relationship," at 297, and "a smooth relationship—certainly in practice," at 301. And also in the U.K. "an equilibrium may have been reached between the ECJ and the U.K. courts as to the requirements of supremacy of EC law" (ibid., 307).

turnover of political personnel in the national governments, and on the division of power between national-level and regional-level governments in the Member States. These ministers sit in the Council in their capacity as members of a Member State executive, national or regional, and in that capacity they are politically accountable to their national or regional parliament, although not to any institution at the EU level (least of all Parliament, which is the other part of the legislative branch). The situation is not unknown in federal bicameral systems, like Germany, but in the latter case it exists only with regard to the less prominent parliamentary house, the Bundesrat. In the Union, however, the situation relates to the most important part of the legislature, thus creating an "accountability gap" that is further enhanced by the role played in the Community's legislative process by COREPER and the various committees and working parties operating under its auspices. COREPER refers to the Committee of Permanent Representatives of the Member States. It is responsible for preparing the legislative and policy work of the Council of Ministers,[43] but in practice it often reaches decisions itself by consensus. In that capacity, it is not politically responsible to any parliament, whether European or national.[44] The issue will be addressed in chapter 7.

Another particularity of the division of competences between the Community and the Member States relates to the executive function of government. As already mentioned, it is in principle for the Member State authorities to implement Community policy and Community law in their state. The phenomenon is known as *executive federalism*, a concept also found in the German Constitution, in which implementation of federal legislation is done by the component states (the Länder).[45] In Community law, the principle flows from Article 10 EC, which obliges the Member States to "take all appropriate measures, whether general or particular, to ensure fulfillment of the obligations arising out of this Treaty or resulting from action taken by the institutions of the Community." The ECJ has construed this obligation as part of the general requirement of good faith that binds Member States and Community

[43] Article 207 (1) EC states that the committee "shall be responsible for preparing the work of the Council and for carrying out the tasks assigned to it by the Council."

[44] On the activities of COREPER, which is assisted by a plethora of working groups composed of national officials and experts from the Member States, see Craig and de Búrca, n. 9 above, 69 and 165–66.

[45] See Chapter VIII, particularly Articles 83–87, of the German Basic Law. The phenomenon is known in Germany as *Vollzugsföderalismus* (federalism in the execution of laws). For a broad comparative analysis, see Vicki C. Jackson and Mark Tushnet, "Federalism: Power Sharing and Minority Protection," in *Comparative Constitutional Law* (New York: Foundation Press, 1999).

institutions.[46] A telling example of executive federalism is the implementation of Community law "directives." As previously mentioned, in contrast to a regulation that is binding "in its entirety," a directive shall only be binding upon each Member State to which it is addressed, "as to the result to be achieved ... but shall leave to the national authorities the choice of form and methods."[47] It is therefore the obligation of all Member State authorities— legislative, executive, or judicial, as the case may be—to implement the directive, at their own expense, within the period of time prescribed in the directive. Any Member State failing to fulfill that obligation correctly and in time may not only be pursued by the Commission (and other Member States) before the ECJ for such failure, but may also be held liable in compensation in a suit initiated before a national court by a private plaintiff who has sustained damage as a result of the state's failure to implement.[48]

In the United States, the situation is totally different. The issue comes up there in the context of state autonomy. Under the current case law of the U.S. Supreme Court, the matter is governed by the so-called "anticommandeering principle," articulated by Supreme Court Justice Marshall in *Hodel*.[49] In that case, Justice Marshall found that the challenged federal legislation did *not* "commandeer . . . the legislative processes of the states by directly compelling them to enact and enforce a federal regulatory program."[50] That dictum left open the possibility that such "commandeering," if ever found, would be invalidated. In later judgments of the Supreme Court, such invalidation occurred, first of federal commands directed at state legislatures in *New York v. United States*,[51] and then of federal commands directed at state or local executive officials in *Printz v. United States*.[52] The reason for these diametrically opposed attitudes may lie in the way in which separation of powers between the federal and national/state levels is classically applied in the United States as compared with the European Union, where, as seen above, the Community and Member State levels are closely intertwined in the European Community

---

[46] See chapter 3 below, p. 139.

[47] Article 249, third para., EC. In contrast, a regulation "shall have general application. It shall be binding in its entirety and directly applicable in all Member States" (Article 249, second para., EC).

[48] Under the so-called *Francovich* jurisprudence (see chapter 3, p. 115).

[49] *Hodel v. Virginia Surface Min. and Reclamation Ass'n, Inc.*, 452 U.S. 264 (1981).

[50] Quoted in Kathleen M. Sullivan and Gerald Gunther, *Constitutional Law*, 14th ed. (New York: Foundation Press, 2001), 179.

[51] 505 U.S. 144 (1992).

[52] 521 U.S. 898 (1997). For a discussion of these and other cases, with excerpts, see Sullivan and Gunther, n. 50 above, 171–97.

at the legislative level (through the Council and COREPER) and at the executive level (as a result of "comitology"). The Member States' heavy participation in the decision-making process means that they have ample opportunity to express their opinions and to influence the outcome of the legislative and administrative process at Community level, and also have the occasion to measure the financial implications of the proposed Community legislation.[53] Another, and even more compelling, explanation can be found in the fact that in the U.S. the federal government has numerous civil servants "on the ground" and can therefore rely on its own employees to implement federal laws in the states, while the Union must necessarily rely on Member State officials to implement most EU policies.[54]

b) The second and third pillars

The complexity of the division of powers—horizontally among Community institutions and vertically between the Community and the Member States—results in a complex system of checks and balances that may lack transparency, and certainly lacks democratic legitimacy. Nevertheless, the system seems to work rather efficiently. That, however, is not the end of the story. Indeed, the complexity of the system, and its lack of transparency and democratic legitimacy, is immensely heightened by the presence, within the European construction, of the second and third pillars. As mentioned before, in these two pillars, relating respectively to a common foreign and security policy (CFSP) and the cooperation between Member State police and judicial authorities in criminal matters (PJCC), the European Council of Heads of State or Government and the Council of Ministers play by far the most prominent role, while the Commission, the European Parliament, and the Court of Justice are kept at a distance. The situation in the third pillar has, however, changed to the benefit of those institutions following the Treaty of Amsterdam which transferred the policies on visas, asylum, and immigration to the first pillar,[55] thereby making the Community decision-making process also applicable to these areas, albeit with certain restrictions.[56]

[53] Recently the Commission has developed a strategy to ensure a better fit between the Community's objectives and the resources needed to fulfill them. As part of the decision-making process, it routinely instigates dialogue with the Council and the Parliament to discuss objectives and resources. See Craig and de Búrca, n. 9 above, 161.

[54] So-called "decentralized" or "shared" management of Community policies by Member States is much more important, and more frequent, than "centralized" or "direct" management by the Commission (see chapter 2, p. 96).

[55] Now to be found in Articles 61–4 EC.

[56] Some derogations from the generally applicable Community provisions are contained in Articles 67 (legislative process) and 68 (judicial process) EC.

With regard to the second pillar concerning the Union's CFSP, it is for the European Council to define, by consensus, the principles and general guidelines, including for matters with defense implications, and to decide on common strategies in areas where the Member States have important interests in common.[57] In that context, it is also for the European Council to frame a common defense policy, "which might lead to a common defense should the European Council so decide."[58] As for the Council of Ministers, it shall make the decisions necessary for defining and implementing the European Council's general guidelines, as well as make recommendations to the European Council to adopt common strategies and, when adopted, implement them, in particular by means of joint actions and common positions.[59] Decisions of the Council are normally made unanimously.[60]

It follows from the preceding that the Council's task under the second pillar is partly legislative and partly executive. In that task the Council is assisted by its secretary-general, currently Javier Solana, who is referred to as the high representative for the common foreign policy and security policy. He assists the Council in the formulation, preparation, and implementation of policy decisions and, when appropriate, conducts political dialogue with third parties.[61] This is particularly important as those decisions also include the performance of "humanitarian and rescue tasks, peacekeeping tasks and tasks of combat forces in crisis management, including peacemaking."[62] Decisions

---

[57] Article 13 (1) and (2) EU.

[58] Article 17 (1) EU. In that case, the European Council shall "recommend to the Member States the adoption of such a decision in accordance with their respective constitutional requirements." Ibid.

[59] Article 13 (3) EU. According to Article 14 (1) and (3) EU, "joint actions" address specific situations where operational action by the Union is concerned; they commit the Member States in the positions they adopt and in the conduct of their activity. According to Articles 15 and 19 (1) EU, "common positions" define the approach of the Union to a particular matter of a geographical or thematic nature; when adopted by the Council, Member States must ensure that their national policies conform to the common position and uphold the positions in international organizations and at international conferences.

[60] They are made with the understanding, however, that abstentions by members present or represented shall not prevent their adoption. Sometimes, when made on the basis of a common strategy, or to implement joint actions or common positions, decisions can be made by qualified majority, and in procedural matters they can even be made by simple majority. Article 23 (1), (2), and (3) EU.

[61] Article 26 EU. The Council is moreover advised by the Political and Security Committee, which monitors the international situation and the implementation of agreed policies (Article 25 EU).

[62] Article 17 (2) EU.

in all these matters are to be made without being prejudicial to the policies and obligations that certain Member States have assumed as a result of their membership of NATO. However, two or more Member States are allowed to develop closer cooperation on a bilateral level, within the framework of the Western European Union (WEU) and NATO, provided such cooperation does not run counter to or impede cooperation decided within the frame of the Union's common foreign and security policy.[63] As for the role of the other institutions under the second pillar, the treaty only mandates that the Commission shall be "fully associated" with the Council's work[64] and that the European Parliament shall be consulted on main aspects and basic decisions and will be kept informed.[65] The Court of Justice has virtually no jurisdiction in matters of common foreign and security policy.[66]

Under the third, or PJCC, pillar also, the Council is the most prominent institution. In that area, its task consists of promoting cooperation between police forces, customs authorities, and other law enforcement services in the Member States, both directly and through the European Police Office (Europol),[67] and between judicial authorities and other competent authorities of the Member States, including cooperation through the European Judicial Cooperation Unit (Eurojust).[68] Where necessary, it must also approximate rules on

---

[63] Article 17 (3) and (4) EU. The latter provision came into the news because of the initiative made by Belgium, France, Germany, and Luxembourg to build up European defense cooperation, an initiative viewed by the Bush administration as unhelpful as it constitutes "a diversion from the very good work that has been done to build up relations between NATO and the European Union" (*New York Times*, April 25, 2003, A15). The extreme tension that the initiative caused proved not to last, however. See P. Norman, *The Accidental Constitution: The Story of the European Convention* (Brussels: EuroComment, 2003), 186–87.

[64] Article 27 EU.

[65] Article 21 EU.

[66] Article 46 EU. See further chapter 3, pp. 118f.

[67] Article 29, second para., first indent, EU, and Article 30 EU. Europol was established by the Convention on the Establishment of a European Police Office of July 26, 1995, [1995] OJ C316/1. Its task is to facilitate the exchange of information and to obtain, collate, and analyze information and intelligence. It started its activities on July 1, 1999, and is located in The Hague. It works with a staff of around 250 people (seconded national liaison officers and Europol employees). See Sabine Gless, "What Kind of Judicial Control Do the New Protagonists Need?" in *L'espace penal Européen: enjeux et perspectives*, ed. G. De Kerchove and A. Weyembergh (Brussels: Institut d'études Européennes, ULB, 2002), 31–45, at 32–34.

[68] Article 29, second para., second indent, EU, and Article 31 EU. Eurojust was established by Council Decision of February 28, 2002, [2002] OJ L63/1. Its task is to promote and facilitate cooperation between judicial authorities in the field of serious

criminal matters in the Member States, and lay down the conditions and limitations under which the police and judicial authorities may operate in the territory of another Member State in liaison and in agreement with the authorities of that state.[69] Although it is for the Member States to coordinate their action, and to establish collaboration between the relevant departments of their administrations, it pertains to the Council, acting as a general rule unanimously on the initiative of any Member States or of the Commission, to adopt common positions defining the approach of the Union in a particular matter, to enact framework decisions or other decisions,[70] and to establish conventions that it shall recommend to the Member States for adoption in accordance with their respective constitutional requirements.[71] As under the second pillar, the other Community institutions have a limited role only: as mentioned, the Commission is given a right of initiative on an equal footing with any Member State and shall be fully associated with the work of the Council; Parliament has the right to be consulted and informed, and obtains limited budgetary powers; and the Court of Justice enjoys limited powers of judicial review and interpretation.[72]

c) The Union as a whole

All of the above conveys an image of the European Union as a rather confusing construction consisting of a large and supranational Community building and two smaller, intergovernmental annexes, well separated from the main building. However, in a groundbreaking article, two legal researchers of the University of Utrecht, Deirdre Curtin and Ige Dekker, have shown that a careful analysis of the objectives, principles, organizational structure, and capacities as provided for in the EU Treaty indicate that the Union is a "layered"

---

crime, especially organized crime, fraud and corruption, money laundering, etc. It is composed of prosecutors, judges, and police officers of the Member States. See further Daniel Flore, "D'un réseau judiciaire Européen à une juridiction pénale Européenne: Eurojust et l'émergence d'un système de justice pénale" [From a European judicial network toward a European penal judiciary: Eurojust and the emergence of a system of penal administration], ibid., 9–30.

[69] Article 29, second para., third indent, Article 31 (e), and Article 32 EU.

[70] Framework decisions that intend to approximate Member State laws are only binding upon the Member State as to the result to be achieved but shall leave to the national authorities the choice of forms and methods; by contrast, decisions that may not pursue approximation of Member State laws are fully binding upon the Member States: Article 34 (2), under (b) and (c), EU.

[71] Article 34 EU.

[72] See Articles 34 (2) first para., and 36 (2), EU (Commission), Articles 39 and 41 EU (Parliament); Article 35 EU (Court of Justice).

international organization with a *unitary* character, and not just a treaty, and that it is wrong to see the second CFSP pillar and the third PJCC pillar as purely intergovernmental additions to the first supranational Community pillar.[73] Indeed, "the fact that the Council, as well as the European Council, decide in principle on CFSP and CJHA [now PJCC] matters by a unanimous vote of all its members does not necessarily mean that its decisions are not decisions of an organ, the forming of the 'common will' not being dependent on one Member State."[74] Curtin and Dekker underpin their conclusions with a remarkable investigation of external and internal legal practices of the European Union that make it clear that the Union behaves on the international scene as one legal person under all three pillars (and is recognized as one person by the other international players),[75] and that, even in the internal decision-making processes, the Council, the Commission, and Parliament take a non–pillar-specific approach.[76] Thus, for instance, the Council has cultivated the practice of adopting second- and third-pillar documents no matter what its configuration might be—even, for example, when it is composed of ministers who are not foreign or justice ministers qualified for second- or third-pillar matters but, say, agriculture ministers qualified for first-pillar matters.[77]

Curtin and Dekkers conclude their analysis as follows: "Although the framers of the Treaty of Maastricht deftly conspired to balance the so-called 'intergovernmental' and 'integration' visions, they in practice provided the institutions in question with the 'space' to act both externally and internally as legally autonomous organs of an international organization rather than as a mere gathering of fifteen sovereign states." Their conclusion is one that later developments certainly have not contradicted, insofar as the draft Constitution intends to abolish the three pillars altogether, and provides in Article I-6, without much ado, that "the Union shall have legal personality."[78]

---

[73] Deirdre M. Curtin and Ige F. Dekker, "The EU as a 'Layered' International Organization: Institutional Unity in Disguise," in P. Craig and G. de Búrca, eds., *The Evolution of EU Law* (Oxford: Oxford University Press, 1999), 83–132.

[74] Ibid., 99.

[75] See ibid., 111–22.

[76] The chapter contains an impressively thorough analysis of the actual practices of the institutions. The authors mention that the same non-'pillar' specific approach is taken by the national parliament dealing with the European Union. They also note that the second- and third-pillar activity of the institutions is far from being marginal or insignificant, some putting its proportion at the time of writing (in the late 1990s) as high as one-third of all EU activity (ibid).

[77] Ibid., 114.

[78] See chapter 6, p. 267. The fact that the Union is regarded as having legal personality as a whole is confirmed by the conclusion, in the aftermath of September 11, of

d) The Court of Justice

At the end of this overview of institutions and competences in the European Union, a word must be said of the European Court of Justice (ECJ). The court is set up in Article 220 EC to ensure that in the interpretation and application of this treaty the law is observed. To fulfill that task, the Court of Justice and the adjacent Court of First Instance (CFI), both located in Luxembourg, are given various competences to arbitrate conflicts between the Community institutions and between the Community and the Member States, and to review the validity of legislative and administrative acts. Moreover, the ECJ may, and in some instances must, be called upon by the Member State courts to decide on the interpretation of Community laws, or on the validity of Community legislation, when those Member State courts need to resolve litigation pending before them in which a question of Community law arises.[79] From the very outset, the Court has used its competences not only to clarify the scope, and the limits, of the powers of the Commission, the Council, and the Parliament, but also to highlight the general principles underlying Community law within a context of the process of European integration to which the Member States had committed themselves.

Examples of such general principles are found in the Court's early judgments in *Costa/ENEL* affirming the precedence of Community law over national laws,[80] and in *Van Gend & Loos* concerning the so-called 'direct effect' of Community law allowing private plaintiffs to rely before a national court on precise treaty provisions and other Community legislation.[81] More recent case law has witnessed the advent of new principles in Community law, such as in *Francovich* where the Court found that the principle of state liability was inherent in the EC Treaty and procured private plaintiffs with a remedy in compensation, to be initiated before a national court, for damage caused by a Member State breaching Community law.[82]

In its endeavor to "ensure that the law is observed," the Court has often

---

international agreements between the Union and the United States: the Europol Agreement concluded on December 20, 2002, and the Judicial Cooperation Agreement on June 25, 2003. For an analysis, see Valsamis Mitsilegas, "The New EU-USA Cooperation on Extradition, Mutual Legal Assistance and the Exchange of Police Data," 8 *European Foreign Affairs Review*, 2003, 515–36.

[79] On the Community courts, and the various procedures that can be initiated before them, see Articles 220–45 EC. See also n. 16 above.

[80] Case 6/64, *Costa v. ENEL*, [1964] ECR 58; see also text accompanying n. 41 above.

[81] Case 26/62, *Van Gend en Loos*, [1963] ECR 1.

[82] Joined Cases C-6 and 9/90, *Francovich and Bonifaci v. Italy*, [1991] ECR I-5357. See chapter 3, pp. 115ff.

used a method of interpretation known as "teleological" interpretation in which it looks beyond the wording and the structure of the text to the purpose of the text. The method is not uncommon in the legal systems of the continental European states, especially in the interpretation of written constitutions, but it has been criticized by lawyers from the common law and Scandinavian countries, which blamed the court for being "activist."[83] Indeed, it cannot be denied that the Court has been proactive in some cases, such as those referred to in the preceding paragraphs. Teleological interpretation tends, however, to be limited to cases in which access to court and judicial remedies on the part of public or private plaintiffs were at stake, or when fundamental rights are involved. By contrast, when the Court is called upon to interpret the meaning of provisions in regulations or directives, it normally uses very orthodox methods of interpretation.[84]

The preceding applies to the role of the Court of Justice under the first pillar, the Community pillar. As already mentioned, under the second pillar the Court of Justice has almost no role to play and, under the third, only a limited role. That does not prevent the Court from promoting, whenever it can, the application of general principles, such as access to documents, across the three pillars. Moreover, as a result of the 1997 Treaty of Amsterdam, the visa, asylum, and immigration policy has been transplanted from the third to the first pillar, thereby bringing this delicate matter almost fully within the normal jurisdiction of the ECJ.[85]

Differences in Levels of Integration: A Europe "à la Carte"?

The development of the European Union has been characterized by some to have happened in the manner of an "à la carte" menu—that is, Member States have been allowed to pick the degree of integration that suits them best.[86] And indeed, *differentiation* between EU Member States has become a

[83] The criticism was first strongly voiced by Hjalte Rasmussen, *On Law and Policy in the European Court of Justice* (Dordrecht: Martinus Nijhoff, 1986). See further Craig and de Búrca, n. 9 above, 96–102.

[84] See further Walter van Gerven, "Community and National Legislators, Regulators, Judges, Academics and Practitioners: Living Together Apart?" in *Law Making, Law Finding, and Law Shaping*, ed. Basil S. Markesinis (Oxford: Oxford University Press, 1997), 13–35, at 28–32. See also van Gerven, "Of Rights, Remedies and Procedures," 37 *CMLRev.*, 2000, 501–36. Actually, since the U.K. has been a member of the EU, its judges have also started to use the teleological method, even in matters of purely U.K. law. See Ian McLeod, *Legal Method*, 3d ed. (Basingstoke: MacMillan, 1999), 281–320.

[85] On this evolution, see Curtin and Dekker, n. 73 above, 124. See also chapter 3, p. 189.

[86] The "à la carte" approach was advocated by former British prime minister John

permanent feature of the European construction. It has two main causes: it is either the result of derogations granted to one or more Member States, or is the result of enhanced cooperation between two or more Member States.[87] The first is the more common source of differentiation. It occurs mainly in the form of transitional arrangements granted to Member States upon accession, or in the form of derogations granted to existing Member States that do not fulfill the criteria for further integration—or, if they do, that choose to stay behind for the time being. Thus, for example, with regard to entry into the third stage of the European Monetary Union (EMU),[88] derogations were granted to Denmark and the United Kingdom, which chose not to enter that third stage of the EMU, and to Sweden, which did not want to participate in the EMU at all.[89] Another example in another domain is the non-participation

---

Major in a speech at Leiden University on September 7, 1994. See further Amaryllis Verhoeven, *The European Union in Search of a Democratic and Constitutional Theory* (The Hague: Kluwer Law International, 2002), 279. Verhoeven examines in her book the decisional and territorial variability in the European Union as a challenge to democratic constitutionalism (193–288) and comes to conclusions similar to those reached below.

[87] On both causes, see Lenaerts and Van Nuffel, n. 18 above, 278–86. Differentiation within the EU as a result of varying degrees of harmonization between Member States should be seen in context with harmonization taking place to a certain degree, and therefore with differentiation, between the EU and a number of *neighboring* states. Switzerland is a prominent example: although the country is not an EU Member State, the Swiss Federal Council nevertheless decided in 1988 to bring Swiss legislation with international implications voluntarily in line with the European standards. Since then voluntary or autonomous adaptation—that is, without any (treaty) obligation to do so for the state concerned—has become normal practice in Switzerland: see Stephan Breitenmoser, "Sectoral Agreements between the EEC and Switzerland: Contents and Context," 40 *CMLRev.*, 2003, 1137–86, at 1139. The same spillover effect occurs in Norway and Iceland (and Liechtenstein), this time, however, on the basis of an obligation that these states have undertaken vis-à-vis the EU, as members of the European Free Trade Association (EFTA), to adopt large parts of EC law. See Carl Baudenbacher, "The EFTA-Court—An Example of the Judicialisation of International Economic Law," 28 *ELRev.*, 2003, 880–99.

[88] From the start of the third stage, the value of the common currency would be fixed and the common currency irrevocably adopted; see Article 118 EC and the following footnote. The criteria to be fulfilled by a Member State to enter the third stage are laid down in Article 121 (1) EC. They imply a high degree of price stability, a sustained budgetary position without an excessive deficit, observance of normal exchange rate fluctuation margins, and durability of convergence being reflected in long-term interest-rate levels.

[89] The third stage began on January 1, 1999, on which date the exchange rates of the participating countries were irrevocably set, and the euro replaced the national cur-

of the United Kingdom and Ireland and the only partial participation of Denmark in the so-called Schengen Protocol, which intended to eliminate checks on persons at the Member State's internal borders.[90] A third example is the United Kingdom opt-out from the Community's Social Protocol.[91]

The second type of potential differentiation (none has occurred yet) results from a decision on the part of some Member States to enhance cooperation between them (and, to that end, to be allowed to make use of the common institutions)—which Union law permits if certain conditions are fulfilled and if the enhanced cooperation involves a minimum of eight Member States.[92] The technique is seen as an instrument for Member States to proceed

---

rencies of the twelve participating countries (eleven at the time, Greece joining in January 2001). Denmark and the U.K. obtained a derogation, the U.K. negotiating an "opt-out" protocol by virtue of which it is not bound to move to the third stage, even if it does meet the convergence criteria mentioned in Article 121 (1) EC. Sweden did not wish to adapt its legislation to comply with the condition concerning the independence of central banks. On all this, see the editorial comments on "The Birth of the Euro," 35 *CMLRev.*, 1998, 585–94.

[90] Because of disagreement between the existing Member States on the meaning and implementation of Article 14 (then 7a) EC, providing for the establishment of an internal market "without internal frontiers" (see para. 2), five of the Member States decided to cooperate *outside* the Community structure in abolishing checks at their shared borders, and on matters of visa policy. To that effect, they signed the Schengen Agreement of 1985 and the Schengen Implementing Convention of 1990. By the end of 1996, thirteen of the then fifteen Member States were adhering to the scheme, with the exception of the U.K. and Ireland. In 1990 all fifteen Member States signed the Dublin Convention concerning asylum applications, which entered into effect on September 1, 1997. All these documents made reference to EC law, but were adopted outside the Community framework; they are designated, in Article 43 EU, under (i), as "the Schengen acquis." Currently, the U.K. and Ireland are not Schengen countries, and Denmark has an intermediate status, as described in another protocol attached to the same treaty; see Article 69 EC. For a detailed description of this complex situation, see Maria Fletcher, "EU Governance Techniques in the Creation of a Common European Policy on Immigration and Asylum, 9 *EPL*, 2003, 533–62, at 543–48.

[91] Following a change of government in the U.K. in 1997, the Social Policy Agreement, which had taken the place of the earlier Social Protocol, was incorporated by virtue of the Treaty of Amsterdam into Articles 136–43 EC, making the British opt-out superfluous.

[92] The provisions on enhanced (or closer) cooperation are set out in Article 43 EU. Under these provisions, as amended by the 2000 Nice Treaty, proposed cooperation must further the objectives of the Union, respect the Union's institutional framework and the *acquis communautaire*, remain within the limits of the Union's power, not concern areas of exclusive competence, not undermine the internal market, and not impede interstate trade or competition. It must involve a minimum of eight Member States (regardless of the total number of Member States), respect the rights and obli-

more quickly when they fear that integration will, to their detriment, slow down as a result of growing enlargement of the Union. The use of it is subject to several restrictive conditions. First, it may only be applied as a last resort, that is, when it is established that the objectives of enhanced cooperation cannot be attained through the normal decision-making channels within a reasonable period. Second, once enhanced cooperation has been established, it should be open to all Member States, and as many as possible should be encouraged to take part.[93] Moreover, on top of these general conditions, there are special conditions relating to each of the three respective pillars.[94] All of these "enhanced cooperation" conditions, general and special, are the result of political compromises that have been fashioned in negotiations between Member States that want to move integration forward, and those reluctant to go ahead. Their purpose is to make enhanced cooperation acceptable to all Member States, as well as to the Union institutions.[95]

Differentiation resulting from covenants between existing Member States or with new Member States, as a result of derogations granted or of enhanced cooperation, surely serves a useful purpose: covenants concluded by current Member States with candidate Member States providing for temporary arrangements facilitate accession; those concluded with old Member States not wishing to enter a new stage of integration allow these states to take into account their citizens' reluctance to proceed with integration too quickly or too far. Both of these covenants are the logical consequence of the *contractual* nature of a Member State's adherence to the Union or its decision to transfer new powers to the Union. Differentiation is therefore inherent in a situation of a gradually enlarged and broadened Union of states, each of them having its own political and cultural past that it cannot and does not wish to abandon in one strike, if ever. In that sense, differentiation belongs to the Union's constitutionalism of a community of states that want their differences not to be

---

gations of the non-participating states, not affect the Schengen acquis, and be open to all Member States that wish to join in accordance with Article 43b EU. On *acquis communautaire*, see n. 3 above; on the Schengen acquis, see n. 90 above.

[93] Articles 43a and 43b EU.

[94] These special provisions provide the procedure to be followed by the Member States seeking authorization and are established in Articles 11–11a EC for the first (Community) pillar, augmenting the role of the Commission and the Parliament in the decision-making process; in Articles 27a–27c EU for the second (CFSP) pillar, emphasizing that enhanced cooperation must assert the Union's identity as a coherent force on the international scene but exclude matters having military or defense implications; and in Articles 40–40b EU for the third (PJCC) pillar, strengthening the role of the Commission.

[95] See further Craig and de Búrca, n. 9 above, 45–49.

obliterated, but to be part of a common future. Nevertheless, too much differentiation may lead to a lack of cohesion that might affect the manageability, if not the structure, of the Union, and must therefore be kept within limits.

These limits are twofold. The first, and most important, limit is "psychological." It implies that a Member State, whatever the agreed-on differences are, must remain committed to the overall European integration process not only by accepting past developments (the *acquis communautaire*), but also by agreeing to consider with an open mind new projects of integration that are proposed by the institutions of the Union or by fellow Member States. On the one hand, that implies that a Member State that does not want to be included in a new and crucial project cannot state categorically that it will never adhere to it but rather should be ready to reconsider its position at regular intervals. On the other hand, it implies that Member States that are to propose enhanced cooperation must first attempt to convince the others to join the initiative within a reasonable period of time and, when they decide to go forward, they must remain ready to take the others on board. The second limit involves the question of whether differentiation remains "manageable" for the institutions of the Union, or, in other words, whether the new form of differentiation does not add a burden to the already significant complexity of the Union's decision-making process such that the overall efficiency of the integration process is endangered. That is a question that must be answered in the first place by the Union's institutions, and in particular by the Commission—which, one might add, has acquired over the years considerable experience managing huge differences.

Present and future differentiation must be assessed in light of these limits. As for enhanced cooperation, the general conditions established in Articles 43–43b EU, and the special conditions under each of the three pillars,[96] are consistent with these limits on the part of both the participating and the non-participating Member States. The participating states agree to further the objectives of the Union and of the Community, and to respect all of the Union's important characteristics and policies. They may only resort to enhanced cooperation when the objectives pursued cannot be attained within a reasonable time through normal procedures, and they shall allow the other Member States to join in if they wish to participate. The non-participating states cannot, following amendments made by the Nice Treaty, veto enhanced cooperation, at least not under the first and the third pillar.[97] Moreover, the decision-

[96] See n. 94 above.
[97] See further Craig and de Búrca, n. 9 above, 46 and 49. Under the second pillar, there is a protective device for Member States that intend to oppose the "enhanced co-

making process authorizing enhanced cooperation involves the Commission, which can thus assess its own ability to take on any additional managerial burden. As for derogations granted to new Member States on accession, or to existing states on entry into a new phase of integration, they have been agreed on with informed consent from all those involved, and there are no indications that the Member States involved have categorically rejected their willingness to reconsider their positions at regular intervals.[98]

As for the requirement regarding the manageability of differentiation, it will be severely tested following the accession, as of May 1, 2004, of ten new states.[99] Apart from the fact that the accession involves a large number of citi-

---

operation" decision in the Council of Ministers "for important and stated reasons of national policy." See Article 27c in conjunction with Article 23 (2), second para., EU, where the device is described: it consists in a referral of the matter by the Council of Ministers, acting by a qualified majority, to the European Council "for decision by unanimity."

[98] The U.K. and Sweden have not indicated that they do not wish to be a full part of the monetary union. On the contrary, the official position of both countries is that they will join when the time is ripe and their people are ready for it. Currently there is no procedure for a Member State that is no longer in a position to agree with the path of integration that the Union intends to follow to leave the Union in an orderly way. That will change with the adoption of the draft Constitution, which provides, in Article I-59 [now Article I-60], that any Member State may decide to withdraw from the Union in accordance with its constitutional requirements. When a Member State announces its intention to withdraw, the Union and the Member State concerned will, under the provisions of that article, negotiate an agreement setting out the arrangements for withdrawal, taking account of the framework for its future relationship with the Union. In other words, upon withdrawal of a Member State, a new (but lesser) form of association may be agreed on.

[99] The Accession Treaty between the EU and the ten candidate Member States was signed at the historic site of the Acropolis in Athens on April 16, 2003. As a result of subsequent ratification by all candidate states in accordance with their constitutional requirements, enlargement became a fact on May 1, 2004. It may be useful to name here, in alphabetical order, first the old and then the new Member States. The fifteen old states are: Austria, Belgium, Denmark, Finland, France, Germany, Greece, Ireland, Italy, Luxembourg, the Netherlands, Portugal, Spain, Sweden, and the United Kingdom. The ten new states are: the Czech Republic, Cyprus, Estonia, Hungary, Latvia, Lithuania, Malta, Poland, Slovakia, and Slovenia. The new Member States have become full members of the Union, but not yet of the euro-zone. Two more states, Bulgaria and Romania, are expected to join the Union in 2007 or 2008. On October 6, 2004, the Commission proposed to start accession negotiations with Turkey in 2005, and the European Council decided on December 17, 2004 to go ahead with the negotiations. However, accession is not expected to occur before 2015. See *European Voice*, October 7–13, 2004, 1, and December 16, 2004–January 12, 2005, 9.

zens,[100] "the scale and nature—in historical, political, and economic terms of the impending enlargement—sets it apart from all previous extensions of Community and Union membership, and the pre-accession process has been an intensive and often contentious one."[101] To be sure, the enlargement operation has been well prepared. As early as 1989, the Community set up its PHARE program providing financial support for Central and Eastern European countries to rebuild their economies. Those countries entered into "Europe Agreements," that is, bilateral free trade agreements with the EU. In June 1993 the Union set out its so-called "Copenhagen" criteria for membership, and in 1997 it presented its Agenda 2000 Programme, in which opinions on candidate countries applications were included.[102] Moreover, the policy of conditionality pursued by the Union has meant that the candidate states were required to adapt their laws and institutions in very significant ways long before any date of accession was set.[103] Furthermore, accession to the Union does not include, from the outset, accession to the monetary union.[104]

II. A EUROPEAN "BODY POLITIC" AND IDENTITY

It will be clear from the foregoing that the European Union stands for *divided sovereignty*.[105] Indeed, with the establishment of the European Economic

---

[100] With the exception of Poland, which has about 40 million people, the other new states have small populations (together less than 40 million). In the enlarged EU of twenty-five countries and 451 million people the seven smallest countries will represent a paltry 1.5 percent of the EU's GDP, as compared with the six largest countries, which will represent 82 percent of the Union's GDP.

[101] Craig and de Búrca, n. 9 above, 27.

[102] Douglas-Scott, n. 18 above, 33.

[103] Craig and de Búrca, n. 9 above, 27.

[104] With the accession of ten new Member States on May 1, 2004, only 48 percent of all Member States belong to the euro-zone. However, by contrast with the situations of the U.K., Sweden, and Denmark, the problem with the new states is "not one of getting them into the EMU, but of persuading them to stay out" (John Wyles in *European Voice*, April 29–May 5, 2004, 12). The author refers to an estimate by Deutsche Bank according to which the eight Eastern European Member States would be ready to join the euro exchange rate mechanism (which is a precondition of qualifying for the euro) between 2004 and 2007, and to join the monetary union between 2007 and 2010.

[105] On sovereignty in the European Union, see also N. MacCormick, *Questioning Sovereignty: Law, State and Nation in the European Commonwealth* (Oxford: Oxford University Press, 1999).

Community in 1957, Member States transferred to the newly created Community some of their sovereign powers for "an unlimited period" of time,[106] and transferred in successive treaty amendments ever-wider areas of competence. As a result of these transfers, an additional layer of government was created on top of the existing political structure of the Member States—some of them being federal states, and therefore already having internally a vertically layered structure of government.[107] Moreover, as pointed out above, in the European Union sovereign powers that are enjoyed by the Union are exercised by the EU institutions with the participation of Member State authorities. That is particularly the case of the Council of Ministers, which is part of the Union's legislative branch, in which national ministers participate, as members of the Council, in the making and preparing of Union laws and policies.

The transfer of sovereign powers by the Member States to the Union has brought the European Court of Justice to state in an early judgment of 1963 that the treaty establishing the European Economic Community

> is more than an agreement which merely creates mutual obligations between the contracting states . . . [as] is also confirmed more specifically by the establishment of institutions endowed with sovereign rights . . . [and] that the Community constitutes a new legal order of international law . . . and the subjects of which comprise not only Member States but also their nationals.[108]

Now that the Community has been transformed into a Union, and more and more sovereign rights have, over the years, been transferred to the Union,

---

[106] Article 312 EC.

[107] Austria, Belgium, and Germany are federal states. Belgium, which became a federal state in 1993, is an interesting example of how states that were formerly highly centralized became the object of federalization under the pressure of constituencies seeking political recognition of their linguistic or cultural diversity. The federalizing trend is also clearly present in Spain, and even in the United Kingdom, where diversity led to a devolution of powers. For a full account, see Koen Lenaerts, "Constitutionalism and the Many Faces of Federalism," 38 *Am.J.Comp.L.*, 1990, 205–63, who distinguishes this form of "devolutive federalism," which also occurred outside the Union in Canada, from the more classic form of "integrative federalism" which occurred in the United States, Switzerland, Germany, and now in the European Union. See also Vicki C. Jackson and Mark Tushnet, n. 45 above, in which the federal structure of a number of states is examined from the viewpoint of power sharing and of protection of minority rights.

[108] Case 26/62, *Van Gend en Loos v. Netherlands Inland Revenue Administration*, [1963] ECR 1. The full text of the last part of the sentence is as follows: "the Community constitutes a new legal order of international law for the benefit of which the states have limited their sovereign rights, albeit within limited fields, and the subjects of which comprise not only Member States but also their nationals."

the question is whether this has transformed the multilayered construction that the Union is into a "sovereign [federal] state," that is, whether the Union has been elevated to the status of statehood.[109]

The European Union: A Political Entity or a State?

To answer that question, it is necessary to define statehood. In the Westphalian understanding, a sovereign state is an entity with exclusive authority within its own geographic boundaries.[110] As such the concept is based on territory, mutual recognition, autonomy, and control; such states have "the authority to act but also . . . can effectively regulate movements across their borders and within them."[111] However eroded the Westphalian concept proves to be,[112] it remains useful as a common reference point to compare the status of the European Community with that of existing "states." It is at the basis of Article 1 of the 1933 Montevideo Convention on Rights and Duties of States, which stipulates that "the state as a person of international law should possess the following qualifications: (a) a permanent population; (b) a defined territory; (c) a government; and (d) a capacity to enter into relations with other

[109] For a broader discussion, see G. Federico Mancini, "Europe: The Case for Statehood," 4 *ELJ*, 1998, 29–42, and J. H. H. Weiler, "Europe: The Case Against The Case for Statehood," 4 *ELJ*, 1998, 43–62.

[110] The Peace of Westphalia, which ended the Thirty Years War in 1648, is rightly or (more likely) wrongly understood as a critical moment in the development of the modern international system composed of sovereign states: thus Stephen D. Krasner, "Rethinking the Sovereign State Model," *Review of International Studies* (2001): 27, 17–42, at 17. Krasner uses the Westphalian concept "in deference to common usage." He mentions that the idea that states ought to be autonomous was only developed in the last part of the eighteenth century by the Swiss international jurist Emmerich de Vattel (p. 17).

[111] Ibid., 18.

[112] Krasner demonstrates that, throughout its history, sovereignty has been continuously breached through conventions, contracts, coercion, or imposition, turning the concept into "a cognitive script [of] rules widely understood but also frequently violated" by which the norms are "decoupled from actual behaviour" (ibid., 17). Conventions are commitments agreed upon by rulers that expose their policies to some kind of external scrutiny, such as human rights scrutiny (23). Contracts are agreements between the authorities in two or more states, or between a state and an international institution; an example is the imposition of changes in domestic policy or economic reform by the IMF or the World Bank as a condition of borrowing arrangements (26ff). Coercion occurs when one state threatens to impose sanctions on another state if it does not accept changes in domestic structures or policies (30ff). Imposition occurs when the rulers of the target state have no choice other than to accept changes (ibid.).

states."[113] It is clear (as could be expected), for example, that the United States has all the characteristics necessary to be a (federal) state.[114] The U.S. government exercises political authority over a defined geographic space, according to the territories of the fifty component states and Washington, D.C. As a state, it is recognized by other independent territorial entities as competent to enter into contractual arrangements, typically treaties,[115] and has full autonomy, so that no external actor enjoys authority within its borders (with the exception of the component states acting within their own territories). It has the authority, legally and effectively, to regulate movements across its borders and within them. All of this obviously takes place according to the scope of its competence as a federal government.

a) The Union is not a state

How does the situation differ for the European Union? At first sight, it does not. Indeed, within the scope of sovereign powers that the Member States have conferred upon the Union, the Union exercises its power within a defined geographic space, which coincides with the territory of the Member States. In addition, it is recognized by other independent territorial entities as competent to conclude treaties, sometimes alone when its competence is exclusive, sometimes together with the Member States when its powers are concurrent. The Union enjoys full authority without regard for any external actor (other than the Member States acting within their own territories), and is empowered, within its sphere of competence, to regulate movements across and within its borders. As in the United States, the Union's ability to act is constrained by the powers that remain with the Member States. Moreover, both the United States and the European Union grant citizenship, and concomitant rights and duties, to the citizens of their component states, notwithstanding that EU citizenship complements, and does not replace, national citizenship.[116]

[113] See Dixon, n. 12 above, 107, where the provision is quoted. The Montevideo Convention on Rights and Duties of States was adopted by the Seventh International Conference of American States and signed on December 26, 1933.

[114] I refer to these characteristics as defined by Stephen Krasner, n. 110 above, 18.

[115] Under Article VI, sec. 2, of the United States Constitution, the president and the Senate share the treaty power, whereas Article I, sec. 10, of the Constitution prohibits the states from entering into any treaty. As part of the "supreme Law of the Land"—thus Article I, sec. 2—a treaty, which is self-executing unless it provides otherwise, overrides conflicting state laws. The treaty power of the federal legislature is, however, subjected to constitutional limitations, and can therefore not be the basis for domestic action affecting individual rights beyond the limits governing other national powers. *Reid v. Covert*, 354 U.S. 1 (1957); Sullivan and Gunther, n. 50 above, 228–32.

[116] See Article 17 (1) EC.

Furthermore, both the United States and the EU have institutions to carry out the basic functions of government and are founded on constitutional values that, for the European Union, are inscribed in Article 6 of the EU Treaty ("liberty, democracy, respect for human rights and fundamental freedoms, and the rule of law") and in the solemnly proclaimed EU Charter of Fundamental Rights of December 2000.[117]

Despite all that, the European Union is not a state because it lacks sovereign powers in matters such as foreign policy, security and defense policy, and criminal matters. Those are powers of coercion, the possession of which would allow the Union to assume the responsibilities expected of states and the ability to cope with the problems of a global society, in proportion to the resources at their disposal. As long as these matters remain subjected to decisions to be made unanimously by Member State representatives in the European Council and the Council of Ministers, the Union is not, as such, empowered to live up to the legitimate expectations that international recognition implies in a global world. This view finds support in the opinion of political scientists according to whom the EU is not a "state" as long as it does not have a monopoly on the legitimate use of coercion, that is, as long as the power of coercion through police and security forces (and, one may add, through military might) remains in the hands of the national governments of the Member States.[118] However, that does not prevent the Union from being a *political system*, as it possesses all the elements needed to be such a system: institutional stability and complexity; powers of government through which citizens and social groups seek to achieve their political desires; a significant impact on the distribution of economic resources and the allocation of social and political values; and a continuous interaction between political outputs, new demands on the system, and so on.[119]

The most important reason why the Union is not a state, however, is that the Member States, and probably their peoples, *do not wish* the Union to be a full-fledged state, because they do not want to see their status, or that of their state, reduced at the international level to that of a component state. Granting statehood to the Union would imply that the Union should obtain full power to impose taxes on its citizens for whatever purpose, including the establishment of its own police and military forces, and to impose penal sanctions and

---

[117] [2000] OJ C364/01. See further chapter 2, p. 123.

[118] In that sense, see Simon Hix, *The Political System of the European Union*, 2d ed. (London: Palgrave, to be published in January 2005). See Working Paper, at http://personal.lse.ac.uk/HIX/WorkingPapers.HTM, Chapter 1, Introduction, at 2–3 under "The EU: a political system but not a state."

[119] Ibid.

procedures, including the creation of a penitentiary system. It would also imply that the Member States would be somehow limited in their capacity to enter into international agreements.[120] It would seem that the Member States, or their peoples, are not ready to embrace such a concept, at least not in the near future, as is made apparent in Article I-5 (1) of the draft Constitution, which stipulates that "the Union shall respect the national identities of its Member States inherent in their fundamental structures, political and constitutional. . . . It shall respect their essential state functions, including those for insuring the territorial integrity of the state, and for maintaining law and order and safeguarding internal security."[121]

b) The Union: A "body politic" in search of democracy

Although the Union is not itself a state, it is, as mentioned above, a political system, a Union of states and peoples that aspires to have an accountable government and good governance. Its goal is well on the way to being realized, as I will show in the following chapters. It is, moreover, a union of states that, like the Union itself, are founded, according to Article 6 (1) EU, on "the principles of liberty, democracy, respect for human rights and the rule of law." Furthermore, to preserve the democratic character of Union membership, a procedure has been put into place to ensure that each Member State remains committed to the aforementioned principles. That procedure, set out in Article 7 EU, was introduced by the 1997 Amsterdam Treaty and can lead to a suspension of a Member State's membership in the Union in the case of a serious and persistent breach by that state of one of the principles referred to above. The procedure was first applied, haphazardly, in 2000 to adopt ad hoc political sanctions against Austria when, in that country, representatives of Jörg Haider's right-wing political party, the FPÖ, became members of a coalition government.

The ad hoc nature of the procedure was so unsatisfactory, however, that it led to huge tensions between Member States, and, ultimately, to the revision of the procedure by the 2000 Nice Treaty. The purpose of that revision was to provide a more detailed procedure according to which the Member State concerned would be given a better opportunity to defend itself, and according to which it would be possible for the Council to call on independent persons to

---

[120] As in the United States, see n. 115 above, where the component states may not conclude treaties. However, a limited competence to conclude an international agreement is not inconsistent with the concept of a federal state, as applied, for example, in Belgium: see Article 167 of the Belgian Constitution after the fourth state reform of 1993.

[121] In the final text of the draft (see Introduction, p. 5), the words "the equality of Member States before the Constitution as well as" were added after the word "respect" in the first line of the quote.

report on the situation.[122] As a result of the revision, the procedure currently starts with a preliminary decision by the Council of Ministers—acting by a majority of four-fifths of its members, and after obtaining the assent of the European Parliament—determining whether there is a clear risk of a serious breach on the part of the Member State. When that risk is established to exist, and when the Member State fails to follow the Council's recommendations to remedy it, the matter will be brought, in a second stage, before the Council, now composed of heads of state or government, which can decide, by unanimous vote, that a serious and persistent breach *has* been committed. That decision may then result, at the discretion of the Council of Ministers, which decides by qualified majority, in the suspension of the rights that the Member State derives from its EU membership, as well as the suspension of that Member State's voting right in the Council.

Obviously, the foregoing procedure constitutes a stark signal that adherence to the principles of democracy referred to in Article 6 EU is a condition of Union membership and the rights flowing from it. It furthermore underscores the inviolable character that the Member States attach to such principles. It has been introduced in the EU Treaty to defend the Union against the emergence of extreme right-wing movements in several Member States, and to preserve the democratic status of the Union. Its aim is to avoid a situation—as occurred in Germany when Hitler was appointed Chancellor on January 30, 1933—whereby the Union would one day find itself hosting an undemocratic state.

c)   "Nation-state": A concept inadequate to define the Union's polity

The proposition underlying the foregoing is that it is possible for an international organization to be a political system, and a democratic one, without being a state; in other words, the proposition challenges "the understanding of the state as the only possible locus of political community and of political identity."[123] But even if the Union were a state, it would not be a "nation-state" in the traditional sense of the word, that is, "a large group of people sharing the same culture, language, or history, and inhabiting a particular state or area;"[124] rather it would be a "citizen-state."

The traditional definition of nation-state has never been able to describe

---

[122] Article 7 (1) EU.

[123] Thus Deirdre Curtin, "Postnational Democracy: The European Union in Search of a Political Philosophy," Inaugural lecture at the University of Utrecht, 1997, referred to in Weiler's article cited in n. 109 above, at 49, fn. 11.

[124] *Paperback Oxford English Dictionary*, ed. Catherine Soanes (Oxford: Oxford University Press, 2002), 560.

countries such as Belgium, Canada, and Switzerland, which are not linguistically homogeneous, and is totally inadequate to define countries such as India
or South Africa,[125] which are neither linguistically nor ethnically homogeneous.
It is, moreover, no longer adequate to define the European nation-states, which,
as a result of large waves of immigration, including from other continents, have
become increasingly multicultural, proving that what ultimately keeps a population together is a formal link of citizenship and a variety of common institutions. All this is not to say, of course, that large numbers of the inhabitants of
these states still share a common history (often a history of oppression, though),
a common culture, if not language, and common ways of life, and that this may
help to strengthen feelings of commonality, provided that these characteristics
are not understood in an introverted, but instead open-minded, manner.[126] Finally, and most importantly, World War II has discredited the concept of nation-state so much[127] that it is no longer appropriate to use the concept in relation to the "supranational" European construction that was set up precisely to
foreclose the atrocities that nationalism has been responsible for.[128]

European Public Space and Public Opinion

With the above I do not wish to suggest that elements of homogeneity in a
population may not be valuable, but simply that they are no longer the distinctive feature of a state, if they ever were. By contrast, homogeneity may be an
element in promoting free debate in public space and in helping public opinion
to emerge. That role was recalled in the Maastricht judgment of the German
Constitutional Court of October 12, 1993.[129] In that judgment the Court examined whether the democratic principle inscribed in Article 20 (1) and (2) of the
German Basic Law, and stated to be unassailable in Article 79 (3), allows the
Federal Republic of Germany to participate in the founding of the European

[125] Thus Mancini, n. 109 above, at 36–37.

[126] In the same sense, see Jürgen Habermas, "Remarks on Dieter Grimm's 'Does
Europe Need a Constitution?'" 1 *ELJ*, 1995, 303–7; and N. MacCormick, n. 105 above,
137–56, at 144–45.

[127] J. Pinder, *The Building of the European Union*, 3d ed. (Oxford: Oxford University
Press, 1998), 3ff.

[128] Compare Jo Weiler, n. 109 above, who finds the notion of a European state un-
appealing in that it does away both with the deep commitment that membership in the
Community entails and with what makes the European postwar experiment so special
(62).

[129] BverfGE (1993) NJW 3047. For an English translation of important excerpts
from the judgment in re *Brunner et al. v. The European Union Treaty*, see 31 *CMLRev.*,
1994, 251–62, with a comment by M. Herdegen, "Maastricht and the German Constitutional Court: Constitutional Restraints for an 'Ever Closer Union,'" at 235–49.

Union by the Maastricht Treaty, and in particular whether it permitted the transfer of sovereign powers which that participation entailed in view of making a European monetary union possible. Following extensive analysis, the Court decided that such participation was permissible under the Basic Law, but at the same time indicated that the democratic principle sets limits to a further transfer of powers to the Union. In that respect, the Court said,

> If the peoples of the individual States provide democratic legitimation through the agency of their national parliaments . . . limits are then set . . . to the European Communities' functions and powers. . . . The States need sufficiently important spheres of activity of their own in which the people of each can develop and articulate itself in a process of political will-formation which it legitimates and controls, in order to give legal expression to what binds the people together (that is, a greater or lesser degree of homogeneity) spiritually, socially and politically.[130]

Earlier in the judgment the Court had emphasized the importance of free debate in the following terms:

> Democracy, if it is not to remain a merely formal principle of accountability, is dependent on the presence of certain pre-legal conditions, such as a continuous free debate between opposing social forces, interests and ideas, in which political goals also become clarified and change course and out of which comes a public opinion which forms the beginning of political intentions. That also entails that the decision-making processes . . . can be generally perceived and understood, and therefore that the citizen entitled to vote can communicate in his own language with the sovereign authority to which he is subject.[131]

The Court added that "such factual conditions, in so far as they do not yet exist, can develop in the course of time within the constitutional framework of the European Union," and that "parties, associations, the press and broadcasting organs are both a medium and a factor of this process, out of which a European public opinion may come into being."[132] It concluded in that respect that it is "decisive . . . that the democratic bases of the European Union are built-up in step with integration, and that as integration proceeds a thriving democracy is also maintained in the Member States."[133]

---

[130] At C, I, 2 (b.2) of the judgment in the English translation referred to in n. 129 above.

[131] At C, I, 2 (b.1). The last sentence has led some German scholars to emphasize the need for citizens, making up the *Staatsvolk* (the state people), to speak the same language. Thus Grimm, "Does Europe Need a Constitution?" 1 *ELJ*, 1995, 282ff, at 295. That is a view I do not subscribe to.

[132] Ibid.

[133] At C, I, 2 (b.2). On the judgment of the German Constitutional Court, see also Gerhard Casper, "The Karlsruhe Republic," *German Law Journal*, 2001, 214–19.

The emphasis in the Constitutional court's judgment on free debate, and public opinion, at both the national and the Union level, is to be welcomed. Indeed, fundamental principles of accountable government, such as political accountability of the executive branch toward an elected parliament, and accountability through the rule of law, which includes the submission of the executive branch to laws adopted by an elected parliament, draw their legitimacy from the people.[134] In that respect, a government in which the executive is accountable to a proactive and well-informed public whose opinions are based on free debate and aided by the free access of citizens and the media to official documents can be considered an even more direct form of democracy than democracy through parliament is. In a thriving democracy, public opinion indeed expresses the will of the people itself. Of course, this begs the questions: 1) whether there is such a European public space where a public opinion can be formed and expressed; 2) whether there is a European people with sufficient common identity to constitute such a public space; and 3) whether there are European media that help a public opinion to be formed

a)   Is there a European public space?

It is often said that, at the pan-European level, there is no public opinion and no free debate on matters of European general interest, and that there are no media worth speaking of that focus on such matters systematically and competently. That there is no public opinion on matters of European general interest is contradicted by empirical research analyzing citizen support for the process of European integration.[135] Moreover, if public opinion and free debate are lacking at the European level, the question can be asked whether the same cannot also be said of public opinion, free debate, and the media in each of the Member States. In other words, the real question is whether public opinion in the Member States is stronger than that at the European level, presumably because of the (more) homogeneous character of the people in that particular state. To be sure, in each of the Member States public opinion can be mobilized by the media around scandals, violence, and accidents, though mainly through tabloid newspapers and magazines. In that respect, "sleaze" at the Community level and the Brussels bureaucracy are no less—and probably

---

[134] See further chapters 2 and 3.

[135] Empirical research carried out on the basis of Eurobarometer surveys, which the European Commission has conducted since the 1970s, shows that public opinion wields real influence: see Russell J. Dalton and Richard C. Eichenberg, "Citizen Support for Policy Integration," in *European Integration and Supranational Governance*, ed. Wayne Sandholtz and Alec Stone Sweet (Oxford: Oxford University Press, 1998), 250–82, at 251. I will return to this issue in chapter 5, pp. 238ff.

more—popular subjects with the public than in the Member States, even though national scandals are often more "juicy," and the bureaucracy of the (much larger) national administrations more exacting.[136]

In addition, notions of "free debate" in the so-called "public space" must be put in perspective. This terminology refers to public debate of the (free, male, and wealthy) citizens of Athens in the agora in ancient Greece.[137] Of course, enlightened public debate among intellectuals and politicians still exists, and radio and television provide outstanding debating groups and instructive talk shows. Nevertheless, the tens, or hundreds, of thousands of listeners and spectators do not really join in the discussion, though they may be given the opportunity to react or ask questions. In the same way, the millions of persons in developing countries do not fully participate in discussions concerning global, environmental, or military subjects, although their futures are as much at stake as those in developed countries. I do not wish to say that public opinion and free debate are nonexistent or, worse, superfluous; quite to the contrary. My point is that free debate and public space are often as problematic at the national and international levels as at the European level, and that on each level we need dynamic, objective, and well-informed media that devote time and resources to less popular, and therefore financially less rewarding, educative and general interest programs.

The latter may, indeed, present more of a problem on the European level since, so far, there are no independent daily media[138] that look systematically at the news from a European viewpoint. This problem should not be exaggerated, however, since it is mitigated by the existence, in each Member State, of regular, and often daily, sections in quality newspapers, which typically employ journalists specializing in European affairs, notwithstanding that those

---

[136] European bureaucracy is a myth. "[It] is in fact tiny, leaderless, tightly constrained by national governments, and almost devoid of the power to tax, spend or coerce. Indeed, the EU lacks nearly every characteristic that grants a modern European state . . . its authority. Of the 20,000 employees of the European Commission, the EU's permanent bureaucracy, only about 2,500 have any decision-making capacity, the rest being translators and clerical workers. The Commission thus employs far fewer officials than any moderately sized European city." Andrew Moravcsik, "Despotism in Brussels? Misreading the European Union" (review of Larry Siedentop's *Democracy in Europe*, in *Foreign Affairs* [May/June 2001]).

[137] On the altered physiognomy of free debate in the public space, see J. B. Thompson, *The Media and Modernity: A Social Theory of the Media* (Cambridge: Polity Press, 1995).

[138] Publications that provide news from such a viewpoint are the periodical *European Voice*, published weekly, and *Arte*, which is essentially a Franco-German cultural television station.

journalists may tend to see European news items through national spectacles. Despite this, Europe still lacks political groups and political parties that attract coverage by the media and that are capable of putting issues and distinct alternatives before the public in terms that can be understood. Surely there are cross-border European political parties in the European Parliament, but the number of politicians in the European Parliament that make Europe their first priority rather than pursuing a national political career is still too small. Consequently, there is an urgent need to make European parties more instrumental in promoting citizen involvement at Union level.[139] I will return to that subject in chapter 7.

b) European identity in historical perspective

The European Union's motto, enunciated in Article IV-1 [now Article I-8] of the draft Constitution,[140] is "United in Diversity." That the European Union is diverse is obvious given the huge differences that exist between the many people from different cultures speaking several languages that form the Union. But what makes the Union united?

In a recent study of the cultural diversity of Europe,[141] one of the contributions was entitled "Europe and Its Values in an Historical Perspective."[142] In that chapter, the authors examine whether a common cultural foundation can be found in the public opinions of the populations of Europe at large. The

---

[139] On the role of political parties at Union level, see Article 191 EC. Not everyone will agree on the role those parties actually play: some consider them "nothing more than clearing houses; providing information, campaign materials, and organizing (poorly attended) conferences and candidate exchanges" (S. Hix, "Parties at the European Level and the Legitimacy of EU Socio-Economic Policy" 33 *Journal of Common Market Studies*, 1995, 527–54, at 535). Others believe that "they are increasingly well-adapted—in their functions and composition—to the demands of the EU's own political arena" (C. J. Lord, "Introduction," in *Transnational Parties in the European Union*, ed. D. S. Bell and C. Lord (Ashgate: Aldershot, 1998), 1–10, at 5. See further chapter 7, pp. 352ff.

[140] See chapter 6, pp. 258–59.

[141] Wil Arts, Jacques Hagenaars, and Loek Halman, eds., *The Cultural Diversity of European Unity* (Leiden: Brill, 2003). The study is part of a large-scale cross-national and longitudinal research project on fundamental values in Western societies, carried out since the late 1970s by a group of social and political scientists. The project was set up at the end of the 1970s by Ruud de Moor of Tilburg University in the Netherlands, and Jan Kerkhofs of Leuven University in Belgium. The most recent survey was published in 2001: Loek Halman, *The European Values Study: A Third Wave, Source Book of the 1999/2000 European Values Study Surveys* (Tilburg: Tilburg University).

[142] Wil Arts, Arnoud-Jan Bijsterveld, and Karel Veraghtert, in *The Cultural Diversity of European Unity*, n. 141 above, 67–85.

theme of the chapter is that Europe's cultural identity is a diverse one that has its roots in the cultural legacy of three treasure houses of antiquity: the ancient Near East, Greece, and Rome. In Israel the religious foundations were established for what later became Christian civilization; ancient Greece has influenced that civilization by way of its philosophy and rationalism; Rome has had an impact via both political principles and systematic law. Because of the importance of the theme for a proper understanding of the Union's motto "United in Diversity," it may be worthwhile to recall the most crucial points of Europe's history.

In Greece in the fifth century B.C., during the Persian Wars, Europe acquired for the first time a cultural identity, at that time mainly identified with freedom and democracy concentrated in free, independent, and democratic city-states. The second time that an emerging European cultural identity made its appearance was during the Roman Empire, with its emphasis on Roman law—which remains the basis of the law in large parts of Europe to this day—as well as on citizenship, individual rights, equity, and the common good. In late antiquity, a unifying cultural framework emerged with Christendom, although that framework appeared to be amenable to differentiation and internal pluralism. In the Middle Ages, Christendom gradually expanded, with the close alliance of ecclesiastical and secular power a distinct feature. At the same time, however, the legacy of Greek and Roman antiquity was preserved, thanks to Muslim thinkers and their stewardship of the inquisitive spirit of Greek science and philosophy, and thanks to the pivotal contribution of early Muslim librarians in preserving the ancient texts.[143] Christendom thus became the heir to the Roman Empire's Greco-Hellenistic and Latin culture, but it also contributed the moral value that protecting only oneself would not result in a humane society, thus merging the biblical values of faith, hope, and charity with the cardinal values of Greco-Roman culture.

Whereas in the Middle Ages Europe was equated with Christendom, during the modern era it was equated with civilization, a relatively new idea that gradually emerged from a complex intellectual process lasting from Renais-

---

[143] Ibid., 72. See also Davies, n. 11 above, who observes, at 349, that the wisdom of the ancients was preserved by Arab scholars at Palermo, Italy, and Toledo, Spain, and that it was the commentaries of Ibn Rusd (1126–98) that turned Aristotle into the philosopher of the Middle Ages. Moreover, Muslim Spain gave Europe decimal numbers and mathematical expertise. More generally, and less peacefully, Islam left a considerable impact on Europe's political future: it destroyed the supremacy of the Mediterranean, eliminated the influence of the post-classical world of Greece and Rome, and passed the political initiative to the emerging kingdoms of the north, especially Francia (p. 257).

sance humanism to Enlightenment rationalism, and adding to the biblical values the singular importance of religious tolerance. This new idea culminated in the eighteenth century with Voltaire stating very emphatically in 1751 that Europe shared common morals and customs.[144] After that, two vast upheavals catapulted Europe into modernity: the French and the Industrial Revolutions, which not only led to the rise of industrial capitalism and parliamentary democracy and to the transformation of religious beliefs into economic and political ethics, but also gave birth to new secular ideologies such as liberalism, socialism, and nationalism. The last of these ideologies was responsible for breaking up Europe into nation-states and national cultures, and in the period 1880 to 1914 taking a dramatic turn, defining a nation in terms of ethnicity and language. In that period nationalism and patriotism increasingly became values of the right, which found its expression on the European continent in the fascist and national-socialistic ideologies of the first half of the twentieth century. These values also proved themselves to be an extremely destructive force, mobilizing the masses and pitting them against one other, and in the process nearly destroying Europe.[145]

This complex history not only explains European cultural identity, but it also explains its diversity by taking heed of the shifting fault lines in European history that are still visible in current European values study surveys. Those fault lines are the marks of cultural diversity, separating Western from Eastern Europe with a wide transitional zone, sometimes called Central Europe, stretching from the Baltic to the Balkans, and separating Catholic Latin Christianity and Orthodox Greek Christianity. But there is also the line between the Western Roman Empire and the Eastern Roman Empire and the Ottoman line marking off the Balkan lands that lived for centuries under Muslim rule, as did part of Spain. There are further the lines dividing the region where Romance languages were spoken, up to the Roman *limes* (boundary), and the regions where Germanic or Slavic languages were spoken; and the lines that appeared in the fifteenth and early sixteenth centuries when the Church of Rome lost its monopoly on power, resulting in fundamental splits in Christendom and the emergence of Catholicism, Anglicanism, Lutheranism, and Calvinism.[146] All of

---

[144] Arts et al., n. 142 above, where it is noted at p. 74 that Voltaire "described Europe as a kind of a great republic divided in several states, some monarchical, some republican, the others mixed, but all corresponding with one another. They all had the same religious foundation, even if divided into several confessions. They all had the same principle of public law and politics, unknown in other parts of the world. So he argued."

[145] Ibid., 76. See further Michael Howard, "Empires, Nations, and Wars," in *The Lessons of History* (Oxford: Clarendon Press, 1991), 21–48.

[146] On all this, ibid., 78–82.

these dividing lines have profoundly affected the values of Europeans, and they are still responsible for many prejudices.

Whatever these differences and resulting prejudices are, the overarching attitude among European peoples remains one of pride for having shared a common history that, in spite of enormous recurrent atrocities, has nurtured and developed the cradle of civilization and culture for more than two millennia. It is a feeling that unites the whole of Europe, within and beyond the (expanding) boundaries of the European Union, and differentiates it from other parts of the world. It explains why the EU Treaty restricts, in Article 49, membership in the Union to European states, but, at the same time, why Turkey and Russia, for example, are seen to be part of Europe, even though they are located in large part in Asia.[147]

c) European identity now and in the future

The question whether Europe currently has a common identity must be seen against the backdrop of this complex history. The basic question is not whether in the end unity or diversity will prevail: they will both survive. The question is whether Europeans will be able to transcend nationalist(ic) feelings and whether, in the words of the culture provision in Article 151 of the EC Treaty, the European Union will succeed in "respect[ing] its national and regional diversity" and, at the same time, "bring[ing] . . . its common cultural heritage to the fore."

In that broad context is it particularly important to gauge whether a European identity is gradually taking shape in the younger generation, thanks to numerous cross-border exchanges in all segments of the population, primarily in the educational field. And, indeed, scientific research shows that, in the long term, public opinion in Europe is moving in a more internationalist and European direction.[148] Not surprisingly, this trend is most conspicuous in the

---

[147] The European Union has always been deliberately vague about where its borders lie. The traditional geographer's answer is that Europe ends at the Ural Mountains, which divide European Russia from western Siberia. The problem with dividing Russia into European and Asian parts is that Turkey also has a European part, ending at the Bosporus Strait, which runs through Istanbul, leaving most of Turkey in Asia. Including the whole of Turkey in the EU, as envisaged, can hardly be a precedent for Russia if that country were to ask for accession: including Russia as a whole would give the EU a border with North Korea, China, and Mongolia. See further Gwynne Dyer, "Where Does Europe End?" in *Baltic Times*, May 10, 2004 (http://www.baltictimes.com/art.php?art_id=9963).

[148] Pippa Norris, "The Global Generation: Cohort Support for European Governance," paper presented at a conference held in Brussels on October 11–12, 2002, not published. But see from the same author on the same subject, "Global Governance

group of baby boomers born after World War II, indicating that a strong generational divide exists between those who favor developments such as international public governance or enlargement of EU boundaries and those who do not. The research supports the conclusion that "if this trend is maintained in future years, then through the gradual process of generational turnover we can expect to see a rising tide of popular support for globalisation and for the European Union in future decades."[149]

The stronger connection of the younger cohorts to European identity is confirmed by other sources. According to interviews, 65 percent of persons under age twenty-five feel "European" to some extent,[150] while only 45 percent of persons over age fifty-five feel similarly.[151] Those figures must be contrasted with the connection to their own state that people in the Member States feel: while 47 percent of the public associate themselves primarily with their locality or their region of the country, only 38 percent identify primarily with their nation.[152] Moreover, 15 percent identify themselves primarily with their continent or "the world as a whole."[153] This 15 percent largely comprises younger, more widely traveled, and therefore more globally influenced respondents

---

and Cosmopolitan Citizens," in *Governance in a Globalizing World*, ed. Joseph S. Nye and John Donahue (Washington, DC: Brookings Institution Press, 2000), 155–77.

[149] Ibid., 1.

[150] Of course, this does not mean that young people in each Member State feel the same way. For example young continental Europeans may be more likely to feel European than young Brits. For the former, crossing borders is much more straightforward; most speak one or more foreign languages; and they have readier access to televised media from other countries.

[151] Eurobarometer 44, published April 1996, at 2.6. According to Eurobarometer 59, published July 2003, 57 percent of EU citizens "see themselves as to some extent European in a near future. The feeling is more widespread among younger respondents" (36). These figures are not contradicted by *The European Values Study: A Third Wave*, referred to in n. 141 above (tables 67–69, pp. 252–54). According to the latter, in total, and without distinguishing older from younger generations, the belonging to a locality or town, or a region, comes first (49.3 + 13.3 percent), before belonging to a country as a whole (27.7), whereas belonging to Europe and the world as a whole (3.2 + 6.5 percent) ranks last. These figures, however, apply to a total of thirty-one countries, including many that are not Member States, nor even candidate Member States, such as Russia, Belarus, and Ukraine.

[152] Norris, n. 148 above, 5. Again, there may be large differences between states: the feeling of belonging to one's own nationality was most strongly felt in the three then most recent Member States: 64 percent for Sweden, 65 percent for Finland, and 50 percent for Austria. They are joined by the British (57 percent) and the Danes (56 percent). Eurobarometer 44, n. 151 above.

[153] Norris, n. 148 above, 5.

who are "backpacking with Eurail passes, volunteering for the Peace Corps, or working with environmental NGOs around the world."[154] These findings confirm not only that the younger generation identifies more with transnational entities, but also, and even more importantly, that a large portion of the older generation see themselves as belonging primarily to their locality or region. In other words, already in the nation-states loyalty to a national community coexists with, or is even superseded by, loyalty to a local or regional community. This phenomenon also occurs at the level of Europe, as a sense of belonging to a regional or national community does not preclude a sense of belonging to the European community as a whole. In other words, feelings of belonging to a European, national, or regional community are not mutually exclusive.[155]

This trend of shared—rather than exclusive—belonging is also confirmed, from a legal point of view, by Article 17 EC, which states that "citizenship of the Union shall complement and not replace national [or, one may add, regional] citizenship," thus taking a firm "combination-of-loyalties view" of European citizenship.[156] "Shared" belonging will become even more evident with the emergence in each Member State, as a result of migration within the Union, of large communities of European citizens who do not have the nationality of the Member State where they reside, or, as a result of migration from third countries, have only recently acquired the nationality of the Member State of residence or of another state. The emergence of such "transnational" communities undoubtedly enhances identification with European society.[157] All of this shows that there is nothing contradictory about being Scot-

[154] Ibid., 6. Indeed, "differences in the extent to which individuals have lived or studied in other member states do seem to correlate with differences in the strength of European identity" (A. Maurits van der Veen, "Determinants of European Identity: A Preliminary Investigation Using Eurobarometer Data," http://www.isanet.org/noarchive/vanderveen.html. The author points out that a sense of European identity is a prominent factor shaping an individual's general support for European integration, much more than vice versa).

[155] See also the research conducted by Thomas Risse, "An Emerging European Identity? What We Know, and How to Make Sense of It," lecture delivered at University of Helsinki on April 25, 2003 (http://www.fu-berlin.de/atasp).

[156] It remains a matter for the Member States to determine who is a citizen of the Union: in principle every national of a Member State is also a citizen of the Union: Article 17 (1) EC. But see the ECJ's judgment in Case 192/99, *Kaur*, [2001] I-1237. On the distinction between nationality and citizenship, see G.-R. de Groot, *Towards a European Nationality Law* (Maastricht: University of Maastricht, 2003).

[157] On the involvement of immigrants in the European landscape, see Riva Kastoryano, "Transnational Participation and Citizenship: Immigrants in the European

tish, British, and European, or feeling Flemish, Belgian, and European, or, transcending civilizations, feeling Muslim and European, just as there is nothing contradictory in feeling Californian and American, or Hispano-American and American.

It is arguable that the recent enlargement of the Union with ten new Member States will slow down the emergence of a transnational European identity (although the strong desire of the new states to become a member of the club points in the other direction). It has certainly accentuated linguistic differences, as the number of official languages has grown from eleven to twenty. That means that EU documents for external use will have to be translated into all these languages; similarly, court proceedings and other official meetings at the institutions of the Union will require simultaneous translation when they are open to the public.[158] Undoubtedly, these processes will increase expenditure, and they may harm efficiency. From that viewpoint, it would be desirable to select a few working languages, or even to limit the number of official languages to the languages of the most populated states,[159] following the model used at the United Nations and the Council of Europe. That is a sensitive matter, however, for which there is no ready solution. The problem should not be overstated, though, as in many services of the EU institutions, one language (often English) is used as the working language. Moreover, language skills are an asset in international relations, particularly when one is working with developing countries, as it facilitates the understanding of cultural differences and sensitivities, and it should therefore remain a high priority on the EU's educational agenda.

Union" (translated from the French by Dominique Lussier), *Cultures et Conflits* 28 (Winter 1997): 59–73, who writes, "As they [activist immigrants] see it, their presence in that web as a transnational community defined by a common fight against racism confers on them a 'right' to participate in the building of Europe on the basis of their commitment towards a new political space that would give everyone the status of citizen of the Union."

[158] In a judgment of September 9, 2003, in Case C-361/01P, *Kik v. OHIM*, [2003] ECJ I-8283, the ECJ has negated the existence of a "fundamental principle of equality of languages," in the sense that every citizen would have a right "to have a version of anything that might affect his interests drawn up in his language in all circumstances" (para. 81), thus recognizing the need for working languages in specific circumstances.

[159] Currently those states are France, Germany, Italy, and the United Kingdom, having a population of 59.2 million, 82 million, 57.5 million, and 59.4 million inhabitants, respectively, followed by Poland (38.6 million) and Spain (39.6 million): *The Economist Pocket World in Figures: 2003 Edition* (London: Profile Books Ltd, 2003).

III. EUROPEAN CONSTITUTIONALISM

The term "constitutionalism" refers to values, traditions, and norms that underlie and substantiate a written constitution. As it is conceived, conceptually and chronologically, before a written constitution, it is possible for a country to have constitutionalism without having a constitution at all. The most famous example is the United Kingdom, which has no written constitution but does have a long history of constitutionalism, based in part upon ancient texts such as the Magna Carta (1215), the Petition of Rights (1628), and the Habeas Corpus Act (1679), which are all perceived to be more fundamental than other laws,[160] as well as upon another fundamental text that was recently added: the Human Rights Act (1998), which facilitates the enforcement by citizens in the U.K. of rights, embodied in the European Convention on Human Rights, before the British courts.

The European Union also has its own constitutionalism, regardless of whether the draft Constitution prepared by the European Convention (further discussed in chapter 6) is ultimately adopted. This constitutionalism is laid out in treaty provisions, in case law of the European Court of Justice, and in "general principles," such as those contained in Article 6 of the EU Treaty and in the 2000 EU Charter of Fundamental Rights.[161] But what are the values that make up European constitutionalism?

European Union Values and Objectives

Europe's diversity notwithstanding, it is not difficult to find a common core of European *values*. They are enumerated in Article 6 (1) of the EU Treaty, which provides that "the Union is founded on the principles of liberty, democracy, respect for human rights and fundamental freedoms, and the rule

---

[160] Gerhard Casper, *Constitutionalism*, Occasional Papers from the Law School, University of Chicago 22 (1987): 1 (referring to Dicey's distinction between the "conventions of the constitution" and the "law of the constitution") and 6. See also Jo Weiler, "European Neo-constitutionalism: In Search of the Foundations of the European Constitutional Order," *Political Studies* (1996): 517ff.

[161] As early as 1986, the ECJ referred, in Case 294/83, *Les Verts v. European Parliament*, [1986] ECR 1339, to the texts of the Community Treaties as the Community's "constitutional charter" (para. 23). The statement was repeated in the Court's Opinion 1/91 on the draft relating to the creation of the European Economic Area [1991] ECR I-6079. The ECJ stated, in para. 21, that "the EEC Treaty, albeit concluded in the form of an international agreement, none the less constitutes the constitutional charter of a Community based on the rule of law."

of law, principles which are common to the Member States." It adds, in paragraph 2, that

> the Union shall respect fundamental rights, as guaranteed by the European Convention for the Protection of Human Rights and Fundamental Freedoms . . . and as they result from the constitutional traditions common to the Member States, as general principles of Community law.

Article I-2 of the draft Constitution repeats these values, stating that "the Union is founded on the values of respect for human dignity, liberty, democracy, the rule of law and respect for human rights," adding, however, that "these values are common to the Member States in a society of pluralism, tolerance, justice, equality, solidarity and non-discrimination." These are values shaped over the centuries during Europe's long and complex history, as has been briefly described above, to which reference is made in the initial text of the draft Constitution's preamble:

> Conscious that Europe is a continent that has brought forth civilisation; that its inhabitants . . . have gradually developed the values underlying humanism: equality of persons, freedom, respect for reason; Drawing inspiration from the cultural, religious and humanist inheritance of Europe, the values of which, still present in its heritage, have embedded within the life of society its perception of the central role of the human person and his or her inviolable and inalienable rights, and respect for law.

The draft Constitution does not stop there. Article I-3 also contains a long (and uninspiring) list of Union objectives. Obviously, objectives cannot be equated with values: they are rather ambitions to put values into practice or make them more effective.[162] I will only quote a few of these objectives. In paragraph 1 of Article I-3, it is thus recalled that "the Union's aim is to promote peace, its values and the well-being of its peoples," and in paragraph 2 it is stated that "the Union shall offer its citizens an area of freedom, security and justice without internal frontiers, and a single market where competition is free and undistorted." Paragraph 3 adds many other objectives, such as

---

[162] According to the explanatory note to Articles I-2 and I-3 of the draft Constitution, "values make the peoples of Europe feel part of the same 'union,'" whereas objectives are "aims justifying the creation of the Union." The reason why the Convention was at pains to draw a distinction between values and objectives was that only values could be used to initiate procedures for sanctioning Member States for serious breach of Union principles and values: Norman, n. 63 above, 82. On this procedure as it currently functions, see the text accompanying n. 122 above.

sustainable development based on balanced economic growth, a social market economy, highly competitive and aiming at full employment and social progress, and with a high level of protection and improvement of the quality of the environment. . . . [The Union] shall combat social exclusion and discrimination, and shall promote social justice and protection, equality between women and men, solidarity between generations and protection of children's rights.—It shall promote economic, social and territorial cohesion, and solidarity among the Member States . . . and shall respect [the Union's] rich cultural and linguistic diversity, and . . . ensure that Europe's cultural heritage is safeguarded and enhanced.

Furthermore, the article states in paragraph 4, again among many other objectives, that

In its relations with the wider world, the Union shall . . . contribute to peace, security, the sustainable development of the earth, solidarity and mutual respect among peoples, . . . eradication of poverty and protection of human rights . . . as well as to strict observance and development of international law, including respect for the principles of the United Nations Charter.[163]

These lists recall values and objectives, most of which are already proclaimed in the preambles of the existing treaties. Many of them will be discussed in the third chapter (the rule of law comprising respect for human dignity and fundamental rights and freedoms) and in the fourth (equality before the law, affirmative action, social justice and solidarity in a welfare state). Some values and objectives that do not figure in the above enumerations— namely accountability and openness of government, as well as efficiency, integrity, and active responsibility in good governance—will also be discussed in later chapters.[164] Other elements that relate to the role of civil society in shaping democracy,[165] and the need for a responsive and responsible citizenry,[166]

[163] Article I-3 (4) of the draft Constitution. The text of the preamble and of Articles I-2 and I-3 (which have not be renumbered) were revised after the European Council meeting of June 17/18, 2004 (referred to in the Introduction, p. 5, and in the Epilogue, p. 375). The changes made to the sentences quoted in the text have not changed the content, though, except that the first sentence of the preamble, quoted at p. 53, has been deleted.

[164] Compare with the "desire," expressed in the preamble to the EU Treaty, "to enhance further the democratic and efficient functioning of the institutions."

[165] Article I-46 (4) [now Article I-47 (4)] of the draft Constitution provides for the possibility of "a significant number of citizens, no less than one million, coming from a significant number of Member States to invite the Commission to submit any appropriate proposal" on matters they consider to be of interest for the implementation of the Constitution.

[166] The concept of citizenship is defined in Article I-8 [now Article I-10] of the draft Constitution, in the same narrow way, however, as it currently is in Articles 17–22 EC

will also be mentioned later as part of democratic accountability and legitimacy.[167]

These values and objectives, spelled out with much rhetoric (and some arrogance) in the preamble and Articles I-2 and I-3 of the draft Constitutional Treaty,[168] stand in stark contrast to the short and powerful preamble of the 1787 U.S. Constitution, which is worth quoting here in full:

> We the People of the United States, in Order to form a more perfect Union, establish Justice, insure domestic Tranquility, provide for the common Defence, promote the general Welfare, and secure the Blessings of Liberty to ourselves and our Posterity, do ordain and establish this Constitution for the United States of America.

Interestingly, the American Constitution names domestic tranquillity and common defense among the primary concerns of the "more perfect Union" that the Constitution wanted to create, while the primary concern of the European Union has been, since the beginning in 1952,[169] economic and monetary integration. In the European Union, the concerns of internal tranquillity or security and common defense came to the fore only with the conclusion of the Treaty on European Union in 1992. That treaty, as we have seen above, added, to the first Community pillar, a second pillar defining a common foreign and security (defense) policy, and a third pillar seeking to provide citizens with a high level of safety by preventing and combating crime and terrorism.[170] Obviously, this basic difference is the result of a different historic background. However, in that respect, the European Union's history could have taken a different turn if the European Defence Community, which was signed in 1952 by France, Germany, Italy, and the three Benelux countries (the

---

Treaty (see chapter 4). In other words, the draft Constitution does not attempt to situate the concept in the wider realm of residents' rights.

[167] The draft Constitution contains, in Title 6 of Part I, Articles I-44 to I-51 [now Articles I-45 to I-52], a number of provisions relating to "the democratic life of the Union." In those Articles the principles of democratic equality, representative democracy, participatory democracy, and transparency are further defined to include, among other elements, an open dialogue with representative associations and civil society, and with social partners, as well as access to documents. See chapter 6, pp. 290–91.

[168] As mentioned in n. 163 above, the text of the preamble has been revised after the European Council meeting of June 17/18, 2004—the first paragraph, starting with "Conscious that," has even be deleted—taking away some of the rhetoric and arrogance, but, unfortunately, not all of it.

[169] That is with the creation of the (now-defunct) European Coal and Steel Community, signed in Paris on April 18, 1951 (p. 7).

[170] Articles 11–28 EU and Articles 29–42 EU, respectively.

U.K. refusing to participate), had not been stopped in its tracks when the French national assembly, wary of German remilitarization, refused to consider ratification.[171] If the European Defence Community had come into existence, it would have provided the Community with a European army, a common budget, and joint institutions, all matters that, more than fifty years later, are still very much on the agenda.

Typically European Values and Objectives?

All in all, the long enumerations in the preamble, and in Articles I-2 and I-3 of the draft Constitutional Treaty, are not very appealing, and they are not of a nature to arouse feelings of attachment to the Union. The values and objectives are too general and too hollow, giving the impression that all of the representatives of the national governments and the various institutions comprising the Convention that prepared the draft Constitution wanted to have their own imprint by adding one or another sentence.[172] Moreover, some important issues have not been addressed, such as, for example, how political accountability of the members of the Commission, and indeed of the Council, to Parliament will be enhanced.[173] Finally, it is not always clear how the Union will live up to the expectations that the draft Constitution has raised. That is particularly true for the objectives of the Union "in its relations with the wider world," mentioned in Article I-3 (4), where, for instance, the Union's intention to contribute to peace and security is not followed up by the adoption of efficient decision-making processes and operational measures in the field.

Most of the values, and the objectives, referred to above do not reflect typical European values or objectives, but are shared by all Western democratic countries.[174] Of course, that does not prevent differences in emphasis

---

[171] Craig and de Bùrca, n. 9 above, 9–10.

[172] Norman, n. 63 above, notes at 83 that because Valéry Giscard d'Estaing (who chaired the Convention preparing the draft Constitution), when introducing a skeleton text, had stressed the important role of objectives in defining the Union, the members of the Convention proposed a mass of additional objectives.

[173] See chapter 2, pp. 83–85, and chapter 7, pp. 349–52 and 360–66.

[174] In his book *The West and the Rest: Globalization and the Terrorist Threat* (Wilmington, Del.: ISI Books, 2002), R. Scruton identifies the following features as characteristic of Western democracies (as opposed to Islamic countries): the freedom of citizens to participate in the political process (based on theories of social contract, from Hobbes to Rawls); separation of religious and secular authority (as already developed in St. Augustine's book *The City of God*); and the creation of a universal system of law, Roman law (1–35). However, also within the Western world, those characteristics, and in particular the second one, are not everywhere accepted in the same way, as was illustrated by the strong differences of opinion at the Convention, and in

from existing. One such difference relates to the vision that the EU and the United States have of a welfare state, an issue that will be discussed in chapter 4. Another difference relates to the way in which government is organized: around parliament, as in Europe, or around the president, as in the United States; this issue will come up again in various chapters, and particularly in chapter 7.[175]

IV. CONCLUSIONS

Over the years the European construction now known as the European Union has developed from a community of six to one of twenty-five Member States. During the same period the sphere of competence of the Union has steadily been broadened. Roughly speaking, it now covers, under the so-called first pillar, the entire economic and financial sector and a large number of policies outside the economic sector that embrace social policy, culture, public health, and consumer and environmental protection; the second and the third pillars cover a common foreign and security policy and police and judicial co-operation in criminal matters, respectively. This does not mean that, in all of these areas, the powers of the Union are equally extensive and are exercised in the same way. Large differences continue to exist with regard to matters falling under the first pillar, in contrast to those falling under the second and the third pillars. A crucial difference is, that, under the first pillar, the three policy-making institutions, the European Commission, the Council of Ministers, and the European Parliament, taken together have true decision- and law-making authority, while, under the second and third pillars, the decision-making power of the Council of Ministers is by far the most prominent. On top of these three institutions there is the European Council of Heads of State or Government, which, on the occasion of regular summit meetings, drives the Union forward, not only in matters falling under the second and third pillars, but also in matters falling under the first pillar. Whatever the formal spreading of competence over the three pillars, analysis of the way in which the institutions function in practice shows that the institutions and the Member States do not attach too much importance to theoretical distinctions, but

---

the ensuing IGC, concerning the reference to God in the draft Constitution: see Norman, n. 63 above, 83–84.

[175] I will not deal in this work with the differences in attitude between Europeans and Americans regarding the use of force in international relations and the commitment to international law—a subject that, as explained in the Epilogue, at p. 385, I intended to discuss in a last chapter. Unfortunately, in order to keep the book to manageable length, I had to abandon that intention.

operate in a way that presents the Union as possessing a multilayered institutional unity.

From a viewpoint of constitutional law, the Union is certainly not an example of a neat separation of power: Under the first, and most important, pillar the legislative power is shared by the Commission, the Parliament, and the Council of Ministers (seconded by a committee of permanent representatives of the Member States, COREPER). The executive power is shared between the Member States and the Union, in accordance with the principle of executive federalism, and is mainly exercised at the level of the Union by the Commission, but with important input from committees in which external experts and Member State civil servants are represented. Only the judicial power is neatly attributed to the European Court of Justice and the Court of First Instance, but with important input from the national courts through the preliminary ruling procedure. Since the beginning, the European Court of Justice has used its power to support the European integration by considering integration as the ultimate aim of the European construction, and applying in its jurisprudence the method of so-called teleological (aim-oriented) interpretation.

Under the second and third pillars this division of powers, which looks complicated but has functioned efficiently in actual practice, does not apply: in areas covered by those pillars, much of the policy- and law-making authority at Union level remains in the hands of the European Council and the Council of Ministers. The crucial question for the future of European integration is whether the procedures applied under the first pillar, known as the "Community method," will, with the passage of time, spill over into the second and third pillars or whether, on the contrary, the procedures applied under the second and third pillars, characteristic of the "intergovernmental method," will spill over into the first pillar. Looking back over the first half century of European integration, there would seem to be no reason to believe that the second scenario will replace the first. That does not mean that "intergovernmental bargaining [would not be] an ubiquitous feature of supranational governance (as it is in many federal polities)."[176] However, what can be expected to continue is that "supranational bodies . . . [will] work to enhance their own autonomy and influence within the European polity, so as to promote the interests of transnational society and the construction of supranational governance."[177]

[176] Alec Stone Sweet and Wayne Sandholtz, "Integration, Supranational Governance, and the Institutionalization of the European Polity," in *European Integration and Supranational Governance*, n. 135 above, 25–26.

[177] Ibid., 26.

This factor has indeed been responsible in the past for European integration becoming broader and deeper.[178]

European integration now faces new challenges, and in particular the recent enlargement of the Union, as of May 1, 2004, from fifteen to twenty-five Member States may subject the Union to a severe test.[179] The way in which these challenges are met will determine whether European integration will develop at the same pace, or whether in fact differentiation will succeed—that is, whether Member States wishing to proceed more quickly in the integration process will be able to make use of the procedures of "enhanced cooperation" and whether they will obtain the approval of the non-participating Member States to go ahead. These procedures will not necessarily be applied, but they can be used as a carrot and stick by the more integration-minded Member States in order to convince their fellow Member States to progress further with the integration process, as has happened in the past with the Schengen Agreement and in the field of social policy.[180] The early reaction of President Jacques Chirac and Chancellor Helmut Schröder when, in December 2003, no agreement could be reached at the IGC meeting on the draft Constitution would

---

[178] Political scientists have devised several theories to explain the process of European integration. Neo-functionalist theories imply that the EU, particularly the EC component, gradually but comprehensively replaces the nation-state in all of its functions. By contrast, intergovernmentalists conceptualize EC politics as a subset of international relations, and they rely on the "principal-agent" analysis to explain how and under what conditions Member State governments delegate authority to Community organs, and how they develop instruments to control the Community institutions. See also chapter 6, pp. 263ff. In an effort to transcend these views, Wayne Sandholtz and Alec Stone Sweet, at that time two political scientists of the University of California, Irvine, examined why policy making sometimes migrates from the nation-state level to the EC, why integration has proceeded more rapidly in some policy domains than it has in others, and to what extent the EC is governed by "intergovernmental" or "supranational" decision making. See their article, n. 176 above.

[179] See Fritz W. Scharpf, "Legitimate Diversity: The New Challenge of European Integration," in *The State of the European Union: Politics and Society*, ed. Tanja A. Börzel and Rachel A. Cichowski (Oxford: Oxford University Press, 2003), 79–104. Besides enlargement, Scharpf examines two other challenges: building common security capabilities and safeguarding European welfare states. He argues that the existing modes of governing the European Union, based on high levels of consensus among member governments and on uniform rules across all Member States, are no longer available to resolve the new challenges, and that we will need to focus on new modes of European governance that are able to accommodate legitimate national diversity. On these new modes of government, see Adrienne Héritier, "New Modes of Governance in Europe: Increasing Political Capacity and Policy Effectiveness?" in ibid., 105–26. See also chapter 4, pp. 167–70 and 197–200.

[180] See nn. 90 and 91 above.

seem to point in that direction. The two leaders threatened to move forward with a "core" Europe if talks on the constitutional draft were not finished by the end of 2004.[181]

The transfer of sovereign powers in limited but ever-wider fields from the Member States to the Union raises the question whether the Union is a political system that is on the way to becoming a federal state, albeit not a "nation-state"—if that concept is taken in its traditional sense of meaning a state with an ethnically, linguistically, and/or culturally homogeneous population—but rather a "citizen-state." I believe that this question is to be answered in the negative, as long as 1) the Union does not possess a plenitude of jurisdiction, including powers of internal and external coercion (police force and military capabilities) and the power to impose taxes to that effect; 2) there is no internal cohesion between the Union and state level, which is typical for a full-fledged federal state; and 3) the Member States and their populations do not wish to reduce the status of the participating states to that of mere component states. This does not mean, however, that the Union is not to be regarded as a political system that has some of the elements that international law considers to be constitutive characteristics of statehood. Nor does it mean that, as a political entity, the Union would not evolve as an entity with democratic legitimacy, thus refuting "the understanding of a state as the only possible locus of political community and of political identity."[182] In the following chapters I will try to show that the Union is well on the way to becoming such a democratic political system.

One of the elements that causes a territorially defined political system to possess democratic legitimacy is the existence of a public space where, in the words of the Maastricht judgment of the German Constitutional Court,[183] "a continuous free debate between opposing social forces, interests and ideas" can take place, and through which public opinion can be formed with the help of responsible media. The question is whether such a public space and public opinion are evident at the level of the European Union, and whether there is a European identity in which such public space and opinion can take root. With the German Constitutional Court, I accept that "in so far as they do not yet exist, [such public space and opinion] can develop in the course of time within the constitutional framework of the European Union"—a dictum dating from 1993—and believe, moreover, that since then European identity has continued to grow, especially with the younger generation. In that respect, one

---

[181] See chapter 6, p. 262.
[182] See Deirdre Curtin, n. 123 above.
[183] See above, p. 41–43.

must keep in mind that European identity, like European citizenship, is not to take the place of national (or often regional) identity but exists in addition to it. Furthermore, what makes the European experiment so special[184] is that, in accordance with the Union's motto "United in Diversity," it will need to resolve in a constructive way the challenge that theories of liberal democracy are confronted with. That challenge is that it no longer suffices to recognize all citizens by attributing them equal rights notwithstanding differences, but that it is also necessary to recognize differences themselves, that is, group values, insofar as individuals identify themselves with those values. In an increasingly multicultural society, as now exists in all Member States, this implies that "newcomers" are ready to respect the basic rules and fundamental institutions of the "natives," and that the latter are ready to respect the former's differences without robbing them of their identity.[185]

In the existing European Treaties and even more so in the draft Constitution (further discussed in chapter 6), values and objectives that are considered "European" are enumerated. Basically, they are founded, according to Article 6 (1) EU Treaty, "on the principles of liberty, democracy, respect for human rights and fundamental freedoms, and the rule of law." Obviously, those values are not exclusively European but are shared by all truly democratic states. Nevertheless, there are differences in emphasis placed on some of these values, as recent events have shown. There will be an occasion to discuss these and other differences in the following chapters.

---

[184] See Joseph Weiler, n. 109 above.

[185] Ibid. See also Herman De Dijn, "Cultural Identity, Religion, Moral Pluralism and the Law," *International Journal of Philosophy and Theology* (2003), with further references.

CHAPTER TWO

Accountable Government

In chapter 1 the European Union was described as a political entity, not a state, in search of democratic legitimacy. To determine whether the Union is making headway in that search, this and the following chapters will examine how democratic EU government has become.

For a political entity to be democratic it must have a democratic government, comply with the requirement of good governance, and do its utmost to involve its citizens in the political process. Democratic government and good governance are twin concepts: the first refers to the organization of public power in a democratic fashion, that is, in a way that makes it answerable to the people; the second refers to the exercise of public power in the pursuit of the public good and justice for all. Both democratic government and good governance entail respect for the rule of law and compliance with the proper procedures. They also require an open government aimed at making citizens and civil servants feel responsible for the common good and keeping them well informed through access to public documents and the media. The subjects discussed in this and the following chapters are thus accountable government (this chapter), the rule of law (chapter 3), good governance (chapter 4), and responsible citizens, open government, and the media (chapter 5).

As in Chapter 1, I will now, and in the following three chapters, focus on the first pillar rather than the second and third. It is indeed under the first pillar that the integration process, driven by a strong executive, the EU Commission, has advanced the farthest, and, accordingly, that accountability, submission to the rule of law, good governance, and open government are most needed.

For a government to be democratic, it must emanate from the people and be answerable to the people. In a representative democracy, this means that the people are represented by men and women elected by universal suffrage and thus empowered to make binding legislation. In a democratic system the executive branch of government must also be responsible to the people, either by having its head elected directly—as in a presidential system—or by making it accountable to an elected parliament—as in a parliamentary system. Political accountability has two meanings: first, it means that the executive branch of government must *render account* to parliament in respect of action undertaken or proposed for the future—an obligation that exists in both the presidential and parliamentary forms of government—and, second, that the executive branch can be *held responsible* by parliament for action that was undertaken in the past. In a parliamentary system, the latter may lead to the resignation of the government as a whole, or of its individual members, if they no longer enjoy the confidence of a majority in parliament. In a presidential system, the second form of accountability does not exist because of the elected president's own democratic legitimacy. I will return to that subject in chapter 7.

For a government to be democratic it must not only be answerable to the people, but it must also be made subject to the rule of law, which is the theme of chapter 3. Submission to the rule of law has many facets. It entails submission of public authority to judicial review by an independent judge, respect for the freedoms and rights of every person, and equality of all before the law. It also requires a clear legal basis for the exercise of public authority, and legal certainty in the application of the law. In this regard, the question arises whether judicial review, as a component of the rule of law, should also extend to the legislative branch, normally an elected parliament. In a sense, the question points to a contradiction between the concepts of democratic legitimacy and the rule of law: whilst the former is based on majority rule, the latter purports to protect the individual. And, indeed, from an analytical point of view, majorities are perfectly able to oppress individual citizens.[1]

Therefore many legal systems, especially those with a strong constitution, take the position that the legislative branch must also be submitted to judicial control. This is the position in both the United States and the European Union. There might even be a causal link between the two concepts, answerability to the people and submission to the rule of law, in the sense that the less democratic legitimacy a system possesses, particularly in its legislative branch, the greater the judicial scrutiny the system should be subjected to. This concept is illustrated by the situation under the Union's first pillar, where the limited democratic legitimacy of the Council of Ministers as a component of the legislature, as exposed in chapter 1, is compensated for by its submission to extensive judicial review. Things are very different under the second pillar

---

[1] Tim Koopmans, *Courts and Political Institutions, A Comparative View* (Cambridge: Cambridge University Press, 2003) 123.

(and, to a lesser extent, under the third), where democratic legitimacy and judicial control are *both* notoriously weak.

As pointed out in the introduction,[2] the assumption made in this and the following chapters is that, ideally, the European Union should, as far as possible, replicate democratic government as it exists in democratic states with a parliamentary regime, thereby combining political accountability of the executive to parliament with the subjection of all public authority to the rule of law. According to this assumption, it should be a political priority to make that happen in the not-too-distant future.[3] This does not mean that the Union should become a state: it is not one currently, and, as explained in chapter 1, neither should it become one.[4] It means, rather, that the EU public authorities should be subjected, in areas where the EU has powers comparable to those of a state, to the same requirements as public authorities in a democratic parliamentary state.

To see whether, and to what extent, that assumption is realized in the Union, I will first examine, in Section I, how executive accountability operates in a democratic state. In doing so I will not only look at the *political* responsibility of members of the executive branch, that is, of cabinet ministers, but I will also describe some other devices through which members of executive government may be held responsible, legally or otherwise. Then, in Section II, I will describe how members of the European Commission are held accountable under the Union's first pillar, that is, under Community law, with special reference to the case of administrative agencies. In Section III, I will draw conclusions.

I. ACCOUNTABILITY OF EXECUTIVE GOVERNMENT

In a democratic system those at the helm of the executive power must be made politically accountable to the people. To put it bluntly, "the basic con-

---

[2] At pp. 2 and 3 above.

[3] That was also the understanding of the Committee of Independent Experts in their two reports (n. 58 and 60 below), as pointed out by Carol Harlow, *Accountability in the European Union* (Oxford: Oxford University Press, 2002), 25–26.

[4] See chapter 1 above, p. 37. In other words, the Union should not replicate the sovereign state "in some new super-state, some new repository of absolute sovereignty," but should transcend it, as pointed out by Neil MacCormick, *Questioning Sovereignty* (Oxford: Oxford University Press, 1999), 191. What the Union needs to replicate, though, are the devices which democratic States with a parliamentary system use in order to gain legitimacy. The reasons why a parliamentary, rather than a presidential, regime is taken as a point of reference are explained in chapter 7.

dition of representative democracy" is that those ruled "'can throw the scoundrels out'—that is replace the Government."[5] In a truly presidential system this means that the head of the executive power must be reelected if he or she wants to continue in office (and the constitution so permits). In a parliamentary system the head and the members of the executive can moreover be asked to resign in between elections by a parliament that has been elected by universal suffrage.[6] Political accountability is not the only device available to hold high officials accountable. To illustrate this, I will concentrate here on a few affairs or scandals during which cabinet ministers in Member States have been held accountable through other means.

Comparing Executive Accountability Regimes

With the notable (and partial) exception of a few Member States such as France and, arguably, Finland and Poland, most EU Member States have a system of "parliamentary democracy." It is characteristic for such a system that the head of government—the prime minister or chancellor—and the members of his or her cabinet, so-called "ministers," can be forced to resign by a majority vote in parliament. To be sure, there are variations on this general rule. For example, in order to enhance the stability of the incumbent government, some countries have instituted constitutional arrangements that require parliament, when it expresses its lack of confidence in the prime minister or chancellor, to (nearly) simultaneously elect a successor (the so-called "constructive vote of no confidence"). In countries with a large number of political parties, and that are therefore ruled by coalition governments, this requirement necessitates sometimes protracted political negotiations—which by their nature discourage governmental change. Moreover, in most states it is the prime minister or the chancellor who dismisses, and replaces, individual ministers when it has become clear that parliament, the public, or the prime minister or chancellor him- or herself has lost confidence in that minister. Furthermore, to balance the system, it is possible for the prime minister or chancellor to request the head of state—the Queen, King, or president—to dissolve parliament and to organize new elections when he or she believes that

[5] J. H. H. Weiler, "The European Union Belongs to Its Citizens: Three Immodest Proposals," 22 *ELRev.*, 1997, 150.

[6] As will be explained in chapter 7, there are different forms of presidential and parliamentary systems. The presidential system referred to herein is a full presidential system with a popularly elected president and without a prime minister. When I refer herein to the power of parliament to ask members of the executive to resign, I mean the house, in a bicameral system, which is composed of members elected by universal suffrage. On bicameralism, see also chapter 7 below, pp. 332ff.

the current parliamentary majority no longer reflects the will of the people. I will return to all of this in chapter 7.

The presidential system of the United States is completely different. Directly elected by the people, the president possesses his or her own democratic legitimacy for the whole period in office and, impeachment aside, cannot be forced by Congress to resign.[7] Moreover, members of the president's cabinet do not bear collective political responsibility with the president, and the president can dismiss them at will. Contrary to the case in parliamentary regimes, in which ministers are generally elected members of parliament, members of the presidential cabinet do not personally have a constituency from which they derive their own democratic legitimacy.[8] This does not mean, however, that in a presidential regime Congress or parliament does not have considerable countervailing powers, especially in the United States, where Congress and its committees have the independence and resources to influence presidential policy, particularly through the power of the purse.

Such are the political structures described in written constitutions, or established in constitutional traditions and covenants, as in the United Kingdom. But, how do these arrangements work in reality? For example, did Tony Blair's position concerning going to war with Iraq make him more vulnerable in his relations with Parliament than George W. Bush's position with regard to Congress? In purely "legal" terms the answer should be in the affirmative since the House of Commons could have sent Mr. Blair home, while Congress was not in a position to do the same to President Bush. There are however, "factual" factors that reinforce the position of the head of government in a parliamentary regime and bring it closer to the executive head in a presidential regime.

Thus, apart from the fact that in the last elections Tony Blair was reelected by a large majority, as reflected in a large parliamentary majority, he is also, like many of his counterparts in the other European states, the de facto leader

---

[7] U.S. Constitution, Art. 2, sec. 4; U.S. Constitution, Art. 1, sec. 2, cl. 5 (giving the House the sole power of impeachment); and U.S. Constitution, Art. 1, sec. 3, cl. 6 (giving the Senate the sole power to try impeachments). Impeachment procedures also can be initiated against the vice-president and "all civil officers of the United States" (Art. 2, sec. 4). Impeachment "shall not extend further than to removal from Office, and disqualification to hold any Office of honor . . . but the Party convicted shall nevertheless be liable and subject to Indictment, Trial, Judgment and Punishment, according to Law" (Art. 1, sec. 3, cl. 7).

[8] In a parliamentary regime a minister may in fact have obtained more votes in the elections than the prime minister, making it almost impossible for the latter to get rid of the minister.

of the political party that won the elections. In that capacity, he is in a position to exercise strong influence on the attitude of "his" political party, also while in office—a factor that is of decisive importance. Indeed, in European parliamentary systems political parties are extremely powerful organizations, able to considerably alter the institutional balance established in constitutional texts or arrangements.[9] They are instrumental in many ways: before the elections, in drafting a coherent political program on which they may win or lose the election; and after the elections, in forming a new government—especially in countries where a coalition government is needed to have a majority in parliament. Political parties are then directly involved in the negotiations to form a new government, and thereafter will make sure that as many political priorities as possible will be reflected in the new government's mission statement. It is this statement that binds together government and the coalition supporting it, and that will be used as a benchmark in the following elections to see whether the government has kept its promises.

The political position of a prime minister or chancellor will thus be safe as long as he or she commands the support of his or her political party both in and outside parliament—and, frequently, as long as he or she has the support of trade unions or other associations affiliated with the political party. Uncertainty as to the prime minister or chancellor's political fate will occur only when political party activists and members of parliament who are not cabinet ministers, sensing the changing mood of the electorate, start to disagree, or at least to pose more questions. This happened to Tony Blair when he was faced with (but survived) an incipient rebellion from his own party for committing British troops in Iraq (and such a rebellion could still happen as, in the aftermath of the war, many infelicities have surfaced). In the case of coalition governments, that uncertainty will be multiplied by a factor equal to the number of parties participating in government.

In the United States, political parties (and trade unions) do not play the same role as in Europe. It would be unthinkable, I assume, for the president's State of the Union address to be cleared in advance by his or her political party, much less by the parties with which a coalition government would be set up (an unlikely situation in the United States, as in the United Kingdom). This does not mean, of course, that there are no strong links between the president and members of Congress of the same party, just as there may also be tensions and occasional flare-ups between the president and Congress, for

---

[9] A state of affairs that, if political parties were to accumulate too much power, would be criticized for turning a system of "demo"-cracy into a system of "party"-cracy.

instance, over the budgetary means the president needs to lay out his policy, which will happen even when both houses of Congress are controlled by the majority that also elected the president.[10]

Having said all this, it remains difficult to say in which of the two systems, the presidential in the United States or the parliamentary in the United Kingdom, congress or parliament yields more countervailing power over the executive. At first glance, it would seem that in the parliamentary system parliament enjoys more countervailing power, since it remains possible for parliament to dismiss the head of government, and the entire cabinet, in the period between elections. Indeed, the power to make those governing resign is a very strong weapon, especially in countries where coalition governments are in power (a state of affairs prevalent in almost all European countries, but not in the UK).[11] This is not, however, so much because parliament actually forces government to step down—something it would not do under normal circumstances, given the political party link between government and the majority in parliament[12]—but because disagreements may arise between the coalition parties in government. When that happens, or is likely to happen, the political parties in opposition will then try to take advantage of these disagreements, and even encourage them in order to force the government to step down on its own initiative. All of this makes one believe that in a parliamentary regime the executive may be under some pressure, but not much more than in a presidential one.[13] I will return to all these points in chapter 7 when discussing the most appropriate form of government for the European Union.

Parliamentary democracy is about representation of the people. From the viewpoint of representative democracy, it is therefore crucial for government (and parliament) to maintain the confidence of the people.[14] The issue came to

---

[10] See Carl Hulse, "Congress and the President: One Party, but Divided," *New York Times*, Feb. 23, 2003, A19.

[11] The reason the U.K. does not have a large array of political parties is its electoral system, which is a single-member plurality or majority system under which the winner takes all, as opposed to a system of proportional representation. See Arend Lijphart, *Patterns of Democracy: Government Forms and Performance in Thirty-Six Countries* (New Haven, Conn.: Yale University Press, 1999), 165, where the two-party system as applied in the U.K. is described at 13–14. For a full account, see chapter 7 below, pp. 330–32.

[12] On this point, see Tim Koopmans, n. 1 above, 124.

[13] See, however, for a view strongly critical of the power of the U.S. Congress, which, in the past few years, has become "less vigilant, less proud and protective of its own prerogatives," Robert G. Kaiser, associate editor and senior correspondent of the *Washington Post*, writing on the contingent nature of institutional evolution in the U.S. robertgkaiser@yahoo.com.

[14] Representative democracy is a difficult concept to define: it may refer to repre-

the fore, in both Europe and the United States, in the weeks before the war in Iraq started, that is, when disagreements came to light between incumbent governments and large segments (perhaps even a majority) of the people. The fundamental question is whether it is correct, as President Bush was heard to say, that "leadership sometimes involves bucking public opinion." Arguments in favor are that political leaders are better informed, and can therefore better judge policy decisions, and that public opinion may be in a constant state of flux. With regard to the latter, a parliamentary regime may be more responsive than a presidential system when the issue is highly controversial, politically and ethically, and when public opinion indicators persistently point in the same direction. That is especially so, again, when a coalition government is in power because conflicting opinions will then be voiced within, as much as outside, the cabinet.

Learning Accountability from Scandals

Political scandals are "potential reputation and 'trust depleters' in a field where vibrant democratic government depends on social trust," and can therefore lead to "a weakened form of democratic government."[15] Consequently, a democracy's forceful reaction to high-level political scandals displays its willingness to maintain trust in the political system. The need to respond forcefully is particularly important since, as mentioned above, political responsibility of cabinet ministers to parliament, as it exists in a parliamentary system, is a strong weapon in theory, but is not often used in practice. Thus it has been observed, for example, that in the Netherlands in the period 1945–96, out of a total of forty-two ministers and secretaries of state who resigned, only ten resigned because a majority in parliament or one of the governing parties had made known its lack of confidence in the policy conducted by the minister concerned.[16] Similarly, in the United Kingdom between 1955 and 1986, only

---

sentation of citizens by an elected parliament, but also to direct participation of citizens in democratic life through political parties, civil society, or public opinion. See, among recent writings on democracy, Amaryllis Verhoeven, *The European Union in Search of a Democratic and Constitutional Theory*, 38 European Monographs (The Hague: Kluwer Law International, 2002), 196–99, and the many references in Carol Harlow, n. 3 above, 101–7. The principles of representative democracy and of participatory democracy are defined in Articles I-45 and I-46 [now Articles I-46 and I-47] of the EU's draft Constitution discussed in Chapter 6, pp. 290–91.

[15] John B. Thompson, *Political Scandal: Power and Visibility in the Media Age* (Cambridge: Polity Press, 2000), 252.

[16] Mark Bovens, *The Quest for Responsibility: Accountability and Citizenship in Complex Organizations* (Cambridge: Cambridge University Press, 1998), 88.

six resignations of senior ministers could be directly attributed to the system of political responsibility of ministers toward parliament.[17] The most conspicuous case was the resignation of Lord Carrington as Minister of Foreign Affairs because his information office had not foreseen the Argentine invasion of the Falkland Islands.[18]

If these trends were proved to exist in other parliamentary regimes as well (as they probably do), that does not automatically mean that political accountability does not work. Indeed, as the cases discussed below show, cabinet ministers often resign voluntarily or are forced to resign by the head of government in the wake of a scandal. In other words, accountability to parliament constitutes a procedure of last resort that heads of government and individual ministers are eager not to apply, the former because they do not wish to see an individual case affect the confidence in the cabinet as a whole, and the latter because they wish to preserve their political future. This means that public opinion and the media play an important role as well, as it is they that will convince the head of government to ask a cabinet member to leave office. Moreover, as the examples referred to below demonstrate, accountability of cabinet members is put into practice not only through political sanctions but also through other means.

a) Open government in Sweden—at the expense of responsible journalism?

There can be no doubt that open government and free access to public documents are crucial in avoiding wrongful behavior by high officials. Within the European Union Sweden is certainly the unchallenged champion of open government. In 1766 the country passed its first constitutional statute on the freedom of the press, establishing a constitutional right for citizens to access and to copy official documents.[19] Under the present system, public officials are free to supply information to the press about the contents of official documents, including confidential items, and a person involved in the production or publication of printed matter is not allowed to disclose the identity of a person who has provided information. To be sure, no causal link can be proven to exist between open government and the prevention of scandals, but

---

[17] Ibid., referring to Colin Turpin, *British Government and the Constitution*, 2d ed. (London: Butterworths, 1994), 432.

[18] Bovens, n. 16 above, 87–88.

[19] The matter is now regulated by the Instrument of Government (the official Swedish Constitution) and by the Freedom of the Press Act of 1949 and the Freedom of Expression Act of 1991. See Ulf Bernitz, "Sweden and the European Union: On Sweden's Implementation and Application of European Law," 38 *CMLRev.*, 2001, 903–34, at 916.

as far as I know,[20] in recent years scandals in Sweden have been limited to the abuse of official credit cards by ministers and, in a recent case, the purchase by a Minister of Justice of an apartment taking advantage of a particular tax scheme (at the time the purchase was perfectly legal, but her political party was ideologically opposed to the tax scheme).[21]

In the latter case, the media over-reacted to such an extent that an independent commentator wondered whether journalists did not behave like "bloodhounds, rather than watchdogs."[22] The issue raises delicate questions concerning the fractious relationship between politics and the media. It is commonplace to observe that mass communication has altered politics, and that "the media have become the essential space of politics,"[23] which includes the politics of scandal. This is particularly so with the growing importance of tabloids (in some countries more than in others), which in recent years have forced political actors "to struggle increasingly . . . to keep their heads above the turbulent waters of media scandal and . . . 'manage sleaze.'"[24]

Obviously, the relationship between politicians and journalists is a delicate one. Those in both professions compete for the favor of people, whether voters or readers, and quite often do so by using doubtful methods—such as making promises that cannot be kept or allegations that cannot be proven, or by focusing on minor but catchy points of interest for the sake of earning votes or readers. Such behavior is not consistent with the common good that both claim to pursue. Moreover, both groups, politicians and journalists, need each other badly: the first need an audience, and the second need scoops. As a

[20] Apart from the appalling sterilization program of "genetically inferior" persons carried out between 1935 and 1976.

[21] These and other cases are described by Alexa Robertson of Stockholm University's Department of Political Science in her paper "Dancing with Doris: Political Contempt and the Media in Sweden," presented at the workshop "Anti-politics and the Media," organized by the European Consortium for Political Research, in Turin in March 2002.

[22] Ibid.

[23] See Manuel Castells, "An Introduction to the Information Age," in *The Media Reader: Continuity and Transformation*, ed. H. Mackay and T. O'Sullivan (London: Sage), 398–410, at 404, quoted by Robertson, n. 21 above, 3.

[24] Robertson, n. 21 above, 3 with further references. See also John B. Thompson, *The Media and Modernity: A Social Theory of the Media* (Cambridge: Polity Press, 1995), 130 and 141ff. The author distinguishes four types of trouble that may make politicians lose grip: gaffes and outbursts, a performance that backfires because of lack of sensitivity to the recipients of a message, leaks whereby insiders cause the dissemination of information that the politician wanted to keep out of the public domain, and scandals.

result, journalists force politicians to make statements about subjects they know little about or about which they have nothing interesting to say.

b) Criminal prosecution in France—playing it rough

In the mid-1980s, France was confronted with a blood contamination scandal. Approximately 1,200 hemophiliacs were infected with HIV following blood transfusions, of whom 250 died. Immense public commotion ensued and all legal avenues were used to placate the victims. A former prime minister and two other ministers were indicted, and a special court, the Cour de Justice de la République, was set up to try them in accordance with common criminal procedures. The former head of the National Transfusion Center, a physician, and several other doctors and civil servants were sentenced to prison by a criminal court in Paris. Several victims sued local transfusion centers and obtained damages. A special fund was created to indemnify victims for pecuniary and non-pecuniary losses. In 1999 the former prime minister and one of the two ministers were acquitted; the other minister, the Secretary of Health, was found guilty, but not punished.

The recourse to criminal law was criticized by many for being an inadmissible change in emphasis from political to penal responsibility. It would indeed be wrong to bring political mismanagement or misjudgment within the realm of criminal law instead of letting constitutional law play its role.[25] It has led, nevertheless, to the so-called Bérégovoy-Balladur rule (after the names of the two prime ministers who applied it to individual ministers), which requires ministers to step down when they are at risk of becoming involved in criminal proceedings.[26] Except for serious breaches, the rule does not apply to the president of the Republic, who, from a political and penal viewpoint, is immune while in office.[27]

Criminal law has also been used in other countries to hold public officials accountable for acts committed while in office. Obviously it is an instrument that has its drawbacks when applied in political cases. To take an extreme example, in Italy the *mani pulite* campaign led to considerable tension between judges and politicians, especially under the leadership of Silvio Berlusconi, the then (and now again) prime minister, who is currently under criminal investi-

---

[25] Olivier Beaud, "Le traitement constitutionnel de l'affaire du sang contaminé" [Constitutional treatment of the affair of contaminated blood], 4 *RDP* 1997, 995, at 997.

[26] Editorial, *Le Monde*, June 14, 2002, 20.

[27] Louis Favoreu et al., *Droit constitutionnel*, 4th ed. (Paris: Dalloz, 2001), 562–64. See further Olivier Jouanjan and Patrick Wachsmann, "La controverse doctrinale autour de la responsabilité du Président de la République," *RFDA*, 2001, 1169–87.

gation, while in office, for alleged bribery. A law of June 2003 granting immunity from trial to the state's five most senior officials, including Berlusconi, tried to change that situation, but the law was struck down on January 13, 2004, by the Italian Constitutional Court.[28]

However delicate their application is, criminal sanctions are often the only remedy left when a minister, prime minister, or chancellor is at the end of his or her political career and therefore no longer fears political sanctions.

c) Tribunals of Inquiry in the UK—playing it softly

In the United Kingdom, as in Ireland,[29] the scrutiny of complex cases of ministerial misconduct is often entrusted to 'ad hoc' tribunals of inquiry, usually chaired by senior judges. This happened in the United Kingdom with the involvement of the Thatcher and Major governments in exports of arms and defense-related goods to Iraq and Iran. The exports had their origin in the Iran-Iraq War, which broke out in September 1980, and in events occurring in the two years preceding the Iraqi invasion of Kuwait in August 1990. A tribunal chaired by Sir Richard Scott investigated the government's complicity or acquiescence in the matter and produced the so-called "Scott Report." After a lengthy and expensive inquiry, the report's conclusions constituted:

> a damning indictment of the Thatcher government, in particular, and of John Major's also. Neither of those individuals was blameworthy of malpractice; but they presided over governments where half truths, suppression of evidence necessary for a criminal defence, and misleading statements and concealed facts were the norm, so that Parliament and the nation were misled.[30]

The Iraq affair together with other scandals (one of them relating to payments demanded by a member of Parliament for asking parliamentary questions on behalf of clients) finally led to the creation of a Committee on Standards in Public Life in 1994.[31] This committee was asked to stem the tide of

---

[28] As a result of the law criminal proceedings against Berlusconi were interrupted, but they can now be reopened. See *The Economist*, January 17, 2004, 41–42. Obviously, it is not a happy situation for Italy that criminal proceedings were initiated against the incumbent prime minister (for events that occurred in the past), but, as the *Economist* journalist notes, "as so often with the Berlusconi government, the suspicion remains that possibly defensible legislation was being proposed for indefensible motives" (41).

[29] See Gary Murphy, "Payments for No Political Response? Political Corruption and Tribunals of Inquiry in Ireland, 1991–2001," paper presented for the conference "Political Scandal: Past and Present," organized by the European Studies Research Institute, Salford University, June 22, 2001.

[30] Patrick Birkinshaw, "Government at the End of Its Tether: Matrix Churchill and the Scott Report," 23 *JLS*, 1996, 406–26, at 407–8.

[31] The committee was set up by Prime Minister Major in October 1994. See Com-

corruption by recommending codes of conduct for ministers and civil servants, independent agencies (quasi non-governmental organizations, better known by the acronym "quangos"), and Members of Parliament. This was unique in a country where the doctrine of supremacy of Parliament is a cornerstone of the constitutional system. The attempt to enforce accountability through soft law devices has its limitations of course, but it also had the merit of stimulating a debate on many delicate issues, such as whether a cabinet minister who has misled Parliament must relinquish his or her position, and whether a minister can be held to account for the serious wrongful action of a subordinate or a third person working under his or her orders. Nevertheless, in the Iraq affair, none of the three ministers was politically sanctioned. Two of them were no longer in office when the Scott Report was finally released, and the third one, who was still in John Major's cabinet, was not forced to resign because resignation was considered to be "constitutionally unnecessary and politically undesirable" by the government.[32]

In the U.K. and Ireland the Tribunal of Inquiry is seen as an essential instrument for exposing and judging the behavior of cabinet ministers involved in political affairs that may develop, or have already developed, into a political scandal. And, indeed, it appears to be an effective way to interrogate not only cabinet ministers who might have a tendency to "pass the buck," but also civil servants. It is also a flexible (but expensive) instrument: it is for the chairman to decide how to conduct the inquiry, whom to call as witnesses, and how long the inquiry will take. A recent example is the Hutton inquiry into the suicide of Dr. Kelly, the British expert who had allegedly said to a journalist that the Blair administration was responsible for consciously misleading the public on the issue of weapons of mass destruction in Iraq. Not only did Alastair Campbell, the prime minister's head of communications, and various civil servants from the Ministry of Defence appear before the tribunal (Campbell resigned in the aftermath), but Tony Blair himself appeared as well, and in his statement took political responsibility for the affair (without, however, admitting personal fault). On January 28, 2004, Lord Hutton's report was published, vindicating the prime minister and his government and putting the

---

mittee on Standards in Public Life, *First Report*, 1995, Cm. 2850, p. 106. For an exhaustive analysis of political scandals and the creation of the committee, see the paper prepared by Robert Kaye, "'Back to Basics' and the Nolan Reforms: Political Scandal and Parliamentary Reform in the UK," presented at the Salford University conference referred to in n. 29 above.

[32] See Adam Tomkins, *The Constitution after Scott: Government Unwrapped* (Oxford: Clarendon Press, 1998), 35.

blame on the BBC.[33] If the tribunal had come to the conclusion that the prime minister was to be blamed personally, his position might have become very difficult.

d) Ministerial responsibility in Germany—in accordance with
the rules of the Basic Law
In contrast to the typically pragmatic British approach, the Federal Republic of Germany relies, with regard to ministerial accountability, on constitutional provisions. Article 64 of the Basic Law provides that federal ministers shall be appointed and dismissed by the federal president upon the proposal of the federal chancellor, who is himself elected by the Bundestag upon the proposal of the president and who must be dismissed by the president when a vote of no confidence in the chancellor is cast by a majority in the Bundestag (Articles 63 [1] and 67 [1]).[34]

The Basic Law reserves a prominent place for the chancellor not only with regard to the selection and dismissal of ministers, but it is also for him to determine and be responsible for general policy guidelines according to which each minister runs his department (Article 65). If a minister is implicated in objectionable behavior, not necessarily an outright scandal, it is therefore for the chancellor to decide whether to ask for his or her resignation. This happened, for example, in 2002 on the eve of parliamentary elections, when the defense minister who had allegedly accepted money and royalties from a public relations firm in violation of ethical and professional guidelines was asked by Chancellor Gerhard Schröder to resign.

Obviously, if the chancellor himself is involved in "objectionable behavior," it is for him to draw that conclusion and to resign when he feels that he might otherwise be subjected to a vote of no confidence in the Bundestag. Such a voluntary resignation occurred in 1974 when Chancellor Willy Brandt took full responsibility for the espionage activities of his personal secretary, Günter Guillaume,[35] and another might have occurred in the case of Chancellor Helmut Kohl if he had still been in office when it became known, in 1999–2000, that he and other officials of his party had been engaged in a network of secret accounts credited with donations above the limit permitted by law.[36]

---

[33] The report is available online at http://www.the-hutton-inquiry.org.uk/content/report/index.htm. See also *The Economist*, Jan. 31–Feb. 6, 2004, 12–13.

[34] See chapter 7, p. 318.

[35] See *Keesings Historisch Archief*, May 17, 1974, 43 *Weekblad*, no. 2229, at 26287–302. Brandt's resignation was also inspired by other reasons, namely growing dissatisfaction, even within his own party, with the chancellor's *Ostpolitik*.

[36] See "Germany in Crisis," Cosmopolis 3 (Feb. 2000), available at www. cosmopolis.ch.

Since World War II, illegal funding has been the Achilles' heel of many parties in Western European states.[37] However, in Germany, the issue aptly demonstrates the important role played by the German Constitutional Court in politics.[38] In a judgment of 1958, the court decided that it is not unconstitutional for the state to make funds available to allow political parties to finance their election campaign. However, in 1966 it changed position, holding that it is not for the state to contribute to the formation of the people's political will, but for the people to determine state politics. Later on, the court changed its position again, now recognizing that many civil organizations are funded by the state and that *private* funding of political parties may have the same, or even a greater, adverse effect on the formation of the people's will as *state* funding. As a result, the court admitted that electoral campaign funding of political parties by the state is permissible if it remains within appropriate limits, and in a later judgment approved legislation based on that principle. That legislation did not prevent many random questions from being submitted to the court, which led to a new position from the court in a judgment of April 9, 1992, and finally to a law of June 28, 2002, by which criteria and limits were set for state funding and for tax-reduction allowances for private donations.[39]

The supervision by the German Constitutional Court of political issues is a structural component of German political life, in contrast with countries that do not have a written constitution or do not have a constitutional court, or one as powerful as the German court.[40] Politically important positions often originate in or have been shaped by the case law of the Bundesverfassungsgericht, both with respect to fundamental citizen rights in relation to the state and to other citizens.[41] Moreover, disputes concerning the respective powers of

---

[37] One possible explanation, suggested by Professor Hayward of Nottingham University and quoted by J. Hooper in *The Guardian* of December 4, 1999, could be that the need for democratic parties to keep strong communist parties from power after World War II has created a conspiracy of silence amongst non-communist politicians who all needed funding badly to influence public opinion.

[38] For a brief overview with references to the judgments of the German constitutional Court (Bundesverfassungsgericht), see Hartmut Maurer, *Staatsrecht I, Grundlagen, Verfassungsorgane, Staatsfunktionen* [Constitutional law, basic principles, constitutional organs, state functions], 3d ed. (Munich: Verlag C. H. Beck, 2003), 360–66.

[39] The judgment referred to is published in *BVerfGE* 85, 264; the law is published in *BGBl.* I, 2268.

[40] The existence of a genuine constitutional court is only one factor, but an important one, that influences the relationship between law and politics. For other factors, see Tim Koopmans, n. 1 above, 282–83.

[41] Maurer, n. 37 above, 654–56.

state institutions may also end up in court,[42] often at the initiative of political parties in opposition arguing that their right to participate in the functioning of government has been curtailed by state organs.[43]

e) Ministerial accountability for civil servants—Primacy of politics in the Netherlands and Belgium

Political accountability of ministers for the wrongful actions of officials in their administration is a controversial matter because of the widespread belief that ministers are responsible for the creation of policy but not for its implementation. That belief is inconsistent with the strict Weberian view, according to which civil servants are hierarchically organized bureaucrats who are not involved in political debate and must be completely loyal to their minister, who, in return, is politically responsible for their behavior.[44]

A tragic illustration of the primacy of politics is the Dutchbat affair, which caused a huge commotion in the Netherlands in the early 1990s and was only concluded in April 2002.[45] In 1993 a Dutch battalion was sent to Srebrenica in East Bosnia to protect the Muslims in an area that was incorrectly designated as a safe enclave by the United Nations. In July 1995 the 490 Dutch troops, with only light weapons and without a mandate to protect the Muslim population, were unable to prevent the Bosnian Serb militia from killing 7,400 Muslim men. In addition, 23,000 Muslim women and children were deported to Muslim territory with the consent of the commander of the Dutch battalion. In that affair, involving the political responsibility of successive prime ministers and ministers of defense, all that could go wrong did go wrong: bad relations between political institutions and international organizations; lack of communication between the minister of foreign affairs and the minister of

[42] See, for instance, on the chancellor's power to issue general policy guidelines, as provided in Article 65 of the Basic law, *BVerfGE* 1, no. 43, 1952, where the court held that Parliament has no power to issue such guidelines except when the Basic Law provides otherwise; quoted by Tim Koopmans, n. 1 above, 186.

[43] Maurer, n. 38 above, 673, where it is noted that political parties have been granted right of appeal by the constitutional court under Article 93 (1), sub 1, of the Basic Law.

[44] On Weber's view, see Mark Bovens, n. 16 above, 150–51. See also, in an American context, Robert D. Benn, *Rethinking Democratic Accountability* (Washington D.C.: Brookings Institution Press, 2001).

[45] For a full description of the initial stage of the affair, see E. Hütte et al., "Srebrenica: een pijnlijke vergissing" [Srebrenica: A painful mistake], in *De Sorry-Democratie* [The sorry democracy], Ed van Thijn a.o. (Amsterdam: Van Gennep, 1998), 28–47.

defense; and lack of communication between successive ministers of defense and their administrations and the armed forces. Only after the full dimensions of the events became known did the Dutch government, under (then) Prime Minister Wim Kok, decide in 2002 to charge an independent research institute, NIOD, with examining the responsibility of all those involved, including prime ministers and ministers in previous governments. When its report came out, finding that successive governments had not been sufficiently alert and that the military had tried to keep information from the minister of defense, the government finally assumed responsibility and resigned on April 16, 2002,[46] on the eve of elections in which the coalition parties suffered heavy losses.

In the Dutchbat affair it took ten years before the government (albeit not the one in charge when the affair unfolded) took political responsibility for what went wrong. The affair is one event among many characterizing what has been called the "sorry democracy."[47] The term refers to the practice, very much in vogue in Belgium in the 1980s and '90s, of ministers who, having been involved in a political scandal, apologize instead of stepping down.[48] This may have changed in recent years under the pressure of public opinion. Two cases demonstrate this transition, one relating to the prison escape of the (then not yet convicted) serial murderer Marc Dutroux[49]—although he was arrested again two hours later—and the other relating to the death of an immigrant "sans papiers" as a result of badly applied police procedures.[50] In the wake of the first affair the minister of home affairs and the minister of justice, and in the wake of the second the minister of home affairs, resigned immediately, even though they were not directly blameworthy for the conduct of low-ranking officials.[51] This change in attitude has raised the question whether

---

[46] *NRC Handelsblad*, April 16, 2002.

[47] Thus the title of the book referred to in n. 45 above.

[48] This occurred notably in the case of the Heizel soccer match tragedy in 1985, when hooligans caused the deaths of thirty-nine spectators. In that case, the minister of home affairs refused to take responsibility for the lack of coordination among police.

[49] On April 23, 1998, Dutroux, then (and still) in custody pending criminal proceedings, escaped from the courthouse as a result of the negligence of two policemen accompanying him.

[50] The illegal immigrant, Semira Adamu, died on a commercial plane flight back to her home country as a result of policemen following procedures that allowed the use of a cushion to silence violent protest by the illegal immigrant.

[51] For a thorough analysis of the Dutroux affair, seen in context with other affairs, and the impact of scandals on policy making, see Jeroen Maesschalck, "When Do Scandals Have an Impact on Policy Making: A Case Study of the Police Reform Fol-

nowadays ministers are not led to step down too easily in situations where they cannot be blamed personally for what has happened.[52]

Although the 'Weberian' principle of primacy of politics still prevails in many European States, as the foregoing examples show, it became more controversial in the second half of the last century.[53] There are two reasons for that. On the one hand, bureaucracy has exploded, particularly in the higher policymaking segments, both as a result of the strong belief in a welfare state and because the issues government is confronted with have become increasingly technical. On the other hand, the fact that policy and operational decisions have become increasingly woven together has led to the "politicization" of a civil service deeply involved in the making of political choices. All of this has led in turn to the "bureaucratization" of cabinet ministers who, because of the growing importance of issues (quantitatively and qualitatively) and their complexity, need more time to understand them, and have little time left to oversee the political dimension of their work. As a result, as ministers become increasingly obliged to rely on their civil servants, their *span of control* becomes very limited.[54]

This evolution raises delicate issues of ministerial political responsibility: how far does the duty of ministers to inform parliament extend, and what should the sanction be when they do not comply? More specifically, must ministers relinquish their positions only when they have knowingly misled parliament? Is it correct to state that ministers are responsible to parliament solely for matters of policy, and that operational matters are the responsibility of civil servants for which they are responsible to the minister and not to Parliament (assuming that policy and operational decisions can be adequately distinguished)? Should a distinction be made between constitutional accountability of ministers and their personal responsibility, whereby the first refers to a minister's duty to account to parliament for the work of his department

---

lowing the Dutroux Scandal in Belgium," presented at the Salford University conference referred to in n. 29 above.

[52] See Paul 't Hart, *Verbroken verbindingen: Over de politisering van het verleden en de dreiging van een inquisitiedemocratie* [Broken links: On politicization of the past and the threat of inquisition democracy] (Amsterdam: De Balie, 2001).

[53] This does not apply, however, in Sweden, for example. See Jacques Ziller, "European Models of Government: A Patchwork with Missing Pieces?" *Parliamentary Affairs* 54 (2001): 102–19.

[54] On all of this, see Ed van Thijn, a former Dutch minister who himself became involved in one of the political crises that occurred in the Netherlands in the 1990s, in *Politiek en bureaucracy: Baas boven baas* [Politics and bureaucracy: Boss above boss] (Amsterdam: Van Gennep, 1997), 9–16.

whilst the second is incurred when the minister is directly and personally involved in a wrongful action for which he can be blamed?[55]

I will return to these questions below. At this stage, I wish only to refer to an exhaustive study prepared in 1993 by a group of experts on behalf of the Dutch Parliament.[56] In that study, three guiding principles were identified. First, a minister is under an obligation to render account to Parliament. This involves more than just supplying Parliament with data; it also entails explaining and defending the ministerial policy. Second, political responsibility remains with the minister alone; in other words, civil servants do not bear political responsibility. Third, ministerial responsibility can only exist with regard to matters for which the minister has corresponding competences.

As for the concrete *scope* of the rule of ministerial responsibility, the report distinguishes the following situations: 1) responsibility for his or her own conduct for which a minister is clearly responsible; 2) responsibility for conduct as a member of cabinet for which a minister may bear collective responsibility with the other ministers; 3) responsibility for conduct of the Queen, whose responsibility is to be covered by a minister under any circumstance; and, most important, 4) responsibility for conduct of a minister's civil servants, or even private persons fulfilling public tasks, for which the minister bears in principle full political responsibility. In each of these situations, the principle of ministerial responsibility must be seen in combination with the principle of confidence, according to which a minister must resign when he or she clearly no longer has the confidence of Parliament. That may happen when a minister is held responsible for conduct as explained above, or for not having rendered sufficient account to Parliament, but also when Parliament is of the opinion that, for whatever reason, it is not in a position to maintain its confidence in a minister's ability to fulfill his or her task adequately in the future.[57]

---

[55] On all these issues, see A. Tomkins, "Ministers and Parliament," in *The Constitution after Scott*, n. 32 above.

[56] Report of the Scheltema Commission, *Steekhoudend ministerschap* [Sound ministership], Tweede Kamer der Staten-Generaal, vergaderjaar 1992–93, and more recently the report of the Holtslag Commission, "De ministeriële verantwoordelijkheid ondersteund" [Ministerial responsibility supported], edited by the Ministry of Interior Affairs, The Hague, 1998, mentioned by M. Scheltema, "Voldoet de ministeriële verantwoordelijkheid nog bij een professionele organisatie?" [Is ministerial responsibility still satisfactory in a situation of a professional organization?], 38 *NJB*, 2000, 1861–67.

[57] On all the foregoing, see chapter 2 of the Scheltema Commission report, n. 56 above, under 2.1 through 2.6.

II. POLITICAL ACCOUNTABILITY OF
EU COMMISSIONERS

On March 15, 1999, the Commission of the European Union, then presided over by Jacques Santer (and therefore called the Santer Commission), collectively resigned after reading the first report of the Committee of Independent Experts.[58] The committee had been created six weeks earlier by the European Parliament to investigate six dossiers with respect to which allegations had been made by Parliament and the press concerning fraud, mismanagement, and nepotism by individual commissioners. The committee's mission was "to examine the way in which the Commission detects and deals with fraud, mismanagement and nepotism . . ." The committee was asked more specifically "to establish to what the Commission, as a body, or Commissioners individually, bear specific responsibility."[59] At the end of its investigation the committee concluded that it had not found any fraud on the part of the Commission itself, or on the part of its members, but that it had established, in two of the investigated dossiers, instances of fraud by a few civil servants of the Commission, and by third persons to whom the Commission had outsourced executive tasks. It also found that individual commissioners, and the Commission as a whole, had not dealt adequately with fraud committed by those persons, and were therefore guilty of mismanagement. Moreover, straightforward nepotism was established on the part of one member of the Commission.

Following the Commission's resignation, the European Parliament mandated that the Committee of Independent Experts prepare a second report formulating recommendations for improving the Commission's practices and procedures, particularly procedures for awarding financial contracts and contracts for temporary staff, procedures for following up allegations of fraud, mismanagement and nepotism, and procedures for treating such cases involving staff.[60] The second report was submitted to Parliament on September 10,

---

[58] Committee of Independent Experts, "First Report on Allegations Regarding Fraud, Mismanagement and Nepotism in the European Commission" 144 (Mar. 15, 1999), hereinafter cited as Committee of Independent Experts, first report, available at http://www.europarl.eu.int/experts/report1_en.htm#procedure. For a brief discussion of the report, see "Editorial Comments," 36 *CMLRev.*, 1999, 269–72.

[59] This from a resolution of the European Parliament adopted on January 14, 1999, as clarified by a statement of the Parliament's Conference of Presidents, quoted in the Committee of Independent Experts, first report, cited in n. 58 above, at 9.

[60] Committee of Independent Experts, "Second Report on Reform of the Commission: Analysis of Current Practice and Proposals for Tackling Mismanagement, Ir-

1999, and formulated ninety recommendations concerning six topics: direct management by the Commission, shared management with the Member States, financial control, fighting fraud and corruption, staff matters, and integrity, responsibility and accountability in European political and administrative life.[61] Many of the recommendations were taken into account by the (then) new Commission, presided over by Romano Prodi, in the preparation of its reform proposals.[62]

The Content of Accountability and Political Responsibility

When the committee communicated its first report to the Parliament and the Commission on March 15, 1999, the latter decided to resign immediately, as a body, without appearing before Parliament to question the committee's conclusions. The Commission's seemingly extreme decision was caused by the committee's conclusion that the Commission as a body was responsible for not having taken measures when it became, or should have become, aware of mismanagement and nepotism in some of its services.[63] The committee also held the Commission responsible for not informing Parliament in a timely manner of the gravity of one situation in which it had to make a decision concerning the renewal of a controversial outsourcing operation.[64] Accordingly, the Commission's resignation must be seen as motivated by its failure, as a body, to deal adequately with the shortcomings of one of its members and those of Commission civil servants and its failure to inform Parliament in good time.

Actually, many of the allegations of wrongful behavior analyzed in the committee's report had been raised and documented in a dossier handed to

---

regularities and Fraud," vols. 1 and 2, 287 (Sept. 10, 1999), hereinafter cited as Committee of Independent Experts, second report, available at http://www.europarl.eu.int/experts/en/default.htm.

[61] For a brief description of the committee's findings, particularly with regard to the last theme, see "Guest Editorial, Ethical and Political Responsibility of EU Commissioners," 37 *CMLRev.*, 2000, 1–6.

[62] See Deirdre Curtin, "The European Commission in Search of Accountability: From Chamber of Secrets to Good Governance?" in *Principles of Proper Conduct for Supranational, State and Private Actors in the European Union: Towards a Ius Commune*, ed. Jan Wouters and Jules Stuyck (Antwerp: Intersentia, 2001), 5–19. See also Paul Craig, "The Constitutionalisation of Community Administration," 28 *ELRev.*, 2003, 840–64; see also below, pp. 95–96.

[63] Committee of Independent Experts, first report, n. 58 above, 138, particularly sub 9.3.4 and 9.3.5.

[64] Ibid., sub 5.8.7.

the Parliament (and later to the committee) by Commission employee Paul van Buitenen—who, later on, received widespread acclaim as a whistle-blower, although not from the Commission. I will return to that matter in chapter 5 when discussing the legitimacy of whistle-blowing.

a) The principle of accountability and political responsibility in
Community law

As pointed out previously, a keystone of constitutionalism in a parliamentary system, as it exists in most of the EU Member States, is the accountability and political responsibility of cabinet ministers to an elected parliament.

This implies that the head of government, the prime minister, and his cabinet ministers must render account of their actions to parliament, which may hold them politically responsible for their shortcomings in the performance of their office. Cabinet ministers are also responsible, through the principle of the primacy of politics, for the shortcomings of civil servants in the performance of their duties. As mentioned above, when these shortcomings cause parliament to lose the confidence that it had in a minister, the prime minister, or the whole cabinet, the parliament may force those persons to resign. Such a vote of no confidence does not occur often, but it nevertheless operates as a deterrent, occasionally causing members of government to resign voluntarily, either at the request of the head of government or at their own initiative, when they fear that a vote of no confidence might be forthcoming. In a presidential system, like that of the United States, in which the president is directly elected by the people, resignation before parliament is not a constitutional option.

All this raises the question of how accountability and political responsibility of the Commission—its president and its members, the commissioners—is regulated in the European Union. Under current Community law, members of the Commission are bound to explain their actions to the European Parliament, and they can be held accountable by Parliament when those actions constitute wrongful behavior. The first requirement follows from Article 197 EC, which gives Parliament the right to hear and interrogate commissioners orally and in writing.[65] The second requirement follows from Article 201 EC, which enables Parliament, by open vote, to censure the Commission, compelling it to resign "as a body" if the motion is carried by two-thirds of the votes cast, representing a majority of Members of the European

---

[65] EC Treaty, art. 197, third para.: "The Commission shall reply orally or in writing to questions put to it by the European Parliament or by its Members."

Accountable Government

Parliament.[66] Furthermore, Article 193 EC gives Parliament the ability to set up temporary committees of inquiry to investigate mismanagement on the part of commissioners or civil servants.[67] Moreover, as of February 2003, the political leadership function of the Commission's president has been strengthened by the Nice Treaty, which granted him or her extensive powers with regard to the other commissioners. Indeed, Article 217 EC, as amended, now provides, in paragraph 1, that the Commission "shall work under the political guidance of its President, who shall decide on its internal organisation," and, in paragraph 2, that the Commission responsibilities "shall be structured and allocated among its Members by the President," and, in paragraph 4, that "a Member of the Commission shall resign if the President so requests, after obtaining the full approval of the College."[68]

It follows from the foregoing that the principle of accountability and political responsibility of the Commission to the European Parliament, which is elected by direct universal suffrage (Article 190 [1] EC), already constitutes a basic element of the European Community's legal order. The involvement of Parliament in selecting and appointing nominees to become president and members of the Commission remains limited, however, and, in fact, parliamentary elections have no impact on the appointment procedure. As set out in Article 214 (2) EC, it is for "the Council, meeting in the composition of Heads of State or Government" to designate by qualified majority a nominee for president and to obtain Parliament's approval of the proposed nominee. Then, it is for the Council of Ministers, also acting by a qualified majority and by common accord with the nominee for president, to adopt the list of the other members of the Commission in accordance with the proposals made by

[66] EC Treaty, art. 201, first para.: "If a motion of censure on the activities of the Commission is tabled before it, the European Parliament shall not vote thereon until at least three days after the motion has been tabled and only by open vote." The first sentence of the second paragraph provides, "If the motion is carried by a two-thirds majority of the votes cast, representing the majority of the Members of the European Parliament, the Members of the Commission shall resign as a body."

[67] EC Treaty, art. 193, first para.: "In the course of its duties, the European Parliament may, at the request of a quarter of its Members, set up a temporary Committee of Inquiry to investigate, without prejudice to the powers conferred by this Treaty on other institutions or bodies, alleged contraventions or maladministration in the implementation of Community law, except where the alleged facts are being examined before a court and while the case is still subject to legal proceedings."

[68] The relevant provisions of the Treaty of Nice, as with other amending treaties, are incorporated in the EC Treaty, in this case Article 217. The word "College" refers to the Commission as a body. It is a literal translation from the French.

each Member State. Finally, it is for Parliament to affirm, by a vote of approval, the nomination of the Commission as a body and for the Council of
Ministers, acting by a qualified majority, to appoint the president and members of the Commission.

To be sure, this complicated procedure gives the Parliament the right to
reject a candidate for president or member of the Commission, but it does
not give Parliament the right to present nominees. Even more important, it
does not require that the Council composed of Heads of State or Government, in selecting the nominee for president, take into account the outcome of elections for the European Parliament, but rather authorizes the
Council of Ministers, in selecting nominees for members of the Commission,
to adopt a list "drawn up in accordance with the proposals made by each
Member State" (Article 214 [2], second para., EC). As a result, the preference
of the Member State government is determinant, not the outcome of democratic elections.

All of the above relates to the Commission, which is the executive branch
under the first pillar, and leaves unanswered the question of whether the principle of accountability and political responsibility should also apply to the
Council of Ministers. The problem with the Council is that, under the first
pillar, it is not part of the executive branch but instead part of the legislative
branch, even though its individual members are, at the level of the Member
States that they represent in the Council, members of executive government
and, in that capacity, only accountable to a Member State national or regional
parliament. This means that—but for judicial review of its action by the Court
of Justice[69]—the Council and its individual members are not politically accountable to any Community institution. I will address that question later, in
chapter 7. Here I will only mention that the problem was not entirely ignored
by the framers of the EC Treaty, who, from the outset, had provided in Article
140 (now 197) EC, that "the Council shall be heard" by the European Parliament "in accordance with the rules laid down by the Council in its rules of
procedure." Moreover, on the occasion of later treaty amendments, now reflected in Article 207 (3) EC, accountability of the Council to the public has
been enhanced by obliging the Council, when "acting in its legislative capacity
. . . to [allow] greater access to Council documents . . . [and making public]
the results of votes and explanations of vote as well as statements in the min-
utes."[70]

[69] See below, chapter 3, pp. 110–13.
[70] On access to public documents, see chapter 5, pp. 225–28.

b) *Commissioners' accountability and political responsibility*
for civil servants

The constitutional scope and content of accountability and political responsibility of commissioners to Parliament should be defined with regard to acts and omissions not only of commissioners, but also of civil servants or third parties falling within their sphere of competence. With respect to civil servants, EU staff regulations provide that "an official in charge of any branch of the service shall be responsible *to his superiors* in respect of the authority conferred on him and for the carrying out of instructions given by him" (Article 21; emphasis added)—which includes the responsibility of the highest ranking civil servants, the directors-general to their superior: the commissioner responsible for their department.[71] By contrast, the political responsibility of commissioners *to Parliament* for their own wrongful action and that of civil servants working under them is not spelled out explicitly—staff regulations apply to civil servants only, and not to commissioners. However, there is no reason to believe that Parliament's right to pass a motion of censure under Article 201 EC would not encompass action taken by Commission civil servants. If that were not the case, the sanction would lose most of its application. This was also clearly the assumption of the Committee of Independent Experts, which, in its first report, held individual commissioners personally responsible for not taking adequate measures to combat wrongful action on the part of Community civil servants.

Political responsibility of commissioners for the actions of their civil servants is an issue that deserves to be studied in depth. As in the Member States,

[71] Article 21, Council Regulation (EEC, Euratom, ECSC) No. 259/68 of February 29, 1968, setting out the "Staff Regulations of Officials and the Conditions of Employment of Other Servants of the Communities," [1968] OJ L56/1, as amended by Council Regulation (EC, Euratom) No. 723/2004 of March 22, 2004, [2004] OJ L124/1. Directors-general are at the head of the Commission services, comprising around 21,000 civil servants. Currently, there are thirty-six directorates-general (DGs) and specialized service divisions, predominantly organized according to policy, e.g., agriculture, competition, etc. Commissioners are not allotted DGs as such, but rather portfolios, which may correspond to more than one DG. The overall Commission administration is overseen by a secretary general, who is supported by a staff of about 350 and is sometimes asked to handle particularly sensitive subjects. Each commissioner has a small private cabinet, headed by a *chef de cabinet*. On all this and more, see S. Douglas-Scott, *Constitutional Law of the European Union* (Harlow, England: Longman, 2002), 57–60. On the status and power of the commissioners' private cabinets, which tend to develop into a parallel administration, see also the second report of the Committee of Independent Experts, n. 60 above, 275–76, paras. 7.12.1–7.12.6.

the issue turns in the first place around the duty of executive officers to inform Parliament, that is, accountability in the sense of rendering account to Parliament by explaining action and giving insight into executive decision making. In that context, the question is often raised whether executive officers (commissioners or ministers) should be blamed only for *knowingly* misleading Parliament, or also for giving inaccurate or incomplete information by *omission* (that is, because they were misinformed by their administration). The issue turns, secondly, around the political responsibility of executive officers to Parliament for past action, whereby the question comes up whether they can be held politically responsible only for so-called policy decisions or also for operational decisions. Thirdly, it turns on whether a member of executive government (commissioner or minister) can be subjected to a political sanction—not forced to resign, necessarily, but also, for example, relegated to a less important department—only when he or she has acted wrongfully, or also when civil servants or third persons have acted wrongly within the sphere of competence for which he or she is responsible.[72]

In the *second* report of the Committee of Independent Experts, the issue of political responsibility was defined as follows:

> Political responsibility concerns the political consequences attached to conduct of holders of public office, or to conduct of civil servants working under them within their sphere of competence, by the institution or person who can hold such holders of public office to account. Although political responsibility exists in all democratic legal systems, it exists in different forms and at different levels depending on the constitutional structure of the legal system concerned.[73]

The report goes on to say, that differences exist:

> (i) "as to the extent of political responsibility: only for individual, personal or functional, misconduct or also for misconduct of subordinate civil servants?" (ii) "as to the nature of the political consequence: dismissal, or other consequences of a lesser nature; imposed collectively, or also individually?" and (iii) "as to the in-

---

[72] In the Member States the problem has taken on a special dimension because of the reallocation of powers, not only between national and local authorities, but also toward independent agencies. As pointed out in a comparative study on the situation in the U.K. and Italy, it is a common experience (not only in those countries) "that accountability can no longer be discussed in terms of political institutions such as Parliament and local authorities but now has to be related to New Public Management strategies, the role of regulators and the introduction of auditing and accounting techniques." See Peter Leyland and Daniele Donati, "Executive Accountability and the Changing Face of Government: UK and Italy Compared," 7 *EPL*, 2001, 217–57, at 218. See also below, pp. 91–97.

[73] Second report, n. 60 above, 279, para. 7.14.15.

stitution or person called upon to impose the political consequence: parliament, president or prime minister?"[74]

Distinguishing between the enforcement of individual and collective responsibility, the report concludes that, with regard to the Community institutions, the latter is a matter for Parliament, while the former is a matter for the president of the Commission, who, however, is answerable to Parliament for any action or inaction on his part.[75]

Already in its *first* report, the Committee of Independent Experts had observed that commissioners have a tendency to evade political responsibility for acts or omissions of their services, on the pretext that they are responsible only for laying down policy while directors-general implement it. The committee rejected such distinction, rightly in my view,[76] for being untenable both in law and in fact. It is untenable in law because it would mean that nobody is accountable to Parliament for implementation of policy decisions, neither the commissioner, nor the head of the administration (nor, a fortiori, his subordinates), who owes responsibility only to his commissioner. The distinction is also untenable in fact because it "is a falsely rigid one, difficult to define in principle and even more difficult to apply in practice."[77] To give only one example, is it a matter of mere implementation, or is it a matter of both policy and implementation, to set up an effective organization, and to provide adequate procedures regarding, for example, division and delegation of work, including assigning work to the private sector, or regarding citizens' rights of appeal against a decision they feel to be unjust? I would suppose that the second is correct and that, therefore, both commissioner and director-general should bear co-responsibility for these matters, albeit that the commissioner alone would be answerable to Parliament.

c) Learning from the Member States

In the absence of a clear doctrine of accountability and political responsibility, one should look for solutions applied in the Member States—notwithstanding that there, also, the issue remains controversial.[78] As noted earlier,[79] the

[74] Ibid., 279–80, para. 7.14.15.

[75] Ibid., 280–81, paras. 7.14.20 and 7.14.21.

[76] Ibid., 271, para. 7.9.1, referring to the first report. I could hardly disagree with the statement, having been one of the five experts and having written the chapter on accountability in the second report.

[77] Ibid.

[78] See A. Tomkins, "Ministers and Parliament," in *The Constitution after Scott*, n. 32 above, 25.

[79] N. 56 above.

Dutch Scheltema report may be a source of inspiration. I will recall some of the report's conclusions here. One is, obviously, that for a minister to bear political responsibility to Parliament—alone or with colleagues, for his own acts or for those of civil servants, as well as for acts of third parties fulfilling public tasks—he must have been attributed competences with respect to matters for which he is being held responsible. Secondly, it is ultimately for Parliament (or for the prime minister, foreseeing Parliament's reaction) to decide whether the event is of such a nature that Parliament should withdraw its confidence in a minister or in the government as a whole because it believes that the minister or government is no longer able to fulfill his or its role.[80] Within these limits, ministers are to be held politically responsible not only for behavior that can be imputed to them personally, but also, it would seem, for behavior for which they cannot be blamed personally because they did not have (nor could be expected to have had) knowledge of the civil servant's or third party's wrongdoing.

It may be worthwhile to recall the national context within which the Scheltema report came about. In 1976 the Dutch prime minister Den Uyl had proposed that a minister not be held responsible for the behavior of subordinates under three conditions: first, the minister must have given general but clear guidelines as to the policy he or she intended to follow; second, he or she must have examined, at regular intervals, whether these guidelines were followed by his civil servants; and, third, the minister must have taken measures to prevent deviation from established policy.[81] The Scheltema report rejected this proposal for restricting ministerial responsibility too much, just as it also rejected the criterion of personal fault to determine ministerial responsibility; it accepted, however, that this element, possibly with others, could be taken into account by Parliament in deciding whether or not it retains confidence in the minister.[82]

The decisive argument in favor of that (broader) position is that if a minister were only responsible for wrongdoings of his civil servants when he is at fault himself (that is, primarily when he knew, or should have known, that something was wrong), a minister might prefer not to be involved in delicate matters, and civil servants might choose not to keep the minister informed. Both of these outcomes would be inconsistent with a proper understanding of

---

[80] To be sure, as was mentioned above, Parliament will only rarely use this weapon, not least because cabinet ministers belong to the same party, or coalition parties, as the majority in Parliament.

[81] On the position of prime minister Den Uyl, see Ed Van Thijn, n. 54 above, 22.

[82] Scheltema report, referred to in n. 56 above, 15, para. 2.5.

democratic control of public administration[83] and with the principle of primacy of politics, as it would have the effect that, to a certain extent, conduct of civil servants would be immune from parliamentary control.[84]

The question is whether, in the present state of Community law, these conclusions can be applied also to members of the Commission. To answer that question, it should be recalled that the Commission is accountable to Parliament, which has the right of hearing and interrogating the individual commissioners, and the right of censuring the Commission and making it resign as a whole, whereas the Commission president has the right to request an individual member of the Commission to resign.[85] Under these circumstances, I do not see why the preceding conclusions cannot be applied to the Commission and its members as well. Surely, the Parliament does not currently have the right to appoint the Commission president and members (but only to approve the persons nominated by the European Council or the Council of Ministers). But this should not prevent Parliament's existing power to maintain or withdraw its confidence by passing or not passing a motion of censure from being interpreted broadly in accordance with the traditions in the Member States.[86]

[83] Ibid.

[84] It has been pointed out by Van Thijn (n. 54 above, 24–25), who agrees with the position taken in the Scheltema report, that this does not imply that resignation must be used as a "catchall" weapon. According to Van Thijn it should only be used under exceptional circumstances, such as 1) when a minister has failed, intentionally or negligently, to give correct or sufficient information to Parliament, with the result that Parliament was unable to fulfil its supervisory task; 2) when the administration's wrongful conduct has had significant adverse consequences, and has done serious harm to the country's reputation abroad; 3) when it led to a serious authority crisis causing senior officials to lose their grip, and no change is foreseeable within a reasonable period of time; 4) when the integrity of public office is manifestly jeopardized; and 5) when a calamity was caused not only by human faults or organizational shortcomings but also by systemic failures, and the responsible minister failed to correct the situation.

[85] See above, pp. 83–84.

[86] The European Parliament's readiness to gauge the political responsibility of commissioners should theoretically be even greater than the readiness of Member State parliaments to assess "their" governments' responsibility, because members of the Commission are deemed to have no political affiliation, or at least to act in complete independence (see Article 213 [2] EC), including independence from any political party or political program, whereas at the national level there is a political link tying government and a majority in parliament together. This is at least the situation de jure, although not de facto, because members of the Commission and the Commission president have almost always had a political career in their Member State before being appointed to the Commission and are therefore *perceived* to belong to a political

d) Accountability under the second and third pillars

All of the above relates to the first, or Community, pillar of the Union to which the relevant EC Treaty provisions specifically apply.[87] By contrast, no similar provisions apply to the second and third pillars, under which both the Commission and the Parliament play only a limited role. Under those pillars, the Council of Ministers, acting under the aegis of the European Council, operates as the driving force, partly with legislative and partly with executive powers. Here also, as under the first pillar, the Council and its individual members are not accountable to any organ of the Union for action undertaken at Union level.

This raises a general question, however, which is not limited to the second and third pillars but arises also under the first pillar: who bears political responsibility for civil servants belonging to Union institutions other than the European Commission, that is, civil servants employed by the Council, the Court of Justice, the Court of Auditors, or Parliament itself? In fact, the question is not specific to the Union, as it also arises at Member State level. The answer to the question can be derived from the historical origin of the principle of primacy of politics. The principle developed in England in the eighteenth century, when ministers were, literally, servants of the Crown. When Parliament took over the prerogatives of the Crown, political responsibility of ministers followed suit. As a result of this origin, political responsibility to Parliament remained limited to the executive branch and its civil servants, and was not extended to the other institutions.[88]

The Special Case of Administrative Agencies

In its 2002 White Paper on European Governance,[89] the European Commission set out to revise the executive process in the Community and proposed to replace committees "in clearly defined areas" with autonomous (pseudo-) regulatory agencies.[90] These agencies would operate with a degree of

---

party—a factor that did play a role, for instance, in connection with the Santer Commission's resignation in 1999. See further S. Douglas-Scott, n. 71 above, 71–72.

[87]These are Articles 197 EC on hearing commissioners, Article 201 EC on censuring the Commission, and Article 193 EC on setting up temporary committees of inquiry; see above, pp. 83–84.

[88] See, on this development, E. J. Janse de Jonge, "Inleiding Hoofdstukken 2–4" [Introduction to chapters 2–4] in A. K. Koekkoek, *De Grondwet* [The constitution], 3d ed. (Deventer: Tjeenk Willink, 2000), 274–76. On the transfer of the powers of the English monarchs into the hands of Parliament, see T. Koopmans, n. 1 above, 18–19.

[89] COM (2002) 428 final.

[90] Ibid., 24.

independence and within a clear framework established by the legislature.[91] Such agencies already exist, mainly as information-gathering entities, though there is a recent trend to grant them some decision-making authority.[92] A similar evolution has taken place in many Member States,[93] where, moreover, genuine independent regulatory agencies have always existed in areas such as banking supervision and competition. These are areas where political independence, technical expertise, and unbiased rule- and decision-making procedures are more crucial than in others.

a) Regulatory agencies

Sweden, especially, is reported to have a long tradition of legally separate and independently managed agencies headed by a government appointee as a general device of executive government. In that country, agencies are bound only by general legislation and bylaws, and through budget allocation.[94] Their independence is guaranteed by the constitution, which provides that

> neither any public authority, nor the Riksdag [the Swedish Parliament], nor the decision-making body of a local government may determine how an administrative authority shall make its decisions in a particular case concerning the exercise of public authority against a private subject or against a commune, or concerning the application of law.[95]

Although the Swedish government, as a body, may quash certain administrative decisions of an agency (though such powers are increasingly being transferred to administrative courts), it cannot give orders to civil servants, nor can it make decisions in the place of the agency's management. Under Swedish law, it is basically for the ombudsman, the courts, and the media to

[91] On agencies, see, among others, Renaud Dehousse, "Regulation by Networks in the European Community: The Role of Agencies," *JEPP*, 1997, 246ff.

[92] P. Craig and G. de Búrca, *EU Law, Text, Cases and Materials*, 3d ed. (Oxford: Oxford University Press, 2003), 106, and Harlow, n. 3 above, 76. One recently created agency is the European Food Safety Authority, established by Regulation No. 178/2002 of January 28, 2002, [2001] OJ L31/1. Another is the European Aviation Safety Agency, established by Regulation No. 1592/2002 of July 15, 2002, [2002] OJ L240. For a full list see the Communication on the Operating Framework for the European Regulatory Agencies of December 11, 2002, COM (2002) 718 final, at 3, fn. 3 to 6.

[93] The United Kingdom, for instance, issued the 1987 report *Improving Management in Government: The Next Steps*, London, HSMO, 1988. See on the situation in the U.K. and Italy, Leyland and Donati, n. 72 above.

[94] See Ziller, n. 53 above.

[95] Chapter 11, para. 7 of the "Instrument of Government," that is, the institutional part of the constitution.

control the agencies' activities and performance.[96] Also, in the United States, independent administrative agencies with extensive regulatory powers assume an important role in the federal structure.[97] They operate as a restriction upon the president's broad executive power, giving rise to the question of whether Congress may constitutionally delegate broad discretionary power to administrative agencies and, more specifically, whether it may immunize subordinate officials from executive control.[98]

In contrast, under the Commission's White Paper on European Governance, as clarified in the ensuing December 2002 Communication on European Regulatory Agencies, regulatory agencies are rather seen to operate as an instrument to *assist* the Commission in exercising its executive power. To be sure, their function would go beyond the task entrusted to merely executive agencies, which, according to the communication, are only responsible for purely managerial tasks. By contrast, EC regulatory agencies would be "actively involved in exercising the executive function by enacting instruments which contribute to regulating a specific sector."[99] That involvement may consist in providing assistance in the form of opinions and recommendations or inspection reports, or in adopting individual decisions that are legally binding on third parties.[100]

In this view, European regulatory agencies are not intended by the Commission to reduce its own executive power but, on the contrary, to provide the Commission with skills and expertise that it does not have itself. They will be called upon "to intervene only in areas where a single public interest predominates," not in areas where they would need "to arbitrate on conflicting public interests, exercise any powers of political appraisal or conduct any

---

[96] Ziller, n. 53 above. Ziller also points out that collective ministerial responsibility, instead of each minister being individually responsible, is a determining feature of the Swedish constitutional system. For a description of the Swedish system, see H. Ragnemalm, "Administrative Justice in Sweden," in A. Piras, *Administrative Law: The Problem of Justice*, vol. 1, *Anglo-American and Nordic Systems* (Milan: Giuffre, 1991).

[97] For a general overview of administrative agencies, see William F. Fox, *Understanding Administrative Law*, 4th ed. (New York: Lexis Publishing, 2000).

[98] See "Where do Administrative Agencies 'Fit' in the Separation of Powers Scheme?" in Geoffrey Stone et al., *Constitutional Law*, 3d ed. (Aspen Law & Business, 1996), 442–45. See also Kathleen M. Sullivan and Gerald Gunther, *Constitutional Law*, 14th ed. (New York: Foundation Press, 2001), 351–85 with references to further literature at 375–76.

[99] Communication on the Operating Framework for the European Regulatory Agencies, n. 92 above, 3.

[100] Ibid., 4.

complex economic assessments."[101] Consequently, regulatory agencies are *not* seen as a device to redesign the executive branch of government, for example, by using them in areas such as competition law, where there is a need for independent agencies that are "distanced as far as possible from capture by either economic agents or protectionist governments."[102] In those areas, regulatory agencies operate as a shield against decision making that may have become too politicized.[103] The European Central Bank is an obvious example of such a truly independent agency.[104]

If genuine *regulatory agencies* were to be created, they should be placed in a constitutional context, as is the case in the United States, where the creation of such agencies is part of the constitutional doctrine of delegation of executive power.[105] Save for a few summary rules,[106] such a constitutional framework does not exist in the Union.[107] Most of the time, agencies are created by secondary legislation adopted on the basis of Article 308 EC (that is, the Union's necessary and proper clause),[108] in which no provision is made with regard to political responsibility for agency acts. To remedy that situation, one commentator has rightly proposed improving the accountability of agencies through legal devices, mainly through procedural scrutiny. Agencies would be "created by democratically enacted statutes which define the agencies' legal authority and objectives"; this would involve, furthermore, "that the regulators are appointed by elected officials; that regulatory decision-making follows

---

[101] Ibid., 8.

[102] Helen Wallace, "Designing Institutions for an Enlarging European Union," in *Ten Reflections on the Constitutional Treaty for Europe*, ed. Bruno de Witte (Florence: European University Institute, 2003), 85–105, at 93.

[103] Ibid.

[104] On this, see Chiara Zilioli and Martin Selmayr, "The European Central Bank: An Independent Specialized Organization of Community Law," 37 *CMLRev.*, 2000, 591–644.

[105] See n. 98 above and accompanying text.

[106] Established in Article 211, fourth indent, EC, and in Article 202, third indent, EC—on the basis of which provision the "comitology" Council Decision 1999/468/EC, [1999] OJ L184/23, has been adopted (see chapter 1, p. 18).

[107] Amaryllis Verhoeven, n. 14 above, 245–46. The author states that delegated rule making operates "in a constitutional near-vacuum," a situation that she seeks to remedy through an institutional balance approach in which she focuses on representativity (who is best placed to decide on a particular matter at issue, taking account of the different interests involved?) and on accountability (how can delegated rule makers be made accountable to the European public?), at 253–54.

[108] As the corresponding provision, laid down in Article I, sec. 8, cl. 18 of the U.S. Constitution, is called in American constitutional terms.

formal rules which often require public participation; finally, that agency decisions must be justified and are open to judicial review."[109]

b) Executive or implementing agencies

The aforementioned solution is second best in the sense that accountability through law can operate as a valuable substitute for accountability through
politics where the latter does not exist or operates inefficiently. Actually, the
device is used in the case of the Commission itself—which institution can be
seen as a (large) species of a genuine regulatory agency.[110]

As was emphasized in the *second* report of the Committee of Independent
Experts, executive or implementing agencies should also be submitted to strict
"accountability through law" devices. In that report, the use of temporary implementing agencies was advocated as a legal instrument to organize and better control the contracting out and funding of Community tasks carried out
by third parties.[111] The report saw this as part of an overall review of the Commission's management of Community policies, *either* through centralized
management, that is, by the Commission itself, *or* through decentralized management, as in the case of the Common Agricultural Policy, that is, by the
Commission and the Member State authorities together ("shared management," as it is called in the report). In the latter case, Commission and Member States each have a distinct but interdependent administrative task in implementing a Community policy program.

Long before the Committee of Independent Experts investigated the
Commission, the outsourcing of purely implementing tasks to private entities
and the funding of these activities by means of Community resources had become an important component of the Commission's direct management, not
the least because, under the pressure of "cost-conscious" Member States, the
Commission's human resources had been regularly subjected to zero-growth
requirements. The practice gave rise to allegations of fraud and nepotism that
were examined by the committee in its *first* report, and led to the resignation

[109] Giandomenico Majone, "From the Positive to the Regulatory State: Causes and
Consequences of Changes in the Mode of Governance," *Journal of Public Policy* 17
(1997): 139, at 160. See also Martin Shapiro, "The Giving Reasons Requirement," *University of Chicago Legal Forum* (1992): 179, who advocates a "hard-look review" of the
courts that requires the agencies to do a perfect job of decision making—in which the
Community courts have now, according to Carol Harlow, succeeded, thanks to the
case law of the Court of First Instance (Harlow, n. 3 above, 160ff).

[110] Cf. G. Majone, "The Rise of the Regulatory State in Europe," *West-European
Politics* 17 (1994): 77–101.

[111] See n. 60 above, 68–69, para. 2.3.27–31, and Recommendation 15 at 7.

of the Santer Commission in March 1999.[112] Asked by Parliament to review the Commission's standing procedures, the committee, in its second report, recommended a drastic change in the Commission's auditing philosophy—which was followed up by the Commission in its White Paper on Reforming the Commission,[113] in which the distinction between direct and shared administration was taken over. This led finally in 2002 to the enactment of a new regulation: Financial Regulation 1605/2002.[114]

The new regulation was hailed by one commentator as a "constitutionalisation" of Community administration in formal terms, in that "the principles governing Community administration have now been enshrined in a norm," as well as in substantive terms, in that the regulation signified "the emergence of overarching principles that frame the entirety of Community administration."[115] The regulation provides a framework for both centralized and shared management. Centralized management covers those activities that the Commission implements either directly through its departments, or indirectly, that is, by entrusting such activities to a new breed of executive agencies, delegating them to networks of national agencies or, exceptionally, contracting them out to private sector bodies. In contrast, shared management, as in the case of the Common Agricultural Policy, encompasses tasks that are entrusted to the Member States in accordance with specific provisions of the new regulation.[116] In the present context, we are only concerned with centralized management undertaken by executive agencies.

Under Regulation 1605/2002, executive agencies are legal entities created to manage a Community program, for which the regulation contains a variety of rules relating to establishment and winding-up, legal status, staffing, tasks, financial arrangements, and review of legality.[117] To set up such an agency, the Commission must undertake a cost-benefit analysis, after which the agency may be created for a determined lifetime upon the approval of a newly estab-

---

[112] See n. 58 above.

[113] COM (2000) 200 final, of April 5, 2000. See also chapter 4, pp. 116f.

[114] Council Regulation 1605/2002, "Financial Regulation Applicable to the General Budget of the European Communities" [2002] OJ L248/1. See also chapter 4, pp. 166–67.

[115] Paul Craig, "The Constitutionalisation of Community Administration," 28 *EL-Rev.*, 2003, 840–64, at 840. In his article Craig analyzes the regulation and puts it in a broader context.

[116] For an overview of the provisions of the new regulation as regards the different forms of centralized management, see ibid., 841–56. In the following pages (856–64) Craig examines the new regulation's provisions concerning shared management, which he explores in the context of the Common Agricultural Policy.

[117] Ibid., 847–51.

lished Regulatory Committee.[118] The operational head of the agency must be a Community official, and the agency's staff will comprise Community officials and non-Community officials recruited on renewable contracts. The agency can be entrusted with any tasks required to implement a Community program, however, with the exception of "tasks requiring discretionary powers in translating political choices into action."[119] In other words, "Policy choices remain for the Commission, implementation is for the agency."[120]

An important novelty is the regulation's provisions concerning legal review of executive agencies' decisions. After some discussion, the system finally adopted consists of an *internal* review by the Commission itself. Pursuant to such internal review, the Commission can suspend implementation of the measure or prescribe interim measures. Moreover, in its final decision, it can uphold the measure, or decide that the agency must modify it in whole or in part. The internal review procedure is complemented by recourse to the *external* review procedure of Article 230 EC before the ECJ.[121] As pointed out by commentator Paul Craig, this new setup of internal versus external review raises important issues of principle. They relate specifically to the role of the Commission sitting as a "judge" in first instance, and the resulting danger of conflict of interest, the agency being responsible only for implementing measures while the Commission remains responsible for policy choices—thus being both party and judge. The setup also raises broader issues of legal design, such as whether tort liability for agency acts should remain with the Commission, which has contracted out activities under a program assigned to itself, or whether it should remain with the agency in order to reinforce within the agency the conjunction of power and responsibility that is central to the new regulation.[122]

The issue is important in the present context because it can be seen as a prefiguration of a debate on how the Commission's accountability and political responsibility for agency acts is to be shaped in the future—a matter that so far remains unresolved.

---

[118] Articles 3 and 24 of Regulation 1605/2002. That committee will be established under Article 5 of the 1999 "comitology" Council Decision 1999/468/EC (n. 106 above). On comitology, see chapter 1, pp. 17f.

[119] Article 6 (1) of Regulation 1605/2002; but see the different formulation in Article 54 (1) and Paul Craig's comment, n. 115 above, at 848–49.

[120] Craig, n. 115 above, at 848.

[121] On all this, see Article 22 of Regulation 1605/2002. As for the agency's liability in damages, see Article 21. For comments, see Paul Craig, n. 115 above, 850–51.

[122] Ibid., 851.

III. CONCLUSIONS

For a government to be democratic, it must emanate from the people *and* be accountable to the people. That means, in a parliamentary democracy, that the executive branch of government is accountable to an elected parliament. Accountability has a double meaning: it means that the executive must render account to parliament of action proposed to be taken and that it remains politically responsible to parliament for action undertaken in the past. Accountability implies that if a majority in parliament does not maintain its confidence in the incumbent government, that government must resign. The assumption made in this chapter and the following is that, for the European Union to have a democratic government, it must adopt the same type of answerability that prevails in the Member States with a parliamentary system (most Member States having such a system, with the notable exception of a few, such as France).[123] Of course, democratic government can also be shaped as a fully fledged presidential system, as in the United States. Applied to the European Union, that would mean that, in addition to the European Parliament, also the president of the Commission, that is, the head of the executive branch under the first pillar, would be directly elected by the people. I will return to that issue in chapter 7.

There exist basic differences between a parliamentary and a presidential system. To establish a clear understanding of these differences, the functioning of the British parliamentary system as compared with the American presidential system was briefly described at the outset of this chapter, against the background of the crisis resulting from the war with Iraq. The comparison shows that, in such a situation, the position of a British prime minister is politically more fragile than that of an American president. Indeed, while Tony Blair was not only obliged to appear regularly before Parliament in order to explain the decisions he had taken, or intended to take, but could also be removed from office by a majority of MPs, the latter could not happen to George W. Bush because, impeachment excepted, the U.S. Congress does not have the power to make the president step down.

In many parliamentary systems, the head of the government is in a position even more fragile than that of the British prime minister, because in most countries, in contrast to the United Kingdom, a coalition of political parties is needed to make up a majority in parliament. This is, for example, the case in Germany, where the political party to which the chancellor belongs does not normally have an absolute majority in the Bundestag. In such a situation res-

---

[123] On the French semi-presidential system, see chapter 7, pp. 315–17.

ignation of the head of government and, with him, the whole government may occur whenever the political parties making up the governing coalition disagree on an important or sensitive policy issue. However, in Germany, as in some other multiparty parliamentary regimes, resignation of the head of state is rendered more difficult through a device known as the "constructive vote of no confidence."[124] Again, the situation is intrinsically different in the United States, where the president is directly elected by the people for a specific period of time and can thus, regardless of the opinion in Congress, remain in office until the end of his term, whatever decision he makes.

At the level of the Member States, political responsibility is not the only instrument with which to hold cabinet ministers accountable. Moreover, it is an instrument that is seldom formally used in the case of individual ministers, and operates mainly as a deterrent or a last resort. Indeed, in most instances, individual ministers will resign voluntarily, of their own accord or at the request of the head of government, whenever they feel they have lost the confidence of their own party or of a majority in parliament—or if they have lost the confidence of the public, induced by, or reflected in, the media, often as the result of a controversy. In such circumstances, it may, indeed, be better for a minister to step down voluntarily if he or she wishes to preserve his or her political future.

In a parliamentary system in which ministerial responsibility is still based on the Weberian concept of primacy of politics, a minister will be politically responsible not only for his or her own wrongful behavior, but also for that of civil servants working under him or her. Because these civil servants are deemed to be politically neutral bureaucrats and cannot be held responsible by parliament in their capacity as civil servants, according to the system's logic, the minister concerned takes political responsibility for their behavior. This is even so when the minister cannot be blamed personally for the civil servant's wrongful behavior, provided that he or she has the legal authority to supervise the civil servant concerned, and that it is unlikely that a majority in parliament will maintain its confidence in the minister. However, as recent examples in the Netherlands and Belgium have demonstrated,[125] the contours of primacy of politics as a principle of political responsibility are not always clear in practice. Therefore it will in most instances be for the head of government to determine whether it is appropriate for a minister (or for him- or herself, when he or she is personally involved) to step down voluntarily. In a country such as the Federal Republic of Germany, where the function and legal

---

[124] See above, p. 65.
[125] See above, p. 77–79.

authority of the chancellor and cabinet ministers is circumscribed in the Basic Law itself and in implementing guidelines, the chancellor's judgment will have to remain within a relatively well-defined constitutional framework and will be supervised, as to its legality, by the Constitutional Court.[126]

In addition to political responsibility, there are other instruments to control ministerial behavior. In that respect, open government and free access to public documents, if broadly applied as in Sweden, are crucial in a democratic society to prevent arbitrariness and to expose unprofessional behavior of cabinet ministers and other high officials. This is particularly so when it is used in combination with investigative journalism. There is, however, a risk that such a combination may "implode" as a result of speculation and overreaction if journalists stray beyond the limits of responsible reporting. Furthermore, in common law countries, tribunals of inquiry are often used as an institutional device to investigate politically sensitive affairs in which ministers or high officials are involved. Usually chaired by a senior judge, these tribunals are useful (though expensive) instruments that, because of their flexibility and high profile, tend to be more helpful than lengthy judicial procedures. This is especially the case when the tribunal can rely on (nonbinding) codes of ethics, so-called Standards in Public Life, which in the United Kingdom are prepared at the initiative of a permanent committee composed of independent persons of high standing.[127] Finally there is criminal law, an instrument of last resort that is often used in cases where ministers have resigned or have abandoned their political career and can no longer be submitted to the sanction of political responsibility. The way in which the tragic blood contamination affair was dealt with in France is a poignant example of this approach.

Turning to the European Union, among these additional techniques, there are two that are also available at Union level. Open government and free access to public documents are instruments that become increasingly important, albeit less than in Sweden, as we will see in chapter 4. The creation of a tribunal of inquiry is also an instrument that can be put to use in the Union, as was illustrated by the Committee of Independent Experts set up by the European Parliament in 1999 to investigate fraud in the European Commission. That instrument could be made more effective, though, if such committees could rely on codes of ethics—rather than codes of conduct[128]—prepared under the su-

---

[126] See above, pp. 75–77.

[127] See above, pp. 73–74.

[128] On the distinction between codes of conduct and codes of ethics, see chapter 4, pp. 162–64.

pervision of a committee of Standards in Public Life.[129] If an appropriate legal framework could be laid out for such committees, they could play a role that parliamentary committees of inquiry (provided for in Article 193 EC) may not be able to fulfill, as was demonstrated in 1999 in the absence, as yet, of a sufficient parliamentary tradition to investigate delicate issues across political party lines.[130]

As for criminal law, the instrument is only partially available at Union level, as long as the Member States refuse to provide the Union with operational competences in the field of criminal investigation and prosecution. Under present law, the Union must rely on the penal authorities, rules, and procedures of the Member State where the offense was committed in order to prosecute criminal fraud, even within its own services. This is different, though, for "in-house" investigation, for which the Union has established a European investigation unit, OLAF, which is empowered to interrogate and investigate the Union's civil servants and officials. Once the investigation has been completed, and apart from internal disciplinary proceedings, the documents and information gathered must, however, be turned over to the competent authorities of the Member State concerned for the purposes of prosecution and adjudication.[131]

As for political responsibility of the Commission as a body and of commissioners individually, Community law already contains basic provisions to make the Commission accountable to Parliament. Parliamentarians may, pursuant to Article 197 EC, put questions to the Commission and hear individual commissioners; furthermore, Parliament is empowered to table a motion of censure under Article 201, which, if adopted, obliges the Commission to resign as a body. To make political responsibility to Parliament fully effective, however, further steps should be taken to strengthen the European Parliament's power over the appointment of the president and members of the Commission. Currently, such power is limited because Parliament is only allowed, under Article 214 (2) EC, to approve persons who have been nominated for president or member of the Commission by the Member State governments represented in the European Council and the Council of Ministers. In the

---

[129] As was suggested by the Committee of Independent Experts in its second report, n. 60 above, 268–69, paras. 7.7.1–7.7.5, and welcomed by the incumbent Commission, but not put in practice: see chapter 4, p. 162.

[130] See pp. 81–82 and 90, n. 85.

[131] On fighting fraud and corruption in the context of the EU and the role of OLAF in that respect, see the 1999 Committee of Independent Experts, "Second Report on Reform of the Commission" (n. 60 above), vol. 2, at 147–201.

Member State parliamentary regimes, the power of national parliaments over the appointment and maintenance in power of the head and members of executive government is made operational through the role that political parties play in political decision making. To make that possible under Community law, major changes in the status and selection of commissioners and in the functioning of political parties at the European level will be needed. This issue is further explored in chapter 7.

The political responsibility of commissioners to the European Parliament must be strengthened by increasing the involvement of Parliament in the appointment of the Commission, and its content must be better defined—for which inspiration can be drawn from the Member States' legal systems. In these systems ministers are politically responsible not only for behavior that can be imputed to them personally, but also for behavior of civil servants under their jurisdiction. At Community level, the latter issue came to the fore with the events leading to the resignation of the Santer Commission in 1999, in which the central question was whether or not commissioners could be held politically responsible for the wrongful behavior of third persons to whom the Commission had assigned implementing tasks. Also in that case the answer should be in the affirmative, again in accordance with the Member State legal systems.

In a similar context, inspiration can also be drawn from the Member States' experience with administrative agencies. So far, agencies at the European level have not been involved in regulatory activities, and the issue of political responsibility for such activities has not come up. As a matter of fact, in the present state of Community law, the constitutionality of entrusting independent agencies with regulatory powers has not really been discussed. As yet, only executive agencies have been set up to assist the Commission in its executive function, in areas where the Community executive should be able to draw on external expertise and information. In that respect, the new Council Regulation 1605/2002 constitutes an important step in the "constitutionalization" of Community administration, and may operate as a test case to explore the content of political responsibility on behalf of the competent commissioner as regards agency activities, and how that responsibility should be constructed in the future.[132]

In the years to come, the need to create truly regulatory agencies may become more acute with the emergence in the Member States, as a result of liberalization, of regulators in the network industries (electricity, natural gas,

---

[132] As mentioned above, the Regulation contains a set of provisions on the review of legality of agency acts: Paul Craig, n. 115 above, 849–51.

telecommunications, rail, and post, for example). This will raise the question sooner or later whether it would not be more appropriate to create regulatory agencies at Community level. The issue raises a series of constitutional and legal issues that will have to be analyzed further relating, for example, to the need for independence, transparency, and accountability of such agencies, and to the relationship between competition and regulation.[133] It also requires further comparative analysis from economic and political science perspectives, with regard to the benefits (specialization and expertise) and drawbacks (breeding grounds for collusion, or interest capture) of such delegation of executive and legislative power to independent agencies.

The above primarily concerns the Union's first pillar, the second and the third pillars raising different issues of political responsibility because of the prominent position that the Council of Ministers occupies under those pillars on the legislative and the executive levels. Except for the European Parliament's right to hear the Council,[134] the Council as a body is not as yet politically accountable to any other institution at Union level, nor are its individual members politically responsible to anyone other than their national parliaments. This issue will be further discussed in chapter 7.

[133] On the relation, for example, between competition and regulation in the telecommunication sector, see Pierre Larouche, "The Bases of EC Telecommunications Law after Liberalization," Ph.D. diss., Maastricht University, 2000, and Wayne Sandholtz, "The Emergence of a Supranational Telecommunications Regime," in *European Integration and Supranational Governance*, ed. Wayne Sandholtz and Alec Stone Sweet (Oxford: Oxford University Press, 1998), 134–63.

[134] See the last sentence of Article 197 EC.

CHAPTER THREE

The Rule of Law

The previous chapter considered the concept of an accountable and politically responsible executive government as an essential element of a democratic political system. The rule of law is another such element. There is a link between the two concepts: the less accountable a government is in a specific instance, the larger the role that the rule of law needs to play.[1] In other words, a higher degree of accountability through law may act as a substitute for a lesser degree of accountability through politics. The rule of law is not a well-defined concept, however,[2] and defining it in a comparative law context is particularly difficult because the English concept has a different meaning and background than the German concept of *Rechtsstaat*. Nevertheless, the two are often used as synonyms, as in Article 6 EU Treaty, where *Rechtsstaat* is translated in the English version as "rule of law."

In Section I, the rule of law and *Rechtsstaat* concepts will be compared with the related concept of judicial review, and, in the following sections, the most important components of the rule of law will be described insofar as they relate to government. Those components are: 1) submission of all public authority to judicial review by an independent judge; 2) respect for human rights and fundamental freedoms; and 3) the existence of a clear legal basis for the exercise of public authority and the need for high-quality legislation. In the following chapter, chapter 4, I will describe the rule of law concept in relation to governance.

[1] See chapter 2, p. 63.
[2] "The concept seems to be a fairly empty vessel whose contents, depending on the speaker, can differ [very much] . . .": G. Casper, "The United States and the End of the 'American Century': The Rule of Law or Enlightened Absolutism?" in *Washington University Journal of Law and Policy*, 2000, 149–73, at 152.

I. RULE OF LAW, *RECHTSSTAAT*, AND JUDICIAL REVIEW

In the United Kingdom the concept of rule of law has never been linked to the idea of the state, but rather has been seen as one of the three overarching principles of British constitutionalism, together with the doctrines of separation of powers and legislative supremacy of Parliament. According to the latter principle, Parliament has "the right to make or unmake any law whatsoever,"[3] which means that it may expressly or implicitly repeal its own legislation without subjection to a higher law. The origin of this proposition lies in the political history of the seventeenth and eighteenth centuries. In the seventeenth century, more particularly in *Bonham's Case*,[4] Parliament's supreme sovereignty was contradicted. In that case, Sir Edward Coke opined that: "when an Act of Parliament is against common law and reason, or repugnant, or impossible to be performed, the common law will control it, and adjudge such Act to be void," thus approving the arguments presented on behalf of the King with regard to royal prerogative.[5] However, Sir Edward's opinion had no follow-up as a general rule of law and, more than a century later, Blackstone expressed the opposite opinion in his authoritative *Commentaries on the Laws of England* (1765–68), stating that the supremacy of the Assembly of Westminster was absolute and that no judge was empowered to review an act of Parliament.[6]

Interestingly enough, while the English courts heeded Blackstone's opinion, Sir Edward's opinion prevailed in the United States Supreme Court. In-

---

[3] As quoted by McLeod, *Legal Method*, 3d ed. (Basingstoke: Macmillan, 1999), 58, from Dicey's influential book *The Law of the Constitution*, first published in 1885. As is well known, the U.K. does not have a written constitution, and is thus the exception in the European Union, all other Member States having a written constitution (including Ireland, the other common law Member State of the Union).

[4] (1610) 8 Co Rep 114.

[5] McLeod, n. 3 above, 59, where some other early cases upholding the royal prerogative are cited. See also T. Koopmans, *Courts and Political Institutions: A Comparative View* (Cambridge: Cambridge University Press, 2003), 17 and 39.

[6] On the historical background of Coke and Blackstone's theories and their impact on American law, see R. C. van Caenegem, *Judges, Legislators and Professors: Chapters in European History* (Cambridge: Cambridge University Press, 1987), 26–31. Casper (n. 2 above) refers in that regard to Thomas Paine, who said of the American tradition, as contrasted with the English at that time, "For as in absolute Governments the King is Law, so in free countries the Law ought to be King; and there ought to be no other." Paine, *Common Sense*, in *The Political and Miscellaneous Works of Thomas Paine*, vol. 1, 1819, at 32.

deed, in *Marbury v. Madison*[7] Chief Justice John Marshall spoke the famous words, "to what purpose are powers limited, and to what purpose is that limitation committed to writing, if those limits may, at any time, be passed by those intended to be restrained?" These words embody the essence of American constitutionalism, which regards a written constitution as superior to legislation as a means of anchoring the organization of government and the protection of the rights and privileges of states and citizens.[8] They have been responsible for the emergence in the United States of a constitutional model that is the opposite of the parliamentary model. In the constitutional model, a parliament cannot be "sovereign" or "supreme" because its legislation has to be compatible with higher law, and in particular with the Constitution, and this compatibility will not be assessed by the parliament but by a judicial body.[9] The essence of a constitutional system, therefore, is judicial review: if a court comes to the conclusion that a statute is unconstitutional, it will 'strike it down,' that is, it will not apply that statute.[10]

Although European observers for a long time saw the American constitutional system as a peculiarity of a federal state, that view changed in the course of the twentieth century. Since then, judicial review has also been considered as an expression of the idea that the protection of civil liberties "might not be in safe hands if wholly entrusted to political institutions."[11] As a result, many European states embraced the American constitutional system, particularly the component of judicial review of statutes by a constitutional court. Particularly after the experience of dictatorships and world wars in Europe, when "faith in the reliability of political institutions, even when democratically elected, began to shrink," the American system of judicial review was adopted in the constitutions of many countries, the Federal Republic of Germany, with its Basic Law of 1949, being a prominent example.[12]

Even in the United Kingdom—where the traditional parliamentary system remains in vogue—the concept of rule of law has come to be understood in a more general way, that is, as "a principle of institutional morality" that guides

---

[7] 1 Cranch 137 (1803).

[8] See G. Casper, *Constitutionalism*, Occasional Papers from the Law School, The University of Chicago, 1987, at 8.

[9] Koopmans, n. 5 above, 35.

[10] In the United States, where each of the fifty states has its own supreme court, examining state laws is a task for each of these courts. However, important cases involving the interpretation of the U.S. Constitution will nearly always be referred to the U.S. Supreme Court in Washington: ibid.

[11] For an overview, see Koopmans, n. 5 above, 41–44. The words quoted are at 41.

[12] Ibid.

"all forms of law-making and law-enforcement. In particular it suggests that legal certainty and procedural protections are . . . fundamental requirements of good governance."[13]

Although such an understanding may bring the British concept closer to the American constitutional concept, there remain, however, large differences, the British concept being understood as a guarantee of good governance, not as a model of democratic government (which remains parliamentary in essence). In the British model, the link between rule of law and democracy is ensured through the doctrine of "conform interpretation" of parliamentary acts. In the words of Lord Steyn, "Parliament must be presumed not to legislate contrary to the rule of law. And the rule of law enforces minimum standards of fairness, both substantive and procedural."[14] That view, however, does not prevent the common law of England from recognizing some statutes, like the European Communities Act 1972, as "constitutional statutes"—which, therefore, cannot be impliedly (only explicitly) repealed.[15]

I turn now to the German concept of *Rechtsstaat*, which, freely translated, refers to a system in which all state authority is governed by law. The concept finds its origin in the *Vernunftstheorie* (theory of rationality), which vests the legitimacy of the state in natural law, and in the "enlightened absolutism" of the late-eighteenth-century Prussian state of King Frederick the Great (1712–86). The Prussian king desired natural law, reason-based codification, administered by a civil service so that, in the words of a commentator, the "messy phenomena of life could be made to fit the Code."[16] Under these theories of rational man and freedom, it is for the state, seen as a liberal state submitted to individual rights and freedoms of its citizens, to support those citizens in their pursuit of personal liberty and self-development. In a later stage, though, emphasis also came to be put, as at present in the United Kingdom, on institutional and procedural aspects guaranteeing decision making in accordance with legal rules, as well as on legality of administrative action and judicial review by an independent judge.[17] Nevertheless, the German view remains cen-

---

[13] Jeffrey Jowell, "The Rule of Law Today," in *The Changing Constitution*, 3d ed., ed. D. Oliver, O. Jowell, and J. Jowell (Oxford: Clarendon Press, 1994), 57.

[14] In *ex p Pierson*, [1997] 3 All ER 577, cited in Patrick Birkinshaw, "Supranationalism, the Rule of Law and Constitutionalism in the Draft Union Constitution," forthcoming.

[15] See Laws LJ in *Thoburn v. Sunderland City Council*, [2002] 3WLR 247 (Queen's Bench Division) and in *Norris Dewar McWhirter et al. v. Home Secretary*, judgment of March 5, 2003 (Court of Appeal).

[16] Casper, n. 2 above, 153. The code he refers to is the Prussian Code of 1794.

[17] On all these aspects, with many references, see P. Popelier, *Rechtszekerheid als be-*

tered primarily on human dignity and a liberal state at the service of its citizens, and therefore places an emphasis on human rights. This differentiates the German constitutional system to some extent from the American system, in which protection of citizen rights was, from the beginning, incorporated not into the (federal) Constitution, but into the ten amendments known as the American Bill of Rights, added to the Constitution in 1791.[18]

With the enactment on May 23, 1949, of the Basic Law of the Federal Republic of Germany, the full significance of the notion of *Rechtsstaat* was recognized.[19] In its first article, the Basic Law recognizes the dignity of man to be inviolable and regards it as a duty for all public authority "to respect and protect it," thus making it clear, in line with the Enlightenment ideas mentioned above, that the state is at the service of its citizens and not vice versa.[20] The Basic Law then starts out with a list of basic rights—which, according to Article 1 (3), "shall bind the legislature, the executive and the judiciary as directly enforceable law"—and establishes a framework for a federal state that, according to Article 20 (1), shall be "democratic and social." It further states that "the legislature shall be bound by the constitutional order, the executive and the judiciary by law and justice" (Article 20 [3]). The Basic Law recognizes all of these principles as being of a higher nature than the Basic Law itself by prohibiting, in Article 79 (3), the amendment of Articles 1 and 20, as well as the division of the federation into Länder (regional states) and their participation in the legislative process. In other words, these principles are the inviolable foundations of the federal state and belong to the essence of constitutionalism, so much so that Article 20 (4) grants "all Germans . . . the right to resist anybody attempting to do away with this constitutional order, should no other remedy be possible."[21]

Under the German law the principle of *Rechtsstaat* encompasses a large

---

ginsel voor behoorlijke wetgeving [Legal certainty as a principle of proper legislation] (Antwerp: Intersentia, 1997), 49–56.

[18] Koopmans, n. 5 above, 44. See also below, pp. 127–28.

[19] Basic Law for the Federal Republic of Germany, promulgated by the Parliamentary Council on May 23, 1949, as amended up to and including December 20, 1993. Official translation revised and updated edition June 1994 (Public Document: Federal Government, Bonn, 1994). For a further updated (non-official) English translation, see Axel Tschetscher, *The Basic Law (Grundgesetz): The Constitution of the Federal Republic of Germany (May 23rd, 1949)* (Würzburg: Jurisprudentia Verlag, 2002). The Basic Law which was enacted for West Germany remained the constitution for the whole of Germany when East and West Germany were united on October 3, 1990, after the collapse of the communist regime in East Germany.

[20] See H. Maurer, *Staatsrecht I*, 3d ed. (Munich: Verlag CHBeck, 2003), 174–75.

[21] Article 20 (1), (2), and (3).

number of rules and institutions, and it may be worthwhile to enumerate them in full. They concern respect for basic rights, separation of powers, submission of all public authority to law, the requirement of a legal basis for all administrative action, judicial protection, state liability, legal certainty, basic principles of criminal law and procedure, and the principle of proportionality.[22] Moreover, as further discussed in chapter 4, Articles 20 (1) and 28 (1) of the Basic Law link the principle of *Rechtsstaat* to the concept of *Sozialstaat*, while Article 23 (as inserted by an amendment of December 21, 1992) makes express provision for the participation of the Federal Republic in the development of the European Union, "which is committed to democratic, rule-of-law, social, and federal principles, as well as the principle of subsidiarity, and ensures protection of basic rights comparable in substance to that afforded by this Basic Law."[23]

It is in light of the foregoing that I will now examine whether the European Union is a political entity that is governed by the rule of law, that is, whether it possesses the characteristics of a *Rechtsstaat*. As will be seen, the answer is in the affirmative for the first pillar, but not unreservedly so for the second and third.[24] In this chapter I will discuss the characteristics of the rule of law that relate to democratic government, drawing inspiration from characteristics embodied in the German concept of *Rechtsstaat*. These characteristics have already been mentioned, and they encompass the submission of all public authority, including the legislature proper, to judicial review through efficient remedies; the duty of all public authority to respect and protect individual (especially human) rights; and the obligation of public authorities to provide legal certainty and to act only when there is a legal basis for it in the EC Treaty. In the following chapter I will discuss some other characteristics relating more specifically to good governance. These are the duty of officials to behave with integrity and efficiency and in accordance with due process requirements, and the pursuit of equality and social justice by officials in the performance of their duties.

[22] Maurer, n. 20 above, 215–38.

[23] The article contains further conditions and modalities for the involvement of the German institutions and Länder in the legislative process of the European Union.

[24] The reason the second pillar cannot be deemed, according to the prevailing opinion, to comply with the concepts of rule of law and *Rechtsstaat* is mainly that judicial review by the Community courts of acts or omissions of the Council, or of the European Council, is unavailable under the second pillar, and limited under the third pillar (see Article 46 TEU, as amended by the Amsterdam and the Nice Treaties). See below, pp. 118–21.

II. SUBMISSION OF PUBLIC AUTHORITIES TO COMMUNITY LAW

Under the Union's first pillar, all Community institutions, including the legislature, and all Member State authorities implementing Community law must act in conformity with the law and can be brought before a court of law, either a Community court or a national court, if they do not comply. That is different, however, under the third pillar, where important limitations apply, and under the second pillar, where judicial review is virtually absent.

Judicial Review by Community and National Courts

a) Judicial review by Community courts
    Article 220, first paragraph, EC states that "the Court of Justice and the Court of First Instance, each within its jurisdiction, shall ensure that in the interpretation and application of this Treaty the law is observed."[25] The following treaty articles set out several legal remedies that allow the Community courts to fulfill their "protective" task.
    The most important of these remedies is laid down in the first and second

---

[25] The Community judicature, which at the outset consisted solely of the ECJ, has, since the 1986 Single European Act, two courts: the European Court of Justice (ECJ) and the Court of First Instance (CFI): Article 220 EC. Since the Nice Treaty, a third layer, consisting of judicial panels with jurisdiction in specific areas, may be created by the Council: Article 225a EC (see chapter 1, p. 12, n. 16). No such third-party layer has been created so far. The ECJ is composed of judges, one per Member State (i.e., as of May 1, 2004, twenty-five judges), and of advocate generals (to remain eight, unless the number is increased by unanimous vote in the Council), all of them "chosen from persons whose independence is beyond doubt" and appointed "by common accord of the governments of the Member States": Article 223 EC. The judges are appointed for a six-year term and are eligible for reappointment. Of the advocate generals, only those appointed from the large (old) Member States can be reappointed; the other advocate generals are appointed from the remaining Member States for one term of six years on a rotational basis. The task of the advocate generals is to give a reasoned opinion, "acting with complete impartiality and independence" (Article 222 EC), on cases brought before the ECJ. The court is under no obligation to follow the advocate generals' opinion. To date, the CFI has as many judges as there are Member States (but more may be appointed), also appointed for six years and eligible for reappointment, but has no advocate generals (a judge may be appointed to act as an advocate general in a specific case). See further S. Douglas-Scott, *Constitutional Law of the European Union* (Harlow, England: Longman, 2002), 200–204, and P. Craig and G. de Búrca, *EU Law, Text, Cases, and Materials* (Oxford: Oxford University Press, 2003), 86–94.

paragraphs of Article 230 EC, according to which the Court of Justice "shall review the legality" of all executive *and* legislative Community acts "intended to produce legal effects vis-à-vis third parties" (first paragraph), "on grounds of lack of competence, infringement of an essential procedural requirement, infringement of this Treaty or of any rule of law relating to its application, or misuse of powers" (second paragraph). In the same vein, Article 232, first paragraph, EC empowers the court to establish a failure to act, "in infringement of the Treaty," on the part of a Community institution. A variety of persons and institutions may bring an action in the Community courts on the basis of those provisions. Thus, actions may be brought in the Court of Justice by a Member State, the European Parliament, the Council, or the Commission without limitation, or by the Court of Auditors and the European Central Bank when needed for the purpose of protecting their prerogatives.[26] Actions may also be brought in the Court of First Instance by any natural or legal person against a decision "addressed to that person" (for example, a decision finding a breach of Community competition rules), or "against a decision which, although in the form of a regulation [that is, an act of a general nature] or a decision addressed to another person, is of direct and individual concern" to the person bringing the suit[27] and, moreover, against a failure of an institution to address a binding act to any natural or legal person entitled to obtain such an act.[28]

The situations in which actions may be brought are very broad. This is, first, because an action can be initiated by an applicant against any binding act, or failure to take such an act, that is inconsistent with Community law and can be attributed to any Community institution, including the European Parliament and the Council of Ministers (that is, the Community legislature). Secondly, this is because the term "infringement of any rule of law" in Article 230 EC has been held by the Court of Justice to include general principles that are part of Community law, including protection of fundamental rights.[29] In

[26] Article 230 and, in a somewhat different formulation, Article 232 EC.

[27] Article 230, fourth para., EC.

[28] Article 232, third para., EC. Roughly speaking, the division of work between the ECJ and the CFI is as follows (for the time being): the CFI hears cases initiated by individual persons, the ECJ hears all other cases, i.e., cases brought by Community institutions or Member States and referrals by Member State courts for preliminary rulings. Moreover, the ECJ hears cases on appeal from the CFI on points of law. For more detail on the internal organization and procedure of the Community courts, see Douglas-Scott, n. 25 above, 204–7.

[29] On the specific case of protection of human rights before Community and national courts, see Bruno De Witte, "The Past and Future Role of the European Court of Justice in the Protection of Human Rights," in *The EU and Human Rights*, ed. Philip Alston (Oxford: Oxford University Press, 2000), 859–97, particularly 875–82.

spite of this broad understanding, the court has nevertheless limited the standing of individual persons before the Community courts in cases involving an alleged breach of fundamental rights by provisions of a *general* nature. In fact, the ECJ has repeatedly refused to give a broad interpretation of the words "of direct and individual concern" in the fourth paragraph of Article 230 EC (quoted above), despite several opinions of the court's advocate generals favoring such a broad interpretation and recent case law of the CFI to this effect.[30] The ECJ's refusal to follow suit is based upon two considerations. The first is that relief can be sought through other procedural means, either, as mentioned below, before the Community courts on the basis of Article 288 EC or before Member State courts that are at liberty, pursuant to Article 234 EC,[31] to ask the ECJ for a preliminary ruling on the validity or interpretation of a general regulation allegedly in violation of an individual's fundamental rights.[32] The second consideration is that, in a situation of such importance, it is for the Member States to revise the text of Article 230 EC if they find the present situation unsatisfactory.[33]

[30] In its judgment of May 3, 2002, the CFI gave a broader reading to that expression with respect to a measure of general application. See Case T-177/01, *Jégo-Quéré et Cie SA v. Commission*, [2002] ECR II-2365. That judgment was in line with the strongly argued opinion of advocate general Jacobs in Case C-50/00 P, *Unión de Pequeños Agriculturos (UPA) v. Council*, [2002] ECR I-6677. Neither UPA nor the appeal from the CFI in *Jégo-Quére* (Case C-263/02 P, judgment of April 1, 2004) caused the ECJ to alter its case law; rather, the court merely confirmed its restrictive position. See *UPA*, paras. 32–47. For a thorough analysis, see John A. Usher, "Direct and Individual Concern— An Effective Remedy or a Conventional Solution?" 28 *ELRev.*, 2003, 575–600.

[31] With respect to Article 234 EC, see below, p. 114.

[32] This is not a satisfactory solution, as it implies that individual plaintiffs may be obliged to break national law allegedly inconsistent with the Community act in order to be able to plead the unlawfulness of the Community act before a national court that then may (or, if a court of last instance, must) ask the ECJ for a preliminary ruling on the basis of Article 234 EC. See A. G. Jacob's opinion in Case C-50/00P, *UPA*, n. 30 above, paras. 36–44. This is not a happy situation, and it is, moreover, inconsistent with the rule of law concept.

[33] See *UPA*, n. 30 above. In fact, this issue arose during the European Convention on the draft Constitution, and a limited amendment was finally proposed in Article III-270 (4) [now Article III-365 (4)] of the final text of the draft Constitution. The amendment allows private plaintiffs to institute proceedings before the Community court "against a regulatory act which is of direct concern to him or her and does not entail implementing measures" (see chapter 6, p. 291). For a discussion of the proposed alteration in light of the *UPA* judgment, see Michael Dougan, "The Convention's Draft Constitutional Treaty: Bringing Europe Closer to Its Lawyers?" 28 *ELRev.*, 2003, 763–793, at 789–91; also John Usher, n. 30 above, 595–98.

The power of Community courts to subject action of all Community institutions, including action from the Community legislature, to judicial review is confirmed in Article 288 (2) EC, which contains another important legal remedy. That article provides for the possibility of individuals bringing before the Community courts actions for compensation against any Community institution, including the legislature, for damage caused to the applicant as a result of a serious breach of Community law. The conditions of this special form of "noncontractual liability"—which, by virtue of Article 235 EC, can be brought before the Court of First Instance, and on appeal before the Court of Justice—will be determined by those courts "in accordance with the general principles common to the laws of the Member States."[34] In this respect, the case law of the ECJ *has* given a broad interpretation to the treaty, holding in its 1971 *Schöppenstedt* judgment that individuals can also obtain damages for Community legislative action of a *general* nature, even when it involves measures of economic policy, when a "sufficiently flagrant violation of a superior rule of law for the protection of the individual has occurred."[35]

The full dimension of this provision became clear in later cases, particularly the 1992 *Mulder* judgment, in which a large number of farmers were awarded compensation for financial losses in connection with a certain milk production quota established by Community legislation in the field of agricultural policy, legislation that was later invalidated for contravening the (unwritten) Community law principle of legitimate expectations.[36] Accordingly, serious violations of "fundamental rights" can give rise to actions for damages brought by a private plaintiff against the Community legislature, provided that the claimant is able to prove actual damage and direct causation (thereby curtailing the effect of the ECJ's aforementioned narrow interpretation of Article 230 EC with respect to the standing of private individuals).

b) Judicial review by national courts in cooperation with Community courts
The jurisdiction of the Community courts is limited in a general manner as they lack competence directly to annul, or set aside, national legislation that is inconsistent with Community law[37]—which, under Community law, remains a matter for the national courts.

---

[34] Article 288, second para., EC.
[35] Case 5/71, *Aktien-Zuckerfabrik Schöppenstedt v. Council*, [1971] ECR 975, para 11. See further Craig and de Búrca, n. 25 above, 547–58.
[36] Joined Cases C-104/89 and 37/90, *J. M. Mulder v. Council and Commission*, [1992] ECR I-3061.
[37] But see Articles 226 and 227 EC, which allow the ECJ to find, at the request of the Commission or of another Member State, that a Member State has failed to fulfill

However, national courts of any standing *may*—and courts of last instance *shall*—ask the Court of Justice for a preliminary ruling on the interpretation of any rule of Community law, or the validity of secondary Community law (that is, not treaty law),[38] when such a question is raised in any litigation before them.[39] The national court must then apply the Court of Justice's ruling in the case giving rise to the question, thus, for example, by annulling, or setting aside, any conflicting national legislation or action. This procedure has allowed the Community court *indirectly* to control any national law or measure that is in breach of Community law. Moreover, the Court, through its long-standing case law on direct effect of Community law, has considerably increased the number of instances in which private litigants, or defendants in criminal proceedings, are able to ask national courts to apply the preliminary ruling procedure in view of annulling, or setting aside, national laws or measures, or correcting national authorities' failures to act.[40]

It is an undisputed fact that the preliminary ruling procedure of Article 234 EC, and "the remarkable trust and co-operation" between national courts and the ECJ within the framework of that procedure, have been responsible for turning Community law into a system with a high degree of legal accountabil-

---

an obligation under Community law—a failure that may consist in not enacting legislation needed to implement Community law, or in maintaining legislation in breach of Community law. If, after a judgment of the ECJ finding an infringement, a Member State fails to comply with the judgment, the Commission or plaintiff Member State can ask the court to impose a penalty on the Member State: Article 228 (2) EC. The Court applied that provision for the first time in Case C-387/97, *Commission v. Greece*, [2000] ECR I-5047. In that judgment, the ECJ outlined its view of the penalty payment and of the way in which the Commission intended to apply Article 228 (2).

[38] When the validity of a Community act is in question, even courts that are not deciding in last instance, have an obligation to refer the question to the ECJ, as was decided by the court in Case 314/85, *Foto-Frost*, [1987] ECR 4199. The ECJ adopted that interpretation of Article 234 EC, which clearly goes beyond the text of the article, in order to prevent Community acts being validated by some national courts judging in first instance, and invalidated by others in the same position.

[39] See Article 234 EC (but also see Article 68 EC containing a limited application of the preliminary ruling procedure in matters of visas, asylum, and immigration, matters that were transferred from the third pillar to the first by the Amsterdam Treaty). Although courts of last instance (and sometimes courts not of last instance: see n. 38 above) have the obligation to refer a preliminary question to the ECJ, that is only so when they do not believe the issue before them to be an "acte clair," i.e., clear and free from doubt. See ECJ in Case 283/81, *CILFIT*, [1982] ECR 3415 and Douglas-Scott, n. 25 above, 244–49.

[40] On the preliminary rulings procedure and the role it has played, and continues to play, in building European law, see Craig and de Búrca, n. 25 above, 432–546.

ity by providing private parties broad access to a court of law.[41] The only significant lacuna left is the one created by the ECJ's narrow interpretation of Article 230, paragraph 4, EC with regard to the standing of private applicants before the Community courts in cases where their fundamental rights have been infringed by a Community act of a general nature. However, as mentioned previously, the preliminary ruling procedure of Article 234 EC, together with the compensation procedure of Article 288 EC,[42] has to some extent been able to fill the lacuna—only to some extent as standing under Article 234 EC depends on the "goodwill" of the national courts to comply with a private claimant's request to refer a question to the ECJ and, moreover, constitutes a "procedural detour" since it does not allow the claimant to attack the allegedly unlawful Community act directly (and immediately after its promulgation), but only after a public authority or a private person has acted in reliance upon it at the national level.[43]

To have framed such a high degree of legal accountability is one of the great achievements of the case law of the ECJ, more particularly in having emphasized the necessity for national laws, and national courts, to broaden extant remedies in order to allow individuals to enforce the rights that they derive from Community law against national public authorities.[44] As a result of that case law, the national courts have been encouraged to broaden the scope of remedies that individuals can use before the national courts in several respects. Thus individuals can now obtain, from Member State authorities, restitution of money paid in breach of Community law, or compensation for harm sustained as a result of infringements of Community law, or interim relief to suspend measures pending the outcome of litigation concerning alleged violations of Community law.

An illustration of this is the Court's case law concerning the principle of state liability that the Court held in *Francovich* to be inherent in the *system* of the EC Treaty: in other words, the ensuing remedy in compensation is not found in the treaty itself.[45] In later case law the remedy has been shaped in par-

---

[41] C. Harlow, *Accountability in the European Union* (Oxford: Oxford University Press, 2002), 153.

[42] See text accompanying n. 32 above and accompanying and following n. 35 above.

[43] See n. 32 above. For an illustration of this "procedural detour," see Case C-466/93, *Atlanta v. Bundesamt für Ernährung und Fortwirtschaft* (no. 2), [1995] ECR I-3799, commented on by de Witte, n. 29 above, 876ff.

[44] See further W. van Gerven, "Of Rights, Remedies and Procedures," 37 *CMLRev.*, 2000, 501.

[45] Cases C-6 and 9/90, *Francovich and Bonifaci v. Italy*, [1991] ECR I-5357, para. 35. The liability created by the court under the principle of State liability is commonly re-

allel with the remedy in compensation that individuals can assert against a Community institution under Article 288, second paragraph, EC, as was mentioned previously.[46] That means in particular that, "in the absence of particular justification," the conditions for liability to arise are the same in both instances. These conditions are: the rule of Community law infringed must be intended to confer rights on individuals, the breach committed by the authority must be sufficiently serious, and there must be a causal link between the breach and the damage sustained.[47] In both instances the rules applied by the courts are based, in the words of Article 288 EC, on "general principles common to the laws of the Member States."

In its famous 1996 *Brasserie du Pêcheur and Factortame III* judgment,[48] the Court applied the doctrine of compensation to breaches of EC law committed by the German legislature (*Brasserie*), and by the British legislature (*Factortame*). The German case concerned the maintenance of national legislation on the brewing of beer that the Court had previously declared to be contrary to Community law. The other case concerned the British Parliament's enactment of the 1988 Merchant Shipping Act, which prevented Spanish fishermen from registering their fishing vessels as British vessels though they were owned by companies incorporated under U.K. law.

The procedural background of the *Factortame* case is of interest as it shows the *interaction* between the Community and the national courts. The case came before the ECJ on three occasions. It was first subjected to the ECJ upon referral from the House of Lords,[49] which wanted to know whether it ought to suspend the Merchant Shipping Act while awaiting the ECJ's pending judgment on the compatibility of the act with Community law. In its referral judgment, the House of Lords noted that, were it not for Community law,

---

ferred to as the "Francovich liability," after the name of one of the plaintiffs in that case.

[46] See above, p. 113.

[47] That means that both lines of ECJ case law can be used back and forth, as a source of inspiration for the courts, both national and Community. See Case C-352/98 P, *Bergaderm*, [2000] ECJ I-5291, paras. 39–44. See further W. van Gerven, "The Emergence of a Common European Law in the Area of Tort Law: The EU Contribution," and Takis Tridimas, "Liability for Breach of Community Law: Growing Up and Mellowing Down?" in *Tort Liability of Public Authorities in Comparative Perspective*, ed. Duncan Fairgrieve, Mads Andenas, and John Bell (London: British Institute of International and Comparative Law, 2002), 125–47 and 149–81, respectively.

[48] Joined Cases C-46/93 and C-48/93, *Brasserie du Pêcheur SA v. Germany and R. v. Secretary of State for Transport, ex parte Factortame Ltd.*, [1996] ECR I-1029.

[49] More accurately, the Appellate Committee of the House of Lords, which acts as the United Kingdom's Supreme Court.

English courts would have no power at all, under the constitutional law doctrine of parliamentary sovereignty, to grant injunctions against the Crown. In
reply to the referral question the ECJ ruled, in *Factortame I*,[50] that the rule of
English law, which precluded interim relief from *ever* being granted against the
Crown (and hence against acts of Parliament), impaired the full effectiveness
of Community law. The House of Lords subsequently granted interim relief in
the specific case. A year later, the ECJ pronounced itself a second time, in
Factortame II,[51] this time on the substance, finding that the British act
breached the Spanish fishermen's Community right under Article 43 EC to be
free from discrimination on the basis of nationality when performing economic services in other EU Member States.

Following these judgments, the case was submitted to the Court of Justice
for the third time, now on referral from the English High Court. That court
wanted to know whether the Spanish fishermen should be allowed compensation for losses caused by the U.K.'s breach of Community law. It was in that
case that the ECJ, applying its "Francovich" doctrine in two joined cases—
Brasserie du Pêcheur and Factortame III[52]—enunciated the guidelines under
which German courts and U.K. courts had to grant compensation in cases
where damage was caused by a national *legislative* act breaching Community
law. According to the ECJ, such compensation was payable even when only
pure economic loss was sustained—that is, economic loss not contingent
upon personal injury or property—a kind of damage that U.K. and German
courts are reluctant to grant under their respective national law. The ECJ's
guidelines were so precise that they left the English and German courts little
choice but to allow such a remedy.[53]

In later cases the "Article 288" and "Francovich" doctrines of noncontractual liability have been further developed by the European courts.
Three specific developments deserve to be mentioned. First, it has been held
that "Article 288" liability may, under exceptional circumstances, also be ap-

---

[50] Case C-213/89, *R. v. Secretary of State for Transport, ex parte Factortame Ltd.*,
[1990] ECR I-2433.

[51] Case C-221/89, *R. v. Secretary of State for Transport, ex parte Factortame Ltd.*,
[1991] ECR I-3905.

[52] N. 48 above. In that judgment the ECJ decided the British and German cases
jointly, hence the name of the case.

[53] It is interesting to note that, as a result of the Community court's case law, Sir
Edward Coke's contention in *Bonham's Case* (1610) (n. 4 above) that an act of Parliament can be inoperative when it "is against common law" became true, almost four
centuries later, in the sense that an act of Parliament can be inoperative when it "is
against Community law."

plied to *lawful* conduct of Community institutions.[54] Second, the ECJ has extended "Francovich" liability to breaches of Community law committed by *judicial* authorities.[55] Third, in a competition case, the Court pointed out that Community law may oblige Member State courts to afford a remedy to a private party whose Community rights have been breached by action from another *private party* on whom Community law imposed a direct obligation (as in Article 81 EC Treaty prohibiting cartel agreements).[56] In the particular case before it, the Court held that its ruling also applied, under certain conditions, when the claimant, as a contracting party, had been found to bear (some) responsibility for the distortion of competition resulting from the prohibited cartel agreement—thus obliging the English court to set aside the unqualified use of the *ex dolo malo non oritur actio*–principle.[57]

The Community Governed by the Rule of Law, but Not (Yet) the Whole Union

It will be clear from the foregoing that, under the first pillar of the Union, judicial review of both Community and Member State action by Community and national courts, often acting in conjunction, has come full circle. As a result of ECJ case law, all public authority is submitted to the rule of law as embodied in Community primary (treaty) and secondary law, as well as in general principles. The submission of all public authority is further enhanced by the principle of Community and/or state liability for injury caused by public authority as a result of infringements of Community law,[58] and by the requirement of full access to court and the right to an effective remedy, as guaranteed by Community law, in line with Articles 6 and 13 of the European Convention on Human Rights.[59]

However, under the second pillar of the Union, judicial review remains

[54] Judgment of the Court of First Instance, Case T-184/95, *Dorsch Consult*, [1998] ECR II-688; upheld on appeal by the Court of Justice, Case C-237/98P, [2001] ECR I-4549.

[55] Case C-224/01, *Köbler v. Republik Österreich*, [2003] ECR I-10239.

[56] Case C-453/99, *Courage v. Crehan*, [2001] ECR I-6297.

[57] In a later (non-competition) case the court made clear that private enforcement of Community law (in that case a regulation), e.g., through claims in compensation, also applies when public authorities have been charged with enforcement at the national level: see Case C-253/00, *Muñoz and Superior Fruiticola*, [2002] ECR I-7289 and the note of Andrea Bondi in *CMLRev.*, 2003, 1241–50.

[58] For a comparison with American law, which is far more restrictive, see James E. Pfander, "Member State Liability and Constitutional Change in the United States and Europe," *Am.J.Comp.L.*, 2003, 237–74. See also chapter 4, n. 128.

[59] Thus, e.g., Case 222/86, *UNECTEF v. Heylens*, [1987] ECR 4097, para. 14.

virtually nonexistent, and under the third pillar it is very limited.[60] To be sure, under the third pillar dealing with police and judicial cooperation in criminal matters,[61] the Council of Ministers may adopt binding legal acts, such as framework and other decisions. However, they are not capable of direct effect[62]—and thus cannot directly be relied on before a national court, even though a citizen's legal position may be affected by national measures taken in implementation of, for example, a framework decision.[63] Furthermore, although a direct action for the annulment of decisions and framework decisions before the ECJ is provided under Article 35 (6) EU, it can be instituted only at the instigation of Member States and the Commission (and not, therefore, at the instigation of the European Parliament, or of private parties). In addition, Article 35 (1) EU gives power to the ECJ to answer references from national courts for preliminary rulings as to, inter alia, the validity of decisions and framework decisions, but the ECJ only has jurisdiction to the extent that a Member State declares that it accepts that jurisdiction, and moreover each Member State may determine whether the power to make reference is to be made available to all national courts, as under Article 234 EC relating to the first pillar, or only to courts of final appeal.[64] It has been noted that these restrictions may give rise to serious problems in Member States (namely Denmark, Ireland, and the U.K.) that have not accepted jurisdiction of the Court of Justice in the third pillar,[65] and they surely constitute an encroachment on the principle of equal access to justice for all Union citizens and others.[66]

Under the second pillar, relating to the Union's common foreign and

[60] See Usher, n. 30 above, 592–95. See also Laurence W. Gormley, "Judicial Review in EC and EU Law: Some Architectural Malfunctions and Design Improvements?" European Law Lecture 2000, Durham Law Institute, U.K.

[61] Chapter 1, pp. 24–25.

[62] See Article 34 (2) EU.

[63] For instance, the Council Framework Decision 2001/500 on Money Laundering, [2001] OJ L182/1: see Usher, n. 30 above, 593.

[64] As to which Member States have made such declaration, and in which way, see ibid., 594. See also Article 35 (5) EU, which prohibits the ECJ from reviewing the legality or proportionality of operations of Member State police or other enforcement services, or the exercise by Member States of law and order and internal security responsibilities.

[65] Usher, n. 30 above.

[66] Gormley, n. 60 above, 6–7. The situation described above is the situation after amendments made by the Amsterdam Treaty. Before those amendments the restrictions on the ECJ's jurisdiction were even more substantial. The ECJ did, however, declare that it had jurisdiction to examine whether action taken under the third pillar was not infringing the powers granted to the court under the first pillar: see Case C-170/96, *Commission v. Council*, [1998] ECR I-2763.

security policy, the jurisdiction of the Court of Justice is even more limited, if not fully nonexistent. Article 46 EU, as amended by the Nice Treaty, contains a restrictive list of competences that are open to examination by the ECJ. However, these are of limited importance, none relating directly to the second pillar. To be sure, that does not exclude the ECJ from verifying, under Article 46, sub (f), and Article 47 EU, whether Council action taken on the basis of the second (or third) pillar should not have been taken on the basis of first-pillar provisions. Arguably, the ECJ may also ensure that Council action under the second (as under the third) pillar does not violate fundamental rights provisions.[67] Nor does it exclude judicial review on behalf of the ECJ when the legal position of third parties, particularly traders, may be affected by action taken under the second pillar, to the extent that it may require implementation by the Member States, or by the Community institutions under the *first* pillar. One such situation is referred to in Article 301 EC, which specifically addresses Community action taken as a result of second-pillar decisions and causing the interruption or reduction of economic relations with one or more third countries. Since measures adopted under Article 301 by the Council of Ministers, on a proposal from the Commission, are normal Community measures, they are also subject to judicial review and the normal remedies of Community law.[68]

In the end, there is no easy answer to the question whether the Union *as a whole* is submitted to the rule of law. To be sure, under the second pillar, relating to the Union's common foreign and defense policy, there is no substantive judicial review. However, that is not a decisive argument in itself, since foreign and particularly defense policy decisions are often considered to be non-justiciable political disputes in the EU Member States (as in the United States), given the complexity of the case and sensitivity of the issues.[69] As for

---

[67] By virtue of Article 6 (2) and Article 46, sub (d) EU: see K. Lenaerts and P. Van Nuffel, *Constitutional Law of the European Union,* ed. R. Bray (London: Sweet and Maxwell, 1999), 607.

[68] Thus Usher, n. 30, 593, with a reference to Case T-306/01 relating to the freezing of assets as a result of Community regulations giving effect to a UN Security Council resolution on sanctions against the Taliban. In that case the president of the CFI rendered an order denying interim relief: *Aden et al v. Council and Commission,* [2002] II-2387. Final judgment is pending.

[69] Thus Koopmans, n. 5 above, 101, where the author examines the political question issue in the United States, France, and Germany at 98–104. Koopmans observes that in those areas the relevant facts, the evaluation of risks, the necessary contacts, and the consequences are often factors that are beyond the area of judicial investigation.

the third pillar, there is clearly a trend, as illustrated by the amendments made to the EU Treaty by the Amsterdam Treaty, to enlarge judicial review, or to transfer matters likely to affect the legal position of persons, such as visa, asylum, and immigration policies, from the third to the first pillar. That same trend is also visible in the draft Constitution, as we will see in chapter 6.[70] All in all, I would conclude that, if the whole Union (as opposed to the first pillar alone) is not yet a political entity governed by the rule of law, it is nevertheless in the process of becoming one.

III. RESPECT FOR BASIC RIGHTS AND FUNDAMENTAL FREEDOMS

A second requirement of the rule of law is that public authorities respect and protect the human rights and fundamental freedoms of all persons, and provide those persons with effective legal remedies before an independent court to protect these rights and freedoms when they have been infringed by a state organ. As pointed out previously, the protection of basic rights is at the center of the German Constitution, but also at the center of other European constitutions, particularly the French Constitution. Thus the attachment to the rights of man and citizen, as defined in the famous 1789 *Declaration des droits de l'homme et du citoyen* (Declaration of the rights of man and the citizen), was confirmed and completed in the preamble of the 1946 Constitution (though not inscribed in the text of the Constitution itself), and was solemnly proclaimed in the preamble of the current 1958 Constitution.[71]

Undoubtedly, the British model reflects some exception to the precedence that other systems give to constitutional enactments of basic rights. In the British model solemn declarations defining the rights of citizens, such as the 1688 Bill of Rights, are not considered by the English courts as overriding the

[70] However, judicial review would not also then be available as regards highly political matters such as foreign policy and defense decisions. On the discussion in the Convention, see Dana Spinant, "Convention Split over Powers for Court," *European Voice*, February 13–19, 2003, 3.

[71] On the French peculiarity of proclaiming the attachment of the French people to basic human and citizen rights in declarations and preambles, see Favoreu et al., *Droit Constitutionnel*, 4th ed. (Paris: Dalloz, 2001), 734. See also Koopmans, n. 5 above, 72–73. From the 1970s onward the French Constitutional Council has upgraded the legal status of those declarations and preambles by systematically examining whether bills submitted to it are compatible with the constitutional protection of civil liberties. On this ongoing evolution, see Koopmans, 72–76.

provisions of a statute: even such a basic document as the 1215 Magna Carta could be abolished by an ordinary statute.[72] In that respect, "British constitutional law occupies a unique place in Europe," in that "there is simply no higher law than the Act of Parliament, and even human rights protection cannot make an exception to that rule."[73] The point was highlighted when British Parliament decided to give effect to the substantive provisions of the European Convention on Human Rights by the Human Rights Act 1998, in which it was made perfectly clear that the act was just another statute that did not supersede a previous statute.[74] However, that does not prevent the English common law from granting those laws the status of constitutional statutes that cannot be impliedly but only explicitly repealed, as was recently decided, for example, with regard to the European Communities Act 1972, as amended.[75]

Interestingly, the particular element of British constitutionalism giving precedence to the supremacy of parliament was not taken over by countries that, in framing their own constitution, closely followed the British model. Thus, for example, when, in 1830, the drafters of the Belgian Constitution attempted to write down the unwritten rules of the British constitutional framework as accurately as possible—an effort that influenced later endeavors of constitutional reform in other European countries—they disregarded this one leading characteristic by accepting that the constitution could be modified only by a special procedure, not by ordinary statute. In doing that, they changed the British model significantly by recognizing that the Constitution's established rules of "higher law" were binding on the ordinary legislature.[76]

---

[72] Koopmans, n. 5 above, 23, referring to a 1920 judgment, *Chester v. Bateson,* [1920] 1 KB 829, which coolly observed of the Magna Carta that "like every other law of England, it is not condemned to that immunity from development or improvement which was attributed to the laws of the Medes and the Persians." The Magna Carta is a charter of liberty and political rights obtained from King John of England by his rebellious barons at Runnymede near Windsor in 1215. It recognized certain rights of landowners, nobles, the Church, and freemen: *Paperback Oxford English Dictionary,* ed. Catherine Soanes (Oxford: Oxford University Press, 2002), 504.

[73] Koopmans, n. 5 above, 23–24.

[74] See Section 4 (6) (a) of the Human Rights Act 1998, where it is stated that a declaration made by a court of incompatibility of a provision of primary legislation with a Convention right does not affect the validity or enforcement of that provision.

[75] See the judgments referred to in n. 15 above.

[76] Koopmans, n. 5 above, 20. In the twentieth century Belgium became a federal state and instituted a constitutional court with extensive powers to review legislation held to be inconsistent with constitutional freedoms. See Patrick Peeters, "The Fifth Belgian State Reform ('Lambermont'): A General Overview," 9 *EPL,* 2003, 1–11.

Protection of Basic Rights and Fundamental Freedoms in the European Union

Since the 1970s it has been a keystone of the case law of the Court of Justice that human rights principles, as laid down in the European Convention on Human Rights (ECHR), are part and parcel of the general principles of Community law.[77] The doctrine was confirmed, and extended to the whole Union, by Article 6 EU Treaty.[78] Furthermore, on December 7, 2000, the EU Charter of Fundamental Rights was solemnly proclaimed in Nice by the three institutions of the Union, the European Parliament, the Council, and the Commission (not, however, by the heads of state or government).[79]

The charter has a very broad scope. It has seven chapters: 1) Dignity; 2) Freedoms; 3) Equality; 4) Solidarity; 5) Citizen's Rights; 6) Justice; and 7) General Provisions. It covers many rights that are not traditionally regarded to be human rights. Thus, for example, the charter refers to the right to medical treatment, and to the right to the protection of personal data (Article 8), the right to education (Article 14), the rights of the child, the elderly, and the disabled (Articles 24–26), workers' social security and social assistance rights (Articles 27–32 and 34), the right to health care and medical treatment (Article 35), the right of access to services of general economic interest (Article 36), environmental and consumer protection (Articles 37 and 38), and others. The breadth of the charter's understanding of human rights actually illustrates the extension of the initial "internal market" concept of citizenship into a broader concept of citizenship that is not only economic but also social, cultural, and

---

[77] In its 1979 *Hauer* judgment (Case 44/79, *Hauer v. Land Rheinland-Pfalz*, [1979] ECR 3727) the court stated that "fundamental rights form an integral part of the general principles of the law, the observance of which the court ensures; that in safeguarding those rights, [it] is bound to draw inspiration from constitutional traditions common to the Member States, . . . and that, similarly, international treaties for the protection of human rights on which the Member States have collaborated or of which they are signatories, can supply guidelines"—after which the court specifically mentioned the ECHR: para. 15.

[78] Article 6 EU has four paragraphs. Only the first two are relevant here. They read: "(1) The Union is founded on the principles of liberty, democracy, respect for human rights and fundamental freedoms, and the rule of law, principles which are common to the Member States. (2) The Union shall respect fundamental rights, as guaranteed by the European Convention for the Protection of Human Rights and Fundamental Freedoms signed in Rome on 4 November 1950 and as they result from the constitutional traditions common to the Member States, as general principles of Community law."

[79] Charter of Fundamental Rights of the European Union, [2000] OJ C364/01.

political. This extension of the citizen concept (which will be dealt with in chapter 4) will also be reflected in the European Constitution, if it is adopted by the Member States, as it is proposed to incorporate the charter under Part II of the Constitution, which would make it a binding text.[80]

As long as this has not happened, the charter is not intended to have binding effect. It is simply a solemn proclamation, joining in that respect the many solemn and glorious proclamations of the past.[81] Moreover, notwithstanding—or rather, because of—its breadth with respect to guaranteed rights, it applies primarily to conduct of the Union institutions and organs (which is why it was signed only by the heads of those institutions), and it applies to the conduct of Member States only when they are implementing Union law.[82] Nevertheless, since the charter must be seen in connection with the ECHR and international law,[83] some of its provisions may already have binding effect on the Union institutions by virtue of Article 6 (2) EU Treaty, that is, insofar as they correspond to provisions laid down in the ECHR, or contained in constitutional provisions or traditions that the Member States share.[84]

The most "visible" effect that the (as yet unbinding) charter may have is

---

[80] Article I-7 (1) [now Article I-9 (1)] of the proposed draft Constitution. See chapter 6, p. 260. Moreover, under Article I-7 (2) [now Article I-9 (2)] the Union shall seek accession to the European Human Rights Convention. As a result of the incorporation of the Charter in the Constitution, the articles of the charter will become Articles II-1 to II-54 [now Articles II-61 to II-114].

[81] On this point, see de Witte, "The Legal Status of the Charter: Vital Question or Non-Issue?" 8 *MJ*, 2001, 81–89.

[82] Article 51 (1), first sentence, of the Charter provides that "the provisions of the Charter are addressed to the institutions and bodies of the Union with due regard for the principle of subsidiarity and to the Member States only when they are implementing Union law." Because of its imprecise wording, the last part of the sentence constitutes a controversial extension of the charter's scope of application: see Leonard F. M. Besselink, "The Member States, the National Constitutions and the Scope of the Charter," 8 *MJ*, 2001, 68–80, at 76–79. For a detailed analysis, see Piet Eeckhout, "The EU Charter of Fundamental Rights and the Federal Question," 39 *CMLRev.*, 2002, 945–94, at 952–79.

[83] Article 52 (3), first sentence, provides that "in so far as this Charter contains rights which correspond to rights guaranteed by the [ECHR], the meaning and scope of those rights shall be the same as those laid down by said Convention." Article 53 provides that "nothing in this Charter shall be interpreted as restricting or adversely affecting human rights and fundamental freedoms as recognized . . . by Union law and international law and by international agreements."

[84] Article 6 (2) EU provides that the Union and its institutions are under the obligation to respect the fundamental rights "as guaranteed by the European Convention [on Human Rights] and as they result from the constitutional traditions common to the Member States."

that its provisions can be used by the Community and the national courts to interpret existing Community and national legislation in conformity therewith.[85] That might even lead to the imposition by the court of so-called "positive obligations" on public authorities in accordance with the case law of the European Court of Human Rights.[86] Obviously, this would be most "beneficial" in areas where the charter goes beyond the current case law of the Community courts. That is particularly so in matters of social law and social security, where positive obligations are most needed to make abstract rights enforceable in concrete cases. However, those are precisely the areas where creative action on the part of courts of law is rather unlikely[87]—if only because of financial implications that such action would entail for the Member States; but also because, in those areas, the scope of application of the charter provisions is greatly reduced, limited as it is to "the cases and under the conditions provided for by Community law and the national laws and practices."[88] In other words, in those areas, it is basically left to the Member States whether they want to give substance to the charter provisions concerned. By contrast, where the charter may have an impact, through the jurisprudence of the courts, is with regard to rights, such as the right to good administration (Article 41) and access to court and to effective remedies (Article 47), that correspond to principles already recognized in Community and national laws and

---

[85] That may also have "freezing" and "inhibiting" effects though, as is explained by de Witte, n. 81 above, 84–87. See also Eeckhout, n. 82 above, analyzing opinions of advocate generals and judgments of the CFI referring to the EU Charter at 946–52.

[86] For a general overview of the Charter, see A. W. Heringa and Luc Verhey, "The EU Charter: Text and Structure," 8 *MJ*, 2001, 11–32, with reference to the concept of "positive obligations." The concept is already used by the European Court of Justice in connection with the freedom of goods: see Case C-265/95, *Commission v. France,* [1997] ECR I-6959. In that judgment France was declared in breach of its obligations under the treaty for having failed to adopt adequate steps to prevent obstacles to the free movements of goods created by actions by private individuals in its territory aimed at products originating in other Member States. These obstacles consisted of disruptive protests of French farmers who blocked roads in order to hinder the free movement of agricultural products. See also the more recent case C-112/00, *Schmidberger v. Austria,* [2003] ECR I-5659.

[87] See De Witte, n. 81 above, 86–87. But see the ECJ's judgment in *Schmidberger,* n. 86 above, where the concept of positive obligation plays a role as a ground of justification to limit the scope of the free movement of goods. See further pp. 134–36 below.

[88] Thus, *mutatis mutandis,* under Chapter 4 on solidarity, in Article 27 (workers' right to information and consultation), Article 28 (right of collective bargaining), Article 30 (protection against unjustified dismissal), Article 34 (social security and social assistance), Article 35 (health care), and Article 36 (access to services of general economic interest).

that may be further developed by the courts with the help of the new Charter provisions.[89]

The Charter is not only broad in scope but also internationally minded in that it purports to accord the benefit of some of the guaranteed rights to non-EU nationals.[90] Unfortunately, it does not always distinguish very explicitly between rights of universal application, rights accorded to EU citizens only, and rights enjoyed by some third-country nationals. For example, Article 15 of the charter, on the freedom to choose an occupation and the right to engage in work, has three separate grants of freedoms. In the first paragraph, the article grants the right to engage in work and to pursue a freely chosen or accepted occupation to "everyone." The second paragraph grants the right to solicit work, to establish oneself and render services in any Member State to every citizen of the Union. Lastly, the third paragraph grants to those nationals of third countries authorized to work in Member State territories the right to work under equivalent conditions as citizens of the Member States.[91] That raises the question how far precisely fundamental rights protection is afforded to non-Union citizens. Moreover, the right of Union citizens of some of the newly acceded Member States to engage in work in the other Member States has also been subjected to significant transitional limitations. These matters will be further discussed in chapter 4.

One final remark. The Charter adds one more list of rights to the existing international and European documents, and to the lists contained in many Member State constitutions. As a result, coherence in the protection of human rights, and still more in the enforcement of protected rights, is presently a far greater problem than lack of protection.[92] As a matter of fact, the numerous lists and declarations may well prove to have a counterproductive effect. Or, in the words of one expert commentator, "The Union does not need more rights on its lists, or more lists of rights. What is mostly needed are programmes and

[89] So far this has not helped the ECJ to abandon its restrictive attitude with regard to the standing of individual persons under Article 230, fourth paragraph, EC (see above, pp. 111–12). That attitude affects mainly the standing of private plaintiffs whose human rights are infringed as a result of general Community legislation.

[90] According to Craig and de Búrca, n. 25 above, 359, the charter constitutes "a creative distillation of the rights contained in the various European and international agreements and national constitutions on which the ECJ had for some years already been drawing."

[91] Deirdre Curtin and Ronald van Ooik, "The Sting Is Always in the Tail: The Personal Scope of Application of the EU Charter of Fundamental Rights," 8 *MJ*, 2001, 102–14, at 104–5.

[92] See further W. van Gerven, "Remedies for Infringements of Fundamental Rights," *EPL*, 2004, 261–84.

agencies to make rights real."[93] That does not mean that the charter is useless, as it may be a helpful instrument, among others, to enhance European awareness, provided that it is put to concrete use. That, however, "requires a clear constitutional document which is judicially enforceable"[94]—which the charter is not, or not yet, as long as the draft Constitution is not adopted.

Protection of Basic Rights and Fundamental Freedoms in the United States

In the United States, the protection of fundamental rights and freedoms was not inscribed in the 1787 Constitution—which consisted of only seven articles establishing the principles governing the division of powers between federal and state institutions and the separation of power between the legislature, the executive, and the judiciary. Fundamental freedoms were guaranteed in ten amendments that were added to the Constitution in 1791. The reason for that delay was that the framers of the Constitution thought that citizens' rights were sufficiently protected by constitutions of the (then thirteen) states and by the limitation of powers attributed to the federal institutions—an opinion which was immediately protested against by Thomas Jefferson (later to become the third president of the United States).[95] The Bill of Rights, as the ten amendments were referred to, also remained loyal to that restrictive philosophy in that the First Amendment secured the liberties of citizens only against possible violations by federal authorities—just as the Fifth Amendment contained a "due process" clause addressed to the federal authorities only—leaving it to the state constitutions to protect the citizens against state actions. Only after the Civil War (1861–65) was that philosophy abandoned with the

---

[93] J. H. H. Weiler, "Editorial: Does the European Union Truly Need a Charter of Rights?" *ELJ*, 2000, 95, at 96. See also Alston and Weiler, "An 'Ever Closer Union' in Need of a Human Rights Policy," in *The EU and Human Rights*, ed. Alston (Oxford: Oxford University Press, 1999), 3ff. But see for a more nuanced view, arguing that human rights should not be understood as the raison d'être of the European Union, Armin von Bogdandy, "The European Union as a Human Rights Organization? Human Rights and the Core of the European Union," 37 *CMLRev.*, 2000, 1307–38. In the field of race discrimination, the European Monitoring Centre on Racism and Xenophobia was established by Council Regulation 1035/97 [1997] OJ L151. The task of the Center, directed by former German employment minister Beate Winkler, is to support Member States in measures to combat and overcome all forms of racism: *European Voice*, February 5–11, 2004, 10. Recently, the Commission has published a consultation paper to the effect of extending the remit of the Center in order to convert it into a Fundamental Rights Agency: COM (2004) 693 final of October 25, 2004.

[94] Eeckhout, n. 82 above, 993.

[95] Koopmans, n. 5 above, 44–45.

adoption of the Fourteenth Amendment in 1868, whereby the protection of citizens' liberties, including "due process" and "equal protection of the laws," was extended to encompass violations of states.

It may suffice here to quote the First Amendment, which reads: "Congress shall make no law respecting the establishment of religion, or prohibiting the free exercise thereof; or abridging the freedom of speech, or of the press; or the right of the people peaceably to assemble, and to petition the Government for a redress of grievances." In accordance with what has been said above, it is not challenged after the adoption of the Fourteenth Amendment that, despite being addressed to Congress, the First Amendment is applicable to all branches of government, and that state infringements are also covered.[96]

Among citizens' rights, by far the most attention is given in the United States to the freedom of speech.[97] Freedom of speech, formulated in absolute terms in the First Amendment, includes the so-called ancillary rights, such as the right to remain silent, freedom of association, political speech in the form of campaign contributions, and freedom of the press.[98] Philosophical justifications for the strong protection thus afforded to free speech have been fiercely debated: among these are the advancement of knowledge and "truth" in the "marketplace of ideas," the facilitation of representative democracy and self-government, and the promotion of individual autonomy, self-expression, and self-fulfillment.[99] The amount of attention thus devoted to freedom of speech, however, has not prevented, and may even have contributed to, the fact that major questions about the scope of the amendment remain unanswered.[100]

---

[96] This was acknowledged by the Supreme Court, which held that freedoms of speech and of the press are among the liberties protected from state infringement under the Fourteenth Amendment: *Gitlow v. New York*, 268 U.S. 652 (1925). Under section 1 of that amendment, it is prohibited for any state to "abridge the privileges or immunities of citizens of the United States; nor shall any State deprive any person of life, liberty, or property, without due process of law; nor deny any person within its jurisdiction the equal protection of the laws."

[97] For example, almost one-third of the fourteenth edition of K. Sullivan and G. Gunther's leading treatise, *Constitutional Law* (New York: Foundation Press, 2001), is devoted to freedom of speech and ancillary rights: pages 956 through 1433, out of a total of 1537 pages.

[98] Ibid.

[99] Sullivan and Gunther, n. 97 above, 959–63.

[100] Such questions include: Are some types of speech more protected than others (for example, political speech over commercial speech), and are some types excluded altogether (such as fighting words, libel, obscenity, and child pornography)? Are restrictions that aim at the content of speech to be better protected than restrictions that aim to protect content-neutral interests, such as peace and quiet, and can government limit speech in its capacity as proprietor, educator, or employer? And, with respect to

Whatever the precise answers to these questions, the trend over the years has clearly been "to withdraw more and more speech and 'speech-plus' from the regulatory and prohibitive hand of government and to free not only speech directed to political ends but also that totally unrelated to any political purpose." Although the application of the First Amendment has never been presumed as absolute as its terms would make one to believe, "the effect has often been indistinguishable."[101]

Illustrations of that liberating trend are, for example, that "commercial speech, long the outcast of the First Amendment, now enjoys a protected if subordinate place in the free speech jurisprudence" and that "freedom to picket, to broadcast leaflets, to engage in physical activity representative of one's political, social, economic, or other views enjoy wide though not unlimited protection."[102] Furthermore, "the possibility of recovery for libelous and slanderous criticism of public officials, political candidates, and public figures, has been reduced by the constitutionalization of the law of defamation, and . . . government's right to prescribe the advocacy of violence or unlawful activity has become more restricted." Moreover, "although obscenity remains abstractly outside the protective scope of the First Amendment, governmental action against the verbal and pictorial representation of matters dealing with sex has been closely confined."[103] Finally, "much governmental regulation of

---

the ancillary right of freedom of the press, does the fact that the freedom of the press is mentioned separately, in addition to freedom of speech, entitle the press to preferential rights under the First Amendment? All of these questions and others are exhaustively examined by Sullivan and Gunther, n. 97 above, in chapters 11, 12, and 13.

[101] Both excerpts are from the introduction to the 1992 edition of 103d Congress, 1st Session (Senate) Document No. 103–6, *The Constitution of the United States of America: Analysis and Interpretation*, prepared by the Congressional Research Service, Library of Congress, ed. Johnny H. Killian and George A. Costello, at xi.

[102] Ibid. On commercial speech, see *Central Hudson Gas & Electricity Co. v. Public Utilities Commission*, 475 U.S. 1 (1986). In that case the court set out a four-pronged test to assess whether commercial speech is entitled to First Amendment protection: the speech must concern lawful activity and not be misleading; the regulation under scrutiny must serve a substantial government interest; it must directly advance the state's asserted interest; and it must not be more extensive than necessary to serve that interest. The test has been applied in later judgments: see Redlich, Attanasio, and Goldstein, *Understanding Constitutional Law*, 2d ed. (New York: LexisNexis, 1999), 484–91. The test shows a striking resemblance with the proportionality principle applied by the European Court of Justice; see below, pp. 140–41 and also pp. 134–37. As for the freedom to *demonstrate*, see *Cox v. Louisiana* (Cox I), 379 U.S. 536 (1965) and *Cox v. Louisiana* (Cox II), 379 U.S. 559 (1965).

[103] Introduction, n. 101 above, ibid. As for the constraint of defamation actions, see the landmark judgment in *New York Times v. Sullivan*, 376 U.S. 254 (1964), where the

campaign finance and of limitations upon the political activities of citizens and public employees has become suspect if not impermissible."[104]

In addition to the freedom of speech clause of the First Amendment, the "due process" clause contained in the Fifth Amendment (relating to federal action), and in section 1 of the Fourteenth Amendment (relating to state action), has also had an interesting history, as will be illustrated further in connection with the interpretation of the interstate commerce clause.[105] Since the beginning of last century, starting with the Supreme Court's 1905 *Lochner* judgment,[106] the clause has been used primarily to protect fundamental economic rights generally, for example to strike down state legislation interfering with the right of contract and with property rights. As a result, the Court invalidated a considerable number of laws, particularly those regulating prices, labor relations, and conditions for entry into businesses.[107] In the 1930s, however, during the New Deal, that line of case law was abandoned in favor of minimal judicial scrutiny of economic regulations.[108] It was, however, revived in the 1960s and 1970s by the Supreme Court to protect certain individual non-economic liberties, such as in the 1965 *Griswold v. Connecticut* judgment,

---

court held that a plaintiff in a defamation action must prove that the defendant published the defamatory falsehood with actual knowledge of its falsity, or with reckless disregard as to its truth or falsity. Regarding advocacy of unlawful objectives, see *Brandenburg v. Ohio*, 395 U.S. 444 (1969), where the court held that the First Amendment did "not permit a state to forbid or proscribe advocacy . . . except where such advocacy is directed or inciting or producing imminent lawless action and is likely to incite or produce such action." As for obscenity, the Supreme Court took a definitional approach in *Miller v. California*, 413 U.S. 15 (1973), setting out a three-pronged test to define obscenity: whether, according to contemporary community standards, the activity concerned (mailing unsolicited, very explicit materials) appeals to the prurient interest, whether the material depicts or describes in a patently offensive way sexual conduct specifically defined by the applicable state law, and whether, taken as a whole, it lacks serious literary, artistic, political, or scientific value. On each of these subjects, see further Redlich, Attanasio, and Goldstein, n. 102 above, 421ff, 367ff, and 495ff.

[104] Introduction, n. 101 above, ibid. As for political campaign financing, see *Buckley v. Valeo*, 496 U.S. 310 (1990), where the Supreme Court distinguished between limitations on contributions and limitation on expenditure; it upheld the former and struck down several of the latter. The court also examined disclosure provisions. See further Redlich, Attanasio, and Goldstein, n. 102 above, 472–79.

[105] See below, pp. 141ff.

[106] *Lochner v. New York*, 198 U.S. 45 (1905).

[107] Sullivan and Gunther, n. 97 above, 466.

[108] Ibid., 469ff. Thus in *West Coast Hotel v. Parrish*, in which the *Lochner* judgment was overruled, the Supreme Court upheld a minimum wage law: 300 U.S. 379 (1937). See also below, p. 143.

which struck down a state ban on the use of contraceptives, and in the 1973 *Roe v. Wade* judgment, which invalidated most state laws that restricted the access of women to abortions.[109]

Judicial Scrutiny in Concrete Cases

At the level of the European Union, there is no real counterpart for the extensive body of case law of the U.S. Supreme Court on protection of constitutional rights against action of state authorities. That is so because, within the Union, the protection of basic rights against state action remains in principle a matter for the Member State constitutions (or comparable higher rules), and thus for the Member State courts, and additionally—but only when domestic remedies have been exhausted (Article 35 [1] ECHR)—for the European Convention on Human Rights and the European Court of Human Rights in Strasbourg established under that Convention.[110] To compare the Supreme Court's case law on *state* action with case law of the European counterparts, for example in the area of freedom of speech, one should therefore primarily look at the case law of the Member States' constitutional courts, and at the case law of the European Court of Human Rights (as we will do briefly in chapter 5), which, as pointed out earlier, is a court that belongs to a different supranational legal order from that of the European Union.[111]

Only in cases involving action taken by *Community* institutions is it for the European Community courts, and for them alone,[112] to address questions re-

[109] 381 U.S. 479 and 410 U.S. 113, respectively. For a (relatively) succinct overview of later case law, both on contraception and abortion, see Redlich, Attanasio, and Goldstein, n. 102 above, 216–29. For an exhaustive account, Sullivan and Gunther, n. 97 above, 510–21 and 521–58. See also chapter 4, pp. 184–86.

[110] As mentioned earlier in chapter 1, p. 12, all Member States have adhered to that Convention, but not the European Union itself, which in the present state of Community law does not have the power to accede to the Convention: ECJ, Opinion 2/94 *Accession by the Communities to the Convention for the Protection of Human Rights and Fundamental Freedoms*, [1996] ECR I-1759, paras. 34–35.

[111] The Court of Human Rights is part of the Council of Europe. See chapter 1, pp. 11–12.

[112] The European Court of Human Rights in Strasbourg has no competence to examine the compatibility of Community acts with the ECHR, but it does have competence over the EU Member States, even when they act in their capacity as EU members in the preparation of Community legislation (which can lead to delicate jurisdictional questions: see R. Harmsen, "National Responsibility for European Community Acts under the European Convention on Human Rights: Recasting the Accession Debate," 7 *EPL*, 2001, 625–49, at 641ff). Accordingly, starting with the ECtHR's ruling in *Matthews v. UK* ([1999] 28 EHRR 361), there has been an increasing trend for applicants to bring proceedings before the ECtHR against all Member States in circumstances where

garding the compatibility of such action with human rights and fundamental freedoms provisions in light of their status as general principles of Community law. However, as discussed above, the scope of the courts' power is limited with respect to Community acts of a general nature because of the ECJ's narrow interpretation of Article 230, paragraph 4, EC.[113] Moreover, the ECJ is occasionally asked, in the context of a preliminary ruling procedure (and thus in cooperation with a national court),[114] to interpret such human rights and fundamental freedoms provisions when Member State action is implementing, or falling within the scope of, Community law.[115]

An early example of a case where the Court of Justice examined whether Community legislation was consistent with human rights principles, in this instance with Article 1 of Protocol no. 1 to the ECHR, which protects one's right to property, is the court's *Hauer* judgment decided in 1979.[116] In that case, the

---

these applicants feel that an act attributable in some respect to the Community has infringed their human rights. A case in point is *DSR-Senator Lines GMBH v. 15 EU Member States* (App. No. 56672/00), mentioned in C. Brown's analysis of the ECJ's *Schmidberger* judgment (n. 86 above) in 40 *CMLRev.*, 2003, 1499–1510, at 1508. The date of the hearing in *DSR-Senator Lines* was fixed by the ECtHR for October 22, 2003, but was cancelled in light of the judgment rendered by the CFI on September 30, 2003, in Joined Cases T-191/98 and 212–214/98, which judgment set aside a fine imposed by the EU Commission for violation of EC competition rules. Other cases are quoted by Harmsen in his article, cited above, at 635–40.

[113] See above, pp. 111–12.

[114] On the preliminary ruling procedure, see above, pp. 114–15.

[115] See, for example, the judgment of the ECJ in Case C-368/95, *Familiapress*, [1997] ECR I-3689, para. 24–25, where the court examined the applicability of Article 10 ECHR guaranteeing the freedom of expression. See also the ECJ's judgment in *Schmidberger v. Austria*, n. 86 above and discussed later at pp. 134–36. In both these cases the ECJ answered the preliminary questions concerning the interpretation of Community law, including fundamental rights general principles, which were submitted by Austrian courts in relation to national law provisions. See also the advocate general's opinion in Case C-168/91, *Konstantinidis*, [1993] ECR I-1191, relating to a Greek national's right to have his name correctly transliterated into Latin characters when doing business in Germany. The advocate general opined that the refusal of the German authorities to have the name correctly transposed was in conflict with a principle drawn from the constitutional traditions of the Member States (at I-1209, para. 39 of the opinion). See further the advocate general's opinion in Case C-159/90, *SPUC v. Grogan*, [1991] ECR I-4685, relating to Irish legislation prohibiting the publication of addresses of British clinics where abortion could be carried out legally. In both these cases, however, the ECJ declined to examine, as was asked by the referral courts, whether Community law was to be interpreted in such a way that it would have affected the validity of the national legislation involved.

[116] Case 44/79, *Hauer v. Land Rheinland-Pfalz*, [1979] ECR 3727.

applicant challenged a Community regulation that placed limitations on the planting of new vines. The Court held that the regulation did not in itself constitute an invalid restriction on property rights, but that it would if the planting restrictions were disproportionate, "impinging upon the very substance of the right to property."[117] The Court thus rested its decision on the principle of proportionality—a principle that the court often applies in cases where the pursuit of a legitimate objective of Community law, or national law, must be weighed against an individual's basic right.[118] For its emphasis on the protection of an individual's property rights against Community legislation, the *Hauer* judgment resembles case law of the U.S. Supreme Court under the Fifth Amendment's due process clause, as we will see later.[119]

There are other instances in which the ECJ has been asked to pronounce itself on an alleged violation, by the EU Commission, of fundamental rights of individuals.[120] One such case was *X v. Commission*,[121] where a person who had applied to the Commission for a job initiated proceedings before the Community courts for breach of his right of privacy. In this case, the Commission had ordered a dissimulated AIDS test to be carried out without obtaining the consent of the person involved. The Court held that, in doing so, the Commission had infringed the individual's right to respect for private life, which included the right to keep one's state of health secret. To be sure, the court held that such right is not an unfettered right and may be restricted by the authority concerned, "provided that the restrictions in fact correspond to objectives of general interest pursued by the Community and do not, taking account of the aim of the restrictions, constitute disproportionate and unacceptable interference, impairing the very substance of the rights guaranteed."[122] As appears from this quotation, the proportionality test was again a key element of its decision.

In another staff case, *Connolly v. Commission*,[123] the freedom of expression

---

[117] Para. 23.

[118] At para. 15 of the judgment. On that principle, see Francis G. Jacobs, "Recent Developments in the Principle of Proportionality in European Community Law," and W. van Gerven, "The Effect of Proportionality on the Actions of Member States of the European Community: National Viewpoints from Continental Europe," in *The Principle of Proportionality in the Laws of Europe*, ed. Evelyn Ellis (Oxford: Hart Publishing, 1999), 1–21 and 37–63, respectively. See also below, pp. 140–41.

[119] See below, pp. 142ff

[120] For an overview and analysis of these cases, see Douglas-Scott, n. 25 above, 437–62.

[121] Court of Justice, Case C-404/92P [1994] ECR I-4737, annulling the judgment of the Court of First Instance in Case T-121/89 and 13/90.

[122] Judgment of the Court of Justice, at para. 18, referring to Case C-62/90, *Commission v. Germany*, [1992] ECR I-2575, para. 23.

[123] Case C-274/99P [2001] ECR I-1611.

of a civil servant was at stake. In that case Bernard Connolly, a senior Community civil servant, had strongly criticized the Community for its dealings in establishing the Monetary Union, in which he had participated as a civil servant. He made his opinion known in a book published during a leave of absence from employment at the Commission. As a result, the civil servant was dismissed by the Commission. On appeal from a judgment of the CFI, the ECJ recognized that officials and other employees of the European Communities enjoy the right of freedom of expression, even in areas falling within the scope of activities of the Community institutions. That right includes the right to express, orally or in writing, dissentient or minority opinions. However, in the opinion of the court, that should not prevent the authorities from imposing obligations upon their employees where needed to preserve a relation of confidence between the institution and its civil servants. Applying these principles to the specific case, the Court held that, in the concrete circumstances, the Commission, in dismissing the civil servant, had struck the right balance between the civil servant's right of expression and his duty of loyalty.[124] I will return to that case in chapter 5.[125]

What becomes clear from this brief overview is that the Community courts, like many other European courts, such as the European Court of Human Rights[126] or the German Constitutional Court,[127] use the proportionality principle to balance fundamental rights or freedoms against each other. A case in point is the recent judgment of the Court of Justice in *Schmidberger v. Austria*.[128] At stake was the decision of the Austrian authorities to allow a thirty-hour demonstration by an environmental association on the Brenner motorway. The objective of the demonstration was to draw attention to the danger to public health caused by the constant increase in the transit of heavy goods vehicles. The demonstration had as its result that heavy goods traffic between Germany and Italy was interrupted for four consecutive days.[129] The chairman of the environmental association and the media had disseminated information

[124] At para. 51ff.

[125] See below, pp. 218–19, where the concrete circumstances of the case are given.

[126] See Jeremy McBride, "Proportionality and the European Convention on Human Rights," in *The Principle of Proportionality in the Laws of Europe*, n. 118 above, 23–35.

[127] For a thorough analysis of several European laws, see N. Emiliou, *The Principle of Proportionality in European Law: A Comparative Study* (The Hague: Kluwer Law International, 1996).

[128] N. 86 above. For comments, see C. Brown in 40 *CMLRev.*, 2003, 1499–1510 (n. 112 above).

[129] Four consecutive days because the thirty-hour demonstration preceded a standard weekend restriction on heavy goods traffic across the Brenner Pass.

concerning the closure of the Brenner motorway and had offered practical information to motorists to avoid the motorway during the period in question. Schmidberger, an international transport undertaking based in Germany, brought an action against the Austrian government before an Austrian court seeking damage on the basis that five of its trucks were unable to use the Brenner motorway during that time.

By questions referred to the Court of Justice the national court wanted to know in the first place whether the Austrian state had infringed Article 28 (ex 30) EC Treaty by not keeping major transit roads clear of all restrictions, inter alia, by not having banned the demonstration, or at least keeping it away from the transit route. To that question, the Court replied that the decision not to ban the demonstration was indeed capable of restricting intra-Community trade in goods, and therefore in principle incompatible with a Member State's Community obligation to take all necessary and appropriate measures in order to ensure that the fundamental freedom of trade in goods is respected on its territory.[130] The second question submitted to the court was more difficult, namely whether the infringement of such a fundamental Community freedom as the free movement of goods could be justified by the concern of the Austrian authorities to allow the demonstration so as to respect the demonstrators' fundamental rights to freedom of expression and freedom of assembly. In its reply, the Court held that this concern could indeed be relied on as justification, taking into account the authorities' wide discretion and the fact that those authorities, including the police, as well as the organizers of the demonstration, had cooperated to ensure that the demonstration went off smoothly. The Court further held that, in the concrete case, the Austrian authorities were reasonably entitled to consider that the legitimate aim of the demonstration could not be achieved by measures less restrictive of intra-Community trade.[131]

In substance, the Court said, the case

> raises the question of the need to reconcile the requirements of the protection of fundamental rights in the Community with those arising from a fundamental freedom enshrined in the Treaty and, more particularly, the question of the respective scope of freedom of expression and freedom of assembly, guaranteed by Articles 10 and 11 of the ECHR, and of the free movement of goods, where the former are relied upon as justification for a restriction of the latter.[132]

---

[130] Paras. 51–64 of the judgment. In that connection, the court referred in particular to its earlier judgment in case C-265/95, *Commission v. France*, n. 86 above.

[131] At paras. 87–94 of the judgment.

[132] Para. 77.

Weighing the free movement of goods and the freedom of expression and of assembly against one another, the Court considered that the exercise of the latter—which, unlike certain other human rights guaranteed in the ECHR, such as the right to life or the prohibition of torture and inhuman or degrading treatment or punishment, are *not* absolute—"may be restricted, provided that the restrictions in fact correspond to objectives of general interest and do not, taking account of the aim of the restrictions, constitute disproportionate and unacceptable interference, impairing the very substance of the rights guaranteed."[133] Weighing all circumstances of the case, the Court ultimately found that the Austrian authorities had not breached Community law in giving precedence to the demonstrators' freedoms of expression and of assembly over the transporter's right to free movement of goods. Accordingly, there was also no ground for the transporter's claim for damages against the Austrian state.

As pointed out by Chief Justice Earl Warren, the U.S. Supreme Court is also bound in difficult cases "to balance two constitutional rights with each other." Thus, for example, in determining whether obscenity is protected by the First Amendment, the Court must consider that the "state and national government [have] a right to have a decent society," but "on the other hand, we have a First Amendment," all of which raises the question of "how far people can go under the First Amendment . . . without offending the right of the government to maintain a decent society."[134] The doctrine of balancing competing interests is not, however, undisputed in the United States. Justice Black, for example, did not subscribe to "the doctrine that permits constitutionally protected rights to be 'balanced' away when a majority of the Court thinks that a state might have sufficient interest to justify abridgment of those freedoms." He believed "that the First Amendment's unequivocal command . . . shows, that the men who drafted our Bill of Rights did all the 'balancing' that was to be [done]."[135] However, on the whole, the "absolutes versus balancing"

---

[133] Para. 80. That is exactly the same "provided" quoted above in the text and appearing in Case C-404/92P, *X v. Commission*, n. 121 above, with a reference to Case C-62/90 *Commission v. Germany*, n. 122 above, and indeed in *Schmidberger* the ECJ refers to both these judgments in para. 80.

[134] In a conversation quoted in G. E. White, *Earl Warren: A Public Life* (1982), 250, cited by Redlich, Attanasio, and Goldstein, n. 102 above, 494. See also the test used in *Central Hudson* with respect to commercial speech: n. 102 above.

[135] *Koningsberg v. State Bar of California*, 366 U.S. 36 (1961) (Black, J., dissenting), quoted by Sullivan and Gunther, n. 97 above, 965–66. In that case, concerning bar admission to an applicant who had refused to answer questions about Communist Party membership, Justices Frankfurter and Harlan, writing for the majority upholding denial, rejected the view that freedom of speech and association are "absolutes": ibid. See also, below, pp. 251–52.

controversy (as it is called) may have been misleading, just like categorization of "protected versus unprotected speech" may have been.[136] Indeed, none of these assertions can themselves be taken as absolutes. In the end, "true balancing" operates only when a court applies some intermediate test of scrutiny, implying that a constitutional right is presumptively protected and that it is for the other side to show a "compelling" state aim and the unavailability of less restrictive means.[137]

This is in fact the quintessence of proportionality, which, as a method of judicial scrutiny, is used by both the European Court of Justice and the European Court of Human Rights, as well as by constitutional or supreme courts in the Member States.[138] But the similarity does not exclude that in some jurisdictions, like in the United States, the presumption in favor of free speech appears to be stronger than in others. This in turn has to do with the fact, as pointed out in *Schmidberger*,[139] that the freedom of expression, provided in paragraph 1 of Article 10 ECHR, is not without limitations. Indeed, the second paragraph of Article 10 sets out a long list of exceptions protecting interests of society that may override the interests of the individual, such as the protection of the rights or freedoms of others. It is for the court (the ECtHR, the ECJ, or a national court) applying the ECHR, to balance those objectives of general interest against the principle of freedom of expression. If, in a specific case, the court finds that the interference with the freedom is no greater than necessary to address the general interest at stake, then the latter would take precedence.[140]

IV. PROVIDING LEGAL CERTAINTY

Legal certainty is a third component of the rule of law concept. It entails, in the first place, that citizens know within which limits, by which authority, and according to which rules their freedom of action can be limited by legislation.

---

[136] Sullivan and Gunther, n. 97 above, 966–67.

[137] Ibid., 967.

[138] See above, p. 134. In the United Kingdom, which has no written constitution, and where proportionality was until recently unknown as a concept of English law, the proportionality test is now applied by British courts when applying Community law (and the Human Rights Act 1998), and it may very well "spill over" from there into other areas of domestic law. Thus, with regard to interim relief in actions involving the State, see *M v. Home Office*, [1994] 1 AC 377, referred to by Mark Brealy and Mark Hoskins, *Remedies in EC Law*, 2d ed. (London: Sweet and Maxwell, 1998), 153, n. 14.

[139] Para. 79 of the judgment quoted in n. 86 above and discussed in the text accompanying nn. 128–33.

[140] On balancing competing fundamental human rights, see chapter 5, pp. 250–52.

In the second place, it means that the rules that have been adopted are such that citizens know exactly what rights and obligations entail, and that changes to those rules will be made in accordance with due process requirements.

The Need for a Clear Legal Basis

In the European Community, and in the European Union as a whole, any legal measure must have a legal basis located in the EC or EU Treaty—which, in the absence of a constitution, constitutes the basic law of the Union. That legal basis must provide the regulating authority with the power to regulate citizens' behavior, in accordance with procedural rules laid down in advance. It is ultimately for the Community courts to verify whether the acting legislature or executive did indeed have the power to legislate or implement legislation, and whether it has used its power in accordance with the appropriate legislative process.[141]

a) The principles of conferral, subsidiarity, and proportionality

As is typical for a federal structure, law making at the higher level is valid only when it falls within the powers that the component states have conferred upon it. This principle of conferral, or attribution, of powers also applies to the European Community, where it is laid down in Article 5, first paragraph, EC, as follows: "The Community shall act within the limits of the powers conferred upon it by this Treaty and of the objectives assigned to it." As a consequence, each Community institution, whether Parliament, Council, Commission, or Court of Justice, shall, according to Article 7 (1) EC Treaty, "act within the limits of the powers conferred upon by this Treaty."

The powers that the treaty confers upon the Community are not all of the same nature: a few are exclusive, in the sense that in a specific area only the Community may legislate and adopt legally binding acts (thus, for example, the power granted the Community in Article 133 EC as regards the Community's common commercial policy). Many others are shared with the Member States, meaning that the Member States may take action as long as the Community has not acted itself (for example, in areas relating to the "internal

---

[141] Such verification is part of the review of the legality of legislation, which the Community Courts undertake under Article 230 EC. As has been mentioned (p. 111 above), private parties can request the Community courts to examine the validity of acts that are of direct and individual concern to them. They can also question the validity of Community law before a national court, in litigation pending before that court. The national court, whether deciding in the last instance or not, must then address, under Article 234 EC, a preliminary question to the ECJ as to the act's validity, unless the answer is that the act is clearly valid. See above, p. 114, and Case 314/85, *Foto-Frost*, referred to in n. 38 above.

market" freedoms: Articles 23–31 and 39–60 EC concerning free movement of goods, persons, services, and capital). Some powers are purely supportive or complementary to state action (as in the field of education, culture, and public health: Articles 149, 151, and 152 EC).

When the Community institutions adopt legislative or other measures within their powers, the rules adopted, or decisions made, will have primacy over the law of the Member States. The principle of primacy is not established in the treaty, but is contained in early case law of the Court of Justice, that is, in the 1964 *Costa/ENEL* judgment.[142] It should be seen in context with the principle of loyal cooperation between Member States and Community institutions. In a federal-like system, primacy of one system over the other must indeed go hand in hand with loyal cooperation. As such, the principle is not inscribed in the treaty, Article 10 EC only providing that Member States are obliged "to take all appropriate measures . . . to ensure fulfilment of the obligations arising out of this Treaty . . . [and to] facilitate achievement of Community tasks," and that they "shall abstain from any measure which could jeopardize the attainment of the objectives of this Treaty."[143]

However, over the years, the Court of Justice has broadly interpreted the principle, giving it a variety of applications, by virtue of which *all* bodies and authorities of Member States are under an obligation to act in good faith at all levels of government,[144] including national legislatures, executives, judiciaries, and administrations.[145] Furthermore, in contrast with the express wording of Article 10 EC, the Court has extended the scope of the principle to impose an obligation also upon the Community institutions to cooperate with the Member States,[146] as well as upon the Community institutions[147] and the Member States[148] to cooperate among themselves.

---

[142] Case 6/64, *Costa v. ENEL*, [1964] ECR 585.

[143] On Article 10 EC, in a context of executive federalism and as compared with the situation in the United States, see chapter 1, pp. 20–22.

[144] See for instance ECJ, Case 85/85, *Commission v. Belgium*, [1985] ECR 1149, paras. 22–23.

[145] See ECJ, Case 80/86, *Kolpinghuis Nijmegen*, [1987] ECR 3969, para. 12.

[146] See ECJ, Case C-2/88 *Imm. Zwartveld and others*, [1990] ECR I-3365, paras. 17–22. See, for an apparent extension of this ruling, Case 275/00, *First & Franex*, [2002] ECR I-10943. For comments, see C. Brown and D. Hardiman, "The Extent of the Community Institutions' Duty to Cooperate with National Courts: *Zwartveld* Revisited" *ECLR*, 2004, 299.

[147] This is particularly true of decision-making processes based on interinstitutional dialogue: ECJ, Case C-65/93 *European Parliament v. Council*, [1995] ECR I-643, para. 23.

[148] For instance, to recognize each other's diplomas and evidence of professional qualifications; ECJ, Case C-340/89, *Vlassopolou*, [1991] ECR I-2357, para. 14.

In addition to the principles of conferral of powers and loyal cooperation, there is the principle of subsidiarity, inscribed in Article 5, second paragraph, EC as follows: "In areas which do not fall within its exclusive competence, the Community shall take action . . . only if and insofar as the objectives of the proposed action cannot be sufficiently achieved by the Member States and can therefore, by reason of the scale or effects of the proposed action, be better achieved by the Community."[149]

The philosophy behind the principle of subsidiarity is that legislation is enacted as close as possible to the citizens—a goal introduced in 1992 by the Maastricht Treaty in an effort to counter criticism that decisions were too readily made at the EC level.[150]

Subsidiarity is a difficult concept,[151] formulated in terms that hardly lend themselves to application in a court of law. To verify whether "action cannot be sufficiently achieved by the Member States and can therefore, by reason of the scale or effects of the proposed action, be better achieved by the Community" indeed requires an input-output analysis that can only be carried out with a sufficient degree of accuracy by regulators, and not by courts. This will explain why the ECJ, in the small number of cases brought before it, has limited its review to procedural "due process" aspects.[152] Moreover, the principle may not be used to upset the Community's "institutional balance" or "the relationship between national and Community law" and "may not call into question powers conferred on the European Community by the Treaty, as interpreted by the Court of Justice."[153] In other words, it cannot allow Member States to take measures in areas where Member State action is prohibited by the treaty, but only in instances where the Community is authorized to take action on a non-exclusive basis.

In addition to the principles of conferral of powers and subsidiarity, Arti-

---

[149] The principle is not applicable, as follows from the first part of the sentence, "in areas which do not fall within the [Community's] exclusive competence." This is a logical exception: were it not provided, and were the principle to apply also to exclusive competences, that competence would no longer be exclusive.

[150] Article 1 (2) EU proclaims that "this Treaty marks a new stage in the process of creating an ever closer union among the peoples of Europe, in which decisions are taken as openly as possible and as closely as possible to the citizen."

[151] For a discussion from an American point of view, see George A. Bermann, "Taking Subsidiarity Seriously: Federalism in the European Community and the United States," 94 *Colum.L.Rev.* 332, 1994, 870.

[152] For a discussion of those cases, see Craig and de Búrca, n. 25 above, 100–101 and 136–37.

[153] Thus the Protocol on the "Application of the Principles of Subsidiarity and Proportionality," added to the EC Treaty by the Amsterdam Treaty, at (2) and (3).

cle 5 EC contains, in paragraph 3, a third principle according to which "any action of the Community shall not go beyond what is necessary to achieve the objectives of this Treaty." The principle is called the proportionality principle. It applies not only to action of Community institutions to which Article 5 EC specifically refers,[154] but also to Member State action. This is particularly so, as seen hereinafter, when the Community internal market freedoms—including free movement of goods and services—have to be balanced against stated justifications or, as seen above in *Schmidberger*,[155] against other, non-economic, fundamental rights. Under certain conditions, such justifications allow Member States to derogate from the internal market freedoms, which is only permissible, however, when the encroachment on the Community freedom is not "disproportionate." The principle has been borrowed from national supreme courts, primarily German courts, and from the European Court of Human Rights.[156]

Under the proportionality principle, the review of the validity of legislation, for example of state action limiting trade between Member States, will take place in three stages. First, the Community or national court will decide whether the state measure concerned was suitable to achieve the (permissible) ground of justification that the state relies on to undertake its action. Second, the court will examine whether the measure was necessary to achieve the objective of the justification, that is, whether the objective could not have been reached as well by other less harmful means. Third, when the measure passes the two previous tests, the court will ask whether the burden imposed by the measure on the internal market freedom of goods was excessive in relation to the objective pursued by the national measure under examination.[157] Clearly, the analysis implies some judicial discretion in assessing the aim pursued by both Community and Member State law.

b) Community jurisdiction regarding interstate trade, in comparison with the United States interstate commerce clause

The Constitution of the United States expresses a principle of federalism similar to that established in Article 5, first paragraph, EC. It implies that the

---

[154] See, for example, Case C-331/88, *Fedesa*, [1990] ECR 4023, para. 13.

[155] Nn. 115 and 128 above.

[156] For an examination of how the principle functions in Community law, and in some Member States' legal systems, see van Gerven, n. 118 above, 37–64. See also chapter 5, pp. 250–52.

[157] For a case where the three stages of proportionality are identified (depending on the concrete circumstances of the case, the court does not always spell out the three stages), see Case C-331/88, *Fedesa*, n. 154 above, and van Gerven, n. 118 above, 38–42.

federal entity possesses only the powers conferred upon it by the Constitution, while residual powers remain with the states. However, in contrast to the EC Treaty, the U.S. Constitution contains an exhaustive list of conferred powers[158] and provides explicitly in the Tenth Amendment [1791] that "the powers not delegated to the United States by the Constitution, nor prohibited by it to the States, are reserved to the States respectively, or to the people." In other words, all non-delegated public powers are reserved to the states.[159] One of the powers explicitly granted to the U.S. Congress is to "regulate Commerce with foreign nations, and among the several States, and with the Indian Tribes."[160] Also in the European Union, the regulation of interstate commerce (in persons, goods, services, and capital) and the preservation of competition from restrictive practices affecting trade between Member States[161] belong to the core of Community competences, however not on an exclusive basis. Because of striking similarities between U.S. and EU legislation and case law as regards interstate commerce, I will hereafter compare the situation in both legal systems. The comparison demonstrates how uncertain the assessment of a clear legal basis may be in actual practice.

In the United States the interstate commerce clause, as the Tenth Amendment is called, has been used to restrict (1) the power of federal and state authorities to impose limitations on individual rights in economic and social affairs and (2) the power of Congress to regulate commerce (a) within a state or (b) at the expense of "state autonomy."

The first subject, imposing *limits on citizen rights*, can be compared with the case law of the European Court of Justice to safeguard economic rights of individuals against Community regulations, as illustrated in the previously discussed *Hauer* judgment.[162] In that area, the interpretation of the interstate commerce clause in case law of the U.S. Supreme Court has changed considerably. Throughout the nineteenth and the beginning of the twentieth century, the interpretation of the clause was consistent with the general doctrine ac-

---

[158] U.S. Constitution, Article I, sec. 8, as compared with Article 10 EC Treaty.

[159] Police powers are primary reserved powers: they clearly include protection of health, order, and public morals, but these traditional subjects do not delimit, but only illustrate, the scope of the state's police power, which may also be deployed to advance public welfare—a concept including the good of society itself: *Berman v. Parker,* 348 U.S. 26 (1954). See further Redlich, Attanasio, and Goldstein, n. 102 above, 50–54, at 53.

[160] U.S. Constitution, Article I, section 8, clause 3.

[161] See Articles 23–38 EC (free movement of goods), Articles 39–60 (free movement of persons, services, and capital), and Articles 81–86 EC (rules on competition).

[162] N. 116 above.

cording to which the due process guarantee of the Fifth and Fourteenth Amendments—the former relating to federal power, the latter to state power—contained a "procedural" *and* a "substantive" content.[163] Applying that interpretation, the Supreme Court found that the due process clause embraced fundamental principles of republican government, law, and natural reason, and used it to impose limitations on the ability of governments to regulate economic and social affairs. In its strongest version, embodied in the *Lochner* decision relating to a New York statute, the doctrine stood for the proposition that legislation, in order to be valid, must be for the public good, making special interest or class legislation unconstitutional.[164] Thus, until President Roosevelt's New Deal, the Supreme Court used the doctrine primarily to protect property rights and freedom of contract as basic constitutional rights.[165] However, that changed in the 1930s, when the Court overruled *Lochner* in *West Coast Hotel v. Parrish*, in which it upheld a state minimum wage law,[166] thus signaling the court's intention that it would preserve certain governmental regulations with redistributive aspects, at both the state and federal levels.

The New Deal case law also entailed a fundamental change in the Supreme Court's interpretation of the power of Congress to *regulate activity* of private persons *within a state*. It started with the court abolishing earlier legalistic distinctions, such as that between "commerce" and "manufacturing," and between "indirect" and "direct" effect,[167] and with the court accepting that Congress had the power to regulate activities that independently had no effect on interstate commerce but, when aggregated together, did have such an im-

[163] As a result of that interpretation, "substantive" due process and fundamental right were used interchangeably in the court's terminology: see, e.g., Pamela S. Karlan, "Some Thoughts on Autonomy and Equality in Relation to Justice Blackmun," 26 *Hastings Const. L. Q.* 59, 62 (1995). With *Lochner* being overruled, the use of "substantive" due process was discredited. Yet, as was mentioned above, on pp. 130–31, in recent years the use of that aspect of due process has flourished again as a haven for fundamental values other than economic ones, such as autonomy and privacy in view of striking down laws restricting abortions and the use of contraceptives. See Sullivan and Gunther, n. 97 above, 451ff.

[164] *Lochner v. New York*, 198 U.S. 45 (1905). See also n. 106 above.

[165] See also above, p. 130.

[166] 300 U.S. 379 (1937).

[167] Thus in *NLRB v. Jones and Laughlin Steel*, 301 U.S. 1 (1937), where the Supreme Court upheld Congress's ability to regulate labor relations at a manufacturing plant operated by a highly integrated manufacturing and interstate sales concern. According to the court, a work stoppage at any single plant would "have a most serious effect upon interstate commerce."

pact.[168] As a result of this expansive interpretation, the Supreme Court de facto recognized Congress's ability to regulate intrastate activities and, indeed, did not strike down a single law based on Congressional interstate commerce authority from 1937 until 1995.[169] That changed, however, when the Supreme Court, in its 1995 judgment *United States v. Lopez*,[170] placed new limits on the power of Congress to regulate interstate activities. In that decision the Court found that Congress lacked the authority to promulgate a federal statute, the Gun-Free School Zones Act, as it was essentially attempting to regulate a (potentially) completely intrastate activity, which, moreover, was not economic in nature. Similarly, in *United States v. Morrison*, decided in 2000,[171] the Court struck down a provision of the 1994 Violence Against Women Act, which Congress had promulgated under the commerce power clause. Although this time Congress had made detailed findings in the legislation to conclude that "gender-motivated violence affects interstate commerce,"[172] the Supreme Court found them insufficient to sustain the law, observing in addition that the activity regulated was non-economic in nature and that it contained no jurisdictional nexus to ensure that the activity affected interstate commerce.[173]

An even more crucial question, from the perspective of the distribution of powers between the federal and state level, is whether *restraints* on Congress's power can also be imposed *due to state autonomy*, as preserved by the Tenth Amendment. The question is, more specifically, "whether a *state's* activities, even though they otherwise relate to commerce, are nevertheless immune from federal regulation, because of external limits stemming from the structural postulates implicit in the federal scheme and reflected in the Tenth and Eleventh Amendments."[174] In the four decades preceding 1976, the "state

---

[168] As in *Wickard v. Filburn*, 317 U.S. 111, 119 (1942), involving the regulation of a farmer's production of wheat for home consumption.

[169] See Sullivan and Gunther, n. 97 above, 135–36. The authors describe the interpretation of the commerce power before the New Deal, from 1824 to 1936 (at 120–37), after the New Deal, from 1937 to 1995 (at 137–49), and in recent case law initiating new limits (at 149–71).

[170] 514 U.S. 549 (1995). In that judgment the court included a brief history of its commerce clause jurisprudence (553–58).

[171] 529 U.S. 598 (2000).

[172] At 614–15.

[173] At 613.

[174] Sullivan and Gunther, n. 97 above, 171. The Eleventh Amendment [1789] provides that "the Judicial power of the United States shall not be construed to extend to any suit in law or equity, commenced or prosecuted against one of the United States by Citizens of another State, or by Citizens or Subjects of any Foreign State." The

autonomy" barrier found little sympathy with the Supreme Court. But in 1976, the Supreme Court found, in *National League of Cities v. Usery*,[175] "that a federal law permissibly based on the commerce power nonetheless infringed impermissibly on state autonomy."[176] However, that judgment was later overruled by a majority of the court,[177] Justice O'Connor strongly dissenting,[178] after which the court abandoned its efforts to impose a "state autonomy" restraint on Congress.[179] Ultimately, Justice O'Connor's dissent would carry the day: in *New York v. United States*,[180] the Supreme Court invalidated a federal law that required states to provide for the disposal of low-level radioactive waste, recognizing that, under the Tenth Amendment, state autonomy can, within boundaries, impose limits on Congress's commerce power. Where those boundaries are, however, remains open for discussion.[181]

For European Community lawyers, it will be clear from the preceding that several parallels can be drawn between U.S. constitutional law and European Community law as regards the interpretation of interstate commerce provisions. As already mentioned, there is a parallel *first* between the U.S. Supreme Court's case law on the protection of fundamental rights under the due process clause of the Fifth and Fourteenth Amendments and the case law of the European Court of Justice as laid down in *Hauer*.[182] A *second* parallel concerns the Supreme Court's case law relating to the limits on the power of Congress to regulate intrastate commerce, and a *third* parallel concerns the limits on the power of Congress flowing from "legitimate interests" of states that Congress

---

amendment thus proclaims the immunity of any component state. The Supreme Court has expanded the scope of that state immunity well beyond the literal meaning of the amendment to include also claims, based on federal law or the Constitution, in a state's own courts by a state's own citizens (*Alden v. Maine*, 527 U.S. 706 [1999]). See further Sullivan and Gunther, n. 97 above, 197–204, and, in comparison with European Community law, the excellent analysis of Pfander, n. 58 above.

[175] 426 U.S. 833 (1976).

[176] Sullivan and Gunther, n. 97 above, 171–72.

[177] In *Garcia v. San Antonio Metropolitan Transit Authority*, 469 U.S. 528 (1985).

[178] In her dissent, Justice O'Connor opined that the "true essence of federalism is that the States *as States* have legitimate interests which the National Government is bound to respect even though its laws are supreme. If federalism so conceived [is] to remain meaningful, this Court cannot abdicate its constitutional responsibility to oversee the Federal Government's compliance with its duty to respect the legitimate interests of the States." Quoted by Sullivan and Gunther, n. 97 above, 177.

[179] Sullivan and Gunther, n. 97 above, 172.

[180] 505 U.S. 144 (1992). For a discussion of the question whether Congress can commandeer the state legislature, see chapter 1, p. 21.

[181] Sullivan and Gunther, n. 97 above, 195–97.

[182] See n. 116 above.

is bound to respect.[183] The third issue, in particular, in conjunction with the second, however, occupies a prominent place in Community law, where the question has been frequently debated in case law of the ECJ as to how far Member States can rely on legitimate interests to justify exceptions to the power of Community institutions to regulate free movement of goods, services, capital, and workers across state borders.

This case law has a long history, and it is characterized by successive judicial interpretations that have much in common with the Supreme Court's interpretations. To demonstrate similarity, I will focus on the ECJ's case law concerning Article 28 EC, which relates to the import of goods from one Member State into another. The starting point for that case law is found in the text of Article 28 EC, which declares that "quantitative restrictions on imports and all measures having equivalent effect shall be prohibited between Member States."[184]

As a starting point, the Court's case law turned on the words "measures having equivalent effect," which refers to any state measure—legislative, executive, or decisional—hindering interstate commerce within the Community internal market. Textually, the prohibition of Article 28 EC concerns only state measures that discriminate against goods *imported* from other Member States, not goods originating in the Member State itself. Indeed, for a long time the ECJ consistently held that Article 28 (and similar free-movement provisions) has no bearing on free movement of goods that are *internal to a Member State*. In recent judgments, however, the court seems to have "been straying from this path . . . despite the strenuous efforts of various Advocate Generals to keep it on the straight and narrow,"[185] essentially indicating a willingness to interpret the free-movement provisions broadly,[186] at least in instances of reverse discrimination[187] or cases involving the protection of fundamental rights.[188]

[183] In the words of Justice O'Connor; see n. 178 above.

[184] As for exports from one Member State to another, see Article 29 EC.

[185] Peter Oliver and Wulf-Henning Roth, "The Internal Market and the Four Freedoms" in 41 *CMLRev.*, 2004, 407–41, at 430.

[186] Thus in Case C-321/94, *Pistre*, [1997] ECR I-2343, the ECJ rendered judgment even though, as highlighted by Advocate General Jacobs, all material facts in this case were confined to France, thereby possibly evidencing a complete reversal of the traditional rule concerning purely internal situations. See Oliver and Roth, n. 185 above, at 431.

[187] In Case C-448/98, *Guimont*, [2000] ECR I-10663, para. 23, in response to a question from a national court, the court ruled that its answer may be useful for that court if it were to hold "that a national producer must be allowed to enjoy the same rights as those which a producer of another Member State would derive from Community law in the same situation." For further references, see Oliver and Roth, n. 185 above, at 431, n. 130.

[188] See Case C-60/00, *Mary Carpenter v. Home Secretary of State*, [2002] ECR I-6279,

Similarly important was the broad interpretation that the ECJ attached to the terms "equivalent effect" in Article 28 EC. As formulated, this provision is aimed at measures discriminating against imported goods, as compared to domestic goods. However, in *Dassonville*,[189] the Court ruled already in 1974 that "all trading rules enacted by Member States which are capable of hindering, directly or indirectly, actually or potentially, intra-Community trade" should be considered to fall under the Article 28 (then 30) EC prohibition on state action. The ECJ thus substituted the criterion of "hindering interstate commerce" for that of "discriminating" between domestic goods and goods imported from other Member States. As a result of that interpretation, many more state measures were brought under the prohibition of Article 28 than originally intended—which, in turn, resulted in greater pressure on the exceptions enumerated in Article 30 (ex 36) EC. The purpose of these exceptions is precisely to preserve Member State autonomy in certain areas by permitting states to maintain "interstate-restrictive" measures for (permissible) reasons of their own. Those reasons, enumerated in Article 30 EC are: "public morality, public policy or public security; the protection of health and life of humans, animals and plants; the protection of national treasures of artistic, historic, or archaeological value; or the protection of industrial and commercial property."

In order to offset the broad *Dassonville* interpretation, and the ensuing broader restrictions on state autonomy, the ECJ was forced to extend this list of exceptions by enumerating, in its 1979 *Cassis de Dijon* judgment,[190] a number of additional grounds of justification, dubbed "mandatory requirements." In its judgment, the Court indicated that the Member States could rely on those additional grounds to justify legislation that is *merely* restrictive of interstate commerce, but not discriminatory. The most important "mandatory requirements"—as they follow from the *Cassis de Dijon* judgment, and from later court judgments—are: prevention of tax fraud, fairness of commercial transactions, consumer protection, protection of the environment, and protection of the plurality of the media.[191]

The story does not end there. As a result of the broad interpretation of the prohibition laid down in Article 28 EC, and the ensuing possibility of con-

---

a case concerning the free movement of persons in the context of the right of family reunification, where the interstate element was held to be present on the most tenuous of bases. See Oliver and Roth, n. 185 above, at 432–33. The judgment is also discussed in chapter 4, pp. 203–4.

[189] Case 8/74, *Procureur du Roi v. Dassonville*, [1774] ECR 837, para. 5.

[190] Case 120/78, *Rewe v. Bundesmonopolverwaltung für Branntwein*, [1979] ECR 649.

[191] Ibid., para. 8. For later case law, also with respect to the other freedoms, see Oliver and Roth, n. 185 above, 434–35.

vincing the court to admit new mandatory requirements, private claimants increasingly attacked restrictive state legislation in their national courts, raising new possibilities of justification that those courts submitted to the Community court. To stem the mounting tide, the Court of Justice finally agreed "to re-examine and clarify its case law," and adopted in its 1993 judgment in *Keck and Mithouard* a much narrower interpretation of Article 28 EC[192] by making a distinction between so-called "product rules" and "selling arrangements."[193]

Although presented in too formalistic terms, the motivation behind the distinction was a correct one, based as it is on the different effect that both categories of state rules tend to have on the functioning of the internal (cross-border) market. Indeed, "product rules" can effectively prevent the access of imported products to the market of the regulating state, as they may compel the producer to adapt his product to the regulation of the state of import. By contrast, "selling arrangements," such as regulations concerning opening hours, selling on Sundays, or prohibiting resale of products at a loss (as in *Keck*), do not normally prevent or impede the access to market of imported products more than they do for domestic products.[194] Accordingly, the Court of Justice submitted these two categories of state rules to a different treatment: while product rules continued to be subjected, in principle, to the broad *Dassonville* "hindering interstate commerce" criterion, selling arrangements were subjected to the narrower "discrimination" standard.[195]

Clearly, a comparison of U.S. and EU case law on interstate commerce evidences a number of similarities as well as differences. One significant point of divergence is that, within the Community, harmonization legislation can be introduced in many areas where Member States could rely, or have relied, on grounds justifying derogation from the "internal market" freedoms (relating to interstate movement of persons, goods, services, and capital). This harmonization legislation, primarily enacted on the basis of Article 95 (1) EC, takes the form of directives that are binding upon the Member States as to the result to be achieved.[196] Such directives are intended to eliminate discrepancies

---

[192] Cases C-267 and 268/91, *Criminal Proceedings against Keck and Mithouard*, [1993] ECR I-6097. The words quoted in the text figure in para. 14.

[193] Ibid., paras. 15 and 16. Product rules lay down "requirements as to designation, form, size, weight, composition, presentation, labeling, packaging" (para. 15).

[194] Ibid., para. 17.

[195] See further Oliver and Roth, n. 185 above, 413–14, where the authors opine that the ruling in *Keck*, thus understood, can also be applied to the other freedoms (services, persons, and capital). In that article, many other issues are examined in light of recent case law of the court.

[196] See Article 249 EC. Harmonization measures under Article 95 EC cannot be

between Member State laws and regulations that hinder the proper functioning of the internal market[197] and have, in fact, brought the laws of the Member
States closer to one another in a large number of areas. Once a harmonization
directive has been enacted, however, a Member State can no longer rely on
Article 30 EC justifications (or *Cassis de Dijon* mandatory requirements) in
order to maintain national legislation that hinders internal market freedom. In
contrast, in the United States, federal legislation cannot force the states to
harmonize laws hindering interstate commerce, although the states could do
so voluntarily.

c) Legal basis, legal certainty, and judicial activism
   The preceding overview may have shown that the case law of both the Supreme Court and the Court of Justice concerning interstate commerce does
have an important constitutional dimension. To quote an author familiar with
both case laws but speaking of the case law of the Court of Justice:

> The Court of Justice has moved into the role of an arbiter between the demands of
> the internal market on the one hand and the effectiveness of a decentralized deci-
> sion-making process on the level of the Member States on the other. The Court's
> jurisprudence concerning the scope and content of the freedoms touches on the
> delicate issue of the competences of the Member States; it has a direct impact on
> the structure and balance of decentralized decision-making in the Union, pre-
> senting hard choices between the promotion of free trade and free movement on
> the one hand and the social choices pursued by the Member States on the other.[198]

The same can undoubtedly be said of the U.S. Supreme Court. The foregoing discussion also demonstrates, though, that the requirement of legal basis, or legal authority, is not necessarily synonymous with legal certainty, of
which it is a component. To be sure, it is for the Constitution, or the Basic
Law, to establish the legal basis for public authority to act, but, in a federal
state or federation of states, it is, in the end, for a supreme court at the helm of

---

taken, however, with regard to fiscal provisions, provisions relating to free movement
of persons, or provisions relating to the rights or interests of employed persons. See
Article 95 (2). For those areas, harmonization is allowed under Article 94 EC, albeit
requiring unanimity in the Council rather than qualified majority voting (QMV) provided under Article 95 EC. With respect to QMV, see chapter 6, pp. 281–84.
   [197] See, e.g., P. J. Slot, "Harmonisation," *ELRev.*, 1996, 378–97; M. Dougan, "Minimum Harmonization and the Internal Market," *CMLRev.*, 2000, 853–85.
   [198] Wolf-Henning Roth, in Oliver and Roth, n. 185 above, 413. In his dissertation of
1977, Roth thoroughly compared EU and U.S. interstate commerce: see *Freier Waren-
verkehr und staatliche Regelungsgewalt in einem Gemeinsamen Markt* [Free movement
of goods and state regulatory power in a common market] (Munich: C. H. Beck'sche
Verlagsbuchhandlung, 1977).

the legal system to define, in concrete cases, the border line between powers belonging to the federal and those belonging to the state authorities. As the preceding overview demonstrates, this implies that those courts are sometimes brought to reexamine existing case law in light of changing attitudes and expectations concerning the correct balance between both levels of government.

The issue unavoidably gives rise, in both the United States and the European Union, to complaints of judicial activism on the part of supreme courts.[199] The issue may be even more visible in the EU than in the United States because of the explicit use by the ECJ of the proportionality principle, which, in the words of the court, "involves weighing the national interest in attaining [the pursued legitimate] aim against the Community interest in ensuring the free movement of goods."[200]

To be sure, letting courts of law decide constitutional issues, shifting power away from elected assemblies to appointed judges, is clearly not in accordance with the principle of democracy, and it raises the question of who controls the court. To that question, there are only tentative answers. One is that the court itself must exercise restraint by limiting its review to (necessarily self-defined) points of law, and by developing its case law cautiously, on a case-by-case basis.[201] Another, more decisive, answer is that there may be a need for a well-balanced and sufficiently flexible—but not too flexible—procedure to amend the Constitution or Basic Law, allowing a constitutional convention, or a parliamentary assembly assuming that role, to reverse judicial interpretations that "the people," represented by the delegates to the convention or the assembly, would not agree with.[202]

In that respect, the existing procedure in the European Union for the amendment of the founding treaties is clearly too inflexible. It is set out in Article 48 EU, which confers upon "the government of any Member State or the Commission" the power to submit proposals for amending "the Treaties on which the Union is founded" to the Council. The Council then must consult with the European Parliament and, if necessary, with the Commission (that is, when a Member State government has made the proposal). Once this has been

---

[199] See also chapter 1, pp. 27–28.

[200] Case C-169/91, *Council of the City of Stoke on Trent and Norwich City Council v. B&Q plc* (one of the Sunday Trading cases decided by the court), [1992] ECR I-6635. See further my article, n. 118 above, 40–41.

[201] On this, see Cass R. Sunstein, *One Case at a Time: Judicial Minimalism on the Supreme Court* (Cambridge, Mass.: Harvard University Press, 1999). On judicial restraint and activism in the United States more generally, see Koopmans, n. 5 above, 51–62.

[202] On the issue of how far judicial decision making can be removed from what a majority of the people thinks right, see Koopmans, n. 5 above, 104–8.

done, the Council may deliver "an opinion in favour of calling a conference of representatives of the Member States, . . . to be convened by the President of the Council for the purpose of determining by common accord the amendments to be made to those Treaties." However, the amendments agreed upon will only "enter into force after being ratified by all Member States in accordance with their respective constitutional requirements."[203] Although that procedure may be adequate for major changes to the treaties, or for enlargement of the Union with new states, it is too inflexible to be used to reverse judicial interpretations of existing treaty provisions. To perform the latter function, a "fast track" amendment procedure would be advisable. Such a procedure should involve representatives of Union institutions and of national parliaments meeting in an assembly.[204] It should provide for decision-making procedures that would make ratification by the Member States superfluous if a decision is made by consensus.[205]

High-Quality Legislation

Legal certainty requires laws and regulations to be well drafted, so that individuals know the legal consequences of their actions in advance, and that the laws are enacted and promulgated in accordance with standards for good legislation. According to Lon Fuller's understanding of the "internal morality" of the law,[206] those standards are, in summary,[207] as follows:

[203] Article V of the U.S. Constitution provides a similar procedure, but it requires a "qualified" majority of the component states: Two-thirds of both houses of Congress or two-thirds of the states' legislatures may cause Congress to call a convention for proposing amendments that shall be valid as part of the Constitution when ratified by the legislatures of three-fourths of the states, or by conventions in three-fourths of the states. So far, twenty-seven such amendments have been ratified.

[204] That assembly could take the form of a convention—an instrument that has so far been used twice, first to prepare the EU Charter of Fundamental Rights, and then to prepare the draft Constitution (see chapter 6). However, the procedure should be made more transparent and established in advance: see A.A., editorial on "The Future of the Convention Method," 28 *ELRev.*, 2003, 573–74. For an exhaustive study, see Lars Hoffmann and Anna Vergés-Bausili, "The Reform of Treaty Revision Procedures: The European Convention on the Future of Europe," in *The State of the Union*, ed. Tanja A. Börzel and Rachel A. Cichowski (Oxford: Oxford University Press, 2003), 127–46.

[205] Such a "fast-track" procedure has been proposed for the adoption of the draft Constitution, but it was rejected by the majority of the Convention preparing the draft Constitution: see chapter 6, pp. 304–5.

[206] Lon L. Fuller, *The Morality of Law*, rev. ed. (New Haven, Conn.: Yale University Press, 1969).

[207] As summarized by N. MacCormick in *Questioning Sovereignty: Law, State, and Nation in the European Commonwealth* (Oxford: Oxford University Press, 1999), 45. In

Law should be *prospective* in operation, should be *published*, and should comprise *general rules*, not individualized directives; but they should also avoid the trap of over-generality and thus extreme vagueness. For laws have to be acceptably *clear* in their terms, in order to serve the function of being guides for the right conduct of rational beings; and this in turn requires reasonable *constancy* through time (not an ever-changing set of rules, so that no one can tell moment by moment what to do) and reasonable *consistency* among laws (for contradictory laws afford no real guidance), and must *not* require people to do *the impossible* (for these, like sets of inconsistent laws, would really be licenses to officials to indulge in arbitrary punishment). Finally, and most crucially, the conduct of legal officials has to be *congruent* with the law as laid down; officials owe the same respect to the same laws as do ordinary citizens, and laws exhibiting the seven characteristics would necessarily limit the scope for official arbitrariness.

Legal certainty thus understood is a problematic issue in the Community's legal system. Complaints concerning the quality of Community legislation are manifold; they are mostly about a lack of coherence between the multitude of Community rules, and a lack of simplicity and intelligibility. To be sure, quality of legislation presents a problem in any jurisdiction, but this is even more so in the Community legal system, where problems arise that do not exist in national legal systems, at least not in the same degree. This is so because Community law is a relatively new legal system, having its own structure and terminology, and is moreover much more fragmented than national laws because of the limited transfer of powers to the Community entailing the need to achieve consistency between laws governing very diverse but limited areas of the law. Moreover, Community laws are now drafted in twenty different official languages, and they are often the result of complex intergovernmental and interinstitutional negotiations.[208]

Improving the quality of European Community legislation remains permanently on the agenda of Community institutions. As recently as June 2002, the Commission adopted a "package" of four documents, one of which takes the form of an action plan on better lawmaking and identifies various measures covering action falling within the Commission's remit, or involving the Community institutions acting jointly or with the Member States.[209] Of the two accompanying communications, the first contains proposals aimed at organizations representing civil society—"which it already consults widely"—

---

the excerpt I italicized the words "not (require) the impossible"—in addition to those already italicized—to make clear that there are eight standards.

[208] On all these points, and many others, see Christiaan Timmermans, "How Can One Improve the Quality of Community Legislation?" 34 *CMLRev.*, 1997, 1229–57.

[209] See the communication from the Commission of June 5, 2002, *European Governance: Better Lawmaking*, COM (2002) 275 final.

while the second describes an integrated method for assessing the *impact* of the Commission's policy or legislative proposals, with particular reference to economic, social, and environmental implications. Other initiatives aim at clarifying executive responsibilities, creating European agencies,[210] taking account of the regional, urban, and local contexts, and setting out a new approach to vetting the *application* of the law are also included. Accordingly, this demonstrates that the problem of improving the quality of Community legislation is as much about legal certainty and cooperation between rule makers at the Community and national levels as it is about efficiency, effectiveness, and compliance. It also shows that the problem is a persistent one warranting permanent attention and that it is unlikely ever to be definitively resolved.

V. CONCLUSIONS

The contents of the rule of law concept may differ between legal systems, each of which is subject to specific constitutional interpretations. In the United Kingdom the concept is seen in conjunction with the principle of democracy, and thus with the supremacy of Parliament. Parliament, however, must be presumed not to legislate contrary to the rule of law.[211] In the United States, the concept is part of the doctrine of constitutional review, which has been imitated in many European countries. In Germany the rule of law concept, inherent in the notion of *Rechtsstaat*, is closely related to the fundamental right of human dignity, demonstrating that the state is at the service of the individual citizens. As one commentator puts it, "the rule of law can be understood as including, at a minimum, the requirement of a clear basis in law for the exercise of public authority, the protection of individual rights, including safeguards against the abuse of power, an independent judiciary and equality before the law."[212]

In this chapter, the emphasis was placed, first, on the subjection of all public authority to independent judicial review (which requires the availability of effective legal remedies); second, on the need to respect basic rights and fundamental freedoms; and, third, on legal certainty, both as a requirement of a clear basis in law for the exercise of public authority and as a need to enact laws in accordance with high standards of legislation. In the following chapter I will examine other components of the rule of law, equality of citizens before the law being the most prominent one.

As for the submission of public authority to judicial scrutiny, and the

---

[210] See Chapter 2 above, at pp. 93ff.
[211] Lord Steyn in *ex p Pierson*, n. 14 above. See also Koopmans, n. 5 above, 243.
[212] Casper, n. 2 above, 152–53.

availability of legal remedies, the analysis of Community law makes it clear that at least the first pillar of Union law almost totally complies with the rule of law concept. This is so because all public power, including the legislature proper, is subjected to judicial review from the Community courts, just like all Member State authorities, including the legislatures proper, are subjected to judicial review before both Community and national courts as regards implementation or application of Community law. In this respect, it has been a constant concern of the Court of Justice, acting in close cooperation with the national courts through the preliminary ruling procedure, to provide individual plaintiffs, of whatever nationality, with legal remedies that they can invoke before the Community courts. There is only one notable exception regarding the protection of basic rights against encroachments by an act of general application.[213] Individuals also have access to extensive legal remedies before Member State courts, where this exception does not apply, although the preliminary ruling procedure, through which questions as to the validity of EU legislation must be referred to the ECJ, does not offer private claimants the same protection as that afforded by direct recourse to the ECJ. The overarching aim of all this is to safeguard the rights that individuals derive from Community law against infringements of Community law by Community institutions and Member State authorities alike.

In this regard, however, constitutional and administrative judicial review is not the only legal remedy available; individuals can also bring actions for damages against Community institutions and against Member State authorities for damage sustained as a result of violations of Community law. Again, this doctrine is applied against all Community and Member State institutions and authorities, including legislatures proper, albeit under less generous conditions when a claim is brought by a private claimant against a public authority that enjoys wide discretion in the matter.

As regards the second and third pillars, the subjection of public authority to the rule of law is more limited under the third pillar than under the first, and virtually nonexistent under the second pillar. However, under the third pillar there is a clear tendency toward broader judicial review, whereas for the second pillar, relating to a common foreign and defense policy, the absence of judicial review is not unusual, as it also exists in the traditional states where foreign policy and national defense matters are often deemed to be non-justiciable.

Also with regard to respect for basic rights and fundamental freedoms, the record of Community law is not insufficient at all. Since the early 1970s, the ECJ has proclaimed the human rights as guaranteed in the ECHR to be general

---

[213] See pp. 112, 113, and 115.

principles of Community law whose observance it must ensure according to Article 220 EC. With the entry into effect of the EU Treaty, the court's doctrine has been explicitly endorsed in Article 6 EU, and it has been broadened, with the adoption in December 2000 of the EU Charter, to include a long list of rights that goes far beyond the traditional human rights embodied in the ECHR. Having said that, the non-binding character of the EU Charter nevertheless shows that the extension of basic rights to, for instance, the social sector is part of a longstanding European tradition of solemn declarations that remain largely academic for lack of competence, if not enforceability devices.

In comparing the way basic, or civil, rights are enforced in concrete cases in case law of the U.S. Supreme Court with the way those rights are enforced in case law of the European Court of Justice and the constitutional courts in the Member States, there seems to be a significant difference in the method of balancing such rights when they are in conflict with other compelling interests. That is particularly so with regard to freedom of speech. In the United States freedom of speech, as guaranteed in the First Amendment, is considered an almost absolute foundation of societal life, as shown by the Supreme Court's case law, which, over the years, has withdrawn more and more speech from the regulatory and prohibitive hand of government. Naturally, in Europe freedom of expression (as it is called there) is also deemed to be a foundation of democracy, but that does not prevent the ECJ and the constitutional courts in the Member States from balancing that freedom against other basic rights or interests with the help of the proportionality principle, as was illustrated in the recent judgment of the ECJ in *Schmidberger*. In that case the Court weighed the fundamental Community law principle of free movement of goods and the freedom of expression of environmental protesters blocking (in a orderly way) cross-border traffic of goods between Member States. In this case the court gave precedence to freedom of expression, but that would have been different if the court had found the protests to be out of proportion with the restriction of interstate commerce.

The principle of legal certainty also plays an important role in the rule of law concept. In the first place there is the requirement of a clear legal basis for the exercise of public authority. As a doctrine "legal basis" takes a prominent place in the case law of the ECJ. The overarching principle is that the EU possesses only those powers that the Member States have conferred upon the Union in the founding treaties, as subsequently amended in later treaties. In other words, all powers that have not been attributed to the Union institutions remain with the Member States. Moreover not all powers conferred on the Union are of the same nature: while only a few powers are exclusive (as in matters of the common policy, and monetary policy within the euro-zone), most powers are shared with the Member States (as is the case with the internal market competences), some others being merely supportive or complementary (as with regard to public health, culture, and education). Furthermore, by virtue of the principle of subsidiarity, powers belonging to the last two categories (shared, and supportive or complementary powers) may only be exercised if the objectives pursued cannot be sufficiently achieved by the Member States and, even then, in accordance with the proportionality principle, the Union institutions may not use their powers beyond what is necessary to achieve the objective pursued by the proposed action.

All that looks clear on paper. In practice, however, it is not always easy to differentiate the powers of the Community institutions from those of the Member States, as, for example, when it comes to weighing the internal market provisions relating to the free movement of persons, goods, services, and capital across Member State borders (borders that have been abolished, economically speaking) against permissible compelling interests pursued by Member States requiring rules that have an impact on interstate commerce. The issue is well known in the United States, where the interstate commerce clause fulfills a similar function. Indeed, a comparison of Supreme Court case law on interstate commerce with case law of the Court of Justice on free movement of goods illustrates how much the judgments of both courts have, over the years, been subjected to similar reconsideration and reversal in interpreting the constitutional restrictions on state autonomy.

Legal certainty also requires high-quality rules enacted in accordance with proper standards of legislation or, in Lon Fuller's terminology, in accordance with standards of "internal morality."[214] Drafting high-quality legal documents is a difficult task for Union lawmakers for the reasons indicated above,[215] and improving legislation is an item that is permanently on the agenda of the Union institutions. In the European Union, as everywhere else, legislative drafting requires a specialized skill that in many Member States has been allocated either to a specialized section of an independent college of jurists, such as the legislative section of the Council of State, or to an office of Parliamentary Counsel.[216] At the level of the Union, no such external review exists.[217]

[214] See n. 206 above.

[215] See p. 152.

[216] On the first alternative, applied in the Netherlands and Belgium, see J. H. van Kreveld, "The Main Elements of a General Policy on Legislative Quality: Dutch Experiences," in T. M. C. Asser Instituut, *Improving the Quality of Legislation in Europe*, ed. Alfred E. Kellermann et al. (The Hague: Kluwer Law International, 1998), 85–100, at 95. On the second alternative applied in the United Kingdom, see Ian McLeod, n. 3 above, 233–51.

[217] According to one author, this is because of mutual trust (which is not, however,

One final remark: In an article under the provocative title "Rule of Law or Enlightened Absolutism," Gerhard Casper examines the actual performance of a democratic system, in this case the American system, concluding that "our performance is often mindless and frequently disproportionate and, at times, even cruel."[218] To illustrate his point, he refers to some concrete examples of how ordinary people are treated in ordinary situations, which "display an insufficient exercise of discretion on the part of government actors, and an insufficient examination of the overall balance of the costs and benefits entailed in governmental decisions."[219] One of the reasons is "the fact that we have no efficient and cheap recourse for those who suffer at the hands of the public authority. Indeed, our judicial process is neither timely nor affordable for most people."[220] The observation refers to a situation that, unfortunately, every country is familiar with. It should at least encourage lawyers, and politicians, to look for practical measures to deal with complaints concerning breaches of citizen rights, rather than multiply the number of solemn human rights proclamations.[221]

---

further defined) between the Member States: L. J. Brinkhorst, "Summing-up of the Conference," in T. M. C. Asser Instituut, n. 216 above, lv.

[218] Casper, n. 2 above, 157.

[219] Ibid.

[220] Ibid., 170. The situation has certainly not improved since 2000, when Casper wrote his article. As a result of the events of September 11, 2001, and the entry into force of the U.S. Patriot Act, the Defense Department was authorized "to develop a project to promote something called 'total information awareness.' Under this programme, the government may gather huge amounts of information about citizens without proving they have done anything wrong. They can access a citizen's records—whether telephone, financial, rental, internet, medical, educational or library—without showing any involvement with terrorism. Internet providers may be forced to produce records based solely on FBI declarations that the information is for an anti-terrorism investigation." Harold Hongju Koh, professor of International Law at Yale Law School, in "Rights to Remember," *The Economist*, November 1, 2003, 24–26, at 24.

[221] In their "An 'Ever Closer Union' in Need of a Human Rights Policy: The European Union and Human Rights" (n. 93 above), Alston and Weiler plead for measures to develop an active human rights policy (p. 3). See also the EU Commission's consultation paper referred to in n. 93 above—it is not yet clear whether the initiative set forth there will enhance enforcement in the field.

CHAPTER FOUR

Good Governance

This chapter and the following are about good governance. The term has several sets of meanings.[1] It has been brought into use in the context of international and transnational organizations where legitimacy does not depend on the organization's subjection to the popular will, in line with the idea of government emanating from the people, but on its capacity to achieve the citizens' goals.[2] While the idea of democratic government implies accountability to the people, submission to the rule of law, and legal certainty—subjects discussed in the preceding two chapters—the idea of good governance, as understood here, refers to the exercise of public power to pursue objectives and attain results in the interest of the people through a variety of regulative and executive processes.[3]

For governance to be "good," public authority must be exercised with integrity and efficiency. Authorities must treat citizens equally, avoid discrimination, and, where appropriate, take affirmative or positive action to remove discrimination. They must pursue social justice for all. These aspects of good governance will be dealt with in this chapter. In the following chapter other aspects of good governance will be discussed, namely civic responsibility, open

[1] Carol Harlow, *Accountability in the European Union* (Oxford: Oxford University Press, 2002), 178.

[2] Ibid. and Fritz W. Scharpf, "Demokratie in der internationalisierten Ökonomie," in *Demokratie—eine Kultur des Westens?* ed. Michael Greven (Opladen, 1998), 81–103, at 99.

[3] Compare Amaryllis Verhoeven, *The European Union in Search of a Democratic and Constitutional Theory* (The Hague: Kluwer Law International, 2002), 199, with further references. For a large variety of articles on problems related to European governance, see Christian Joerges and Renauld Dehousse, eds., *Good Governance in Europe's Integrated Market* (Oxford: Oxford University Press, 2002).

government, citizen involvement, and freedom of the press. Together with accountable government, these two sets of characteristics are vital to confer legitimacy on any political entity, especially a multilayered organization such as the European Union.

In such a multilayered organization "lines of authority duplicate and overlap, functions are performed in fragments by many subsystems; sometimes authority flows sideways and upwards, at other times the flow is downwards."[4] While public authority was traditionally organized pyramidally along hierarchical lines, it is now also organized through numerous networks of public and private nuclei of power,[5] making power move both vertically and horizontally.[6] This paradigmatic shift in governance is reflected as well in the EU Commission's recent White Paper on European Governance.[7] Although the paper in-

[4] E. Haas, "Is There a Hole in the Whole? Knowledge, Technology, Interdependence and the Construction of International Regimes," 29 *IO*, 1975, 827, at 856, quoted by S. Douglas-Scott, *Constitutional Law of the European Union* (Harlow, England: Longman, 2002), 78. For an earlier work, see E. Haas, *Functionalism and International Organizations* (Stanford, Calif.: Stanford University Press, 1964).

[5] For a recent analysis of that paradigmatic change, with reference also to the European Union, see François Ost and Michel Van de Kerchove, *De la pyramide au réseau?* [From pyramid to network?] (Brussels: Publications Universitaires Saint-Louis, 2002). The notion of a networked (or fused) administration is not new, as Haas's writings in the preceding note show. See also Karl-Heinz Ladeur, "Towards a Legal Concept of the Network in European Standard-Setting," in *EU Committees: Social Regulation, Law and Politics*, ed. Christian Joerges and Ellen Vos (Oxford: Hart Publishing, 1999), 151ff.

[6] Whereas in a theocracy a divinity is at the top of the hierarchical structure, in a monarchy the king or queen is at the helm. With the arrival of the Enlightenment, power shifted to the bottom, first to an elitist parliament and later on, when society embraced democratic ideas, to a parliament elected by all citizens. On this evolution, see Verhoeven, n. 3 above, 21–30.

[7] Commission of the European Communities, *European Governance: A White Paper*, dated July 25, 2001, COM (2001) 428 final, [2001] OJ, C287/5. In that paper the Commission defines "governance" in a loose way (and in a footnote!) to refer to "rules, processes and behavior that affect the way in which powers are exercised at the European level, particularly as regards openness, participation, accountability, effectiveness and coherence" (8). The paper has not been received with great enthusiasm and has been defined as "a no-win text," "an impatient document . . . [that] provides us with seemingly easy answers . . . and refuses to take the thorny legitimacy challenge posed by transnational governance seriously." Christian Joerges, "The Commission's White Paper on Governance in the EU—A Symptom of Crisis?" 39 *CMLRev.*, 2002, 441–45, at 442 and 443. Indeed, and unfortunately enough, the paper does not examine the Commission's own democratic accountability: see my review of Carol Harlow's book, n. 1 above, in 40 *CMLRev.*, 2003, 1281–87, at 1285.

sists on the need to maintain the so-called "Community method," based on "the formal hierarchies of the traditional constitutional framework," it emphasizes at the same time the need for social dialogue and the involvement of civil society: this implies "connecting with networks . . . linking businesses, communities, research centres, and regional and local authorities."

This shift goes hand in hand with a different emphasis in decision-making instruments. Whereas the "Community method" is based on binding legislation[8]—which was crucially important during the first decades of European Community history, and is still useful, to harmonize Member State rules hindering the establishment of an internal market[9]—there is now a need for new forms of governance. That need became apparent in the 1990s when "the European integration project ha[d] reached a stage where the core activities of the member states are directly addressed—that is those activities related to employment policy, social policy, migration, criminal prosecution, and education. These are areas where member-state political support for harmonization through legislation is very difficult to gain."[10]

In contrast with the traditional method based on binding legislation, those new forms of government are guided by "principles of (1) voluntarism, that is, non-binding targets and soft law, without formal sanctions; (2) subsidiarity, that is, measures are decided by member states or private actors; and (3) inclusion, that is, the actors concerned participate in defining the policy goals and the instruments to be applied."[11] However, they do not replace the old forms of governance, which continue to be used in areas where binding legislation is imperative. Moreover, in between the traditional and the new methods of governance, new uses of old instruments have developed, such as so-called "framework directives" aimed at allowing Member States more flexibility, and

[8] Pp. 11–15 of the White Paper, referred to in n. 7 above. The "Community method" is described on p. 8. According to that method legislation is most frequently adopted by the Council of Ministers and the European Parliament at the proposal of the Commission. For a recent account and assessment of what is called "the traditional model of EC constitutionalism"—from which I have taken the quotation in the text— see Gráinne de Búrca, "The Constitutional Challenge of New Governance in the European Union," 28 *ELRev.*, 2003, 814–39, at 817–21, with many references to literature from the 1990s.

[9] "Internal market" is defined in Article 14 (2) EC as "an area without internal frontiers in which the free movement of goods, persons, services and capital is ensured."

[10] Adrienne Héritier, "New Modes of Governance in Europe: Increasing Political Capacity and Policy Effectiveness?" in *The State of the European Union*, ed. Tanja A. Börzel and Rachel A. Cichowski (Oxford: Oxford University Press, 2003), 105–26, at 105. See also n. 14 below.

[11] Ibid., 106.

at the same time making the legislative process at Community level more efficient.[12] Whatever the method used, all of them entail more consultation with stakeholders, the occasional provision of forms of co- and self-regulation, or the involvement of social partners in decision making.[13] One of the new methods of governance, the so-called open method of coordination (OMC), will be further discussed in Sections I and III below.[14]

I. INTEGRITY AND EFFICIENCY

As pointed out at the outset, good governance is about aims, results, and proper procedures in the exercise of public authority. In this section, I will discuss two aspects of proper procedures: standards of ethical behavior in public life, and methods to ensure efficiency and effectiveness.

Encouraging Ethical Behavior

Integrity is an essential characteristic of good governance. The subject received much attention in the first report of the Committee of Independent Experts because of that committee's decision to assess the behavior of members of the Commission in light of Standards in Public Life similar to those in effect in the U.K.[15] In its second report, the committee also referred to the

---

[12] An example is the legislative procedure applied in the European Securities Markets, following the recommendations made in the Final Report of the Committee of Wise Men on the Regulation of European Securities Markets of February 15, 2001 (the so-called Lamfalussy Report). The report was adopted by the March 2001 European Council summit meeting in Stockholm and was endorsed by the European Parliament. It provides a four-level approach (framework principles adopted by the Council and Parliament, implementing measures adopted by the Commission, networking among Member State securities regulators, and enforcement procedures) to speed up the legislative process and to allow the regulatory process to react speedily to changing market conditions. For the text of the report, see http://europa.eu.int/comm/internal_market/securities/lamfalussy/index_en.htm.

[13] See further Norbert Reich, in collaboration with Christopher Goddard and Ksenija Vasiljeva, *Understanding EU Law: Objectives, Principles and Methods of Community Law* (Antwerp: Intersentia, 2003), 290–93. The author points out that, in its White Paper on European Governance, the Commission was quite critical of the new methods of governance, and in particular the open method of coordination (OMC) (291). He shares that criticism to some extent because the use of that method may affect the binding force of the *acquis communautaire* (293).

[14] See below, pp. 167–70 and 196–200.

[15] Committee of Independent Experts, First Report on Allegations Regarding Fraud, Mismanagement, and Nepotism in the European Commission (March 15, 1999), 12–13, para. 1.5.4. See chapter 2, p. 81.

Principles for Managing Ethics in the Public Service established by the Organization for Economic Co-operation and Development (OECD), and it underlined the need to create a standing Committee on Standards in Public Life.[16] The task of that standing committee would be to encourage all Community institutions to adopt codes of conduct containing specific rules for each institution in line with general standards in public life applicable to all. The Santer Commission followed up this recommendation by issuing three codes of conduct before its resignation in 1999, one of them relating to the behavior of the commissioners themselves, and another relating to the behavior of civil servants.[17] The codes were, with minor changes, confirmed by the incumbent Prodi Commission. In its White Paper on Reforming the Commission, the commission also announced the establishment, via an interinstitutional agreement, of the Committee on Standards in Public Life,[18] promised to be effective by December 2000. This has not happened.

In the EC Treaty itself there are only a few provisions concerning the behavior of the senior executive officials, the commissioners. They are contained in Article 213 (2) EC, which provides that "Members of the Commission shall, in the general interest of the Community, be completely independent in the performance of their duties . . . [that] they shall neither seek nor take instructions from any government or from any other body." Furthermore, they "shall refrain from any action incompatible with their duties . . . [and] may not . . . engage in any other occupation, whether gainful or not." The aforementioned code of conduct relating to commissioners contains other prohibitions concerning outside activities, financial interests and assets, activities of spouses, confidentiality, rules for missions and governing receptions, acceptance of gifts, and the like. With the exception of a rule on the composition of the commissioners' private offices, these rules are of a "bureaucratic" type, setting forth prohibitions rather than values, aspirations, and ideals. They are therefore of a different nature than the rules contained in the U.K. Standards in Public Life, or in the OECD principles mentioned above.

[16] Committee of Independent Experts, Second Report on Reform of the Commission (Sept. 10, 1999), 260–65 and 268–69, sections 7.4, 7.5, and 7.7. See chapter 2, pp. 81–82. In the meantime, a new OECD document on the topic has been issued: *Trust in Government: Ethics Measures in OECD Countries* (2000).

[17] The third code concerns the relations between commissioners and commission departments; see Documents Sec (1999) 1479, 1481, and 1494 of September 16, 1999, published by the commission's secretariat-general.

[18] Commission of the European Communities, *Reforming the Commission, A White Paper, Part II, An Action Plan*, at chapter II, 3. That part is the second part of the document referred to in n. 27 below.

The difference between codes of prohibitions and codes of values is one of attitude. It is best explained by reference to the distinction, made by Lon Fuller in *The Morality of Law*, between "morality of duty" and "morality of aspiration."[19] Morality of duty, in Fuller's words, "starts at the bottom of human achievement. It lays down the basic rules without which an ordered society is impossible . . . or must fail of its mark. It is the morality of the Old Testament and the Ten Commandments. It speaks in terms of 'thou shalt not' and, less frequently, of 'thou shalt.'"[20] By contrast, and higher on the scale of moral issues, is the morality of aspiration: "It is the morality of the Good Life, of excellence, of the fullest realization of human power. . . . [It is] recognized, of course, that a man might fail to realize his fullest capabilities. As a citizen or as an official, he might be found wanting. But in such a case he was condemned for failure, not for being recreant of duty; for shortcoming, not for wrongdoing."[21]

The difference in attitude reflects a difference in *ethos* that, as pointed out in American literature, is responsible for two different kinds of codes: *bureaucratic* codes of *conduct* versus *democratic* codes of *ethics*. The first

> focuses on mechanisms of external control, the moral minimum. Laws, rules, and regulatory codes of conduct detail what a public servant must do to . . . stay out of trouble. . . . In contrast, the democratic, developmental approach relies on cultivating internal controls, the moral maximum. It is concerned . . . with . . . the protection and the advancement of the public interest. . . . [T]he emphasis . . . is on the cultivation of virtues, integrity, and character . . . ; the public servant is not seen as a bureaucratic functionary, but rather as a moral agent capable of transcending particular interests in pursuit of the larger social good."[22]

The codes that the commission issued in 1999 are of the bureaucratic type; that is, they primarily contain prohibitions, not goals, values, or aspirations, and they correspond to the narrow view that an administration might have with regard to phenomena known as "whistle-blowing," or "civil disobedience."[23] The problem with a bureaucratic, as opposed to democratic, vision of administration is that it fails to address the real issue, which is the democratic

[19] Lon L. Fuller, *The Morality of Law* (New Haven, Conn.: Yale University Press, 1969).

[20] Ibid., 5–6.

[21] Ibid., 5.

[22] James S. Bowman, "From Codes of Conduct to Codes of Ethics," *Handbook of Administrative Ethics*, 2d ed., ed. Terry L. Cooper (New York: Marcel Dekker, 2001), 335. The author discusses the 1994 American Society for Public Administration (ASPA) Code.

[23] See chapter 5, pp. 217ff, especially pp. 219 and 223–24.

legitimacy of the European executive. Instead it concentrates on better steering tools and managerial instruments, as evidenced by the White Paper on European Governance,[24] as well as on integrated human resources with an emphasis upon management quality and merit-based sustained performance, which are the key concepts used in the recent 2004 Reform of the EU Civil Service.[25] Certainly, these are not unimportant issues, but they do not focus upon the maintenance of high ethical and democratic standards of selflessness, integrity, and honesty, nor upon accountability, openness, and transparency, all of which are virtues capable of building public trust in the European institutions. The creation of a Committee on Standards in Public Life, as recommended by the Committee of Independent Experts (see above), might have been able to place these virtues at the heart of institutional reform, not only in the Commission, but also in the Council and European Parliament.

Ensuring Efficiency and Effectiveness

While integrity is about "accountability through ethics," efficiency and effectiveness are about "accountability through audit."[26] For governance to be good, it must be efficient and effective, as the EU Commission emphasizes in its 2000 White Paper on Reforming the Commission.[27] The paper indicates a wish to promote "activity-based management," a managerial system in which decisions about policy priorities and corresponding resources are taken together.[28] The aim of such a system is to improve *efficiency*, understood by the Commission as a "correct relationship between output of goods, services and

[24] For a comment on the Commission's White Paper on European Governance (n. 7 above), see the site of the Academy of European Law online: http://www. jeanmonnetprogram.org/papers/01/012401-01.html. See also Joerges's comments, n. 7 above.

[25] On March 22, 2004, the Council definitively adopted the Commission proposals for the modernization of the EU Civil Service. See Council Regulation (EC, Euratom) No. 723/2004 amending the Staff Regulation of Officials of the European Communities and the conditions of employment of other servants of the European Communities, [2004] OJ L124/1, of April 4, 2004. At the heart of this system is a structure that "provides for career progress in which pay rises depend much more on sustained proven performance, and much less on length of service." Commission Press Release dated March 22, 2004.

[26] Thus Harlow, n. 1 above, 108.

[27] Commission of the European Communities, *Reforming the Commission, A White Paper—Part I*, dated April 5, 2000, COM (2000) 200 final/2. The second part of that paper, entitled *Reforming the Commission, A White Paper, Part II, An Action Plan*, was published on March 1, 2000, COM (2000) final.

[28] Ibid., Part I.

other results, and resources used to produce them," and *effectiveness*, "the relationship between the intended and the actual impact of action undertaken."[29] The Commission sees efficiency and effectiveness as crucial devices for enhancing an organization's "output legitimacy" (that is, legitimacy that depends on a political system's "capacity to achieve the citizen's goals and solve their problems effectively and efficiently").[30] In other words: "the higher the capacity, the more legitimate the system."[31] In contrast to output legitimacy, "input legitimacy" is about a system's capacity to achieve "legitimacy by the way decisions are made (and not by the results these decisions produce)."[32]

a) *"Input" and "output" legitimacy of the budgetary*
  and accounting process

In a democratic system, "input legitimacy" is realized through binding (often constitutional) legislation in which it is left to an elected parliament, acting in concert with the executive, to define citizens' goals and expectations, and to determine the size and allocation of the resources needed to meet them. This happens in the Community as well, though the budgetary procedure is more complicated there than elsewhere because of the "three-headed" structure of the Community legislature and executive (Parliament, Council, and Commission). The procedure for drawing up, and approving, the budget annually is set out in Article 272 EC and is the subject, since a 1993 interinstitutional agreement,[33] of a carefully balanced interplay among the Commission, the Parliament, and the Council.[34] Once the budget is adopted,[35] it is for the

[29] Ibid., at the Annex 3 Glossary in Part I.

[30] F. Schimmelfennig, "Legitimate Rule in the European Union: The Academic Debate," in *Tübinger Arbeitspapiere zur internationalen Politik und Friedensforschung*, working paper no. 27 (Tübingen, 1996), 19.

[31] Ibid. Output legitimacy helps to legitimate actions of international organizations where input legitimacy is less obviously present.

[32] Ibid., 20.

[33] European Parliament, Council, and Commission, *Budgetary Discipline and Improvement of the Budgetary Procedure*, Interinstitutional Agreement of May 6, 1999 [1999] OJ C172/01.

[34] The discharge of the budget is laid out in a detailed procedure in Article 276 EC. In its final report on simplification, Working Group IX of the Convention for the Future of Europe (see chapter 6 below) observed "that practice ha[s] rendered null and void the articles of the EC Treaty devoted to the budgetary procedure . . . [especially] the distinction between compulsory and non-compulsory expenditure, which is one of the principal causes of the complexity of the budgetary procedure [and] no longer reflects a real difference in nature." European Convention Secretariat, *Final Report of Working Group IX on Simplification*, Doc. CONV 424/02, Nov. 29, 2002, at 18.

Commission to implement it, and thereafter annually to obtain discharge from the two other institutions, predominantly from Parliament. As is not unusual in a democratic system, Parliament has used its budgetary power gradually to strengthen its overall political impact on Community affairs.[36]

From a viewpoint of "output legitimacy," the implementation of the General Budget of the European Communities is entrusted to the Commission (Article 274 EC). To that effect, the Commission has set up an *internal* auditing system to monitor whether revenues have been received and expenditures have been made in accordance with legal, administrative, and budgetary provisions. As a result of severe criticism by the Committee of Independent Experts in its second report,[37] the existing auditing system was completely overhauled.[38] Instead of focusing on the granting of permission for specific expenditures, the new system emphasizes evaluating an organization's managerial performance, and that of each of its departments (directorates-general). It finally led to the replacement of the previous 1977 Financial Regulation by a new 2002 regulation applicable to the General Budget of the European Communities.[39] The new system is based on a separation of the duties of the authorizing officer and the accounting officer, with the emphasis on the authorizing officer, whose function is central to the whole scheme: he or she must establish the organizational structure and internal management and control procedures suited to the performance of the duties assigned to the in-

---

The group recommended a simplification and updating of the budget procedure based on a number of principles outlined in the report. See further chapter 6, p. 302.

[35] To give an idea of the amounts involved, in 1999 the EC budget amounted to 83,978 billion euros, representing 1.2 percent of the Community GNP. The largest revenues came from Member State contributions, which were based on a uniform rate applied to net Value Added Tax (VAT) receipts (31.3 billion euros) and the relative gross national products of Member States (37.3 billion euros). The largest expenditure programs were the Common Agricultural Policy (CAP) schemes to support farmers and agricultural markets (39.8 billion euros) and the program of regional or structural funding to reduce regional disparities of wealth between Member State regions (26.6 billion euros): see Harlow, n. 1 above, figure 5.1 at 117. See also chapter 6, pp. 301 and 304.

[36] See Craig and de Búrca, *EU Law, Text, Cases and Materials* (Oxford: Oxford University Press, 2003), 108.

[37] Committee of Independent Experts, Second Report on Reform of the Commission (Sept. 10, 1999), n. 16 above.

[38] For a full account, see Harlow, n. 1 above, 116–23.

[39] Council Regulation 1605/2002 on the Financial Regulation Applicable to the General Budget of the European Communities, [2002] OJ L248/1. For a discussion, see Paul Craig, "The Constitutionalization of Community Administration,"28 *ELRev.*, 2003, 840–64.

stitution, whereas the accounting officer is responsible for payments, collection of revenue, and keeping the accounts, for example.[40]

In addition to internal auditing within the department responsible for the revenue or expenditure, the European Court of Auditors carries out an *external* audit for all of the Community institutions and bodies. Article 248 EC states that the court (which is not a court of law) "shall examine the accounts of all revenue and expenditure of the Community" and "examine whether all revenue has been received and all expenditure incurred in a lawful and regular manner and whether the financial management is sound." Consequently, the Court of Auditors should concentrate on the legality of budgetary operations, but also on managerial performance of the organization. That does not prevent criticism of the procedure applied by the court as being too bureaucratic and time-consuming, mainly because of the ("lawyerlike") contradictory nature of the procedure, which gives the services examined ample opportunity to water down the Court of Auditors' initial findings.[41]

b) New modes of governance

Setting up a procedure to approve and discharge the budget and checking whether the budget is correctly implemented, therefore ensuring *efficiency* in the use of resources, is one thing, and it is not easy to accomplish. It is even more difficult, however, to assess whether funds have been able to fulfill the goals and expectations of the citizenry, in other words to assess the *effectiveness* of the system of governance in terms of actual effect of intended action. Obviously, the conventional method of checking whether the correct processes were followed in budgeting and implementing public action ("accountability for process") can hardly be applied as a method for checking whether the goals set by a specific agency were actually met ("accountability for results").[42] Indeed, process is different from performance: the former is about compliance with rules and processes, the latter about fulfillment of expectations (in other

---

[40] Ibid., 846. The new system abolishes the system of *ex ante* visas, which, according to the Committee of Independent Experts, led to a culture that denuded officials of responsibility. By contrast, the new system is aimed at giving officials control over the activities for which they are responsible: ibid., 846–47. Regulation 1605/2002 distinguishes different methods of implementation of the budget: either by centralized management by the Commission directly or indirectly, or by shared or decentralized management with the Member States, or by joint management with international organizations: ibid., 841–42. See also chapter 2, pp. 95–97.

[41] See Harlow, n. 1 above, 126.

[42] Thus Robert D. Behn, *Rethinking Democratic Accountability* (Washington, DC: Brookings Institution Press, 2001).

words, "our, the citizens', desired results"). The former can be laid down in rules and processes, while the latter cannot be codified.[43]

Improving (policy) effectiveness is part of the new methods of governance that, as mentioned above, have been developed since the early 1990s in areas where the traditional method of governance based on binding and uniform legislation is less useful or inappropriate. Those are areas where the interests and preferences of the Member States are less convergent. In the beginning, economic integration "was the proximate goal of the Original Six and the dominant motive of later accessions," whereby the Member States allowed the European institutions to "achieve a degree of market integration, economic interaction, and transnational mobility that has gone far beyond the original aspirations of the governments that had concluded the Treaty of Rome."[44] However, since the 1990s less convergence of Member State interests is found in policy areas of the second and the third pillars, or in areas of the first pillar where the emphasis is on policies rather than on rules, as in monetary and social matters. In those areas, national preferences have sufficiently high political salience to prevent agreement on strictly uniform European policies, and therefore differentiated European policies had to be developed to accommodate divergent national problems and preferences.[45] Hence, the need for new modes of governance—which in general refers to methods, such as "enhanced cooperation" (or "closer cooperation," as it is also called), the conclusion of "voluntary accords with and by private actors," and, most important, the "open method of coordination" (OMC).

Of these three methods, "enhanced cooperation"—an instrument already discussed in chapter 1—has not yet been applied but may gain importance after the forthcoming enlargement.[46] The second instrument, "voluntary ac-

---

[43] Ibid., 113. To create accountability for the fulfillment of citizens' expectations, Behn proposes a new concept of accountability, a "compact," or ethical commitment, of mutual, collective responsibility, "an understanding in which every member makes a mutually supportive commitment to every other member and to their common purpose" (125–56 and 198). Under such a compact, "people are not merely evaluated by their hierarchical superior. They are also evaluated by their subordinates, their peers . . . by their internal and external customers as well as their internal and external suppliers." This, Behn adds, "requires us to escape from our simple dichotomous world occupied by accountability holders and accountability holdees" (204).

[44] Fritz W. Scharpf, "Legitimate Diversity: The New Challenge of European Integration," in *The State of the European Union*, ed. Tanja A. Börzel and Rachel A. Cichowski (Oxford: Oxford University Press, 2003), 79–104, at 85–86. The Treaty of Rome referred to in the quotation is the EEC Treaty, now the EC Treaty.

[45] Ibid., 99.

[46] See above, pp. 30–31 and 32–33.

cords," is particularly used in the area of social policy: for instance, Articles 137–39 EC foresee consultation of management and labor at Community level as a means of involving organizations of employers and trade unions in the decision-making process. The third instrument, OMC, was introduced for the first time in the Maastricht Treaty to coordinate economic policies of Member States[47] and appeared again, this time for the coordination of employment policies, in the Amsterdam Treaty.[48]

The method "implies that member governments should agree to define certain policy purposes or problems as matters of 'common concern', whereas the actual choice of effective policies should remain a national responsibility. Its core is an iterative procedure."[49] The successive components of that procedure are: first, a report from the Commission to the European Council; then, guidelines of the Council based on a Commission proposal; followed by national action plans and subsequent reports on action taken by national governments; and, thereafter, evaluation in light of comparative benchmarks by the Commission and by a permanent committee of senior civil servants. This all finally leads to new guidelines, or—the only formal sanction—to specific recommendations of the Council,[50] after which the whole procedure may start again. The vocabulary of this new method is: negotiation of policy targets and time schedules; diffusion and learning of good practices; benchmarking; persuasion and standardization of knowledge about the implementation of policies; and repetitive processes of monitoring and target readjustment.[51]

Political scientists have examined the usefulness of the new methods of governance from a viewpoint of political capacity (or efficiency) and policy effectiveness. To that effect, a political process "is considered to have political capacity (a) when a decision can be reached without long negotiations, and (b) when it enjoys the political support of all actors concerned and therefore has a high consensus capacity."[52] Policy effectiveness is defined, by contrast, "as the use of particular policy instruments, in such a way as to increase the chance to achieve the defined policy target."[53] Theoretical and empirical analysis indicates[54] that both the political capacity and policy effectiveness of the

---

[47] Articles 98–99 EC.
[48] Articles 125–30 EC.
[49] Scharpf, n. 44 above, 101.
[50] Ibid., 101–2.
[51] Héritier, n. 10 above, 106.
[52] Ibid., 107.
[53] Ibid., 113.
[54] The theoretical argument is based on political transaction costs theory, on principal-agent theory, and on the theory of negotiating democracy; the empirical analysis

new modes of governance depend on the particular type of problem dealt with in the policy-making process. More specifically, problems that are unlikely to lend themselves to the new modes are: redistributive problems that trigger differences between those who lose and those who benefit from a policy measure; "prisoner's dilemma" problems, where one actor profits from the rule-abiding behavior of the other actors, but where free-riding may occur at the level of implementation; and problems involving policies that are institutionally deeply entrenched, embedded in longstanding national traditions. By contrast, the new modes lend themselves better to distributive, coordinative, or network goods policies that are equally beneficial to all concerned, as well as policy areas where diverse, highly complex/uncertain, or discrete problems are at stake.[55]

The overall conclusion is that new methods of governance are useful under the right circumstances but they need the support of a legally binding instrument such as a "framework" directive, that is, a directive that simply contains core principles, thus leaving more room for the discretion of national policy makers than is normally true of EU directives.[56] Indeed, if, for instance, policy effectiveness is to be achieved, basic binding legislation, or at least the threat of it, must go on to play an important role in underpinning the process.[57] That conclusion is not different from the one reached by legal analysis, which emphasizes that the rule of law concept requires legal support for the new methods.[58] Unsurprisingly, the conclusion is strongly underlined by EU lawyers whose work (and interest) focuses on binding legislative and administrative measures and on judicial rulings.[59] Unfortunately, this was also the focus of the Convention members drafting a constitutional treaty, who rejected a general clause on OMC and agreed only on some references in specific areas, thus forgoing the chance of providing the new instruments of governance with a solid basis in law.[60]

---

is based on three case studies: the Temporary Workers Agreement/Directive, the European Employment Strategy, and the Auto-Oil Programme.

[55] Héritier, n. 10 above, 123–26.

[56] Scharpf, n. 44 above, 102. Under the first pillar, the legal notion of framework directive does not exist in the sense indicated. This does not prevent the instrument from being used in practice, for instance in the area of European securities markets: see the Final Report of the Committee of Wise Men on the Regulation of European Securities Markets (the so-called Lamfalussy Report) of February 15, 2001, at 22–25; see also n. 12 above.

[57] Héritier, n. 10 above, 125.

[58] Reich et al., n. 13 above, 292–93.

[59] Thus de Búrca, n. 8 above, 815; see also chapter 6, pp. 258, n. 8, and 274–75.

[60] Ibid., 837–38, and chapter 6.

II. EQUALITY IN LAW AND AFFIRMATIVE ACTION

Good governance, as we understand it here,[61] is not only about procedures but also about aims and results. An important aim is equal concern for citizens in helping them to achieve their personal goals. It requires public authorities to treat citizens—and residents[62]—alike before the law, to eliminate discrimination, and, where appropriate, to take "affirmative action," as it is called in the United States—"positive action," as it is also called in the EU—to remove consequences of past discrimination. Equality in law and affirmative action in the EU in comparison with the United States are the subjects discussed in this section. In the EU, equal concern is understood to imply also that public authorities should regard human dignity and the pursuit of social justice as an aim of the welfare state—a theme discussed in the following section.

Equal Protection in the European Union and the United States

Article 20 (1) of the EU Charter of Fundamental Rights states: "Everyone is equal before the law."[63] In EU law, the principle of equality began life as a limited prohibition on discrimination on the basis of *nationality*, insofar as free movement of goods, services, enterprises, and workers across state borders was hindered thereby, and as an equally limited prohibition on discrimination on the basis of *gender*, insofar as equal pay of workers was concerned. As such, it played a role in the initial "common market"–oriented European Community as a market-unifying device only. Over the years, the prohibition on discrimination was transformed, however, into a general constitutional right to equal treatment[64]—an evolution that was the result of a complex process of interaction between complaints and pleas of litigating parties, case law of Community and national courts, pressure groups, Council legislation, and treaty amendments.

The evolution turned around three themes. The first theme arose very early in the Community's existence. It consisted of the development of case

---

[61] See above, p. 158.

[62] The focus in this section and the following will be on citizens. For the protection of (legal and illegal) residents, see below, pp. 206–7.

[63] Charter of Fundamental Rights of the European Union, [2000] OJ C364/01, Art. 20 (1).

[64] For a history of the principle, see Gillian More, "The Principle of Equal Treatment: From Market Unifier to Fundamental Right?" in *The Evolution of EU Law*, ed. Paul Craig and Gráinne de Burca (Oxford: Oxford University Press, 1999), 517–53.

law allowing "peripheral" market participants such as part-time workers, artists, students, and tourists from other Member States to benefit, within certain limits, from equal treatment with the nationals of a Member State. One example is the ECJ's seminal judgment in *Cowan* concerning a British tourist who had been attacked in Paris. The Court held that the French administration's refusal to grant the tourist relief under the French criminal compensation scheme was inconsistent with the principle of free movement of services laid down in Article 59 (now 49) EC.[65]

The second theme related to discrimination in equal pay for male and female workers, prohibited by Article 119 (now 141) EC. This theme also developed very early in the Union's life, first as a result of legislation and case law concerning that treaty provision that gradually turned the specific prohibition on unequal pay into a more general prohibition ensuring men and women equal treatment with regard to a variety of issues such as access to employment, vocational training, promotion, working conditions, and social security benefits.[66] Later, the 1997 Amsterdam Treaty incorporated this general discrimination prohibition in Article 3(2) EC, which requires Community institutions, in all their activities, "to eliminate inequalities, and to promote equality, between men and women." Around the same time, the ECJ referred to the principle in its case law as a fundamental human right that it is bound to ensure, even in relations of employment, for example with regard to retaliatory measures adopted by an employer against an employee who had sued the employer before a court of law.[67]

At a later stage, the principle of equal treatment was finally expanded into an even more general principle, now unconnected with nationality or gender. Article 13 EC, inserted by the 1997 Treaty of Amsterdam and amended by the 2000 Treaty of Nice, empowers the Council to "take appropriate action to combat discrimination based on sex, racial or ethnic origin, religion or belief, disability, age or sexual orientation."[68] This led in 2000 to the enactment of

---

[65] Case 186/87, *Cowan v. Le Trésor Public*, [1989] ECR 195.

[66] See, among others, Council Directive 76/207 [1976] OJ L39/40 (access to employment and working conditions) and Council Directive 79/7 [1979] OJ L6/24 (social security).

[67] Case C-185/97, *Coote v. Granada Hospitality Ltd.*, [1998] ECR I-5199. In *Coote* the ECJ relied on an earlier judgment in which it had proclaimed the right not to be discriminated against to be a fundamental right. In that case it found in favor of a worker who had been discriminated against because he had informed his employer of his intention to undergo, and then had undergone, a gender-reassignment operation: Case C-13/94, *P. v. S. and Cornwall County Council*, [1996] ECR I-2143.

[68] Now Article 13 (1) EC.

three implementing documents: a directive prohibiting any discrimination on grounds of race or ethnic origin; a second directive prohibiting discrimination on grounds of religion, belief, disability, age, or sexual orientation in the field of employment;[69] and an action plan to combat discrimination on all grounds listed in Article 13.[70]

Equal protection in the United States is based on the Fourteenth Amendment [1868].[71] The amendment provides that no state shall "deny to any person within its jurisdiction the equal protection of the laws." Although literally it applies only to state action, judicial interpretation has made it applicable to the federal government as well, as an aspect of Fifth Amendment due process.[72] Equal protection has for a long time focused mainly on racial discrimination, to the extent that in early cases the Supreme Court even suggested that racial concerns exhausted the meaning of the clause.[73] Since then, the clause has been applied in many contexts outside race discrimination, not the least in gender discrimination cases. This does not mean, though, that the concept of equal protection is applied in all instances with the same vigor. A remarkable aspect of equal protection in the United States is indeed the variation in judicial scrutiny, depending on the area involved. The Supreme Court uses three types of scrutiny: 1) strict scrutiny, as applied in race discrimination, 2) rationality review, which is the most deferential form of review, as applied with re-

---

[69] The first directive ("Race") is Council Directive 2000/43, implementing the principle of equal treatment between persons irrespective of racial or ethnic origin, [2000] OJ L180/22. The directive is particularly broad in scope and content and contains, apart from general and final provisions, provisions on remedies and enforcement as well as on the creation of bodies for the promotion of equal treatment. The second directive ("Framework Employment") is Council Directive 2000/78 and establishes a general framework for equal treatment in employment and occupation, [2000] OJ L303/16.

[70] The action program was laid out in Council Decision 200/750, [2000] OJ L303/23. For comments, see Lisa Waddington and Mark Bell, "More Equal Than Others: Distinguishing European Union Equality Directives," 38 *CMLRev.*, 2001, 587–611. For a more recent analysis by the same authors, see Mark Bell and Lisa Waddington, "Reflecting on Inequalities in European Equality Law," 28 *ELRev.*, 2003, 349–69.

[71] In 1923, an Equal Rights Amendment to the U.S. Constitution was proposed according to which "Equality of rights under the law shall not be denied or abridged by the United States or by any state on account of sex." Later approved by Congress, the amendment is not yet in effect as it has only been ratified by thirty-five of the thirty-eight states required. More information is available at http:/www.equalrightsamendment.org/.

[72] Sullivan and Gunther, *Constitutional Law*, 14th ed. (New York: Foundation Press, 2001), 601, n. 1.

[73] Ibid., 601, with a reference to the *Slaughter-House* cases, 83 U.S. 36 (1872).

gard to economic regulations,[74] and 3) intermediate review, which is a heightened form of review in between the two other forms, and is seemingly applied in cases of gender discrimination, and of discrimination against aliens.[75]

Each of these forms of scrutiny is characterized by methodological differences: 1) the lowest form of judicial scrutiny, rationality review, requires the legislation under scrutiny to pursue "legitimate" ends through "reasonably" related means; 2) strict scrutiny requires legislation to be justified by "compelling" ends, and requires the means employed to be "necessary" (that is, no other less restrictive means must be available), and 3) the intermediate form is satisfied with "important" ends, and with "substantially" related means.[76] Although the distinction is relatively clear in theory, its application to specific areas is not always straightforward (with the exception of race discrimination, where strict scrutiny is invariably used). Gender discrimination is a case in point. Until the 1950s, the Supreme Court applied at best a rationality standard.[77] Then, in 1971, it applied heightened scrutiny in *Reed v. Reed*,[78] though using simple rationality test language. Later, in 1973, the Court attempted, in *Frontiero v. Richardson*, to extend the strict scrutiny test from race to gender discrimination by making classifications based on gender "inherently suspect."[79] But in *Craig v. Boren*, already referred to, the Supreme Court ended up devising a middle-tier analysis.[80] That ruling was clarified in later judgments to mean that the legislation under scrutiny must have an "exceedingly persuasive justification."[81]

[74] For an example, see *Williamson v. Lee Optical Co.*, 348 U.S. 483 (1955), where the Supreme Court rejected an equal protection as well as a due process clause challenge to Oklahoma's scheme for the regulation of opticians, and *McGowan v. Maryland*, 366 U.S. 420 (1961), where state Sunday closing laws were sustained against challenges based not only on the religion clauses of the First Amendment, but also on equal protection.

[75] For an overview, see Sullivan and Gunther, n. 72 above, 602–4.

[76] Thus in *Craig v. Boren*, 429 U.S. 190 (1976), a case concerning gender differential in age in a state statute prohibiting the sale of "non-intoxicating" 3.2 percent beer.

[77] For instance in *Goesaert v. Cleary*, 335 U.S. 464 (1948), in which the court upheld a Michigan statute prohibiting a woman from being a bartender unless she was the wife or daughter of the male owner of a licensed establishment.

[78] 404 U.S. 71 (1971), striking down a statute that preferred male estate administrators assuming that they had more business experience than women.

[79] 411 U.S. 677 (1973); quotation at 682.

[80] N. 76 above. All these examples come from Redlich, Attanasio, and Goldstein, *Understanding Constitutional Law*, 2d ed. (New York: LexisNexis, 1999), 287–90, with many more references in the following pages.

[81] See particularly *United States v. Virginia*, 518 U.S. 515 (1996), excerpted and discussed in Sullivan and Gunther, n. 72 above, at 659ff.

Discrimination against aliens offers another interesting point of comparison with Community law. As mentioned above, in Community law the principle of equal treatment was primarily developed in the areas of nationality and gender discrimination. From a comparative viewpoint, it is therefore noteworthy that the U.S. Supreme Court has similarly used the "strict scrutiny" standard to invalidate state laws that excluded "resident aliens from the legal profession, denied them welfare benefits, prevented them from becoming notaries public, barred them from all other classes of state competitive civil service jobs, and restricted their access to financial aid."[82] However, the Supreme Court has declined to apply strict scrutiny to federal laws because of the involvement of federal government with immigration and naturalization, and it also makes an exception for state laws with regard to "political functions."[83] With respect to illegal aliens, the Supreme Court has used the Equal Protection Clause as well, this time to strike down a Texas law denying free public education to undocumented school-age children.[84]

However brief, the preceding overview shows some interesting points of comparison. This holds particularly true for the Supreme Court's use of three different standards of scrutiny in a variety of areas—as may also become the case in the European Union, now that Article 13 (1) EC and related implementing legislation prohibit a large number of discriminatory practices unconnected with nationality or gender. As is well known, the EU courts, both the ECJ and the CFI, as well as the European Court of Human Rights (ECtHR) and the supreme courts of most of the EU Member States, use a similar standard of scrutiny, embodied in the principle of proportionality, which also has a different content depending on the matter at hand.[85] Other issues of common interest are those relating to burden of proof, remedies at the disposal of the courts to redress discrimination, equal protection in private relations

[82] Redlich, Attanasio, and Goldstein, n. 80 above, 326, with references for each of these categories. In the leading case, *Graham v. Richardson*, 403 U.S. 365 (1971), the Supreme Court, using preemption as an alternative basis, held a University of Maryland rule denying lower in-state tuition to resident aliens unconstitutional. This case is to be compared with the ECJ's judgment in Case 293/83, *Gravier v. City of Liège*, [1985] ECR 593, which related, however, to a national of another Member State.

[83] Ibid., 326–27.

[84] In *Plyer v. Doe*, 457 U.S. 202 (1982).

[85] See Craig and de Bùrca, n. 36 above, 373–74, who see a distinct use of the proportionality principle, i.e., with a varying degree of scrutiny depending on the subject matter. Thus, in cases involving policy choices, there is a more deferential approach; in cases challenging penalties imposed, the scrutiny is more intense; and in cases of administrative action interfering with an individual's Community rights, the proportionality test is applied with the most vigor.

(mainly employer/employee relations), and the significance of equal protection for illegal aliens.

Affirmative Action Correcting Race and Gender Discrimination

It is one thing for citizens to be equal before the law, but it is quite another for them to be equal in practice. Although it is impossible for any state or political community to achieve the latter, no government can be regarded as legitimate if it does not, in Dworkin's words, practice the sovereign virtue of "show[ing] equal concern for the fate of all those citizens over whom it claims dominion and from whom it claims allegiance."[86] Such equal concern may imply a duty, under certain conditions, to redress current factual inequalities that are the consequence of unequal treatment imposed or permitted in the past by a dominant culture, and the law supporting it. That may include an obligation to take "affirmative action," or "positive action" as it is called in Europe, in favor of disadvantaged groups. In the United States such affirmative action relates primarily to race differences, while in the European Community positive action was first undertaken—because of the historically "market-related" origin of the equality principle[87]—with respect to gender discrimination in pay and, later, working conditions.

In the United States, the legality of affirmative action under the Equal Protection Clause[88]—"benign" discrimination, as it is called[89]—is assessed in accordance with Justice Powell's judgment in the case *Regents of California v. Bakke*,[90] decided by the Supreme Court in 1978.[91] In that case the Medical

[86] Ronald Dworkin, *Sovereign Virtue: The Theory and Practice of Equality* (Cambridge, Mass.: Harvard University Press, 2002), 1, adding that "when a nation's wealth is very unequally distributed, as the wealth of even very prosperous nations now is, then its equal concern is suspect."

[87] See above, p. 171.

[88] Title VII of the Civil Rights Act of 1964 is the principal federal statute dealing with discrimination, as regards employment, based on race, gender, and certain other impermissible criteria. While the Equal Protection Clause concerns public action, broadly understood, Title VII also protects private employees.

[89] "Benign" because racial classifications are used for "benign" purposes, that is, to aid rather than disadvantage minorities. See Sullivan and Gunther, n. 72 above, where many pervasive questions that arise in a context of "benign," or "reverse," discrimination are listed (750–51).

[90] 438 U.S. 265 (1978).

[91] Four justices concurred as to the result, namely, invalidating the program, albeit for different reasons. For an overview, see Redlich, Attanasio, and Goldstein, n. 80 above, 308–13, from which I have borrowed the elements mentioned in the text. See also Sullivan and Gunther, n. 72 above, 752, where large excerpts are reproduced from Justice Powell's judgment for the court, and from the opinions of the other justices,

School of the University of California at Davis had designed an admission program to admit sixteen minority students into the entering class of one hundred. A special admissions committee reviewed applicants who identified themselves as minorities (defined as Blacks, Chicanos, Asians, and American Indians). The committee recommended minority candidates until the prescribed number of spaces was filled. As a result of the system, *Bakke*, a white applicant, was rejected twice by the regular admissions committee, although minority applicants with significantly lower grade point averages had been admitted by the special admissions committee.

Announcing the judgment of the Court in *Bakke*, Justice Powell rejected the argument that white males did not merit special Fourteenth Amendment protection. He held that each group having to struggle to overcome prejudices, either of a monolithic majority or of a majority composed of various minorities, was entitled to invoke protection. To assess the university's program, he applied the strict scrutiny test (though there remained some doubt because of the use of the word "substantial" rather than "compelling" to justify the end pursued by the contested measure). Justice Powell rejected three of the four interests posited by the university to justify its special program:[92] 1) the historic deficit of traditionally disfavored minorities in medical schools and in the medical profession; 2) curing societal discrimination suffered by particular minorities; and 3) promoting health care services to underserved communities.[93] But he accepted the fourth, which is that a diverse student body encourages a robust exchange of ideas, thus engaging the First Amendment interest in freedom of speech. He found, however, that the university's admission program did not constitute the necessary means of achieving that end. He suggested that a program like that used at Harvard College was a more acceptable method of achieving diversity because it considered a number of factors such as economic disadvantage, race, and ethnicity along with geographical location and special talents, all of which contributed to the diversity of the university.

Bakke is understood to allow universities to offer a "plus factor" to minority students if the purpose of the system is to improve racial diversity among

concurring and dissenting in part (Powell's judgment therefore being "a majority of one").

[92] See Redlich, Attanasio, and Goldstein, n. 80 above, 311.

[93] The reasons for rejecting these grounds of justification were that the first amounted to preferring one group for the sake of race, that the second aided members of the victimized groups at the expense of innocent people, and that, for the third, there was no evidence on record to prove that the program would effectuate the goal pursued: ibid.

students, provided that it does not stipulate fixed minority quotas but takes race into account as one factor among several.[94] The doctrine became a cornerstone of affirmative action, which, as appears from an analysis of a large number of admission records,[95] succeeded in the most selective colleges and universities "in educating sizable numbers of minority students who have already achieved considerable success and seem likely to in time occupy positions of leadership throughout society . . . and [resulted in making] academically selective colleges and universities . . . highly successful in using race-sensitive admissions policies to advance educational goals important to everyone."[96] The doctrine was nevertheless challenged recently following an announcement by President Bush in January 2000 that his administration would seek the invalidation before the Supreme Court of race-sensitive admission policies of the University of Michigan.[97] In the minds of many, it would have been unfortunate if *Bakke* had been reversed.

In its judgment rendered on June 23, 2003, in the first of these cases, *Grutter v. Bollinger,* the Supreme Court has paid heed to these considerations holding, with regard to the University of Michigan Law School's program, that it narrowly tailored use of race in admissions decisions to further a compelling interest in obtaining the educational benefits that flow from a diverse student body and is therefore not prohibited by the Equal Protection Clause. In that judgment the Court endorses Justice Powell's view, in *Bakke,* that student body diversity is a compelling state interest in the context of university admissions.[98] In its second judgment of the same date, *Gratz v. Bollinger,* the Supreme Court applies Justice Powell's opinion again, now however to reach the opposite conclusion, and to reject the admission program of the University of Michigan's College of Literature, Science, and the Arts, "because it was not narrowly tailored to achieve the respondents' asserted interest in diversity . . . [as] it automatically distributes one fifth of the points needed to guarantee

[94] See Dworkin, n. 86 above, 387.

[95] See William G. Bowen, Derek Bok, and Glenn C. Loury, *The Shape of the River* (Princeton, N.J.: Princeton University Press, 2000).

[96] Dworkin, n. 86 above, 390–91.

[97] The cases were argued before the court on Tuesday, April 1, 2003. Excerpts from arguments in one of the cases, *Grutter v. Bollinger,* were reproduced in the *New York Times,* April 2, 2003, A12. The plea, in both cases, of the white applicants who were not admitted was supported, on behalf of the Bush administration, by the U.S. solicitor general, Theodore B. Olson. The administration's position was that the Michigan programs are unconstitutional because the university had failed to show that it cannot achieve diversity through a race-neutral alternative: ibid., A13.

[98] See http://caselaw.lp.findlaw.com/scripts/getcase.pl?court=US&vol=000&invol= 02–241, *Grutter v. Bollinger et al.,* at pp. 9–13.

admission to every single 'underrepresented minority' applicant solely because of race."[99] In the end, the *Bakke* test thus survived as a principle which, in practice, may lead to different applications.[100]

In the European Union, positive action has been used principally under Article 2 (4) of Council Directive 76/207 of February 9, 1976, mainly "to promote equal opportunity for men and women, in particular by removing existing inequalities which affect women's opportunities"[101] as regards employment opportunities, vocational training and promotion, and working conditions. The 1997 Amsterdam Treaty has confirmed this position in more general terms in Article 141 (4) EC. The article now permits Member States to maintain or adopt measures "providing for specific advantages in order to make it easier for the underrepresented sex to pursue a vocational activity or to prevent or compensate for disadvantages in professional careers." It also features in the new directive combating discrimination on grounds of racial or ethnic origin[102] and in the Framework Employment Directive.[103]

The ECJ has decided several cases under Article 2 (4) of the 1976 directive.[104] In the *Abrahamsson* judgment, the Court considered the appointment of Elisabeth Fogelqvist to the chair of Hydrospheric Sciences at the University of Göteborg. The appointment was made in accordance with a provision of Swedish law, which provided that a candidate for a public post belonging to the underrepresented sex must be given preference over a candidate of the opposite sex when "the difference between the merits of the candidates of each sex is not so great as to result in a breach of the requirement of objectivity in making appointments."[105] The Court found this provision to be inconsistent with Article 2 (4) of the Directive, arguing that the provision as formulated

[99] See http://caselaw.lp.findlaw.com/scripts/getcase.pl?court=US&vol=000&invol=02-516, *Gratz v. Bollinger.*

[100] For a comment on the judgments, see Mark Tushnet, "United States: Supreme Court Rules on Affirmative Action," 2 *International Journal of Constitutional Law*, 2004, 158–73.

[101] N. 66 above.

[102] Article 5 Racial Equality Directive referred to in n. 69 above. The article allows Member States "with a view to ensuring full equality in practice . . ." to maintain or adopt "specific measures to prevent or compensate for disadvantages linked to racial or ethnic origin."

[103] Article 7 Framework Employment Directive referred to in n. 69 above.

[104] For an analysis of the underlying concepts of equality, and the differences in treatment and approaches in the Community equality directives, see Bell and Waddington, n. 70 above.

[105] Thus in the ECJ's judgment in Case C-407/98, *Katarina Abrahamsson and Leif Anderson v. Elisabeth Fogelqvist,* [2000] ECR I-5539.

grants an automatic preference to a candidate whose merits are inferior to those of a candidate of the opposite sex.[106]

In earlier cases the ECJ had dealt with recruitment disputes in which the male and female candidates possessed the same qualifications. Perhaps the most interesting case, because of the outspoken nature of the court's underlying reasoning, is *Marschall*.[107] In that case, a German regional law required women to be given priority over men for promotion to a higher grade post in the event of equal suitability, competence, and professional performance, unless reasons specific to an individual male candidate tilted the balance in his favor. The Court upheld the law, arguing that "it appears that, even where male and female candidates are equally qualified, male candidates tend to be promoted in preference to female candidates particularly because of prejudices and stereotypes concerning the role and capacities of women in working life and the fear, for example, that women will interrupt careers more frequently, that owing to household and family duties they will be less flexible in their working hours, or that they will be absent from work more frequently because of pregnancy, childbirth and breastfeeding."[108]

The *Marschall* judgment is unique because it openly describes "prejudices and stereotypes" that continue to prevail while illustrating a more permissive approach toward positive action than earlier case law. The Court was clearly more permissive, for example, than it was in *Kalanke*,[109] in which it held that positive action legislation was a "derogation" from the right to equal treatment, and therefore must be strictly scrutinized. In fact, the Court followed its *Marschall* judgment with an even more permissive approach in *Badeck*,[110]

---

[106] The court was specifically concerned with an unclear objectivity requirement that was not amenable to review. It stated that the law did not "obviate any arbitrary assessment of the qualifications of the candidates," and did not allow an "objective assessment taking account of the specific personal situations of all the candidates." Furthermore, the court found that the criterion used was "ultimately based on the mere fact of belonging to the under-represented sex": paras. 52, 49, and 53 of the judgment.

[107] Case C-409/95, *Hellmut Marschall v. Land Nordrhein Westfalen*, [1997] ECR I-6363.

[108] Para. 29 of the judgment. For excerpts from this and other related judgments, and for a discussion of positive action, see Craig and de Búrca, n. 36 above, 888–94.

[109] Case C-450/93, *Kalanke v. Freie Hansestadt Bremen*, [1995] ECR I-3051. *Marschall* is seen by many as an instance of the court taking heed of vociferous criticism of *Kalanke*, the facts of which were less readily distinguishable from *Marschall* than the court makes out.

[110] Case C-158/97, *Badeck v. Landesanwalt beim Staatsgerichtshof des Landes Hessen*, [1999] ECR I-1875.

where the court found that even rather strict forms of positive action, such as quotas, were permitted at the *pre*-selection stage, such as quotas for women for training places and for interviews for open positions.

The European Court's attitude can be summarized as follows. First, affirmative action cannot be based on the mere fact that a group is underrepresented; only specific measures genuinely designed to reduce de facto inequalities and to compensate for disadvantages in the professional or educational life of persons belonging to the underrepresented group are permitted. Second, specific measures must be based on transparent and objective criteria that are amenable to review in order to obviate arbitrariness. Third, measures must contain sufficient flexibility to allow the personal situations and individual qualifications of a person not belonging to the underrepresented group to be taken into account. Fourth, specific measures to reduce inequalities and to compensate for disadvantages may not be "disproportionate to the aim pursued."[111] This implies that differences in qualifications between sufficiently qualified candidates belonging to the underrepresented group and candidates of the opposite sex who would otherwise have been selected should remain limited.

It would be audacious, after this succinct overview, to compare positive action in the case law of the ECJ with affirmative action in that of the U.S. Supreme Court—for example, comparing *Abrahamsson* with *Bakke*, both cases having been rendered in the educational field in favor of a candidate with lesser qualifications. The first judgment relates to gender, the second to race discrimination.[112] Nevertheless, there are some "methodological" similarities that deserve to be mentioned here. In both instances, the tests applied by the two courts imply a high degree of scrutiny and operate both ways, that is, traditionally dominant males/whites may also complain about being discriminated against on the basis of gender or race. Moreover, in both cases the test implies justification of the discriminatory measure in light of the end pursued, and of the means applied to reach that end. The major difference, though, concerns the *nature* of the end deemed to justify discrimination. In the Euro-

---

[111] *Abrahamsson*, n. 105, para. 55. In this statement, the ECJ is referring to Article 141 (4) EC, indicating that the provision comes into play only when the court has found that national "positive action" legislation is inconsistent with more specific directive provisions, such as Article 2 (4) of Directive 76/207. See n. 66 above.

[112] In *Bakke* Justice Powell referred to the materially different contexts of race and gender discrimination: preferential programs premised upon sex present less analytical and pragmatic problems because only two possible classifications are involved, and race discrimination has a long, odious, and tragic history: Redlich, Attanasio, and Goldstein, n. 80 above, 308.

pean gender discrimination cases, such as *Abrahamsson* and *Marschall*, removing inequalities affecting the opportunities of women is openly mentioned as justification for positive action. In the American race discrimination cases, at least in educational cases like *Bakke* and the subsequent *Bollinger* cases, the only ground of justification is the "compelling interest in obtaining the educational benefits that flow from a diverse student body."[113]

No such difference exists, however, with regard to sex discrimination cases, as is made clear in *Johnson v. Transportation Agency*,[114] a case decided by the U.S. Supreme Court that presents a striking resemblance with the *Marschall* judgment of the European Court of Justice.[115] In *Johnson* the Supreme Court upheld an affirmative action plan intended to remedy underrepresentation not only of racial minorities, but also of women in certain positions. Although 76 percent of the office and clerical workers at the agency were women, they held less than 10 percent of administrative, professional, and technical positions. The agency's action plan set aside no specific positions for minorities or women, but authorized consideration of ethnicity or gender as a factor when evaluating qualified candidates. Writing for the Court, Justice Brennan noted that this feature supported the legality of the plan because, as in *Bakke*, these criteria were not the sole factors in choosing an applicant. Moreover, the disparities between the scores of the women and the rejected male applicant were small.[116]

The preceding overview shows that equality in law is as much a concern of good governance in the European Union as it is in the United States and that, following the example of the United States, the Union is equally prepared to take affirmative or positive action. The overview also shows that the courts in both jurisdictions are ready to validate such action within certain limits, and along similar lines. To be sure, historically and institutionally different backgrounds explain why the emphasis is on race discrimination in the United States while the focus has been on discrimination on the basis of nationality and gender in the European Union. That may change, however, now that the EC law principle of equal treatment has been expanded by the ECJ in recent years into a general principle, unconnected with nationality or gender.[117]

---

[113] Thus in the ruling of *Grutter v. Bollinger et al.*, n. 97.

[114] 480 U.S. 616 (1987). For an overview, see Redlich, Attanasio, and Goldstein, n. 80 above, 314ff.

[115] N. 107 above.

[116] Redlich, Attanasio, and Goldstein, n. 80 above, 316.

[117] A case that raises similar problems in both jurisdictions is the case of stable homosexual relationships. In *D. v. Council*, the ECJ had to pronounce itself on the question whether a same-sex partner of a civil servant employed by the Council of Minis-

III. SOCIAL JUSTICE AND THE WELFARE STATE

Is social justice a matter to be pursued by the welfare state as an objective of good governance? The answer to that question will differ from one country to another, depending on the goal that it assigns to social welfare policy. In that respect there are large differences between Europe and the United States. In the United States, social welfare policies, including general assistance programs that give money or food to qualifying individuals, are ostensibly designed to benefit the poor and the elderly. In European states, social welfare programs are set up to help the general public through social insurance that covers income losses due to illness, unemployment, and retirement. The difference relates to an even more basic difference in political culture and the values it advances.[118] In the United States, there is an emphasis on self-reliance and rugged individualism. These are values that encourage individuals to seek remedies from within themselves rather than from government or society.[119] In Europe that philosophy does not prevail.

The different attitudes regarding social welfare policy point to an even more fundamental difference in mentality. This mentality is analyzed by Har-

---

ters could be denied a household allowance under the provisions of the Community's staff regulations: Cases C-122 and C-125/99P [2001] ECR I-4319. The ECJ decided that it could not "interpret the Staff Regulations in such a way that legal situations distinct from marriage are treated in the same way as marriage" (para. 37 of the judgment). To reach that conclusion, it stated that "it is clear, that apart from their great diversity, such arrangements for registering relationships between couples not previously recognized in law are regarded in the Member States concerned as being distinct from marriage" (para. 36). It added that this is a matter for the legislature, in that case the Union legislature, for example by amending the provisions of the staff regulations (para. 38). In the United States, the recognition of gay marriages by state laws is a controversial matter. Recently, the Massachusetts Supreme Court ruled—in response to a request by the Massachusetts Senate asking whether a bill gave same-sex couples the same rights and benefits of marriage even though their relationships were called civil unions—that such a bill "would have the effect of maintaining and fostering a stigma of exclusion that the (Massachusetts) Constitution prohibits." *New York Times*, February 5, 2004, 1 and 23. In a statement issued by the White House, President Bush found the ruling "deeply troubling," leaving little doubt that he is heading toward backing a change to the U.S. Constitution: ibid.

[118] For an excellent analysis with further references, see Stella Z. Theodoulou, from California State University, *Policy and Politics in Six Nations* (Upper Saddle River, N.J.: Prentice Hall, 2002). Social welfare and health care are two policies, among others, that she examines in Brazil, Germany, the U.K., Japan, Sweden, and the United States. On social welfare, see 101–33.

[119] Ibid., 128.

vard professor Mary Ann Glendon, who describes the "lonely rights bearer" mentality of American society, as compared with a society of citizens bound together in a community of solidarity. The latter view is typical, she believes, of the German constitutional order where the Federal Republic of Germany is proclaimed, in Article 20 (1) of the Basic Law, to be "a democratic and social federal state."

A Citizenship of Lonely Rights Bearers?

In *Rights Talk*, published in 1991, Glendon paints a gloomy picture of the "impoverishment of political discourse" in the United States and the effect of the "sound bite" on serious and sustained political discussion.[120] She notes that "in the home of free speech, genuine exchange of ideas about matters of high public importance has come to a virtual standstill." "Our current American rights," she goes on to say, "is . . . set apart from rights discourse in other liberal democracies by its starkness and simplicity, its prodigality in bestowing the rights label, its legalistic character, its exaggerated absoluteness, its hyper-individualism, its insularity, and its silence with respect to personal, civic, and collective responsibilities."[121]

Glendon describes the history of the American version of privacy as a distinctive feature of the American rights dialect, and opines that "its extraordinary homage to independence and self-sufficiency, based on an image of the rights-bearer as a self-determining, unencumbered individual, a being connected to others only by choice,"[122] contrasts with the European view. In the words of the German Constitutional Court, she adds, this view, especially the German version of it, is a "concept of man [that] is not that of an isolated, sovereign individual," but rather of a citizen that is related and bound to the community without detracting from his individuality.[123] As an illustration thereof, she refers to the U.S. Supreme Court's abortion case *Roe v. Wade*,[124]

---

[120] Mary Ann Glendon, *Rights Talk, The Impoverishment of Political Discourse* (New York: MacMillan, 1990), 1.

[121] Ibid. She believes that, in contrast with the stark emphasis on rights, there is an overwhelming silence in the United States about responsibilities, which is illustrated by the "no-duty-to-rescue" rule of American tort law (76–108).

[122] Ibid., 48.

[123] Ibid., 71 (referencing the judgment of the Constitutional Court of July 7, 1970).

[124] 410 U.S. 113 (1973). In that decision the Supreme Court invalidated a Texas law that made it a crime to procure or attempt an abortion except to save the life of the mother. Delivering the opinion of the court Justice Blackmun premised the right of the mother to choose an abortion on the constitutional right of privacy that derived from the concept of personal liberty in the Due Process Clause of the Fourteenth

and compares it with the German abortion judgment of February 25, 1975.[125] Whereas in Germany a woman's personal right to abortion is embedded in an array of counseling, medical care, and social assistance arrangements, in America, pregnant women have their constitutional right to privacy and little else.

Glendon attributes the difference in attitude to American legal education, which emphasizes a sharp distinction between law and morality. This reflects, in her view, distant divergences in the attitudes toward law taken by English and continental philosophers of natural rights:

> Rousseau's vigorous embrace—at a crucial juncture in European history—of the classical notion that law can and should help to shape society and to make good citizens of the individuals who compose it, together with Kant's emphasis on the ability of human beings to create and follow ethical norms, still figure importantly in the intellectual horizon of continental jurists. American lawyers, by contrast, have more fully accepted the Hobbesian idea of law as command, together with the strict separation—postulated by Hobbes and elaborated by John Austin—between law and morality.[126]

I am not in a position to judge the correctness of Mary Ann Glendon's assessment. To be sure, the American "rights culture" in litigation is perceived by many European lawyers as proof of a vindictive society, in which contingency fees, juries, class actions, and punitive damages play an excessive role in the adjudication especially of tort claims, emphasizing extreme restorative justice at the expense of distributive justice.[127] However, that in itself does not warrant Glendon's severe statement that American rights talk "seems to con-

---

Amendment. See further Sullivan and Gunther, n. 72 above, 521–31, where later cases are discussed in the following pages. See also judgment in *Casey*, n. 130 below.

[125] BVerfG, 39, 1. For a translation in English, see Robert E. Jonas and John D. Gorby, "West German Abortion Decision: A Contrast to Roe v. Wade," in *9 John Marshall J. of Prac. & Proc.* 605 (1978).

[126] Glendon, n. 120 above, 86.

[127] Recently there have been some developments to the contrary, such as the Bush administration's plan to limit medical malpractice liability by imposing a cap on compensation for non-physical damage and the Supreme Court's recent judgment to limit punitive damages in *Virginia v. Black*, No. 01–1107 (reported in the *New York Times* of April 8, 2003, A1 and A16). Furthermore, on May 22, 2003, a Florida appeals court threw out a landmark $145 billion punitive damage award against the nation's cigarette makers saying the case should never have gone forward as a class action suit on behalf of 300,000 smokers in the state, but rather as separate claims brought by individual smokers, because each one had started, and continued, to smoke for a different reason: *New York Times*, May 22, 2003, A21.

done acceptance of benefits of living in a democratic social welfare state, without accepting the corresponding personal and civic obligations."[128] Moreover, the 1975 judgment of the German Constitutional Court she refers to has in the meantime been overruled by another judgment of May 28, 1993,[129] and also *Roe v. Wade* has been followed by other judgments, more particularly *Casey*,[130] which has brought the American and German approaches much closer together.[131]

Mary Ann Glendon's analysis may nevertheless bear witness to a basic difference between American and European political thinking as regards the concept of welfare state. In a recent interview,[132] Michael Sandel, also a Harvard law professor,[133] was asked about the differences in European and American

[128] Glendon, n. 120 above, 1. As pointed out in chapter 3, pp. 115–18, in European Community law also there is a trend to reinforce individual rights by granting private parties remedies in tort against Community institutions and national public authorities, thus doing away with any kind of immunity even for legislatures. In that respect, the relevant case law of the European Court of Justice takes a much more rights-oriented approach than the U.S. Supreme Court. In the words of an American author, "for all of its rhetorical commitment to the rule of law . . . , the Supreme Court of the United States has recently forged quite a robust, constitutional doctrine of state sovereign immunity . . . that begins [with the Court's decision in] *Seminole Tribe v. Florida*": James E. Pfander, "Member State Liability and Constitutional Change in the United States and Europe," in *Am.J.Comp.L.*, 2003, 237–74, at 237. The *Seminole* judgment, 517 U.S. 44 (1996), broadens the state immunity from suit under the Eleventh Amendment. In that judgment, a suit was dismissed brought by an Indian tribe to compel Florida to perform its duty provided in a federal statute passed under the Indian Commerce Clause (Article I, § 8, U.S. Constitution) to negotiate in good faith with an Indian tribe toward the formation of a compact between the tribe and the pertinent state.

[129] BVerfG, 39, 1. Judgment of May 28, 1993. For a summary and a discussion in English, see Gerald L. Neumann, "*Casey* in the Mirror: Abortion, Abuse and the Right to Protection in the United States and Germany," 43 *Am.J.Comp.L.*, 1995, 273.

[130] *Planned Parenthood of Southeastern Pennsylvania v. Casey*, 505 U.S. 833 (1992). For a comparison of American and German (and Canadian) abortion cases, see, in addition to the articles referred to in the preceding notes, Vicki C. Jackson and Mark Tushnet, *Comparative Constitutional Law* (New York: Foundation Press, 1999), 1–143.

[131] The major difference is that in Germany the state has a positive duty to protect the life of the fetus, and to do so not only by prohibiting abortion but through counseling: Jackson and Tushnet, n. 130, 142. That is not so in the United States, where, since *Casey*, informed consent and counseling requirements are permissible but not required. See further Redlich, Attanasio, and Goldstein, n. 80 above, 225–28.

[132] In the Belgian newspaper *De Standaard*, July 11, 2002, in *Standaard der Letteren*, 8–9.

[133] Known for his books *Liberalism and the Limits of Justice* (Cambridge: Cambridge University Press, 1st ed. 1982, 2d ed. 1998) and *Democracy's Discontent* (Cambridge, Mass.: The Belknap Press of Harvard University Press, 1996).

attitudes. Sandel explained the prominence of the freedom of choice in America. That freedom of choice, he said, is closely related to the tradition of American individualism and freedom, seen not only as independence from any history or inherited status but also as freedom from any community. It implies choosing your own values and objectives in life, unhindered by public authorities and unencumbered by the past. That explains, according to him, differences in attitude with regard to the necessity for the state to set up public safety nets, for instance. Whereas in Europe such safety nets are regarded as instruments of solidarity between members belonging to the same political community, their necessity is recognized in America only insofar as they allow citizens to make their own choices. Sandel agrees that this may be a shortcoming in present American thinking, and believes that there is a need for a new "formative project," a new political vision of humans and society that is less individualistic and more concerned with the substantive content of a morally good life.[134]

Different Conceptions of the Welfare State

Whatever the merit of Sandel's "formative project,"[135] his analysis is an interesting point of departure for what may be seen as a basic difference in opinions in the United States and Europe on the role of a state in a democratic society.[136] In Europe, the notion is closely linked to the existence of a comprehensive (and expensive) social security system. The social security system is intended to combat poverty and adverse conditions for the less wealthy in

[134] It is not easy for a European to grasp the American spirit of far-reaching individualism. Although, according to an American author, that may be a valid claim, it is also a misleading one unless carefully qualified: see Everett Carl Ladd in what is known as "The Ladd Report," of which an excerpt is reprinted in *The Lanahan Readings in the American Polity*, ed. Ann G. Serow and Everett C. Ladd, 3d ed. (Baltimore, Md.: Lanahan Publishers, 2003), 26–39, at 34. According to that report, "The drift and consequences of American individualism are collectivist, though certainly not of a state-centered variety. It's a collectivism of citizenship. The value of each individual's shareholding depends upon the beliefs and behavior of millions of others. . . . We Americans have been less inclined than our counterparts in other democracies to turn to government for answers—in part because we've sensed that only the quality of our shared citizenship, expressed through a vast array of self-formed and self-managed groups, can sustain the type of societal life to which we aspire": ibid. See also in the same book the excerpt from Louis Hartz, *The Liberal Tradition in America* (New York: Harvest Books, 1955), 11–16.

[135] See the critical remark of Dworkin, n. 86 above, 219–20.

[136] On the main types of welfare state regimes, their perspectives, goals, and tools, and on the several approaches used by governments in the provision of welfare policy, see Theodoulou, n. 118 above, 101–4.

times of economic recession and unemployment, to redistribute income, to reduce excessive differences in income, and to provide all citizens with equal access to health care, education, and public utilities, including the Internet and banking facilities.[137]

The aspiration to see such a system realized at the European level was confirmed by the EU Charter of Fundamental Rights adopted in Nice on December 8, 2000, which recognizes in Article 34 (1) of the charter a citizen's entitlements to a large array of social security benefits and social services—adding, however, that these entitlements are recognized "in accordance with the rules laid down by Community law and national laws and practices." However, the Union does not itself have the power to confer social security benefits (except to its staff members), but can only prohibit Member States from discriminating, in terms of the benefits they offer, between citizens of the regulating Member State and citizens of another Member State. Thus, it will be for the Member States individually to live up to the standard established in the charter, which, it may be recalled, they have not ratified themselves.[138] In other words, the charter is no more than an encouragement to the Member States to bring about a certain conception of the welfare state that the Union itself cannot achieve for lack of law-making authority in this field, as will be illustrated below.

The situation is different in the United States, where social welfare programs are a joint responsibility of all levels of government, federal, state, and local. The *federal* government is involved in policy formulation through deciding the types of programs to be adopted and the social issues to be addressed, and through providing funding to states to support delivery of welfare services.[139] Implementation, including the drafting of rules for eligibility and providing supplementary welfare assistance through their own general assis-

[137] As recognized in much detail in Articles 34–36 of the EU Charter of Fundamental Rights proclaimed in Nice in December 2000.

[138] See chapter 3, text accompanying n. 79, As observed by Piet Eeckhout, in "The EU Charter of Fundamental Rights and the Federal Question," 39 *CMLRev.*, 2002, 945–94, at 952, it is remarkable that many provisions of the charter, although only applicable to the Union institutions, have been drafted as if they were aimed at the Member States.

[139] Medicaid provides health benefits to fifty million people a year and is financed jointly by the federal government and the states. This does not work out without difficulty, federal officials saying that states have used creative bookkeeping and other ploys to obtain large amounts of Medicaid money without paying their share. See the *New York Times* of February 16, 2004, A1, and February 23, 2004, A17. See also "Governors Resist Bush Plan to Slow Costs of Medicaid," *New York Times*, May 25, 2003, A1.

tance programs, is left to the *states*. For its part, *local* government decides whether an individual is eligible and what amount he or she should receive. As appears from this short description, the engagement of the federal government is essential; however, it has evolved over the years, with ups and downs, due to deep-rooted political conflicts revolving around questions as to the nature and causes of poverty (whether individuals themselves or systemic factors are to blame), the role of government in social policy, and the appropriate burden to be borne by taxpayers.[140]

It was only after the Great Depression, which began in 1929, that the 1935 Social Security Act was adopted under President Franklin D. Roosevelt. The act established two main mechanisms: social security and unemployment compensation. Under President Lyndon Johnson's Great Society and War on Poverty programs, two more health insurance programs were introduced: Medicare for the elderly, and Medicaid for the poor. The situation changed dramatically, however, under the Nixon administration in the 1970s and the Reagan administration in the 1980s, when many of President Johnson's War on Poverty programs were dismantled under the influence of Milton Friedman, who argued that a broad social policy approach created disincentives and encouraged welfare dependency.[141] As a result, by 1992 welfare was seen by many, Republicans and Democrats alike, to be the root of America's problems, and was regarded as a failure that cost too much and discouraged individuals from working. In 1995 both houses of Congress passed resolutions to roll back welfare, resolutions that were signed into law in 1996 by President Bill Clinton.[142]

It follows from the foregoing that the American situation is different from the European in two respects. First, while social welfare is dimly regarded in the United States, and seen as a system that at best should alleviate the condition of the elderly and the poor, the system is regarded in the EU and its Member States as a cornerstone of the "social market" doctrine that they all have in common. According to that doctrine, social security is made necessary by the instability that is inherent in capitalist economies. That is not negated by the fact that, in many Member States, reform has been adopted recently, or is underway, to cut the cost of the system; indeed, reform is seen as inevitable, not because the system has lost its attraction, but in order for the system to survive.[143] Second, in the United States social welfare is the joint responsibility

[140] Theodoulou, n. 118 above, 132–33.
[141] Ibid., 130.
[142] Ibid., 131.
[143] For example, in France, proposals were presented by the Raffarin government

of the federal government and the states, whereas in Europe the Union has only limited, supportive competences. The main concern for the Union is to see to it that Member State laws on social welfare do not hinder the free movement of persons, primarily of workers and their families (but also citizens more generally) and of recipients of services, across Member State borders.

a) Health care in the United States and the European Union

Also in matters of health care, the European approach is in stark contrast with the American approach. This is, first, because the former is based on a comprehensive system aimed at the whole population and, second, because it leaves health care services only marginally to the market. By contrast, the American approach is more incremental and more entrepreneurial. Characteristic of the U.S. approach is the focus on welfare programs for the elderly, the disabled, and the poor, and the facilitation of the development of private insurance by generous tax exemptions.[144] The drawback is that it leaves a large group of people uninsured—those who cannot benefit from a welfare program and, if unemployed, do not have sufficient income to take out private insurance.[145]

It is true that, in the past, attempts have been made by several Democratic presidents to establish a comprehensive public insurance system,[146] but each of them failed, as was the case with both President Johnson's Great Society strat-

---

in May 2003 to reduce early pension retirement systems for the public sector (which led to strong resistance). To defend his proposals, Prime Minister Raffarin pointed out that, confronted with the demographic reality of retirees who are living longer and the prospect of waves of baby boomer retirees, the system becomes financially unbearable: in 1960, Raffarin said, four workers financed each pensioner, with two in 2000 and one by 2020: *New York Times*, May 9, 2003, A3. In Germany, the Bundestag approved, on September 26, 2003, a proposal by Chancellor Gerhard Schröder to cut 5 percent (23 billion euros) of the total health care budget, requiring patients to contribute more and abolishing the reimbursement of some dental services: *De Standaard*, September 27/28, 2003, 10.

[144] See Theodoulou, n. 118 above, 167–68.

[145] With the result that from 2000 to 2002, the most recent year for which official figures are available, the number of uninsured shot up more than 9 percent, to 43.6 million, the Census Bureau says: see the *New York Times*, February 7, 2004, A7, reporting a meeting with journalists of the U.S. Senate majority leader Bill Frist. Those millions of uninsured people depend on hospital emergency room care, the cost of which is absorbed by the hospital or passed on to the rest of the citizenry.

[146] Such attempts were also made by Theodore Roosevelt in 1912, Franklin D. Roosevelt in the 1930s, Harry S. Truman in the '40s and '50s, and John F. Kennedy in the '60s. See further Theodoulou, n. 118 above, 166–71.

egy in the 1960s and President Clinton's health plan in the 1990s.[147] The latter plan had two objectives: to extend medical coverage to the 15 percent of Americans who were uninsured and to stop the spiraling cost of medical care. The plan was formally submitted to Congress in October 1993, but it never emerged as legislation.[148] It left the United States in the paradoxical situation that—according to a 2000 analysis by the World Health Organization of the health systems of 191 nations[149]—the country with the greatest proportion of high-tech services, more employees per bed than any other country, and arguably the best medical research and training in the world, and, moreover, the country that spends a higher proportion of its GDP on health care than any other nation, ranks only 37 out of 191 nations worldwide in terms of overall performance. Great Britain ranks 18, Sweden 25, and Germany 27.[150]

By contrast, in Europe health care is regarded not as a privilege of employment and income but as a right of citizenship.[151] Characteristic for this approach is the Swedish Constitution (entitled "Instrument of Governance"), which provides that "personal, economic and cultural welfare of the private person shall be fundamental aims of public activity . . . it shall be incumbent

[147] See Jacob S. Hacker and Theda Skocpol, "The New Politics of Health Policy," 22 *J. Health Pol'y & L.*, 1997, 315, at 319. For a complete description of the Clinton health plan, see Nicholas Laham, *A Lost Cause* (Westport, Conn.: Praeger, 1996), 29–36.

[148] Theodoulou, n. 118 above, 170–71. On January 14, 2004, a panel of the National Academy of Sciences, a non-partisan body, concluding three years of work, urged Congress to begin work immediately to achieve health insurance coverage for all Americans by 2010. The cochairman of the panel said, "The economic cost to the country from the poorer health and premature death of uninsured people is in the range of 65 billion to 130 billion dollars a year": *New York Times*, January 15, 2004, A17.

[149] *The World Health Report 2000—Health Systems: Improving Performance*, WTO, Geneva, 2000. The systems were measured against five performance indicators: overall level of population health; health inequalities within the population; overall level of health system responsiveness (a combination of patient satisfaction and how well the systems acts); distribution of responsiveness within the population; and the distribution of the system's financial burden within the population. See Theodoulou, n. 118 above, 135.

[150] Ibid., 166. Those are the three European countries that Theodoulou compared with the United States. For a lucid analysis of the situation, see the opinion of Paul Krugman, "The Health of Nations," *New York Times*, February 17, 2004, A23, who writes in an op-ed piece, "It's true that the U.S. spends far more on health care than any other country, but this wouldn't be a bad thing if the spending got results. The real question is why, despite all that spending, many Americans aren't assured of the health care they need, and American life expectancy is near the bottom for advanced countries."

[151] Laham, n. 147 above, 8.

upon the public institutions to secure the right to work, housing and education, and to promote social care, social security, and a good living environment."[152] Although the same "rights" approach prevails in the other Member
States, too, and in the EU Charter of Fundamental Rights, that does not prevent huge differences from existing between the EU Member States,[153] depending on which of the two models they have chosen, the "Beveridge model"
or the "Bismarck model."[154]

The "Beveridge model" is based primarily on state funding, and on health
providers (doctors, pharmacists) who are engaged by a public health authority.[155] The model recognizes a universal right for the whole population to receive medical care (almost invariably) for free. Under the "Bismarck model,"
coverage is dependent on the exercise of some activity or membership in a
group and is mainly financed through the payment of premiums (mainly by
employers and employees). Health services are either supplied by a provider
designated and paid directly by a social security institution, or by a freely chosen provider paid by the patient, who is then reimbursed by the social security
institution.[156] Both models are opposed to the market (or "entrepreneurial")

[152] Swedish Constitution, chapter I, art. II, para. 2. Compare this with Article 35 of
the EU Charter, which reads: "Everyone has the right of access to preventive health
care and the right to benefit from medical treatment under the conditions established
by national laws and practices. A high level of human health protection shall be ensured in the definition and implementation of all Union policies and activities." For a
description of the Swedish system in a policy perspective, see Theodoulou, n. 118
above, 160–65. The author discusses some of the problems the system is currently
coping with: lack of physicians and increasing costs, which puts pressure on the government to make cuts while still being perceived as committed to a system that is accountable, accessible, and equitable (165).

[153] For a description of the social security systems, including health care, of the 25
(old and new) Member States, see D. Pieters, *The Social Security Systems of the Member
States of the European Union* (Antwerp, Oxford, New York: Intersentia, 2002) and *The
Social Security Systems of the States Applying for Membership of the European Union*
(Antwerp, Oxford, New York: Intersentia, 2003).

[154] William Henry Beveridge (1879–1963) was a British economist and social re-
former who was at the basis of much of the welfare legislation on which the U.K. is
founded. Otto Eduard Leopold von Bismarck (1815–89) was chancellor of the German
Empire (1871–90) and was the driving force after the unification of Germany.

[155] This system is found in the U.K., Ireland, Spain, Italy, Portugal, Greece, Denmark, Finland, and Sweden. For a description of the U.K. system, and a discussion of
future outcomes and policy weaknesses, see Theodoulou, n. 118 above, 149–56.

[156] The first system is found in Austria, Germany, and the Netherlands, the second
in Belgium, France, Germany, and Luxembourg. For a description of the German system and a discussion of the challenges ahead, see Theodoulou, n. 118 above, 143–49.
She refers more specifically to the problems that Germany was confronted with as a

model, where both funding and providing of health services remain private, with relatively little interference from the state, as in the United States.

Although systems can be recognized on the basis of their main character-istics as belonging to one of these models, most countries have a mixed system situated between the two extremes, the "public" U.K. system and the "private" U.S. system. Thus, under both the Beveridge and the Bismarck systems pa-tients must pay for some services themselves, or part of the fee charged, just as some state funding and management will occur under the market system. Most of the industrialized states do have a comprehensive health care system for the large majority of the population—even though large differences exist with respect to the scope and range of health provisions and the personal contribution patients must pay themselves. Moreover, all systems increasingly cope with funding problems, the affordability of the system becoming ques-tionable everywhere as a result of an aging population and technological prog-ress in the medical field.[157]

*b) The impact of EU internal market freedoms on Member State health
care systems*

As mentioned previously, and partially in contrast with the United States, in the EU social security remains basically a matter for the Member States.[158] In the areas of both social security and public health, the Union has been em-powered by the states only to support and complement Member State activi-

---

result of the unification of East and West Germany—which, some authors argue, is "equivalent to the U.S. incorporating Mexico within its health care system" (148).

[157] Regardless of whether the system is a more "public" (as the U.K. system) or a more "private" system (as the U.S. system). See notes 148–50 above and accompanying text.

[158] In that context, it should be mentioned that, within the EU, the capacity of na-tional governments to influence the course of their national economies and to shape their social orders has been greatly reduced by the creation of the monetary union, which has deprived the Member States within the euro-zone of the ability to respond to economic problems with a revaluation of the currency, and which moreover has se-verely restrained them in their choice of fiscal policy responses by the conditions of the Stability and Growth Pact. See further Fritz W. Scharpf, n. 44 above, 91–94. It may be recalled that at the end of November 2003 the Stability and Growth Pact, which is the euro-zone's foundation, was the subject of sharp tensions between Germany and France and the other euro-zone states when the former two states announced their intention not to comply (for the third consecutive year) with the pact, and more par-ticularly with the deficit ceiling of 3 percent of GDP. See *The Economist*, November 29, 2003, 29–30. One of the reasons for non-compliance is the necessity for Germany and France (and also for the other states) to finance their social security system by means of budgetary deficits.

ties and to encourage cooperation between Member States.[159] Apart from that, the EU institutions, in line with the internal market philosophy of free movement of services within the Union, are mainly concerned with eliminating Member State restrictions on access to their social security systems for both providers and recipients of health care services coming from other Member States.

Since the early 1960s, this has led to a large volume of Community law regulations and directives that have been adopted both to ensure that workers (and their families) moving within the Union continue to receive social and health care benefits and to organize the equivalence and mutual recognition of diplomas and other qualifications so that providers of health care services can work in Member States other than their own state.[160] Similarly, this has led to ECJ case law declaring that health services fall within the ambit of the Community internal market freedoms even when they are provided in the context of a social security scheme.[161] In effect, through a series of judgments, the Court has paved the way for care providers to operate, and for patients to obtain the best available service, in any one of the Member States.[162]

Two recent judgments illustrate the (incremental) impact that internal market freedoms may thus have on the Member States' social security schemes.[163] *Vanbraekel* concerned a Belgian woman who underwent orthope-

---

[159] See Article 137 (1), sub c, (2) and (4) EC, as regards social security; and Article 152 (1), (2), and (5) EC, as regards public health.

[160] See Vassilis G. Hatzopoulos, "*Killing* National Health and Insurance Systems but *Healing* Patients? The European Market for Health Care Services after the Judgments of the ECJ in *Vanbraekel* and *Peerbooms*," 39 *CMLRev.*, 2002, 683–729, at 685–88. With respect to the first category, the main legislative text is Regulation 1408/71 of June 14, 1971, on the application of social security schemes to employed persons, to self-employed persons, and to members of their families moving within the Community, which was reissued and updated by Council Regulation 118/97 of December 2, 1996, OJ L28/1, 1997.

[161] Joined cases 286/82 and 26/83, *Luisi and Carbone*, [1984] ECR 377, para. 16. For further developments, see Hatzopoulos, n. 160 above, 688–94.

[162] Health care services and medical workers have also been held to fall under the Community rules on free competition, and they may, in principle, even fall under the Community rules on state aid and public procurement. On all these points, see Hatzopoulos, n. 160 above.

[163] Case C-368/98, *Vanbraekel*, and C-157/99, *Geraerts-Smits and Peerbooms*, [2001] ECR I-5363 and 5473, respectively. The two judgments are analyzed by Hatzopoulos in his article quoted above. They have been followed by other judgments, as, for example, by the judgment in Case C-326/00, *Idryma Koinonikon Asfaliseon (IKA) v. Vasileios Ioannidis*, [2003] ECR I-1703 (dealing with the rights of pensioners, as opposed to workers, to receive health care services while in other Member States, and defining the

dic surgery in France notwithstanding the refusal by the Belgian sickness fund to authorize such surgery—which authorization she needed in order to have her medical expenses reimbursed by the Belgian fund. The refusal was based on the absence of a document certifying that the surgery could be performed under better circumstances in France. In its judgment, on a preliminary question from a Belgian court, the ECJ held that Ms. Vanbraekel was nevertheless entitled, under Council Regulation 1408/71 on social security and Article 49 (ex 59) EC Treaty on free movement of services, to be reimbursed by the Belgian sickness fund by an amount equivalent to what she would have obtained if she had received treatment in Belgium (where reimbursement was more advantageous than in France). The Court brushed aside the argument that the Belgian legislation prescribing authorization was intended to prevent the financing of the Belgian social security system from being undermined. The Court observed in that regard that reimbursement in accordance with the Belgian rules could not have that effect since it did not impose any additional burden on the Belgian sickness insurance scheme.

In *Smits and Peerbooms*, a Dutch national who fell into a coma following a road accident in the Netherlands was transferred in a vegetative state to the university clinic in Innsbruck, Austria, in order to be submitted there to neuro-stimulation. The technique was used experimentally in the Netherlands at two medical centers, but not for patients over the age of twenty-five. As a result of the therapy, the patient came out of the coma and was able to leave the clinic and continue his rehabilitation in the Netherlands. The Dutch health care insurer (CZ), which was asked to reimburse the costs of treatment at the Austrian clinic, rejected the claim, arguing, first, that the therapy was not regarded as normal within the professional circles concerned and, second, that even if it were, adequate treatment was available in the Netherlands without undue delay (a finding that in fact was contradicted by a court-appointed expert witness).

The Dutch court stayed the proceedings and submitted preliminary questions to the ECJ asking whether Dutch legislation was permitted 1) to subject reimbursement to prior authorization of the treatment by the sickness insurance, and 2) to make the granting of authorization, and the reimbursement of medical costs, dependent on the "normality" of the treatment in professional circles, and on the "necessity" for a patient to go abroad for lack of adequate treatment without undue delay in the Netherlands.[164] In answer to these ques-

---

corresponding rights and obligations of funds and hospitals in the home and host states). For comments, see Vassilis Hatzopoulos, 40 *CMLRev.*, 2003, 1251–68.

[164] On the requirement of prior authorization, see also the judgment of May 13,

tions, the ECJ held that Articles 49 (ex 59) and 50 (ex 60) EC on free movement of services did not preclude the Dutch legislation at issue, provided that
it regards treatment as "normal" when it is sufficiently tried and tested by international medical science (and not just in the Netherlands), and that "necessity" should be applied to refuse authorization only if the same or equally
effective treatment can be obtained without undue delay from an establishment with which the patient's sickness fund has contractual arrangements.
The Court added, in connection with the last point, that although the conditions of "normality" and "necessity" constituted a barrier to the freedom to
provide and receive services, the restriction could be objectively justified in
the interests of "maintain[ing] an adequate, balanced and permanent supply
of hospital care on national territory and [of] ensur[ing] the financial stability
of the sickness insurance system."[165]

Both judgments demonstrate the *potential* disruptive effects that "the rig-
ours of the (EC) Treaty rules" may have upon "some of the core aspects of
national welfare systems," even though their ultimate outcomes are not
alarming.[166] This is evidenced by the fact that, in both cases, the ECJ was willing to accept that Member States may justify, subject to the principle of proportionality, national restrictions on internal market freedoms based upon the
need to ensure the financial stability of the national (public) sickness insurance fund and to maintain a balanced and manageable national health care
system. In other words, disruptive effect there may be, but within limits.

The Union's Social Policy and Social Citizenship

Three subjects are discussed herein. The first subject concerns the gradual
extension of the powers of the Union in areas of social policy. The second is
the transformation of citizenship in the Union from a pure market citizenship
into a more general political and social citizenship. The final subject concerns
the status of long-term residents in the Union coming from third countries.

*a) Community supportive action in the sphere of social policy: Social
exclusion as an example*

As mentioned above, the powers of the Union institutions in the area of
social security (and public health)—and in many other social policy fields[167]—
are intended purely to *support* and *complement* the activities of the Member

---

2003, in Case C-385/99, *Müller-Fauré and Van Riet*, [2003] ECR I-4509 with a comment
from M. Flear, *41 CMLRev.*, 2004, 209–33.

[165] *Smits and Peerbooms*, para. 97.
[166] Craig and de Búrca, n. 36 above, 810.
[167] See Article 137 (1) (b) EC.

States.[168] Autonomous regulatory powers have been kept to an absolute minimum.[169] As specified in Article 137 (2) (a) EC, the Council may adopt measures "to encourage cooperation between Member States through initiatives aimed at improving knowledge, developing exchanges of information and best practices, promoting innovative approaches and evaluating experiences, *excluding* [however] any harmonisation of the laws and regulations of the Member States" (emphasis added). Moreover, none of these measures may "affect the right of the Member States to define the fundamental principles of their social security systems and must not significantly affect the financial equilibrium thereof," nor should they prevent "any Member State from maintaining or introducing more stringent protective measures."[170]

The new modes of governance, and in particular the open method of coordination (OMC) referred to above,[171] must be seen in this context: they are the most significant instrument that the Community institutions can use, in the absence of regulatory powers, to have an impact on the development of social policy at the Union level. Combating social inclusion is an example of a field where OMC is applied.[172] The objective was fleshed out after the European Council meeting at Lisbon in March 2000, during which the European Council recognized that "the number of people living below the poverty line and in social exclusion in the Union is unacceptable . . . [and that] [s]teps must be taken to make a decisive impact on the eradication of poverty."[173] The

---

[168] The first recognition of the need for Member States to grant some competences to the Community in the sphere of social policy came at the 1972 Paris Summit, which concluded that economic expansion was not an end in itself and should result in improvements to quality of life as well as standards of living. The summit was followed by the 1974 Social Action Programme laid down in the Council Resolution of January 21, 1974, OJ C13, 1–4. An important step was taken with the Treaty of Amsterdam when the United Kingdom agreed to incorporate into the EC Treaty the broader powers provided for in the Social Agreement. That agreement had been concluded in 1992 by the other (then eleven) Member States, and was repealed by the Treaty of Amsterdam. For further developments, see K. Lenaerts and P. Van Nuffel, *Constitutional Law of the European Union*, ed. R. Bray (London: Sweet and Maxwell, 1999), 226–28; Kenneth A. Armstrong, "Tackling Social Exclusion through OMC: Reshaping the Boundaries of European Governance," in *The State of the European Union*, ed. Tanja A. Börzel and Rachel A. Cichowski (Oxford: Oxford University Press, 2003), 170–94.

[169] See Article 137 (2) EC.

[170] Article 137 (4) EC.

[171] See above, pp. 167–70.

[172] See Article 137 (1) (j) EC. The article enumerates many other social policy fields in which the Community institutions may take supportive and complementing measures.

[173] Quoted by Armstrong, n. 168 above, 170. In a report on social inclusion pub-

Community's concern about fighting poverty goes back to its multi-annual Poverty Programmes starting in the 1970s. However, lack of a specific legal basis, leading even to a legal challenge of measures taken by the Commission,[174] has made it difficult for the Community institutions to provide concrete action. This changed only with the amendment of Articles 136 and 137 EC by the Amsterdam and Nice Treaties.[175]

These changes made it possible for the Council and the Parliament to adopt, by Decision 50/2002,[176] the Community Action Programme, with a budget of 75 million euros to be allocated to activities in three respects: 1) to enhance knowledge about poverty and social exclusion; 2) to promote policy cooperation, exchange of information, and best practice, for example through Member States volunteering to have projects evaluated by two or three other Member States; and 3) to promote participation and dialogue, and to mobilize all relevant actors, including financing NGOs such as the European Anti-Poverty Network and the European Federation of National Organisations Working with the Homeless.[177] The action plan aims at the achievement of four objectives endorsed by the Nice European Council: to facilitate participation in employment, and access by all to resources, rights, goods, and services; to prevent the risk of exclusion; to help the most vulnerable; and to mobilize all relevant bodies.[178]

From a theoretical point of view, the OMC used in the area of social exclu-

---

lished on December 17, 2003, the Commission found 21 percent of Irish citizens face the threat of falling below the breadline, more than twice the percentage for Sweden, which has the lowest risk of poverty in the EU. Although the average proportion of people at risk fell across the Union from 17 percent in 1995 to 15 percent in 2001, one in ten Member State children live in a household in which neither parent has a job: *European Voice*, December 18, 2003–January 14, 2004, 6. These figures add perspective to the figures mentioned in n. 145 above as to the number of American citizens who have no health insurance.

[174] Case C-106/96, *United Kingdom v. Commission*, [1998] ECR I-2729. In that judgment the court held that, with the exception of non-significant expenditure, a basic legal act had to be adopted for the implementation of budgetary expenditure in addition to the existence of a budget line in the EU budget: see Armstrong, n. 168 above, 175.

[175] Ibid.

[176] Council and European Parliament Decision 50/2002, [2002] OJ L10, 1–7.

[177] Armstrong, n. 168 above, 186–87. In that article the functioning of the open method of coordination to prevent social exclusion is thoroughly analyzed. The article more specifically regards the organizational, procedural, and substantive levels of policy development (180–87) and the role of all relevant actors, particularly the role (and limits) of civil society actors (187–93).

[178] Ibid., 180.

sion has all characteristics of the new modes of government:[179] 1) participation and power sharing: involvement of all public and private actors and stakeholders, civil society included; 2) multilevel interaction: both horizontal and vertical engagement of Community, Member States, and subnational actors; 3) decentralization and diversity: coordinating Member State policies rather than imposing Community solutions; 4) deliberation: problem solving through debate and dialogue; 5) flexibility: a preference for "soft law" solutions (nonbinding instruments) that can be revised in light of experience; 6) experimentation and knowledge creation: governance processes viewed as productive of knowledge and consciously experimental.[180]

It has been pointed out that the use of the OMC with regard to social inclusion and other social policies breaks with the "rights discourse" usually applied in Community law.[181] Indeed, from the very outset, the position of individual citizens has been viewed through the possession of legal rights, mainly economic rights—the right not to be discriminated against on the basis of nationality (the internal market freedoms)—but also social rights—the right not to be discriminated against on the basis of gender (equal treatment with regard to pay and the working environment)—and now also general rights—the right not to be discriminated against on other grounds (the non-discrimination provision of Article 13 EC).[182] This "rights discourse" has culminated in the EU Charter of Fundamental Rights, where it was extended to include a wide array of specific rights, for instance, in connection with combating social exclusion and poverty, "the right to social and housing assistance so as to ensure a decent existence for all those who lack sufficient resources, in accordance with the rules laid down by Community law and national laws and practices."[183]

Formulating the situation in such general terms, one may contemplate the merit of such a catalogue of rights at the EU level when it is not accompanied by regulatory competences and financial resources allowing the Union to supplement the national social security systems by minimal Union social security instruments. Seen in this perspective, the American incremental approach of having *federal* safety nets in specific areas may be more attractive than would

---

[179] As identified by Joanne Scott and David M. Trubek, "Mind the Gap: Law and New Approaches to Governance in the European Union," *ELJ*, 2002, 1–18, referred to by Armstrong, n. 168 above, 171.

[180] Armstrong, n. 168 above, 171.

[181] Ibid., 176–78.

[182] On this evolution, see above, pp. 171–73. See also, in a broader context, de Búrca, n. 8 above, and chapter 6, pp. 274–75.

[183] Article 34 (3) EU Charter.

appear at first glance, provided, however, that it is underpinned by comprehensive social security systems at state level (as would be the case in Europe).

b) From market citizenship to political and social citizenship

As mentioned previously,[184] it was at the 1972 Paris Summit that European
economic integration was put into a broader perspective of social welfare.
Since then, the neo-liberal philosophy that was at the basis of the European
Economic Community (and still is, to a large extent, at the basis of the European Community, that is, the first pillar of the Union) was gradually turned
into a more socially oriented philosophy. From a perspective of citizen rights,
this means that the rights that citizens enjoy by virtue of EC law are no longer
only "market rights" but have been enlarged to include "political rights" as
well, and slowly also "social rights" in the broad sense of the word, that is,
rights (and duties) concerned with people's welfare generally, including work,
education, health, and quality of life.[185]

This transformation started with the incorporation, by the Maastricht
Treaty, of a new part II in the EC Treaty, entitled "Citizenship of the Union"
and composed of Articles 17–22 (ex 8–8e) EC. According to Article 17 (1) EC,
citizenship in the Union, "complement[ing] and not replac[ing] national citizenship," is established and accorded to every person "holding the nationality
of a Member State." The rights enjoyed by Union citizens are, according to
Article 17 (2), "the rights conferred by [the EC] Treaty . . . subject to the duties
imposed thereby." Those rights are in the first place the internal *market* freedoms (in the exercise of which discrimination on the basis of nationality is
prohibited) and related consumer and worker rights specified elsewhere in the
treaty. Then, in Articles 18 to 21 EC, a limited number of rights are enumerated, starting with the general right to move and reside freely within the territory of the Member States and followed by a number of specific *political*
rights: the right to vote and stand as a candidate at municipal and European
Parliament elections, the right to diplomatic protection in a third country,[186]
the right to petition the European Parliament and to address complaints to the
European Ombudsman. In Articles 39–46 of the (as yet non-binding) EU
Charter of Fundamental Rights, this list of citizen rights was consolidated, and

---

[184] See n. 168 above.

[185] See Douglas-Scott, n. 4 above, 502. For a broad overview of this development,
see Reich et al., n. 13 above, 54–88.

[186] To be assured by any Member State to any Union citizen whose own Member
State does not have diplomatic representation in the particular third country concerned: Article 20 EC.

it was expanded with the rights to good administration and access to documents.

The enumeration of these lists of rights in the EC Treaty, as amended, and in the EU Charter may seem rather symbolic,[187] many of the rights mentioned being already specified in other treaty provisions. However, the fact should not be overlooked that the rights enumerated in Articles 18 to 21 EC are granted to all citizens, that is, they are unconnected with the exercise of any economic activity. That obviously holds true for the political rights, but it is also becoming increasingly true, as we will see below, for the general right of citizens, established in Article 18 EC, to move and reside freely within the territory of the Member States.

Among the rights conferred by other treaty provisions are the rights that *workers* from other Member States—and by extension members of their family (so-called "dependents")—enjoy in the Member State where they work.[188] These rights remain connected, however, to the status of "worker" in the sense of Article 39 (1) EC (relating to freedom of movement for workers), as interpreted by the ECJ in numerous judgments. It means, in concrete terms, that nationals from one Member State who want to work in another Member State need a residence permit, for which they must produce proof of engagement from an employer. Similarly, family members, whether from a Member State or a third country, must produce proof of their relationship with the worker.[189]

---

[187] Thus Gráinne de Búrca, "The European Court of Justice and the Evolution of EU Law," in *The State of the European Union*, ed. Tanja A. Börzel and Rachel A. Cichowski (Oxford: Oxford University Press, 2003), 48–75, at 70.

[188] Under the accession agreements with the ten Member States that joined the EU on May 1, 2004, the old Member States are allowed to restrict the access of workers from the new Member States to their labor markets. These agreements provide for a differentiated transition regime: for two years after accession, the old Member States can autonomously decide how much access they grant; after this two-year period, Member States may notify the Commission that they intend to continue to apply national measures for another three years and can thereafter invoke an additional two-year period of restrictions in case of serious disturbances of the labor market or threat thereof. See further Reich et al., n. 13 above, 81–84. Most of the old Member States have already announced their intention to apply one or another form of control. See *De Standaard*, February 21–22, 2004, 10 (information taken from the *Financial Times*). The restrictions thus imposed on free access have been strongly criticized for being both needless and against the interests of the present Member States: see Dana Spinant, "Why Eastern Europeans Will Not Move En Masse—and Why EU-15 Will Need Them," *European Voice*, March 4–10, 2004, 7.

[189] For an overview of the ECJ's extensive case law on the Community law concept of "worker" and on the formal requirements for workers to enter another Member

At first sight, Article 18 (1) (incorporated into the EC Treaty in 1992) did nothing to change the status quo: although Article 18 (1) grants to all EU citizens "the right to move and reside freely within the territory of the Member States," that right is *"subject to* the limitations and conditions laid down in this [EC] Treaty and by the measures adopted to give it effect" (emphasis added).[190]

However, after some hesitation,[191] the ECJ has been willing, in *Grzelczyk*,[192] to accord more substance to the general right to free movement and residence enshrined in Article 18 EC by using the notion of citizenship as an autonomous (and not just a residual) basis to grant nationals of other Member States certain social and other advantages on a basis equal to that of the host Member State's own nationals. More specifically, in that case the Court ruled that a French student living in Belgium who was seeking entitlement to a non-contributory minimum subsistence allowance could plead the principle of non-discrimination in any situation covered by the material scope of the treaty, as defined *in part* by the free movement and residence right of Article 18 EC. Accordingly, and despite secondary legislation requiring that, in order to be permitted residence, non-economically active persons should not be-

---

State to work or search for work, see Craig and de Búrca, n. 36 above, 704–14 and 728–34, respectively.

[190] The most important of these measures are: Council Directive 68/360, containing formal requirements for workers and their family members, and Council Regulation 1612/68, concerning the substantive rights and social advantages that workers and their family members enjoy. Further directives relating to rights of residence granted to categories of persons *other* than genuine workers are: Directive 90/366, replaced later by Directive 93/96, covering students exercising the right of vocational training; Directive 90/365, dealing with persons who have ceased to work; and catch-all Directive 90/364, governing all those persons who did not already enjoy a right of residence under Community law. These three residency directives have in common that the persons involved must have adequate resources not to become a financial burden on the social assistance schemes of the host Member State and must be covered by sickness insurance. For references, see Craig and de Búrca, n. 36 above, 756. The scope of these directives was reconsidered by the ECJ in its *Grzelczyk* and *Baumbast* judgments mentioned later in the text. See also further n. 208.

[191] See Case C-193/94, *Skanavi and Chyssanthakopoulos*, [1996] ECR I-929, where the court treated Article 18 (then 8a) EC as residual and apparently secondary to other more specific rights.

[192] Case C-184/99, *Rudy Grzelczyk*, [2001] ECR I-6193. See also Case C-224/98, *D'Hoop*, [2002] ECR I-6191, where the court extended its reasoning to a national being withheld an allowance in her own state because she had received her secondary education in another Member State.

come a financial burden on the host Member State,[193] the student's right of residence was directly based on Article 18 EC,[194] with the effect that he was entitled in Belgium to financial assistance available to Belgians.[195]

In fact, not only EU citizens but also third-country nationals enjoy social rights under certain conditions, principally when they are family members of migrant workers,[196] or migrant workers from countries with which the EU has special agreements.[197] In this context, the *Mary Carpenter* case deserves to be mentioned: it concerned the right, under EU law, of the non-EU spouse of a U.K. national to remain with him in the United Kingdom, despite her having violated immigration rules.[198] The ECJ ruled in that case that, since the depor-

[193] See n. 190 above.

[194] In that respect, the court went further than in an earlier judgment in Case C-85/96, *Martinez Sala*, [1998] ECR I-2681. In that case, a Spanish national who lived in Germany was seeking entitlement to a child-raising allowance. The court relied on her status as Union citizen to recognize the applicant's right on the same conditions as German nationals, regardless of whether she was a migrant worker. However, Ms. Sala *had* been granted a right to residence in Germany, so there was no need to base the applicant's right to the allowance directly on Article 18 EC.

[195] Subsequently, the ECJ issued another strong ruling in Case C-413/99, *Baumbast and R v. Secretary of State for the Home Department*, [2002] ECR I-7091. In that case, the court declared that Article 18 was directly effective and gave independent residence rights to an EU national who was no longer a worker. In that ruling, the ECJ also broadly interpreted the right of access to education of children of migrant workers, holding that the right is not lost by the mere fact that the parent citizen no longer lives within the Member State in question and none of the other family members are EU citizens. For an analysis of this and other recent judgments, see Norbert Reich and Solvita Harbacevica, "Citizenship and Family on Trial: A Fairly Optimistic Overview of Recent Court Practice with Regard to Free Movement of Persons," 40 *CMLRev.*, 2003, 615–38. On *Baumbast*, see also below in the text, pp. 204–5.

[196] On that subject, see Regulation 1612/68 referred to in n. 190 above, and Craig and de Búrca, n. 36 above, 739–43.

[197] Obviously, non-nationals also enjoy rights other than "national" rights on the basis of other treaty provisions, such as consumer rights, rights of access to public documents, sex equality rights, and so on: see further Reich et al., n. 13 above, 70–71. The author also discusses the possibility of using the notion of permanent legal residence as a substitute for nationality (85–88).

[198] Case C-60/00, *Mary Carpenter v. Secretary of State for the Home Department*, [2002] ECR I-6279. See de Búrca, n. 187 above, 71–73. From a methodological point of view, the judgment has been rightly criticized for extending the scope of application of the freedom to provide services too far under the influence of the concrete circumstances of the case: see "Editorial Comments: Freedoms Unlimited, Reflections on *Mary Carpenter v. Secretary of State*," 40 *CMLRev.*, 537–43.

tation of his spouse (who cared for children from his previous marriage) could adversely affect the husband in the exercise of *his* (EC) right to provide services in other Member States, the situation fell within the scope of EC law. Furthermore, the Court held that although a Member State may limit the right to provide services on grounds of public policy or public security (as mentioned in Article 46 referring to Article 55 EC), the Member State concerned is bound to observe the human rights requirements embodied in EC law— including respect for the right of family life, as laid down in Article 8 ECHR. Citing the *Boultif* judgment of the Court of Human Rights, the ECJ held that the U.K. would be violating the right to respect for family life if it expelled Mrs. Carpenter without a more significant public policy reason than violation of immigration laws.[199]

The ECJ's case law deriving social rights for Union citizens from the free movement and residency right embodied in Article 18 EC raises the delicate issue of how far the ECJ can go in imposing financial burdens on Member State social security systems in the name of solidarity between Union citizens.[200] The issue is underlying many recent judgments, but is most apparent in *Baumbast*.[201] In that case, the ECJ ruled that Article 18 (1) EC is sufficiently clear and precise to be directly applicable (and directly effective), and this despite the fact, as pointed out previously, that the article submits the free movement and resident right "to the limitations and conditions contained" in the treaty and in secondary legislation.[202] The question at issue was whether the U.K. immigration authorities could reject Mr. Baumbast's application for renewal of his residence permit on the grounds that he and his family were not insured for emergency treatment in the U.K., where the family lived (although they were covered by comprehensive medical insurance in Germany, of which Mr. Baumbast was a national). Such a residence permit is needed under the three EC directives granting rights of residence to categories of persons other than workers. These directives provide that rights of residence are subject to two conditions: first, the applicant must possess sufficient resources, and, second, he or she must

---

[199] De Búrca, n. 187 above, 72 (with references to other judgments), and Reich and Harbacevica, n. 195 above, 621–22 (also with references to other judgments). The ECJ referred to the *Boultif v. Switzerland* judgment of the Court of Human Rights of August 2, 2001, in para. 42.

[200] The issue is examined by Michael Dougan and Eleanor Spaventa in "Educating Rudy and the (Non-) English Patient: A Double-bill on Residency Rights under Article 18 EC," 28 *ELRev.*, 2003, 699–712.

[201] See n. 190 above. It also came up in the two health care judgments, *Van Braekel* and *Geraerts-Smits*, discussed previously and referred to in n. 163 above.

[202] At paras. 84–86 of *Baumbast*, n. 195 above.

have comprehensive medical insurance for all risks.[203] It was clear, as the court observed, that Mr. Baumbast had sufficient resources, but it was equally clear that he had no health insurance for emergency treatment within the U.K.

In its judgment, the ECJ ruled that the refusal of the British authorities was unfounded. It recognized that the requirements in the directives were permissible, being based on the idea that exercise of the Union citizen's right of residency can be subordinated to the legitimate financial interests of the Member State—including the fact that foreign nationals should not become an "unreasonable burden" on the public finances of the host state. Nevertheless, those limitations and conditions, laid down in secondary Community legislation, must be applied in compliance with general principles of Community law, and in particular with the principle of proportionality. The Court then found that to deny Mr. Baumbast residence solely on the grounds that he lacked medical insurance for emergency treatment within the United Kingdom would be a disproportionate interference with the exercise of his residency right under Article 18 (1) EC.[204]

The difficulty with the ECJ's case law in this case, but also in other "social rights" cases,[205]

> is that the Court, and the EU, "cannot simply grant full rights of residency to all its citizens, because it cannot foot the consequent welfare bill, especially in respect of economically inactive individuals. The aspiration towards a supranational form of social citizenship, which many see embodied in Article 18, must therefore remain sensitive to domestic conceptions of belonging to (and being excluded from) the welfare society."[206]

Apart from this basic question, many other issues of a more specifically legal nature arise, such as which general principles other than proportionality will be permitted to qualify restrictions imposed by secondary Community legislation. The question is most acute with regard to economically inactive and financially dependent persons: What are the benefits of Union citizenship for them? Should they not be able to derive residency rights from fundamental rights provisions, such as respect for private and family life and for human dignity? Should these rights not have an impact upon the ability of Member

---

[203] See n. 190 above. The directive at issue here was Directive 90/364, on general right to residence, [1990] OJ L180/26. Mr. Baumbast, living in the U.K. and also working there first, was later employed by German companies to carry out work in Lesotho and China and was therefore not considered a worker under Article 39 EC. See further Dougan and Spaventa, n. 200 above, 701.

[204] At paras. 91–93 of the *Baumbast* judgment, n. 195 above.

[205] For a full account, see Dougan and Spaventa, n. 200 above, 701–2.

[206] Ibid., 704.

States to expel individuals who would otherwise be considered an unreasonable burden upon the public purse?[207] A straight answer to that question would be to grant Union citizens who have been lawfully resident in another Member State, for example, at least five consecutive years "permanent resident" status regardless of their economic or financial status—as is proposed by the Commission in a draft general directive which, if adopted, would replace much of the existing secondary legislation.[208]

c) From citizen to resident rights

For many centuries Europe has been an area of emigration; during the twentieth century, however, all Member States have gradually become countries of immigration, as explicitly recognized by the European Council at its 1999 meeting in Tampere, Finland. At that meeting the Council stated that "a common approach must be developed to ensure the integration into our societies of those third country nationals who are lawfully resident in the Union."[209] The issue is important for several reasons: first, the sheer number of persons concerned[210] will steadily grow in the future; second, those persons

[207] Ibid., 710–11.

[208] Proposal for a European Parliament and Council Directive on the Right of Citizens of the Union and their Family Members to Move and Reside Freely within the Territory of the Member States: COM (2001) 257 final. For a discussion see Craig and de Búrca, n. 36 above, 761–62; Reich et al., n. 13 above, 76. The proposal was adopted by the European Parliament and the Council on April 29, 2004 as Directive 2004/38/EC, [2004] OJ L229/35. The aim of the new directive is to simplify and consolidate existing legislation, not to extend citizen rights. As a result of the directive, the legislation, referred to in n. 190 above, will be repealed with effect from April 30, 2006.

[209] Quoted by Kees Groenendijk and Elspeth Guild, "Converging Criteria: Creating an Area of Security of Residence for Europe's Third Country Nationals," 3 *EJML*, 2001, 37–59, at 52. Another, even more controversial, issue with respect to immigrants from third countries is the action to be taken in regard to *illegal* immigration. In that matter, agreement was reached at the 2002 European Council meeting in Seville, Spain, on a common policy concerning asylum and illegal immigration. The purpose is to stop the "leaking dike syndrome," that is, to avoid the situation in which one Member State tightens up its immigration laws, leading immigrants to find another, easier, way through another Member State to enter into the Community. See Caroline Forder, "Editorial: Common Minimum European Standards in Immigration Matters," 9 *MJ*, 2002, 221–29, where the author emphasizes that common minimum standards applicable to all Member States must comply with the case law of the ECtHR, which she describes in her contribution. Asylum and immigration are, of course, areas that are especially subject to changes in the overall political climate, and the emphasis after September 11 has been on security: see Craig and de Búrca, n. 36 above, 753–54.

[210] In 1998 approximately 10 million nationals of third countries were legally resident in one of the then fifteen EU Member States: Groenendijk and Guild, n. 209 above, 39.

intend, by and large, to stay in the Union; and third, the Union should not be conceived of as an exclusionary organization concerned solely with citizens of its own Member States and not with legal residents from third countries.[211] Moreover, from a study requested by the Commission as to the state of the law in each of the Member States, it appeared that there was already a large convergence among the Member States on the essential issues, and that the legal status of legal residents was already set out in case law of the ECJ, the common thread being that third-country legal residents in the Union had acquired a status approaching, but not yet equal to, citizenship.[212]

It was therefore not surprising that on November 25, 2003, Directive 2003/109 was adopted, granting persons who have resided legally and continuously for five years in the territory of a Member State the "right" to claim the status of long-term resident, conditional upon their possession of stable and continuous resources to support themselves and members of their family so as not to become a burden to the social assistance or sickness insurance systems.[213] To obtain that status, they should lodge an application with the competent national authorities. They will in due course receive an official EC residence permit. Long-term resident status will guarantee equal treatment with citizens in the Member State of residence, including access to employment, working conditions, access to education and vocational training, recognition of professional diplomas, entitlement to social security and core benefits, tax benefits, access to public housing, and free access to the entire territory of the resident state. With regard to residence in other Member States, long-term residents will be allowed access to the labor market, but there may be safeguard clauses attached to such access.

[211] Ibid., 39–40.

[212] Ibid., 40–41. For an overview of how a common European Policy on Immigration and Asylum came about in the past and should be developed in the future, possibly with the help of the open method of coordination, see Maria Fletcher, "EU Governance Techniques in the Creation of a Common European Policy on Immigration and Asylum," 9 *EPL*, 2003, 533–62. The common European policy on visas, asylum, and immigration is based on Title IV of the EC Treaty (Articles 61–69 EC), which was transferred from the third pillar to the first pillar by the Treaty of Amsterdam and for that reason still contains features that distinguish it from the rest of the treaty. See further Craig and de Búrca, n. 36 above, 30–32.

[213] Directive on the Status of Third-Country Nationals Who Are Long-Term Residents, [2004] OJ L16/44. For an analysis of the directive, see Steve Peers, "Implementing Equality? The Directive On Long-Term Third-Country Nationals," 29 *ELRev.*, 2004, 437–60.

IV. CONCLUSIONS

Good governance is about aims and results in pursuing citizens' aims, and about procedures in the exercise of public power. More specifically, it is about integrity and ethical behavior, about efficiency and effectiveness, and about the pursuit of equality of citizens and social justice for all. The question examined in this chapter was whether the European Union can be deemed to enjoy good governance in that sense.

According to Article 213 EC members of the Commission shall, in the general interest of the Community, be completely independent in the performance of their duties and behave with *integrity*.[214] The duties of commissioners and civil servants are spelled out in codes of conduct, which, in the terminology of Lon Fuller, are expressed in terms of morality of duty, and not (unfortunately) in terms of a code of ethics, which, in Fuller's terminology, is about morality of aspiration. The existing codes of conduct are of a bureaucratic nature, containing prohibitions, whereas they should be ethical codes of a democratic nature, that is, focused on goals, values, and aspirations. The difference becomes readily apparent, as we will see in the following chapter, in the way in which institutions deal with whistle-blowing and civil disobedience. Regrettably, the Commission has not been able to create a Committee on Standards in Public Life, as this would have helped to bring the issue of accountability through ethics to the foreground.

In its 2000 White Paper on Reforming the Commission, the European Commission aimed at improving the institution's efficiency and effectiveness. *Efficiency* is understood as a correct relationship between output of services and the resources used to produce them. *Effectiveness* concerns the relationship between the intended and the actual impact of action undertaken. Together, they are crucial for measuring an organization's output legitimacy, which depends on the capacity of the organization to achieve citizen goals. The European Community is organized along the *traditional mode of governance*: it is the task of an elected Parliament, acting in concert with the Council and the Commission, to define citizen goals and to determine the size and allocation of budgetary means needed to achieve these goals, while it is for the Commission to implement the budget and, thereafter, to obtain discharge from the Parliament. The process of implementation is made subject to an internal and

---

[214] Article 213 mentions the duty of integrity (and discretion) only in the context of commissioners engaging in any occupation after their term in office. But there can be no doubt that they are also bound, a fortiori, to act with integrity and honesty during their time in office.

external auditing system. Internal auditing, as embodied in the new Council Regulation 1605/2002, leaves behind the bureaucratic system of *ex ante* visas, which led to a culture denuding officials of responsibility, and delegates responsibility instead to officials who are commissioned to establish the organizational structure and management and the control procedures suited to the performance of the duties assigned to the organization. External auditing is carried out by the European Court of Auditors. Although it is designed to examine both legality and managerial performance, it is still perceived as being too bureaucratic and time-consuming.

In recent years *new modes of governance* have been put in place in order to increase the output legitimacy of the European construction in policy areas, such as social policy, where the interests and preferences of the Member States are less convergent than they were (and still are) in the area of economic integration, and for which Member States do not wish to abandon too much of their sovereignty. These new methods, and particularly the so-called "open method of coordination," are aimed at enhancing the European Union system's political capacity and policy effectiveness. Whereas the traditional method is based on binding and uniform legislation, the new methods are based on principles of voluntarism (non-binding targets and non-binding rules without formal sanctions), of subsidiarity (with targets agreed at Community level, and implementing measures decided, in a decentralized way, by states and private actors), and of inclusion (all actors participating in defining policy goals and determining the instruments to be applied). Negotiation, experimentation and learning, persuasion, sharing good practices, monitoring, and target readjustment are the mechanisms used at the European level.[215]

Among the citizen goals pursued in a democratic society, and therefore a primary concern of good governance, *equality in law* takes a prominent place. In Community law, the principle of equality has been the subject of an evolution that came about in three stages. The principle started its career as a limited prohibition on discrimination on the basis of nationality as regards the internal market freedoms (persons, goods, services, and capital), and an equally limited prohibition on discrimination on the basis of gender as regards equal pay. As a result of case law of the Court of Justice, and accompanying Community legislation, the first prohibition was gradually extended to encompass "peripheral" market participants, such as tourists in their capacity of beneficiaries of services, and the scope of the second prohibition was broadened to encompass all inequalities between men and women. Finally, as a result of treaty amendments, the principle was turned into a general principle

---

[215] Héritier, n. 10 above, 106.

unconnected to nationality or gender. As such, it became a principle offering equal protection at the federal and state levels, in a similar way as the Fourteenth Amendment in conjunction with the Fifth does in the United States.

A brief comparison of the equality principle in American and European law shows interesting similarities between the standards of judicial scrutiny that are used to define discriminatory behavior: on the American side, strict scrutiny, rationality scrutiny, and intermediate scrutiny; on the European side, the proportionality test. Similarities also exist in the way in which *affirmative or positive action* is constructed in both jurisdictions, in the United States primarily to correct race discrimination, in the European Union mainly to correct gender discrimination. A prominent example is the way in which diversity is promoted in the United States in university admission policies, and the way these policies are assessed in the Supreme Court's judgments in *Bakke*, and more recently in *Grutter v. Bollinger* and *Gratz v. Bollinger*. In these judgments diversity in the composition of the student body is seen as a compelling interest to allow affirmative action, provided the university's admission program is narrowly tailored to achieve that interest.

The Court of Justice also has examined the permissibility of affirmative action in its case law regarding gender inequalities, as, for example, in *Abrahamsson*, where the Court admitted that a female candidate for a public post in a Swedish university can be given preference over a candidate of the opposite sex when the difference between the merits of the candidates of each sex is not too disproportionate.[216] It appears from the court's case law that affirmative action cannot be based on the mere fact that a group is underrepresented, and that only specific measures that are designed to reduce de facto inequalities and to compensate for disadvantages in professional or educational life are permissible—provided that they are based on transparent and objective criteria that 1) are amenable to review, 2) contain sufficient flexibility to allow personal situations to be taken into account, and 3) are not disproportionate to the aim pursued. It appears from this brief overview that equality in law is as much a concern of good governance in the European Union as it is in the United States and that, in both jurisdictions, courts are equally prepared to validate affirmative or positive action within certain limits and along similar lines.

The pursuit of social justice by enabling dignified living for all is seen in Europe as an objective of good governance. For example, both the French and the German constitutions consider the characteristic of a social state an essen-

---

[216] See text accompanying n. 111 above.

tial part of the state structure.[217] It has been put forward, in this respect, that there is a profound difference between the American and the European mentalities. "Rights talk" would be typical for the American political discourse, and a citizenship of lonely rights bearers typical for American society. By contrast, Europe would have a different mentality, that is, the idea that citizens can be related and bound to the community without detracting from their individuality.[218] Although there may be some truth in this view, American society being perceived as a more "rights vindictive" society, with a more pronounced litigation culture than European society, the difference may lie primarily with a different perception of the freedom of choice, which in the United States, more than in Europe, is closely related to a tradition of independence from any history, inherited status, or even any community. That would explain why in the United States the need for safety nets, or at least safety nets of a state-centered variety, is felt less.[219]

Indeed, social security schemes, particularly within the health care sector, are organized differently in Europe and the United States. In Europe safety nets are considered a political priority and the foundation of the "social market" philosophy shared by all Member States. Consequently, Member States and the European Union are united in their ambition to provide a comprehensive social security system, of which health care is an essential part. In the United States, however, the approach is different. Americans do not rely upon the state to take care of their needs and envision social security only as a substitute for those persons who cannot, or can no longer, take care of themselves, that is, the less well-off, the elderly, and the disabled, for whom special programs have been instituted. That said, within the Union, the ambition set down in the EU Charter of Fundamental Rights to establish a comprehensive safety network for all Union citizens and residents still remains a matter for the individual states, as the EU itself has only limited competences in the area of social policy, and has hardly any resources. In other words, notwithstanding the long list of social rights enshrined in the EU Charter of Fundamental Rights, it remains for the Member States alone to make these rights effective, with the result that large differences in the social security systems of the now twenty-five Member States will continue to exist for quite some time.

The foregoing should not make one forget that there are a number of uni-

---

[217] Article 2 of the French 1958 Constitution and Article 20 of the German 1949 Constitution.

[218] See Glendon, n. 120 above, 127.

[219] See Michael Sandel in an interview referred to on pp. 186–87, and "The Ladd Report," referred to in n. 134 above.

fying factors at work. One of them is the impact that the internal market free-doms exercise on the Member State health care systems through EU legisla-tion and ECJ case law. The objective is to ensure that workers and their fami-lies, and providers and recipients of services, including providers and recipi-ents of medical services, can go to other Member States and enjoy there the same advantages as nationals of the host state, without losing the advantages they are entitled to in their own state. Another unifying factor is that Member States are encouraged to take advantage of each other's knowledge and experi-ence in areas of social policy through the so-called open method of coordina-tion, as exemplified in the area of social exclusion. The method is aimed at en-gaging Union and Member State institutions and private actors jointly in the fight against poverty. A third unifying factor is the growing importance of European citizenship, which, as a result of recent case law of the ECJ, comes to the fore as an autonomous source of social rights for Union citizens and their families who reside in a Member State other than their own.

New legislation is in the process of being adopted that will simplify the ap-plicable conditions and administrative formalities concerning the existing right of all EU citizens to travel and reside freely throughout the Union; how-ever, in the aftermath of the recent 2004 enlargement of the EU with ten new Member States, certain—and controversial—limitations regarding workers and their families from newly acceded Member States have been put in place for a long transitional period.[220] In contrast, a directive has recently been adopted granting the EU status of long-term resident to third-country nation-als. This directive illustrates the EU's desire to make Union citizenship not a divisive line but a cohesive one by treating long-term legal residents on a par with EU citizens.

[220] See n. 188 above.

CHAPTER FIVE

Open Government

Democratic government and good governance are empty concepts if civil servants are not encouraged to feel responsible for the common good and citizens are not stimulated to become involved in public affairs. This can only be achieved by allowing civil servants to speak freely on matters of general interest and providing citizens and the press with free access to public documents within limits that should not be drawn too narrowly. Only then will it be possible for vibrant public opinion and open government to emerge, both of which are needed to preserve democratic legitimacy and good governance. In this chapter, I will examine to what extent these elements are already part of the European Union's political culture.

I. CIVIC RESPONSIBILITY

Republicanism Correcting Individualism

The understanding of responsibility as a moral virtue is the quintessence of republicanism as I understand it, that is, as a political doctrine that emphasizes the need to care for the *res publica*, the common good. As such, this understanding is not antagonistic to liberalism, which is rightly regarded as the keystone of a democratically organized society, but is instead complementary to it. The function of republicanism is to prevent liberalism from being perverted by excesses of individualism.[1] According to the French writer Alain Renaut, there

---

[1] See further Alain Renaut, "Républicanisme et Modernité," in *Libéralisme et républicanisme: Cahiers de Philosophie de l'Université de Caen* 34 (2000): 165–88. Renaut defines liberalism in terms of its basic components: the necessity of limiting state action, the sovereignty of the people through its elected representatives, the recognition of the individual and his rights as a leading principle, and the neutrality of the state in matters of

are three versions of modern republicanism. The first is a moral version, as embodied in Rousseau's thinking, which regards the moral education of individuals as essential to reeducating them in appraising the general interest, and in exercising their right to participate in the exercise of sovereign power. The second
is a cultural version advocated by "communitarian" authors, such as Charles
Taylor and Michael Walzer,[2] who seek to cure the "malaise of modernity."[3]
These authors see republicanism as a counterweight against individuals with-
drawing into themselves and failing to invest in the public sphere. They regard
republicanism as an instrument to encourage a feeling of belonging to a community of traditions and values, which, in a pluralist society, must be multicultural.[4] The third version of republicanism is the political one, as proposed
by Habermas, which views republicanism not as the conscious belonging to a
community, but as the creation of more participatory political structures and
procedures. These structures and procedures are meant to convince citizens
that it is useful and worthwhile for them to engage in the public sphere.[5]

This is not the place to discuss these versions further, or to examine how
introspective and self-interested individuals can be encouraged to change their
attitudes and act more like responsible citizens. I have only two remarks on the
subject. First, recent research shows that membership in voluntary civil society
associations is important in promoting responsive and responsible citizenship
and that its impact grows with the level of education of the association members.[6] Second, the research also shows that civic responsibility should no longer
be understood exclusively in terms of interpersonal relations but also in terms
of universal values, such as sustainable development of the earth or concern for
poverty.[7]

---

religious and moral convictions. For a recent work on republicanism, see P. Pettit, *Republicanism: A Theory of Freedom and Government* (Oxford: Clarendon Press, 1997).

[2] C. Taylor, *Multiculturalism and the Politics of Recognition* (Princeton, N.J.:
Princeton University Press, 1992); M. Walzer, *Spheres of Justice: A Defence of Pluralism
and Equality* (Oxford: Blackwell, 1983); M. Walzer, *Thick and Thin: Moral Argument at
Home and Abroad* (Notre Dame: University of Notre Dame Press, 1997).

[3] Such is the title of one of Taylor's books.

[4] See W. Kymlicka, *Politics in the Vernacular: Nationalism, Multiculturalism and
Citizenship* (Oxford: Oxford University Press, 2001).

[5] On all this, see Renaut, n. 1 above, 173–77.

[6] On that subject, see M. Hooghe and D. Stolle, eds., *Generating Social Capital:
Civil Society and Institutions in Comparative Perspective* (New York: Palgrave, 2003), es-
pecially Hooghe's contribution "Voluntary Associations and Democratic Attitudes:
Value Congruence as a Causal Mechanism," 89–111, at 96–97.

[7] On this dimension, see J. B. Thompson, *The Media and Modernity: A Social Theory of the Media* (Cambridge: Polity Press, 1995), 261–62.

Instead, I will focus on the attitude of the EU organization toward civil servants who feel responsible for the proper functioning of the organization to which they belong.

Five Conceptions of Responsibility in Complex Organizations

In his book *Quest for Responsibility* Dutch legal and political scientist Mark Bovens distinguishes between five conceptions of responsibility that are characteristic of complex organizations, whether public or private:[8] 1) the hierarchical conception, in which the emphasis is on strict loyalty to one's own organization, particularly to one's superiors; 2) the personal conception, in which personal ethics and loyalty to one's own conscience are predominant; 3) the social conception, in which norms of decency and loyalty to one's peers are at the center; 4) the professional conception, in which the emphasis is on professional ethics and loyalty to one's own professional group; and 5) the civic conception, in which the emphasis is placed on civic values, such as democratic control, and focus on loyalty to parliament and to the public cause. Bovens discusses the merits and deficiencies of each of these conceptions. I will mention some.

Loyalty to superiors is the classical conception of organizational responsibility developed by, among others, Frederick Taylor and Max Weber.[9] Weber emphasizes the need for efficiency; he emphasizes that officials must be subordinate to democratic control by politicians; and he also stresses officials' duty of neutrality, and the impartiality of the rule of law. The concept of loyalty to superiors has lost some credibility in the last fifty years, as a result of the Nuremberg and Tokyo trials, in which Third Reich and Japanese high officials and generals invoked *"Befehl ist Befehl"* (commands have to be followed up) as an excuse for atrocities committed. Moreover, this hierarchical conception has become progressively more difficult to apply: the relationship between civil servants and their superiors has changed substantially in recent times as civil servants have become more educated, and the pyramidal form of

---

[8] M. Bovens, *The Quest for Responsibility: Accountability and Citizenship in Complex Organisations* (Cambridge: Cambridge University Press, 1998), 148–63. See also, by the same author, *De vierde macht revisited: Over ambtelijke macht en publieke verantwoording* [The fourth power revisited: About "civil service" power and public accountability] (Utrecht: Utrecht School of Governance, 2001).

[9] F. W. Taylor, *Principles and Methods of Scientific Management* (New York: Harper, 1911); Max Weber, *Politik als Beruf* (Munich: Duncker and Humboldt, 1919). See Mark Bovens, n. 8 above, 149–56, with further references to Henri Fayol, Woodrow Wilson, and Frank Goodnow. See also Robert D. Behn, *Rethinking Democratic Accountability* (Washington D.C.: Brookings Institution Press, 2001), 40–61.

hierarchy in complex organizations has flattened accordingly. Of course, this does not mean that the idea of loyalty to superiors should be abandoned: it remains, within limits, a basic virtue in public administration.[10]

On the other hand, the concept of *loyalty to conscience*, relied upon by conscientious objectors and whistle-blowers to justify their disobedience to superiors, can hardly be presented as a general alternative to the hierarchical conception. This concept is indeed at loggerheads with principles of legal certainty, equal treatment, and efficiency: in extremis, one's treatment by an organization would depend on the personal values of the person handling one's case. Again, this does not mean that the concept should have no role within an organization. An organization that permits individuals to express personal convictions and stand up for the ethical commitment of "their" organization, shows an openness on the part of management without which an organization cannot function properly within a democratic society.[11]

Loyalty to social values, such as decency, collegiality, and trustworthiness, has a clear advantage over loyalty to one's own conscience in that it offers a common ground for debate and allows scrutiny from third parties. However, it may also give rise to an excessive form of esprit de corps, such that a group such as a police force may become abusive if left unchecked.[12] In comparison, *loyalty to professional ethics*, as demonstrated by doctors, lawyers, and accountants working in an organization, constitutes an improved form of loyalty, as it introduces external moral considerations into the working environment, and it allows third parties to appeal to external obligations and standards. However, professional codes often function as an instrument to enhance professional status, to preserve bias, and to shield against outside interference.[13]

Finally, there is the *loyalty to citizens* embodied in the civic conception: "It proceeds on the assumption that when employees or civil servants pass through the company gate or up the stairs in the morning, they [do not] lay aside their citizenship and only retrieve it [as in the hierarchical conception] at the end of the working day, when they leave the organization behind and go home."[14] In that conception, the democratic constitutional state itself sets the limits as to what an organization can demand of its officials in terms of obedience and confidentiality. An organization cannot command its officials to violate their commitment to democracy when basic general interests are at

---

[10] See further Bovens, n. 8 above, 149–56.
[11] Ibid., 157–60.
[12] Ibid., 160–61.
[13] Ibid., 161–63.
[14] Ibid., 163.

stake, "such as the preservation of the rule of law, the enhancement of democratic control, the prevention of a violation of the law, of mismanagement, or
of the large-scale waste of government resources." By the same token, however, a large number of forms of disloyal behavior on the part of officials will
be illegitimate, for example, when they pursue party-political or personal interests at the expense of the interests detailed above.[15]

The Civic Dimension of Whistle-blowing

a) Whistle-blowing (and civil disobedience) in the European Union and
    in the United States

There are certain forms of behavior that are clearly inconsistent with the
hierarchical conception of responsibility but may be justifiable under the civic
conception of responsibility. Whistle-blowing is one such behavior.

This is well illustrated by the case of Clive Ponting, a senior civil servant in
the Ministry of Defence under the government of Margaret Thatcher. The case
concerned a British nuclear submarine's torpedoing of the Argentinean war-
ship General Belgrano in May 1982. The event resulted in the loss of life of 368
crew members and marked the beginning of the Falkland Islands conflict.[16]
The minister of defense asked Ponting to prepare answers to the questions
Parliament was expected to ask about the incident, but failed to use them
when Parliament indeed raised the questions. Shocked by the minister's behavior, Ponting sent a brief anonymous note to the Labour MP who had asked
the questions, encouraging him to press on. When a new series of questions
remained unanswered, and the undersecretary of defense gave intentionally
misleading information to the standing Commission of Foreign Affairs,[17]
Ponting sent his draft answers to the MP. The MP's questioning finally forced
the government to admit that Parliament had been misled on a number of
crucial points.

Clive Ponting was criminally prosecuted for breach of the Official Secrets
Act by communicating confidential information to a person "other than a person to whom he is authorized to communicate it, or a person to whom it is in
the interest of the state his duty to communicate it."[18] Ponting argued before

---

[15] Ibid., 168ff.

[16] For a thorough discussion of the case, see Bovens, n. 8 above, 146–48.

[17] Specifically, the undersecretary failed to relay the information that the Belgrano,
at the time of its sinking, had already changed course and was on its way back to its
home port. It was therefore no longer a threat to the British fleet.

[18] S. 2 (1) Official Secrets Act, quoted in N. MacCormick, Questioning Sovereignty
(Oxford: Oxford University Press, 1999), 33. The Ponting case is discussed from a constitutional law point of view at 28–48.

the court that, as a civil servant, he "must ultimately place his loyalty to Parliament and the public interest above his obligation to the interests of the Government of the day."[19] At the close of the trial, the presiding judge directed the jury that Ponting's defense depended on a misinterpretation of the law. In spite of this direction, the jury found Ponting "not guilty."[20] The decision implies, correctly in my view, that a minister's dissemination of misleading information to Parliament is inconsistent with basic democratic accountability.[21]

The European Union also has notorious cases of whistle-blowing. As mentioned in chapter 2,[22] the actions of civil servant Paul van Buitenen led to allegations of mismanagement and nepotism against Commissioner Edith Cresson and ultimately caused the resignation of the European Commission in 1999.[23] Although many of the allegations proved to be correct, van Buitenen's superiors did not appreciate his whistle-blowing. They first suspended him, then reduced his salary by half, and then began disciplinary proceedings against him. He finally left the Commission service.

Civil disobedience, or in a broader sense civil disloyalty, is another behavior that is in direct opposition to the hierarchical conception of responsibility. The issue is different from that arising in a whistle-blowing case. In the latter case, there is a conflict between a civil servant's duty of confidentiality and the general interest in disclosing alleged wrongdoing. In contrast, in a civil disloyalty case, the conflict is between a civil servant's freedom to express an opinion different from the opinion of the institution in which he works and his obligation to obey orders—which, if he fails to do, amounts to civil disobedience in the strict sense of the word. This is exemplified by the Connolly case that occurred in 1995. Bernard Connolly, a senior civil servant of the European Community and an active participant in the preparation of the European Monetary Union,[24] wrote a book called *The Rotten Heart of Europe: The Dirty War for Europe's Money* while he was on leave from the Commission. He pub-

---

[19] Quoted by Bovens, n. 8 above, 147.

[20] Referenced in MacCormick, n. 21 above, 30.

[21] I would have found it more appropriate, though, if Ponting had submitted the information directly to the chair of the standing Committee on Foreign Affairs rather than to an individual Member of Parliament, especially so because the MP in question was a member of the opposition, and therefore Ponting's action may have at least given the impression that it was motivated in part by party politics.

[22] See pp. 81–83.

[23] For a description of the event, see S. Douglas-Scott, *Constitutional Law of the European Union* (Harlow, England: Longman, 2002), 71–73.

[24] The monetary union refers to the Union's monetary policy, and the institutions in charge of it, regulated in Articles 105–124 EC.

lished the book without having obtained the permission of the Commission, as is prescribed by the staff regulations for civil servants. Except for that omission, Connolly's case did not involve wrongdoing or mismanagement. It rather concerned a publicly aired difference in opinion regarding an issue that he had worked on in the performance of his duties.

When Connolly returned to work, the Commission initiated disciplinary proceedings against him and removed him from his post for conduct involving a serious and irremediable breach of trust. The case finally ended up in the Community courts, where the removal decision was confirmed notwithstanding the European Court's recognition that "officials and other employees of the European Communities enjoy the right of freedom of expression . . . even in areas falling within the scope of activities of the Community institutions."[25] In the concrete circumstances of the case, the court found that the Commission had struck a reasonable balance between the requirement of allegiance and the freedom of expression of employees.[26] In the recently amended Staff Regulations for Community officials, the issue of disobedience —that is, not complying with orders —is addressed in the following terms: Article 21a grants an official the right of informing his superiors in writing—first his immediate superiors, then the hierarchical authority—that he or she considers orders to be irregular or likely to give rise to serious difficulties; if the superiors confirm the orders, the official shall carry them out unless they are "manifestly illegal or constitute a breach of the relevant safety standards."[27] By contrast, the Staff Regulations do not specifically deal with civil disloyalty—that is, publicly expressing a dissenting opinion—leaving the matter to be decided by the Community courts case by case.

Whistle-blowing has received more attention from the EU institutions than has civil disloyalty. In its second report (referring to the case of van Buitenen), the Committee of Independent Experts emphasized the impor-

[25] Case C-274/99P, *Bernard Connolly v. Commission*, [2001] ECR I-1611, para. 43. See also Case C-100/88, *Oyowe and Traore v. Commission*, [1989] 4285, para. 16.

[26] At para. 51ff. As for the concrete circumstances of the case, the court noted, in paragraph 62, "that Mr Connolly was dismissed not merely because he had failed to apply for prior permission . . . or because he had expressed a dissentient opinion, but because he had published, without permission, material in which he had severely criticised, and even insulted, members of the Commission and other superiors and had challenged fundamental aspects of Community policies which had been written into the Treaty by the Member States and to whose implementation the Commission had specifically assigned him the responsibility of contributing in good faith." On the permission to publish, see now Article 17a of the amended Staff Regulations referred to in n. 37 below.

[27] See Council Regulation (EC, Euratom) No. 723/2004 of March 22, 2004, referred to in n. 37 below.

tance of whistle-blowing in the following terms:

> The events leading up to the resignation of the former Commission demonstrated the value of officials whose conscience persuades them of the need to expose wrongdoings encountered in the course of their duties. They also showed how the reaction of superiors failed to live up to legitimate expectations. Instead of offering ethical guidance, the hierarchy put additional pressure upon one such official.

The Committee added a caveat, though:

> This does not mean that officials must be encouraged to come forward in all instances where they believe that superiors or colleagues have not acted correctly. The duty of loyalty and discretion must not become an empty concept. But neither must it be used to install a conspiracy of silence.[28]

The question, then, is how to strike the correct balance between loyalty to an individual's institution, superiors, and colleagues and loyalty to one's own conscience and the public's general interest in preventing serious shortcomings in government.

In the United States the right of civil servants to criticize government finds protection in the First Amendment on free speech.[29] Thus in *Pickering v. Board of Education*, decided in 1968, the Supreme Court held that a public school teacher could not constitutionally be dismissed for criticizing, in a letter to a newspaper, the school board's handling of revenue measures for the school, and its allocation of financial resources.[30] Speaking for the court, Justice Marshall stated that government employees do not relinquish "the First Amendment rights they would otherwise enjoy as citizens to comment on matters of public interest," but noted also that "the State has interests as an employer in

---

[28] Second Report on Reform of the Commission: Analysis of Current Practice and Proposals for Tackling Mismanagement, Irregularities and Fraud (Brussels, Sept. 10, 1999), paras. 7.6.9 and 7.6.10. See chapter 2, p. 81.

[29] Compare with the protection under Article 10 of the ECHR. The ECtHR has not yet had the opportunity to decide on whistle-blowing, but it has had the occasion to rule that civil servants enjoy the protection of Article 10 ECHR: see, for instance, *Vogt v. Germany*, judgment of September 26, 1995, Series A-323, para. 31 (concerning the dismissal of a schoolteacher actively engaged in the Communist Party). However, the court allows states a large margin of appreciation to apply the exceptions enumerated in Article 10 [2]: see *Ahmed et al. v. United Kingdom*, judgment of September 2, 1998, Reports 1998-VI (allowing a prohibition on political activities), with a joint dissenting opinion, however, of Judges Speilmann, Pekkanen, and Van Dijk. See further L. Vickers, "Whistleblowing in the Public Sector and the ECHR," *PL*, 1997, 594–602; and F. B. Ronkes Agerbeek, *Zeg ik dat goed? EU ambtenaren en hun vrijheid van meningsuiting* [Do I say it correctly? EU civil servants and their freedom of expression of opinion] (Leiden: E. M. Meijers Instituut, Leiden University, 2003), 69.

[30] 391 U.S. 563 (1968).

regulating the speech of its employees that differ significantly from [those concerning] the speech of the citizenry in general. The problem is to arrive at a balance."[31] In this respect, the content of the communication may be highly relevant, as a civil servant's criticism lacks constitutional protection if it does not involve a matter of public concern.[32]

As for whistle-blowing specifically, Congress adopted in 1978 the Civil Service Reform Act, which accorded special protection to federal employees facing adverse action for reporting agency misconduct.[33] The act explicitly prohibits federal institutions from imposing disciplinary measures or other sanctions on a civil servant in cases involving justifiable forms of whistle-blowing, namely "a disclosure of information by an employee or applicant which the employee reasonably believes evidences (i) a violation of any law, rule, or regulation, or (ii) mismanagement, a gross waste of funds, an abuse of authority, or a substantial and specific danger to public health or safety."[34]

b) Dealing with whistle-blowing properly

On the basis of the American Civil Service Reform Act and other sources, Bovens analyzes the grounds that can make disclosing information legitimate. He names the following grounds: having knowledge of 1) serious penal offences

[31] On speech and association by public employees and contractors, see Sullivan and Gunther, *Constitutional Law,* 14th ed. (New York: Foundation Press, 2001), 1258–74.

[32] *Connick v. Meyers,* 461 U.S. 138 (1983). See also *United States v. National Treasury Employees Union,* 513 U.S. 454 (1995), where the Supreme Court invalidated a ban on honoraria that civil servants received from making speeches or writing articles. Justice Stevens, writing for the majority, indicated, however, that the ban might have been appropriate if Congress had demanded a nexus between the speaker's employment and the subject of the expression.

[33] The act was adopted under President Carter, who had campaigned for an ethically clean administration. As a result of criticism, as well as lengthy hearings and reports, Congress later concluded that the act had not met all stated expectations. See Bovens, n. 8 above, 202–6. In 1989 the Whistleblower Protection Act was adopted to strengthen the position of whistle-blowers, but a subsequent 1992 survey indicated that the effect of that amendment remained similarly restricted; ibid., 206. Accordingly, in 1994, new amendments were made to the act.

[34] Quoted by Bovens, n. 8 above, 202. For a discussion, see Robert G. Vaughn, "Statutory Protection of Whistleblowers in the Federal Executive Branch," *U.Ill.L.Rev.,* 1982, 615. Recent American whistle-blowing cases in the public and private sectors concerned three women named by *Time* magazine the Persons of the Year for 2002: Coleen Rowley, the FBI agent whose pleas before the September 11 attacks were ignored by her superiors; Cynthia Cooper, the internal auditor at WorldCom who alerted the firm's board of directors of accounting irregularities; and Sherron Watkins, the Enron vice president who warned the company's chairman that the firm could collapse as a result of extensive false accounting.

or other serious violations of laws or regulations; 2) substantial and specific danger to public health, safety, or the environment; 3) gross waste, or unauthorized use of public funds and other large-scale forms of mismanagement; 4) the misleading of controlling or supervising bodies, particularly parliament.

Bovens also describes the standards of care with which whistle-blowers must comply when disclosing information. They must reasonably believe that something improper has occurred, or was about to occur, and that the competent authorities were not already dealing with the matter in an appropriate way; and no other less far-reaching means must have been available to the whistle-blower to deal with the situation, including the possibility of raising the matter internally. Moreover, the interest that the whistle-blower intends to serve must be weighed against the possible damage to the legitimate interests of the public service, colleagues, and involved third parties, and to the public interest of a general or specific nature. Furthermore, the whistle-blower must try to restrict the damage resulting from the disclosure; and he or she must turn to the appropriate body to make the disclosure, which implies that he or she must be prepared to come forward and should "be aloof and unresponsive in his or her relations with the media."[35]

In the aftermath of the EU Commission's 1999 resignation, the new European Commission exposed its attitude toward whistle-blowers in a communication presented in 2000 by the Commission's vice president, Neil Kinnock, entitled *Raising Concerns about Serious Wrongdoings*.[36] The communication took a broad view of the usefulness of whistle-blowing and stated that, "if an organization ensures that there are acceptable and safe ways in which an employee can raise a concern about wrongdoing, this will have a deterrent effect," and that the effect of such arrangements will be "that a more open and self-disciplined culture is encouraged." Following the communication, the Commission formulated amendments to the Staff Regulations, applicable to all officials of the European Communities, which were finally adopted by the Council on March 22, 2004.[37]

---

[35] For a further discussion of both the grounds justifying disclosure and the standards of care that whistle-blowers must comply with, see Bovens, n. 8 above, 207–9 and 209–11. The author adds that "media attention, however effective, often causes much damage to legitimate interests and offers few possibilities for a substantive and procedurally careful consideration of the matter in hand" (211). In a sense, Bovens's standards of due care incorporate a proportionality test similar in approach to that applied by the ECJ.

[36] Consultative document of November 29, 2000, SEC (2000) 2078.

[37] Council Regulation (EC, Euratom) No. 723/2004 of March 22, 2004, amending the Staff Regulations of Officials of the European Communities and the Conditions of

According to Article 22a of the amended Staff Regulations, it is the duty of any official of a Community institution to inform without delay one of the persons mentioned below of "any presumption of possible illegal activity detrimental to the interests of the Communities, or relating to the discharge of professional duties which may constitute a serious failure" to comply with official obligations by an official, a member of the institution (for example, a commissioner), or a person carrying out work for the institution. The information should be communicated to the whistle-blower's immediate superior, his or her director-general, or the secretary-general of the institution (or a person holding an equivalent position). The whistle-blower should also transmit any evidence of which he or she is aware directly to the European Anti-Fraud Office (OLAF). If the official concerned "honestly and reasonably believes that the information disclosed, and any allegation contained in it, is substantially true," he or she may, according to Article 22b, go outside his or her institution and disclose the information to either the president of the Commission, the Court of Auditors, the Council, the European Parliament, or the European Ombudsman; however, he or she may only take such action after allowing the institution concerned or OLAF a period of time decided upon by the institution or office (unless he or she can prove the period unreasonable) within which to take appropriate action. Pursuant to both these articles, an official who has complied with the foregoing provisions shall not suffer any prejudicial effects on the part of the institution concerned as a result of having communicated information.

Unfortunately, neither the 2000 communication (or subsequent documents) nor the amendments in Articles 22a and 22b of the amended Staff Regulation delineate the specific grounds that may be relied upon in order to justify whistle-blowing or specify the duty of care with which a whistle-blower must comply. The only guideline is that he or she must act "reasonably and honestly."[38] Requiring a whistle-blower to go to his or her own superiors and to the European Anti-Fraud Office before proceeding to the president of the institution concerned or to the European Ombudsman is understandable; however, the strictly hierarchical nature of the procedure, involving the highest level of the institution concerned, may in fact discourage many potential whistle-blowers.[39] Further, it means that neither confiding in an individual

---

Employment of Other Servants of the European Communities, [2004] OJ L124, 1.

[38] Thus, Articles 22a (3) and 22b (1) (a) of the Staff Regulations, n. 37 above. Article 22c adds that the official may still incur personal liability under the relevant national law.

[39] It is not clear from the text whether the whistle-blower may go to the president of an institution other than his or her own, for example, for a Commission official to go to the president of the European Parliament or the Court of Auditors. In a press release published on March 22, 2004, the Commission does not clarify this point.

Member of Parliament (as whistle-blower van Buitenen did) nor, a fortiori, going to external persons or organizations, particularly going to the media, is permissible under any circumstances. It is therefore unlikely that the system, thus conceived, would have been of any assistance to whistle-blowers such as Ponting or van Buitenen. In short, it is designed predominantly with the institution's interests in mind and shows too much faith in the capacity of a complex organization to police itself. It also ignores the extreme pressure of conscience under which honest whistle-blowers may labor when it becomes clear to them that their complaints will not be heard, acted upon by their immediate superiors, or paid attention to by the head of the organization.

To be of real assistance to whistle-blowers, the adopted measures should provide whistle-blowers with more legal certainty by spelling out the grounds of justification on which they can rely and the standard of care with which they must comply.[40] They should spell out some rule of proportionality, such as 1) there must be cause, or good reason, for whistle-blowing; 2) the whistle-blowing action must be indispensable and be kept within limits of necessity; and 3) its aim must be weighed against other compelling interests. The measures should, moreover, come to terms with a basic question that has not been properly addressed in the adopted measures, namely, whether a potential whistle-blower should be enabled to have recourse, at an early stage of the process, to an external body of impartial and experienced persons with the legal and moral authority to look into the matter and give advice on how to handle the situation further. Without such advice, it will be impossible for a whistle-blower to fully come to grips with the situation, and unrealistic to expect an individual under extreme pressure to assess the proportionality of his or her action correctly.

However, for such a procedure to be workable, this external body must be completely unbureaucratic. It must be able to give the whistle-blower fast and personal guidance, and offer the assurance that following such guidance will not result in disciplinary action. If these conditions are not fulfilled, the system would be dilatory, and it would actually discourage bona fide whistle-blowers from taking advice.[41]

Clarity is also lacking at another point, i.e., where the press release states that "to provide assistance to officials who feel unclear about their duty . . . , the Commission is ensuring that all staff have access to confidential and impartial advice without making it compulsory." It remains ambiguous how this statement will be implemented.

[40] That would also be in accordance with the recommendation of the European Ombudsman in van Buitenen's case: see *The European Ombudsman Annual Report*, 2000, 19.

[41] Compare with the considerations of Bovens, n. 8 above, stating that the American Civil Service Reform Act "is so long winded and full of safety clauses that not only

II. FREE ACCESS TO PUBLIC DOCUMENTS

In chapter 1, reference was made to open government as a Swedish invention, as that country passed its first constitutional statute on freedom of the press and access to public documents in 1766. The European Union did not provide for similar access until 1997, when the principle was inscribed in Article 255 EC Treaty by the Amsterdam Treaty. The first paragraph of Article 255 states that "any citizen of the Union, and any natural or legal person residing or having its registered office in a Member State, shall have a right of access to European Parliament, Council and Commission documents." The article goes on to require the Council, acting jointly with Parliament, to determine the "general principles and limits on grounds of public or private interest governing this right to access." It was only after protracted discussions that the Community institutions were able to comply with that requirement through Regulation (EC) No. 1049/2001.[42] Actually, this was after Article 42 of the EU Charter of Fundamental Rights had already elevated the right of access to a fundamental "citizen" right.[43]

Conflicting Views on How Much Free Access

Opinions as to the extent to which citizens (and the media) should be granted access to public documents vary widely from one jurisdiction to another. Notably, the difference in access afforded to the public between a Member State like Sweden and the European Union was illustrated by a 1998 case before the Court of First Instance.[44]

The case was initiated by the Swedish Journalists Association against the EU Council. It turned on the refusal of the Council's General Secretariat to

---

troublemakers and spies but even bona fide whistleblowers are effectively kept at bay" (213).

[42] Regulation 1049/2001 on Public Access to Documents, [2001] OJ L145/43. For a comprehensive account of the development of transparency in the EU, see S. Peers, "From Maastricht to Laeken: The Political Agenda of Openness and Transparency in the EU," in *Increasing Transparency in the European Union*, ed. Veerle Deckmyn (Maastricht: EIPA, 2002).

[43] This article prevents arguments that only Member States would have standing in court to claim a right to information. See Alasdair Roberts, "Multilateral Institutions and the Right to Information: Experience in the European Union," 8 *EPL*, 2002, 255–75, at 274.

[44] Case T-174/95, *Svenska Journalistförbundet v. EU Council*, [1998] ECR II-2289. For comments on this and other CFI judgments, see the annotation of I. Österdahl in 36 *CMLRev.*, 1999, 1059–77.

grant the association access to twenty documents, all relating to the European Police Office (Europol) and thus falling within the third pillar. The Secretariat originally granted access to only two documents, but agreed to give access to four documents after a "confirmatory application" had been made. In the meantime, the association had been granted access to eighteen of the *same* twenty documents through an application to the Swedish authority, which had obtained the documents from the EU Secretariat. The Swedish Journalists Association subsequently filed suit with the Court of First Instance asking for the annulment of the EU Council's refusal. Although the CFI granted the association standing in court under Article 230 EC,[45] even though the documents requested were third-pillar police documents, it did not rule on substantive law issues, such as the potential violation of a citizen's right to access. It nevertheless annulled the Council decision; it did so, however, on due process grounds, ruling that it had been inadequately motivated.

Regulation 1049/2001, adopted by the European Parliament and the Council on May 30, 2001, must be seen against this background. It came about after the Council had unilaterally amended its own 1993 decision adding two new categories of mandatory public interest, one based on "the security and defense of the Union or one of its Member States" and the other on "military or non-military crisis management."[46] The amendment had been concocted during the summer of 2000 when the European Parliament was in recess. The amendment was bitterly received by Parliament and by some national governments, especially the Dutch government. It was only after grueling negotiations between the Commission, Council, and Parliament that the Swedish presidency of the Council could secure a compromise: Regulation 1049/2001.[47]

I will not explain in detail the scope of the right of access contained in the regulation;[48] rather, I will concentrate on the most important points. The

[45] Despite the ECJ's narrow interpretation of the right of private plaintiffs to initiate proceedings under that provision; see Douglas-Scott, n. 23 above, 363ff.

[46] The doubtful action of the Council was called the Solana "coup," after the head of the Council's General Secretariat, and was made to satisfy the EU's NATO partners: see Douglas-Scott, n. 23 above, 146–47.

[47] Ibid., 147.

[48] The regulation, n. 42 above, mostly confirms the CFI's ruling in the Swedish Journalist Association case. However, a compromise was reached in Article 5 of the regulation with regard to the communication of documents received from outside sources. Article 5 requires the Member State *either* to "consult with the institution concerned in order to take a decision that does not jeopardize the attainment of the objectives of this regulation" *or* to "refer the request to the [Community] institution [concerned]."

regulation is broad in purpose, scope, and beneficiaries. Article 2 (1) provides any citizen or legal resident of the Union, in accordance with Article 255 EC, with a right of access to European Parliament, Council, and Commission documents. The article further grants the institutions the ability to confer the same right upon non-residents. Section (3) of the article makes the regulation applicable to all documents "held by an institution, that is to say, drawn up or received by it and in its possession, in all areas of activity of the European Union." It therefore applies to documents concerning all three pillars of the Community. Furthermore, Article 3 defines the term "document" broadly, encompassing any content, whatever its medium.

However, after this promising start, Article 4 (1) and (2) of the regulation sets out a long list of exceptions. These exceptions are designed to protect the following public interests: 1) public security, 2) defense and military matters, 3) international relations, 4) the financial, monetary, or economic policy of the Community or a Member State, 5) the privacy and the integrity of the individual, 6) commercial interests, including intellectual property, 7) court proceedings and legal advice, and 8) inspections, investigations, and audits. If an institution asserts any of these exceptions, it must prove, under Article 4 (1) and (2), that disclosure would "undermine the interest" protected by the exception. With regard to the last three exceptions, Article 4 (2) requires a further (balancing) test: the institution must grant access even when disclosure would harm the protected interest if the applicant can show "an overriding interest in disclosure." Thus, for instance, when an institution asserts the protection of privacy and the integrity of the individual, proof of harm suffices to *refuse* disclosure; however, when an institution asserts the commercial interests of a person or company, including those related to intellectual property, disclosure *cannot* be refused if the applicant can show an overriding interest in disclosure.

Clearly, Regulation 1049/2001 constitutes a compromise between conflicting views and can be seen as an illustration of a free debate between institutions and public authorities. At the outset, the accessibility of documents prepared by the services of the Council and the Commission was very limited in scope and content. This provoked within the Union a fierce debate between the advocates and opponents of openness. Among the advocates of openness were the European Parliament, the Community judiciary (especially the CFI and advocates general of the ECJ), the European Ombudsman, and some Member States, mainly the Nordic states and the Netherlands. They demanded, and finally obtained, greater transparency despite the efforts of those opposing transparency, including the Commission, the Council, and some of the larger Member States, like France, Germany, Italy, and Spain.[49]

Parliament, for example, succeeded in broadening the scope of transparency, reversing many of the limitations on transparency that the Commission and the Council had proposed in the draft text of the regulation. The European Ombudsman was able to prevent the Council from altogether excluding from disclosure the so-called "Presidency Documents," which are the records produced by the Member State holding the presidency of the Council.[50] For its part, the Court of First Instance found a right of access to documents in many of its judgments.[51] The ECJ upheld most of these judgments, and advocates general later used the judgments to emphasize the necessity, in a democratic society, of turning the right of access into a general principle. In addition, many of the CFI and ECJ judgments were later confirmed in legislation. All of these actions were strongly supported by the Nordic states, particularly Sweden and Finland, which had made transparency a condition for their accession to the Union.

The debate between institutions and Member States on the text of Regulation 1049/2001 remains illustrative of the vast differences in opinion on openness between and among Member States and Community institutions. To be sure, the EU's approach to transparency is no longer that of a standard international organization, as was the case in the early Community, but it remains uncertain whether transparency has actually become an overarching principle that can be enforced before the Community courts.[52]

Freedom of Information in the United States

Prior to the enactment in the United States of the 1966 Freedom of Information Act, § 3 of the Administrative Procedure Act (APA) "gave the agencies a virtual *carte blanche* to withhold information from whomever they pleased and to set up what amounted to a *de facto* presumption against disclosure.

[49] For an astute analysis of this situation, see Roberts, n. 43, 271–73.

[50] Ibid., 262–63, where the relevant decisions of the ombudsman are quoted in the footnotes.

[51] For references, see Jan Wouters, "Institutional and Constitutional Challenges for the European Union: Some Reflections in the Light of the Treaty of Nice," 26 *ELRev.*, 2001, 342–56, at 349, n. 49. For a brief overview, see Ian Harden, "Citizenship and Information," 7 *EPL.*, 2001, 165–93, at 178–79.

[52] P. Craig and G. de Búrca, *EU Law, Text, Cases and Materials*, 3d ed. (Oxford: Oxford University Press, 2003), 395, where the role of the ombudsman as a key player in the development of openness and transparency is highlighted. See also the description of the function and task of the ombudsman in Article 195 EC.

Agencies read §3 as permitting them to do almost anything they wanted with their data."[53] That changed dramatically when Congress adopted the Freedom of Information Act.[54] Since then, any person may request information from any agency—including independent regulatory commissions, the executive office of the president, all other executive departments, all government corporations, *and* the military—without demonstrating, as required under the old version, that it is properly and directly concerned. Disclosure may be obtained of any agency record, a term that the Supreme Court has broadly construed, emphasizing that an agency resisting disclosure carries the burden of proof that information in its hands is not an agency record.[55] Where some part of the document is protected, any "reasonably segregable" portion shall be provided.[56]

The Freedom of Information Act was amended by Congress in 1974 to make information even more easily obtainable.[57] The act now contains a list of nine exemptions, concerning 1) national security information, 2) internal personnel rules and files, 3) separate statutory exemptions, 4) commercial/financial information and trade secrets, 5) inter- and intra-agency memoranda, 6) personnel, medical, and other files, disclosure of which would violate personal privacy, 7) law enforcement and investigation files, 8) data on financial institutions, and 9) certain geological and geophysical information on oil and natural gas wells. According to a commentator, "the exemptions are supposed to protect as little as possible, consistent with the exemption's [carefully specific] language, and are to be read in light of the fundamental purpose and presumption of the [act] favoring disclosure of information."[58]

In the aftermath of the Watergate scandal, Congress was concerned with too much government decision making taking place in secret. It enacted in 1976 the Sunshine Act (or Open Meeting Act) requiring agencies, headed by a collegial body, to conduct their meetings in a format that is open to the public, and to publish meeting times and topics in advance in the Federal Register. In addition to the nine exemptions referred to above, an exemption was added, however, allowing for a closed meeting if openness would "significantly

---

[53] William F. Fox, Jr., *Understanding Administrative Law*, 4th ed. (Lexis Publishing, Matthew Bender, 2000), 365.

[54] The act is incorporated in §552 of the Administrative Procedure Act (APA). Excerpts from the latter are reproduced in Fox, n. 53 above, 395–437.

[55] *Department of Justice v. Tax Analysts*, 492 U.S. 136 (1989).

[56] Fox, n. 53 above, 370; see § 552 (b), *in fine*, APA.

[57] Ibid., 373.

[58] Ibid., 374.

frustrate implementation of a proposed agency action."[59] Though the idea is "healthy in concept . . . [it is] completely unworkable in practice . . . , true deliberations tak[ing] place elsewhere—in hallway conversations or exchanges of memoranda."[60] Another reaction to the Watergate scandal consisted in the adoption in 1974 of the Federal Privacy Act. This act restricts the manner in which government may collect and disseminate personal information, provides penalties for wrongful disclosure, and gives a person a statutory right to correct or supplement information. The upshot of the act is to establish a presumption *against* disclosure, and to provide exceptions under which applicants are given the right to obtain data.[61]

It is difficult to access the impact of the USA Patriot Act passed by Congress in 2001, weeks after the September 11 terrorist attack, on the foregoing. Concerns have been expressed over the loss of the public's right to access official information and its right to privacy. Although this new legislation has indeed affected access, there is evidence indicating that it is not strictly enforced.[62]

III. CIVIL SOCIETY, PUBLIC OPINION, AND CITIZEN PARTICIPATION

Civil society, public opinion, and citizen access to political power are three interrelated concepts. Together with freedom of the press, dealt with in the following section, they give voice to the realm of organized social life, autonomous from the state and standing between the private sphere of individual and family life and the public sphere represented by the state and other public entities.

The Importance of Civil and Civic Society

The concept of *civil* society refers nowadays to the role of nongovernmental organizations (NGOs) in the implementation of national or international governmental policies. In the jargon of the European Union, it en-

---

[59] § 552b (c) (9) (B) of the Administrative Procedure Act.

[60] Fox, n. 53 above, 380.

[61] Ibid., 381.

[62] See Paul Bellamy, Background paper no. 27 on Access to Official Information, May 2003 (Paul.Bellamy@parliament.govt.nz); and Dahlia Lithwick and Julia Turner, "A Guide to the Patriot Act," Parts I, II, III, and IV, posted on *Slate*, Sept. 8–11, 2003: http://slate.msn.com/id/2088106/. See also David Cole, "Enemy Aliens," 54 *Stanford Law Review*, 2002, 953–1004, at 966–74.

compasses the various private law groups, so-called "stakeholders," that have an interest in one or another governmental project and are therefore eligible to be consulted, often via digital means.[63] Intermediate organizations as part of civil society have deep roots in Western political thinking on both sides of the Atlantic: "Rooted in aristocratic criticisms of royal absolutism [it] describes civil society as an intermediate sphere of voluntary association and activity standing between the individual and the state."[64] This political thinking

> is closely identified with the work of Alexis de Tocqueville, but its roots can be found in the Baron de Montesquieu's fear of modernity's centralizing monarchies, Jean-Jacques Rousseau's preference for an intimate small-scale republic, and Edmund Burke's attack on the French Revolution. All three came together in Tocqueville's remarkably influential body of thought, whose anti-statist thrust . . . explain[s] its contemporary popularity.[65]

Civil society remains at the center of modern political thinking. It is recognized to supplement the impact that the political elite has on democracy in developmental terms, that is, democracy understood as "a political system that emerges gradually in fragments or parts, and is always capable of becoming more liberal, inclusive, responsive, accountable, effective, and just."[66] In political sociologist Larry Diamond's terms, "Civil society is the realm of organized social life that is open, voluntary, self-generating, at least partially self-supporting, autonomous from the state, and bound by a legal order or set of shared rules."[67]

[63] Thus the Commission's White Paper on European Governance of July 25, 2001, COM (2001) 428 final (discussed in chapter 4, pp. 159–60 and 164), stating that "Introducing change requires effort from all the other Institutions, central government, regions, cities, and civil society in the current and future Member States." For a concrete example, see the involvement of civil society in the open method of coordination on social exclusion: chapter 4, pp. 197ff.

[64] John Ehrenberg, *Civil Society: The Critical History of an Idea* (New York: New York University Press, 1999), 144.

[65] Ibid. A great admirer of the United States, de Tocqueville, addressing himself to his fellow Frenchmen, described American society in 1835 as follows: "Nothing struck me more forcibly than the general equality of condition among the people" and "the prodigious influence that this primary fact exercises on the whole course of society . . . extends far beyond the political character and the laws of the country, and . . . has no less effect on civil society than it has on government." Quoted by Ehrenberg, n. 64 above, 160–61, from Alexis de Tocqueville, *Democracy in America* (New York: Random House, 1990), 1: 3.

[66] Larry Diamond, *Developing Democracy: Toward Consolidation* (Baltimore, Md.: Johns Hopkins University Press, 1999), 219.

[67] Ibid., 221.

Civil society organizations are distinct from other groups in society in five respects: 1) civil society is concerned with public ends rather than private ends; 2) it relates to the state in some way but does not seek to win control over or position within the state; 3) it encompasses pluralism and diversity in that, by contrast with religious fundamentalism or ethnic chauvinism, it does not seek to monopolize a space in society, crowding out all competitors and claiming that it represents the only legitimate path; 4) it does not seek to represent the complete set of interests of a person or a community; and 5) it should be distinguished from *civic* community or society: whereas the latter (in Robert Putnam's understanding) consists of "interpersonal" trust-building associations, such as neighborhood associations and choral societies, and is more democracy enhancing; civil society groups, by contrast, have an explicitly civic (public) or political purpose, for instance to reform the polity or advocate human rights.[68]

In Diamond's view, five features are important for a democratic civil society, that is, a civil society that seeks to foster and deepen democracy. These are: 1) self-government in accordance with democratic principles of transparency, accountability, participation, deliberation, representation, and rotation of leadership; 2) goals and methods that are not maximalist and uncompromising, and do not reject the rule of law and the authority of the democratic state; 3) organizational institutionalization along established procedures that are widely and reliably known and regularly practiced and that are opposed to personalized, arbitrary, and unpredictable modes of operation; 4) pluralism allowing multiplicity as to alternatives within each arena or interest sector; and 5) a large number of associations representing a wide range of societal interests, and the ability of citizens to have more than one membership.[69]

As mentioned above, according to Diamond, *civil* society should be distinguished from *civic* community, or civic society. The former refers to organizations that seek to promote democracy by, for instance, defending collective rights and values (such as human rights or environmental organizations), or by pooling resources and talents to improve the quality of life (such as organizations fighting poverty or attempting to enhance the functioning of the political system). By contrast, civic society refers to (often unstructured, and, if not, then horizontally structured) organizations that bring together citizens for any purpose around ties that are more or less mutual, cooperative, and trusting. The distinction is not that easily made, and civic communities may become engaged in civil society goals, for instance, when a church community

[68] Ibid., 223–27.
[69] Ibid., 227–33.

organizes itself to fight poverty.[70] Civic community turns around the notion of social capital, advocated by Robert Putnam, which, unlike physical capital (which refers to physical objects) or human capital (which refers to properties of individuals), "refers to connections among individuals—social networks and the norms of reciprocity and trustworthiness that arise from them. In that sense social capital is closely related to what some have called 'civic virtue.' The difference is that 'social capital' calls attention to the fact that civic virtue is most powerful when embedded in a dense network of reciprocal social relations."[71]

Social capital as generated in civic communities is widely recognized to have profound implications for the quality and consolidation of democracy. Both for economic development and effective democracy, voluntary cooperation is crucial: such cooperation "is greatly facilitated by interpersonal trust and norms of reciprocity, and these cultural orientations in turn are fostered by (but also deepen) 'networks of social engagement,' in which citizens are drawn together as equals in 'intense horizontal interaction.'"[72] In Putnam's words, social capital generates "active participation in public affairs; widespread political equality; norms of solidarity, trust, and tolerance; and a thick structure of associations with multiple memberships [that] correlate highly with one another."[73] Putnam's insights have been deepened by other research, which has shown that multiple or overlapping personal memberships in voluntary associations are indeed related to the development of civic attitudes. Not all types of associations have the same effect, however: social and hobby groups, for example, have less democracy-fostering effect than more value-oriented groups. Recent research also shows that, in addition to civic communities, government policy and institutions play a role in this development as well.[74]

To sum up, civil *and* civic society are strong instruments to foster and

[70] Ibid., 225–26.

[71] Robert D. Putnam, *Bowling Alone: The Collapse and Revival of American Community* (New York: Simon and Schuster, 2000), quoted in Ann G. Serow and Everett C. Ladd, eds., *American Polity*, 3d ed. (Baltimore, Md.: Lanahan Publishers, 2003), 17–26.

[72] Larry Diamond, n. 66 above, 225, referring to Robert Putnam et al., *Making Democracy Work: Civic Traditions in Modern Italy* (Princeton, N.J.: Princeton University Press, 1993).

[73] N. 71 above, quoted by J. Ehrenberg, n. 64 above, 227, where references are also found to works of other "communitarian" theorists.

[74] Hooghe and Stolle, n. 6 above, at 11. The authors caution, however, "about unwarranted optimism: institutional effects do not work overnight, rather long established institutional patterns and policies are behind successful cases of social capital."

deepen democracy—particularly so in a "body politic" like the European Union, which is in search of democratic legitimacy. It is therefore essential to let them play their role, which should be done by involving *civil* society in the European political process and by reinvigorating *civic* education about Europe in schools, encouraging youth associations, and promoting community-based television programs.[75] How this might be achieved is discussed below.

Citizen Access to the Political Process

The participation of citizens in the political process has a double meaning. It refers to a citizen's participation through elected representatives (parliament) *and* non-elected actors (political parties and public interest or social action groups), but it also refers to the personal involvement of citizens. Such personal involvement can be direct, as through voting, campaigning, standing as a candidate and, if elected, exercising a political mandate. It can also be indirect, for example by participating in civil society organizations or actively seeking information, knowledge, or opinion formation concerning the political process. Ultimately, the political process is about winning control of a political entity, and the direct involvement of citizens is often about winning some position within this process.[76] It is assumed that, where many citizens have some personal experience with politics, whether active or passive, this may help to enhance the legitimacy of democracy.[77] The focus here is on citizen participation through *non*-elected actors, that is, through political parties and interest groups.[78]

Within the European Union, political citizen rights are embodied in Articles 19–21 EC, "Citizenship of the Union." The central core of any notion of citizenship "embodies community, with allegiance, cultural and personal identity and a sense of belonging [to that community]." In other words, it is used "to define who are, and who are not, members of a given society," therefore "effectively erecting a protected enclosure around insiders, separating them from, and shutting off, outsiders," and "defining who shall not have access to political power within it; in other words, citizenship is used in an inclusive and an exclusive way, that is to grant or deny groups political 'voice.'"[79]

---

[75] Ibid.

[76] Diamond, n. 66 above, 221.

[77] Ibid., 171, with further references.

[78] For a general and exhaustive overview, see Carol Harlow, "Citizen Access to Political Power in the European Union," Working Paper RSC No 99/2, European University Institute, Florence.

[79] Ibid., 13–14.

a) Elections and political parties in the EU

The most important political rights—the rights to vote and to stand as a candidate at municipal elections in the Member States and in elections to the European Parliament—are guaranteed in Article 19 EC to all EU citizens, even when residing in a Member State other than their own. That does not prevent the average voter turnout across the Union from being (relatively) low, voter participation having gradually declined since the first election in 1979 from 63 percent to 59.5 percent in 1994.[80] These figures should be put in perspective. As a rule, turnout is high only when voting is compulsory in the Member State concerned; if voting is not compulsory, turnout is higher in a system with proportional representation, and it often depends on accidental factors, such as whether elections take place on a Sunday, which may improve turnout.[81] Turnout varies greatly from one state to another, and from one group of the population to another. In the United States, for example, turnout is very low, especially among less affluent and younger segments of the population and among minority groups. Although the 1993 National Voter Registration Act, intended to make voter registration easier and less expensive, has produced an unprecedented increase in voter registration, turnout did not rise. Four years into the new system, it had even fallen another 2.8 percentage points, from 38.8 percent in 1994 to 36 percent in 1998.[82] Hope exists that electronic voting may improve turnout—but it may also increase the underrepresentation of the less wealthy among the electorate.

Political parties are the most prominent instrument to involve citizens in the political process. In the Member States' parliamentary regimes they have taken the lead, "not only in voicing policy programmes but also in the recruitment and selection of politicians . . . and in . . . link[ing] government and parliament to each other according to party political loyalties."[83] Thus far, political parties at the European level (so-called "Euro-parties")[84] do not yet play

[80] See Douglas-Scott, n. 23 above, 494. In the June 2004 elections—the first in which the ten new Member States participated—voter participation across the twenty-five countries even declined to 45.5 percent. See http://en.wikipedia.org/wiki/European_Parliament_election_2004.

[81] Franklin, van der Eijck, and Oppenheim, "The Institutional Context: Turnout," in C. van der Eijck, M. Franklin et al., *Choosing Europe? The European Electorate and National Political Processes* (1996), quoted by Harlow, n. 78 above.

[82] Frances Fox Piven and Richard Cloward, "Why Americans Still Don't Vote" (2000), excerpt reproduced in *American Polity*, n. 71 above, 507–14, at 509.

[83] S. van Bijsterveld, *Democracy and the Rule of Law in Transition* (Utrecht: Lemma Publishers, 2002), 159.

[84] Until recently, Euro-parties were no more than groups of MEPs belonging to national political parties that share some kind of general philosophy but do not nec-

a similar role in designating members of government, that is, the president and members of the Commission, or in linking government and parliament, as political parties in the Member States do. Individual candidates for the European Commission and its president are indeed de facto designated by the Member State governments without much involvement of the Euro-parties, and there is no direct link, based on same party affiliation, between the European Commission and the political majority in the European Parliament, thus making the former politically independent from the latter. That may have to change in the future, as discussed in chapter 7.[85]

b) Citizen access through other means

In addition to voting, campaigning, and forming political parties, there are other ways that citizens attempt to influence government.[86] Some are individual, such as individuals contacting an official or parliamentary representative, and others are cooperative, such as citizens working together by forming informal groups or formal organizations to influence government officials. Some are self-interested; others are acting in the general interest. With the growing importance of the Union, pressure groups and lobbyists have concentrated resources on Brussels, where the EU Commission is located, adhering to the advice "Shoot where the ducks are."[87] Many Euro-associations such as consumer or banking associations, mostly made up of national associations operating in the Member States, sometimes with very different traditions, and often with competing interests as well, have thus been formed.[88] In its relations with interest groups, the Commission distinguishes between profit and non-profit organizations, and demands certain standards from such groups relating to their dissemination of information, their behavior, and the way in which they represent themselves. It will consult such groups on an ad hoc basis and elicit their views in preliminary position papers, called Green Papers, on one issue or another.[89] Profit-making lobbying groups outnumber non-profit

---

essarily have the same attitude vis-à-vis the process of European integration. For a detailed description of the existing Euro-parties, see Douglas-Scott, n. 23 above, 86–89; also Stephen Day and Jo Shaw, "The Evolution of Europe's Transnational Political Parties in the Era of European Citizenship," in *The State of the European Union*, ed. Tanja A. Börzel and Rachel A. Cichowski (Oxford: Oxford University Press, 2003), 149–69.

[85] At pp. 352–60.

[86] Harlow, n. 78 above, 17, with reference to S. Verba et al., *The Modes of Democratic Participation: A Cross-National Comparison* (1971).

[87] Craig and de Búrca, n. 52 above, 164.

[88] Ibid., with further references.

[89] When the issues described in a Green Paper have been further clarified, after

groups and have far more significant resources[90]—making the "political voice" of interest groups unequal and often biased.[91]

As pointed out previously,[92] consultation of "civil society" groups in the preparation of legislation and policy has become part of the Commission's and Parliament's political culture, particularly so where new modes of governance are used—which assume the involvement of private actors in defining policy goals and instruments. An example thereof is the role assigned to civil society actors—as distinguished from social actors, such as employers' associations and trade unions—in the open method of coordination project on social exclusion.[93] The project, aimed at fighting poverty in the Union, wishes to draw on the experience of victims of social exclusion and their associations, such as the European Anti-Poverty Network (EAPN) and national and local anti-poverty groups, in shaping policy instruments. Although an assessment of the first action plans has highlighted several inefficiencies, such as the lack of concrete measures to promote the participation and self-expression of people suffering exclusion, there is generally optimism and support from the national and local groups to persevere with the project.[94]

Involvement of private actors within the loose framework of the open method of coordination has its limits, though. First, it creates fluid boundaries between governmental and non-governmental actors, not the least with Parliament, which sees the emphasis on the participation of civil society in the elaboration of policy as a threat to its institutional position as guarantor of legitimacy. Second, there is the danger that NGOs, in their engagement with EU processes, will become increasingly "governmentalized" and compromise their own communicative potential. Third, since these NGOs are to a certain extent subsidized by the EU, there is also a risk that they may become bureaucratized and excessively dependent on EU funding, and that they may

---

broad consultation, and if it is decided to take the matter further, a so-called White Paper will be prepared that is more definitive (and also more concrete), although it will still be submitted, before being finalized, to further consultation from the public.

[90] Craig and de Búrca, n. 52 above, 165.

[91] Harlow, n. 78 above, 17. On interest groups in the United States, see the classic work of Theodore Lowi, *The End of Liberalism* (1969), excerpted in *American Polity*, n. 71 above, 468–74, also with excerpts from more recent publications on the same subject at 474–503.

[92] Above, pp. 196ff.

[93] See Kenneth Armstrong, "Tackling Social Exclusion through OMC: Reshaping the Boundaries of European Governance," in *The State of the European Union*, n. 84 above, 170–94, at 187–93.

[94] Ibid., 189.

enter into competition with other NGOs in neighboring areas of interest.[95] As Diamond warns in general, "To the extent that hierarchy and suspicion rule [a civil society] organization, cooperation becomes difficult, both among members of the organization and between it and other organizations. The organization then becomes dependent on a leader or ruling clique and may manifest a debilitating contradiction between its internal style of governance and the goals it professes to seek for the policy."[96]

A Vibrant Public Opinion on European Integration

Like civil society, to which it gives "voice," public opinion as a concept has a long history.[97] It goes back to Kant's crucial 1784 pamphlet *What is Enlightenment?*, in which the author defines Enlightenment as the emancipation of human beings who leave behind their self-inflicted incapacity to make use of their intelligence without someone else's assistance.[98] For Kant and the other Enlightenment thinkers, the worst imaginable form of despotism is a political model in which civil society cannot express a public voice and cannot impose itself as a participant in the formation of political will.[99] Developing Kant's ideas, Hegel defines civil society as an autonomous sphere within which shared communal values and norms (which he calls "Sittlichkeit") come to fruition, and which offers citizens a framework that allows them to develop their individual political and ideological preferences in equality before the law. That common ethos binds individuals in spite of differing preferences; it permits civil society to exist and flourish, and individuals to transcend their selfishness.[100] However, for such a society of equal citizens to last, instruments must be put into place that foster mutual respect and recognition and enable citizens to join in participatory citizenship. These instruments must be firmly anchored in political organizations and legal institutions that are not governed by individual preferences or partisan strategies, but rather by the common ethos.[101]

---

[95] On all these limits, see ibid., 191–93.

[96] N. 66 above, 226.

[97] For a brief but illuminating overview, see René Foqué, "Referendum en Publieke Opinie" [Referendum and public opinion], in *De Re Ferenda*, ed. F. Fleerackers (Brussels: Larcier, 2001), 101–29.

[98] In the original version, *Was ist Aufklärung?*, the text reads as follows: "Der Ausgang des Menschen aus seiner selbst verschuldeten Unmündigkeit," i.e., "das Unvermögen, sich seines Verstandes ohne Leitung eines anderen zu bedienen." Quoted in ibid., 109.

[99] Foqué, n. 97 above, 109–10.

[100] Ibid., 110–11.

[101] Ibid., 111–12.

It is on these foundations of an emancipated, autonomous citizenship, and of a civil society mediating, within a frame of shared values and norms, between the private lives of individuals and the general perspective of the state, that public opinion is called on to operate as a significant political force.[102] To fulfill that function, public opinion must be able to rely on autonomous, reflexive, and responsive citizens who are receptive to a better argument, are encouraged to make their judgments and insights known in order to shape the political community's general interest, and in the process escape their own particularities and peculiarities.[103] For such a civil society to become operational, there is a permanent need for a well-organized center field, a public space operating as a "training ground" for individual citizens to involve themselves in making decisions about the general interest. In that process small societies, such as the English coffeehouses, the German *Tischgesellschaften*, or the French *salons* in the seventeenth century, played an essential role.[104] These societies offered educated (then exclusively male) elites of the new bourgeoisie the opportunity to interact and discuss issues of general, social, and political significance that were increasingly brought to the attention of a larger public in new periodicals.[105]

How can this romantic view of a bourgeois civil society as a debating club for gentlemen, and of a public opinion that was expressed in periodicals with a limited number of readers, be reconciled with modern society? Today's society is one in which mass media, driven by profit, have taken the place of periodicals focusing on general interest issues[106] and citizens have become readers and spectators, "disconnected from the kind of dialogical exchange characteristic of face-to-face conversation."[107] To be sure, the traditional and the new forms continue to coexist in modern society, and the new forms of communication are also to a certain extent interactive (think of readers' letters in newspapers). But television has created a form of "mediated public-ness," establishing a new link with the public (at a much more global level), but in one direction only: the spectators remain invisible and unheard, notwithstanding efforts to involve the public in panel discussions and through electronic communication.[108]

---

[102] Ibid., 112.

[103] Ibid., 114–15.

[104] Ibid., 121.

[105] John B. Thompson, n. 7 above, 70.

[106] Or in Habermas's words, a public opinion that no longer discusses but consumes culture, "vom Kulturräsonierenden zum kulturkonsumierenden Publikum": *Strukurwandel der Öffentlichkeit* (Neuwied: Luchterhand, 1962), 176, quoted in Foqué, n. 97 above, 123.

[107] Thompson, n. 7 above, 125–26.

[108] On these developments, ibid., 129–30. The author observes, "we shall not arrive

Despite the preceding remark, and contrary to what is often propounded, public opinion does play an important role in the shaping of European Union policies. This point has been made and documented by two American researchers, Russell Dalton and Richard Eichenberg, who analyzed the role of public opinion as a societal actor in the European integration process.[109] To be sure, at the outset that role has been underestimated, because, as they found, public opinion was only seen as having provided political leaders with considerable *latitude* in carrying out the European project ("permissive consensus"). Later, however, it became clear that, even during the first decades of European integration, public opinion had *guided* the "elite" in defining national preferences and defending them in the bargaining process.[110] It also became clear that, throughout the existence of the Community, public opinion in the Member States has moved the integration process along the continuum from intergovernmentalism to supranationalism.

A prominent example of how public opinion steered governmental decision making in the Member States is the public debates that occurred in France and Germany in the 1990s over the monetary union, and the ensuing public reactions to proposed cuts in government spending to meet the monetary union's targets. It is undeniable that in these and other developments public preferences in the Member States have conditioned the actions of interest groups, political parties, and elites toward proposed EU policies.[111] Dalton and Eichenberg's core argument is that the influence of public opinion does not come from a broad movement on all fronts, but expresses itself in reactions toward specific initiatives in specific areas. Only by focusing on the specific policy preferences of Europeans does overall progress become visible.[112]

The authors' research is based on the Eurobarometer surveys that the Commission has conducted since the 1970s. However, it has only been since

---

at a satisfactory understanding of the nature of public life in the modern world if we remain wedded to a conception of publicness which is essentially spatial and dialogical in character, and which obliges us to interpret the ever-growing role of mediated communication as a historical fall from grace" (132). Thompson sees the solution in, among other things, the renewal of politics through "deliberative" democracy (ibid.), and in "regulated pluralism" (237–43).

[109] Russell J. Dalton and Richard C. Eichenberg, "Citizen Support for Policy Integration," in *European Integration and Supranational Governance*, ed. Wayne Sandholtz and Alec Stone Sweet (Oxford: Oxford University Press, 1998), 250–82.

[110] Ibid., 250, where several factors are mentioned that contributed to an increased awareness of the significance of public opinion.

[111] Ibid., 251.

[112] Ibid., 252–53.

the mid-1980s that the survey question has been formulated in terms of whether particular policy areas should be decided *jointly* within the EU, instead of *either* at the national level *or* at the European level.[113] Only the then twelve Member States are included in the research (which was conducted prior to the accession of Austria, Finland, and Sweden in 1995). The authors review six policy areas in depth: developing countries, scientific research, foreign policy, environmental protection, asylum regulations, and immigration policies. They find that, across all policy areas, support for policy integration is about 50 percent, but that support varies widely on specific policy issues. For example, in the 1990s support for cooperation with developing countries was almost 80 percent, for foreign policy with third countries around 70 percent, for political asylum around 55 percent, and for cultural policy only about 40 percent.[114] Moreover, as could be expected, variations across nations are also found to be very substantial with regard to specific policy issues. Not surprisingly, it appears from the survey that the greatest net support for European-level action is found among the six founding nations, although Germany falls noticeably below the other founding nations. A hesitancy toward policy integration is displayed among the (then) newer states: in nineteen of the twenty-two areas, the Danes and British express less support than average for integration, and support is equally restrained in Greece, Spain, and Portugal.[115]

After having studied three specific areas (environmental policy, a common security and defense policy, and economic and monetary union) in more depth,[116] the authors draw some conclusions. The first concerns the importance of disaggregating the integration process: "Although European integration may be a general process, it is comprised of specific steps on specific policy matters. . . . The building of a European Union progresses by the cumulation of policy integration, and the factors affecting policy integration may vary from issue domain to issue domain."[117] A second conclusion concerns the importance of values, culture, and identity: "To the extent that this experiment [of European integration] impinges on the substratum of cultural and national identification built over hundreds of years, it is likely to meet resistance."[118] A third con-

---

[113] Ibid., 257.

[114] Ibid., Table 9.1 at 258–59.

[115] Ibid., 262 and Table 9.2, at 263.

[116] Ibid., 264–80. At 276–77 the authors observe that EU efforts to fight unemployment enjoy majority support in most Member States, but the same is not true of support for joint decision making in the areas of health and social security.

[117] Ibid., 281.

[118] Ibid.

clusion is that there is general support for the liberalization of the market and for the instruments for managing that market.[119]

Obviously, ten years later, research with new data, and on many more Member States than the original twelve, will surely require shifts in emphasis. It is unlikely, however, that the aforementioned conclusions would be proven to be incorrect, the main conclusion being that public opinion in the Member States concerning European integration is a powerful factor that the national leaders are bound to take into account when negotiating new developments at the European level. That public opinion in the Member States remains a powerful factor is best illustrated by the strong reactions of the peoples in all Member States over the war in Iraq, and their impact on the Member States' attitudes in the areas of foreign and defense policy. A Eurobarometer poll, carried out between mid-February and mid-March 2003 in the (then) fifteen Member States, found 63 percent of EU citizens favoring a common foreign policy (with 22 percent against) and 71 percent backing a common defense policy (with 17 percent against). Surely, there was a divergence in enthusiasm, as Peter Norman reports, between countries such as Greece, Italy, and Luxembourg, which were strongly in favor of both policies, and traditionally neutral countries like Finland, Sweden, Austria, and Ireland, where support was significantly below the Union average. But only in Britain did more people oppose a common foreign policy than support it.[120]

IV. FREEDOM OF THE PRESS: A MARKETPLACE FOR IDEAS

Free access to public documents is a strong instrument for controlling political power, especially when used in combination with the freedom of the press and, as in Sweden, with the right of civil servants to give information to the press. This point has never been proven better than by Carl Bernstein and Bob Woodward's investigation of the Watergate affair,[121] which forced President Nixon to step down. Investigative reporting has never been as popular in

---

[119] Ibid.

[120] Peter Norman, *The Accidental Constitution: The Story of the European Convention* (Brussels: EuroComment, 2003), 236.

[121] See Gerald Gunther, "Judicial Hegemony and Legislative Autonomy: The Nixon Case and the Impeachment Process," 22 *UCLA Law Review*, 1974, 30. On the Watergate story told by the then owner and publisher of the *Washington Post*, Katharine Graham, see the excerpt from her book *Personal History* (1997), quoted in *American Polity*, n. 71 above, 629–42.

Europe as in the United States, although there have been some cases where it has exposed important abuses of power with considerable political consequences.[122] At the level of the EU, the media were crucial in providing a public forum and moral support to whistle-blower van Buitenen when he became engaged in his lonely fight against the institutions.[123] Nevertheless, the European attitude toward the media has been much more reserved than in the United States,[124] particularly so when rights of third parties are at stake, as in criminal proceedings.[125]

a) Freedom of the press under the European Convention of
Human Rights (ECHR)
In Europe the protection of freedom of the press is primarily ensured by the Member State courts and, when procedures before the national courts have been exhausted, by the European Court of Human Rights in Strasbourg. By contrast, the ECJ and CFI only occasionally pronounce themselves on matters of freedom of the press,[126] for example with regard to journalists' right of access to public documents,[127] or with regard to the right of a Member State

---

[122] See, for instance, the role played by *El Mundo* in the 1990s in breaking the political scandals in Spain surrounding the possible involvement of Felipe Gonzalez's socialist government in the murders of Basque separatists by the terrorist group GAL. The newspaper *El Mundo* was founded in 1989 by a journalist who had been at the *Washington Post* during the Watergate affair. It "quickly became the standard bearer of investigative journalism in Spain": Karen Sanders, Tim Bale, and María José Canel, "Managing Sleaze: Prime Ministers and News Management in Conservative Great Britain and Socialist Spain," *European Journal of Communication*, 1999, 461–86, at 468.

[123] Above, pp. 82–83. When van Buitenen was suspended by the Commission just before Christmas 1998, he agreed to be interviewed by the Belgian newspaper *De Morgen*. The interview was published on January 4, 1999, and forced Commission president Jacques Santer to hold a news conference on January 6 to refute the allegations. Instead of silencing the press, it had the reverse effect.

[124] That attitude may have changed, journalistic accountability having become stricter after the resignation in May 2003 of Jason Blair, who was found to have fabricated or plagiarized parts of articles published in the *New York Times*, and the resignation in January 2004 of Jack Kelley, a journalist of *USA Today* who is under investigation for similar conduct: see the *New York Times*, January 19, 2004, C1 and C9.

[125] See the Recommendation of the Committee of Ministers of the Council of Europe to Member States of the Council, including the EU Member States, adopted on July 10, 2003. See also n. 151 below.

[126] On the relationship between the two supranational courts, the ECJ and the ECtHR, and the conflicts that can arise in the protection of human rights by both courts, see Craig and de Búrca, n. 52 above, at 363–68. See also chapter 3 above, n. 112.

[127] Now governed by Regulation 1049/2001: n. 42 above.

to rely on pluralism of the press as a ground for justification of state action limiting interstate commerce in services.[128]

Save for these infrequent cases, the protection of a free press and free speech from state interference is a matter for the Member State courts to decide, acting on the basis of their national constitutional provisions, or for the European Court of Human Rights (ECtHR) when the plaintiff is not satisfied with the relief he or she obtained and cannot obtain further relief in a domestic court. In that Court private parties can also, on the basis of Article 10 (1) ECHR, initiate proceedings for violation of their Convention rights by a state authority.[129]

Article 10 (1) ECHR is formulated as follows:

> Everyone has the right to freedom of expression. This right shall include freedom to hold opinions and to receive and impart information and ideas without interference by public authority, and regardless of frontiers. This Article shall not prevent States from requiring the licensing of broadcasting, television or cinema enterprises.[130]

Article 10 ECHR contains a second paragraph, though, in which a large number of exceptions are enumerated by virtue of which the contracting states are enabled to subject the exercise of the freedom of expression[131] to "such formalities, conditions, restrictions or penalties as are prescribed by law and are necessary in a democratic society." Those exceptions are:

[128] See Case C-368/95, *Familiapress v. Heinrich Bauer Verlag*, [1997] ECR I-3689, para. 18, with references to earlier cases in that and later paragraphs.

[129] As pointed out in chapter 1, pp. 11–12, all EU Member States (new and old, and other European States as well) have accepted the jurisdiction of the ECtHR. The court has no jurisdiction, though, over EU institutions when one of them infringes an individual's fundamental right; in such a case, that individual can bring suit before the ECJ or the CFI. However, as pointed out above, the ECtHR in principle has jurisdiction over the Member States that have participated in the enactment of a Union measure that allegedly infringes the plaintiff's right: ibid., and chapter 3, p. 131, n. 112.

[130] The first two sentences of Article 11 (1) of the EU Charter of Fundamental Rights (see chapter 3, pp. 123f) use identical wording as Article 10 (1) ECHR. Moreover, in accordance with Article 6 (2) EU Treaty, the Community courts will apply the provisions of the ECHR as part of the rule of law concept established in Article 6 (1) EU Treaty. All this, however, does not prevent differences in interpretation from existing, mainly because the EU courts take an "integration"-oriented approach, whereas the ECtHR takes a purely "human rights protection"–oriented approach. For differences in interpretation, see Craig and de Búrca, n. 52 above, 367–68.

[131] In other articles of the ECHR there are similar (but usually shorter) lists relating to other human rights: see Article 8 (the right to respect for private and family life), Article 9 (freedom of thought, conscience, and religion), and Article 11 (freedom of assembly and association).

the interests of national security, territorial integrity or public security, the pre-vention of disorder or crime, the protection of health or morals, the protection of the reputation or rights of others, to prevent the disclosure of information re-ceived in confidence, maintaining the authority and impartiality of the judiciary.

The ECtHR has rendered numerous judgments applying Article 10 ECHR to interference of states, or state agencies, with the freedom of expression of journalists or authors of newspaper articles.[132] One of them is *Castells v. Spain*, in which the Court stated:

> the freedom of expression . . . constitutes one of the essential foundations of a democratic society and one of the basic conditions for its progress. Subject to paragraph 2 of Article 10, it is applicable not only to "information" or "ideas" that are favorably received or regarded as inoffensive or as a matter of indifference, but also to those that offend, shock or disturb. Such are the demands of that plural-ism, tolerance and broadmindedness without which there is no "democratic soci-ety."[133]

The Court went on to say:

> In this respect, the pre-eminent role of the press in a State governed by the rule of law must not be forgotten. . . . Freedom of the press affords the public one of the best means of discovering and forming an opinion of the ideas and attitudes of their political leaders. In particular, it gives politicians the opportunity to reflect and comment on the preoccupations of public opinion; it thus enables everyone to participate in the free political debate which is at the very core of the concept of a democratic society.[134]

In *Castells*, the newspaper writer concerned was an elected politician repre-senting a Basque nationalist party who had seriously criticized the Spanish authorities for an alleged lack of investigation into a series of murders, amounting, he maintained, to total immunity for the perpetrators of the crimes.[135] In connection with those allegations, the Spanish public prosecutor's office brought criminal proceedings against the politician for having insulted the government and its civil servants. After being convicted by the Spanish courts, the politician initiated proceedings against Spain before the ECtHR.

---

[132] It is important to note that, in the ECtHR (unlike in the ECJ), judges are al-lowed to express dissenting and concurring opinions: see Article 45 (2) ECHR and Ar-ticle 74 (2) of the Rules of Procedure of the ECtHR of November 4, 1998, which reads: "Any judge who has taken part in the consideration of the case shall be entitled to an-nex to the judgment either a separate opinion, concurring with or dissenting from the judgment, or a bare statement of dissent." In contrast to the ECJ, the ECtHR is not as-sisted by advocates-general.

[133] *Castells v. Spain*, Publ. Court, Series A-236, para. 42 of the judgment.

[134] Ibid., para. 43.

[135] See n. 133 above.

In its judgment the ECtHR was asked to weigh the politician's freedom to express an opinion in the press against the government's legitimate aim of "prevent[ing] disorder" and "protect[ing] the reputation . . . of others." These two goals figure in the list of exceptions contained in Article 10 (2) ECHR, and are regarded by the Convention as possible grounds of justification for a contracting state to limit freedom of opinion, including the freedom of the press.[136] Before the Court, the defendant state, Spain, relied on these exceptions to excuse its action, a defense that the court refused to accept holding that, in the circumstances of the case,

> the limits of permissible criticism are wider with regard to the Government than in relation to a private citizen. . . . In a democratic system the actions or omissions of the Government must be subject to the close scrutiny not only of the legislative and judicial authorities but also of the press and public opinion.[137]

Although the ruling demonstrates the ECtHR's willingness to give high priority to freedom of expression, and to give precedence to it over legitimate aims pursued by state agencies, it also indicates that the court does not intend to grant freedom of expression absolute priority over and against other freedoms. That, indeed, would have been inconsistent with the enumeration of exceptions in Article 10 (2) ECHR, which allow the contracting states to abridge the freedom of expression under certain circumstances. By contrast, the First Amendment to the U.S. Constitution does not contain such an enumeration, leaving it therefore to the Supreme Court itself to read grounds of justification into the text of the First Amendment, as we will see hereinafter.

Another illustration of the high (but not absolute) priority that the European Court of Human Rights attaches to the freedom of expression and the freedom of the press is the court's judgment in _De Haes and Gijsels v. Belgium_.[138] In that case, the Court permitted severe criticism of judges by investigative journalists, notwithstanding harm done to "the reputation of . . . others"—which, as mentioned above, is another ground of justification included in the list of Article 10 (2) ECHR. To reach that conclusion, the ECtHR took into account the seriousness of the circumstances of the case, and of the issues involved,[139] and noted that the magazine articles contained precise, and duly

---

[136] Ibid., para. 39.
[137] Ibid., para. 46.
[138] Judgment of February 24, 1997 (1998) 25 EHRR 1.
[139] _De Haes and Gijsels v. Belgium_ concerned a complaint of journalists of _Humo_, a Belgian magazine, against the Kingdom of Belgium for having infringed their freedom of the press. The case related to an award of damages by Belgian courts to judges whom the journalists had, in their articles, accused of bias in awarding custody of minor children to a father accused by his wife of incest and child abuse.

checked, information. In that regard, the court distinguished statement of facts from value judgments: while the veracity of the former can (and ought to) be proven, the latter cannot. Furthermore, in an earlier judgment, *Goodwin v. U.K.*,[140] the Court held that journalistic sources must be protected, stating that

> having regard to the importance of journalistic sources for press freedom in a democratic society and the potentially chilling effect an order of source disclosure can have on the exercise of that freedom, such a measure [of compelling the journalist to disclose his or her sources] cannot be compatible with Article 10 of the Convention unless it is justified by an overriding requirement in the public interest. . . . In sum limitations on the confidentiality of journalistic sources call for the most careful scrutiny by the Court.[141]

b) Freedom of the press in the United States

As pointed out in chapter 3, the First Amendment [1791] of the U.S. Constitution prohibits the abridgment of the freedom of speech or the press. The specific reference to the press has raised the question whether the media are entitled to specific constitutional protection. According to Justice Stewart, the answer is in the affirmative. He argued that "the Free Press guarantee is, in essence, a *structural* provision of the Constitution. [It] extends protection to an institution . . . the only organized business that is given explicit constitutional protection. [If] the Free Press guarantee meant no more than freedom of expression, it would be a constitutional redundancy."[142] Stewart's view is not the prevailing opinion, though, and was contradicted by Chief Justice Burger, who argued that no support could be found for that interpretation in the history of the clause that would suggest that the authors contemplated a "special" or "institutional" privilege, and who argued that the clause was not redundant either, since freedom of the press merited a special mention simply because it had often been the object of official restraints.[143]

The Supreme Court's case law relating to the First Amendment contains a strong presumption against prior restraints. In a leading case, *Near v. Minnesota*, the Court struck down a Minnesota statute permitting state authorities, with judicial consent, to prohibit the owner or publisher of a newspaper, magazine, or other periodical to "engage in the business of regularly publishing . . . malicious, scandalous and defamatory material" where the publication

---

[140] Judgment of March 27, 1996 (1996) 22 EHRR 123.

[141] Paras. 39 and 40 of the judgment.

[142] Stewart, "Or of the Press," 26 *Hast.L.J.* 631 (1975), quoted by Sullivan and Gunther, n. 31 above, 1392.

[143] In a dictum in his opinion in *First National Bank of Boston v. Bellotti*, 435 U.S. 765 (1978): ibid.

could not be proven to be accurate and to be published with good motives and for justifiable ends. Speaking for a narrow 5–4 majority, Chief Justice Hughes characterized the Minnesota law as "the essence of censorship."[144] The court did not exclude, however, that it may uphold injunctions to publish in some instances, particularly where national security considerations are at stake.

The question came up in *New York Times v. United States* (the Pentagon Papers Case),[145] in which a majority of 6–3 held, however, that the government failed to meet the "heavy burden" of showing justification of prior restraint. Consequently, the court rejected the government's plea for imposition of an injunction on the *New York Times* and *Washington Post* from publishing classified government documents, stolen from the Pentagon, on the Vietnam war. The opinion of Justice Stewart represented the most protection that a majority of the court was prepared to afford against prior restraints. Justice Stewart was found ready to allow the president to seek prior restraints to protect sensitive information relating to defense and international relations. However, in the case at issue, he opined that the government had not established that disclosing any of the documents would "surely result in direct, immediate and irreparable damage to our nation or its people."[146]

Tim Koopmans, a former judge in the European Court of Justice, has remarked that, from a comparative point of view, the judgment shows how U.S. Supreme Court decisions are normally devoid of any kind of deference to the political institutions, even to the point that some of the concurring opinions showed the justices' distaste for the Vietnam war.[147] He quotes Justice Black saying, "Only a free and unrestrained press can effectively expose deception in government. And paramount among the responsibilities of a free press is the duty to prevent part of the government from deceiving the people and sending them off to foreign lands to die of foreign fevers and foreign shot and shell." Koopmans adds, "There is little doubt that in most other countries the government's interest in keeping war information secret would have prevailed."[148]

---

[144] 283 U.S. 697 (1931). For a discussion, see Redlich, Attanasio, and Goldstein, *Understanding Constitutional Law*, 2d ed. (New York: LexisNexis, 1999), 394–95.

[145] 403 U.S. 713 (1971). For a discussion of the separate concurring opinions of the six justices making up the majority, see ibid., 395–97.

[146] 403 U.S. 713, at 730.

[147] Tim Koopmans, *Courts and Political Institutions: A Comparative View* (Cambridge: Cambridge University Press, 2003), 195.

[148] Ibid. The author contrasts this case with the "Spycatcher book" judgment decided by the House of Lords (*AG v. Guardian Newspapers Ltd.* [1990] 1 AC 109). The book, containing confidential information about the actions of the counterespionage

Questions of unconstitutionality submitted to the Supreme Court do not always involve prior restraint. They can also involve *post hoc* sanctions, such as in *Landmark Communications, Inc. v. Virginia*, where the Virginia courts had imposed criminal sanctions on a newspaper for having accurately reported a pending confidential inquiry.[149] A unanimous court reversed the imposition, finding that the state's interests in confidentiality did not outweigh the First Amendment right to publish truthful information about confidential proceedings. The issue concerns press access to judicial proceedings (pretrials, criminal proceedings, testimony in sex offenses), which came up in several other cases.[150] In *Landmark* the question arose whether the state's asserted legitimate interests—promoting efficient inquiries, protecting the reputation of Virginia's judges, and maintaining the institutional integrity of its courts—outweighed the right to publish truthful information. Chief Justice Burger commented that "injury to official reputation is an insufficient reason 'for repressing speech that would otherwise be free.'" In that regard, the opinion is comparable with the aforementioned judgment of the ECtHR in *De Haes and Gijsels*. It would seem, however, that in the right circumstances a legitimate interest, such as fairness of the proceedings or protection of third parties' rights, including those of the suspect in criminal proceedings, would carry the day under Article 10 (2) ECHR.[151]

Another issue concerns journalistic privilege (as opposed to immunity)

---

branch of the British Security Service, was published in Australia and later in the United States, after which English newspapers started to serialize it. The House of Lords held that it was too late to grant an injunction on publication, but granted damages to the Crown (195–96).

[149] 435 U.S. 829 (1978).

[150] See further Sullivan and Gunther, n. 31 above, 1397–1403.

[151] See in that regard the Recommendation on Provision of Information through the Media in Relation to Criminal Proceedings, adopted on July 10, 2003, by the Committee of Ministers of the Council of Europe to the member states of that organization: www.coe.int/T/E/Human_Rights/media. As mentioned previously in chapter 1, pp. 11–12, that Committee of Ministers belongs to the same European supranational organization as the ECtHR, and, indeed, the committee's recommendation draws on the ECtHR's case law in an attempt to reconcile three distinct fundamental rights: the freedom of expression guaranteed by Article 10 ECHR, the right to respect for private and family life protected by Article 8 ECHR, and the right to a fair trial and the presumption of innocence laid down in Article 6 ECHR. According to Principle 14 of the recommendation, live reporting in the courtroom is only allowed "as far as expressly permitted by law or by competent judicial authorities"—an authorization that should only be given "where it does not bear a serious risk of undue influence on victims, witnesses, parties to criminal proceedings, juries or judges." Moreover, Principle 10 requires police and judicial authorities not to supply information "which bears a risk of substantial prejudice to the fairness of the proceedings."

with regard to demands from public authorities to disclose information that journalists have obtained in the course of their newsgathering activities. As mentioned, the question came up before the ECtHR in *Goodwin*. The leading American case is *Branzburg v. Hayes*, where the Supreme Court, framing the issue narrowly, decided that a reporter who had been subpoenaed to testify before a grand jury about knowledge he had acquired concerning criminal activities was not exempted from burdens imposed by a generally applicable civil or criminal statute.[152] In his concurring opinion, Justice Powell made it clear, however, that, although no express privilege was granted, a reporter could not be required to give information that was only remotely or tenuously relevant to the grand jury investigation, or that revealed confidential sources without a legitimate law enforcement need. Justice Powell's opinion, which offers more journalistic protection, was actually followed by most lower court judges. Moreover, in response to *Branzburg*, many state legislatures have enacted press "shield" laws providing at least a qualified privilege against revelation of journalists' sources.[153]

c) Comparing ECtHR case law with case law of the U.S. Supreme Court

Comparing case law of the ECtHR with case law of the U.S. Supreme Court in an area as diverse as free press and free speech is a matter that needs more than just a few references. Nevertheless, it is worth noting how courts protecting citizens' constitutional or fundamental rights apply similar methods of scrutiny when dealing with comparable issues. There remain striking differences, though, the most important, as already pointed out, being that the ECtHR, in judging whether state action interfering with a fundamental right can be justified, can rely on a list of grounds explicitly and exhaustively enumerated in the ECHR itself. Thus, Article 10 ECHR, which protects freedom of expression in its paragraph 1, specifies in paragraph 2 that the exercise of the freedom may be subjected by the contracting states to such formalities, conditions, restrictions, or penalties as are prescribed by law, and are necessary in a democratic society in the interest of a large number of compelling interests (mentioned earlier in the text). Protection of national security and of the reputation or the rights of others are among these interests, as well as maintaining the authority and impartiality of the judiciary.[154]

Accordingly, for state action limiting freedom of opinion and of the press

---

[152] 408 U.S. 665 (1972).

[153] Sullivan and Gunther, n. 31 above, 1410. Justice Powell's opinion is reproduced at 1408–9.

[154] Similar lists of grounds potentially justifying interference with fundamental rights and freedoms are contained in Articles 8, 9, and 11 ECHR.

to be legitimate under the ECHR, 1) it must have been prescribed by law, which must not necessarily be statutory law, provided that the provision is formulated with sufficient precision, 2) it may only pursue one of the aims specified in the second paragraph of Article 10, and 3) it must be necessary in a democratic society—which means that the action taken must be "in response to a pressing social need, and that the interference with the rights protected is no greater than is necessary to address that pressing social need."[155] The latter requirement seems to correspond with the method of strict scrutiny applied by the Supreme Court, which requires a compelling end and necessary (i.e., the least restrictive) means.[156]

Because of the explicit enumeration of potential grounds of justification in the text of Article 10 (2) ECHR, there is in Europe no room left, as there is in the United States, for a debate as to whether free speech and ancillary rights are "absolute," or rather subject to the balancing of competing interests.[157] Only the latter position is consistent with Article 10 (2) ECHR. In the United States, both opinions have their defenders. It is apt to quote two proponents with differing opinions, first Justice Black, then Justice Frankfurter. Justice Black believed "that the First Amendment's unequivocal command that there shall be no abridgment of the rights of free speech and assembly shows that the men who drafted our Bill of Rights did all the 'balancing' that was to be [done]."[158] By contrast, Justice Frankfurter believed that "the demands of free speech in a democratic society as well as [countervailing governmental interests] are better served by candid and informed weighing of the competing interests, within the confines of the judicial process, than by announcing dogmas too inflexible for the non-Euclidean problems to be solved."[159]

The ECHR approach has the advantage that, in view of "balancing," the competing interests are exhaustively enumerated, although being worded with sufficient flexibility—thus allowing the courts to apply the scrutiny test in a flexible but not totally discretionary way. This approach reflects the European inclination to reconcile opposing compelling interests. Thus, for example, the rulings of the German Constitutional Court, which refuse to give privileged status to the freedom of the press when it conflicts with one's *Persön-*

---

[155] F. G. Jacobs and R. C. A. White, *The European Convention on Human Rights*, 2d ed. (Oxford: Clarendon Paperbacks, 1996), 306.

[156] See chapter 4, pp. 173–74.

[157] On that point see Sullivan and Gunther, n. 31 above, 965–66.

[158] Black, J., dissenting, in *Konigsberg v. State Bar of California*, 366 U.S. 36 (1961), excerpt in ibid., 965.

[159] Frankfurter, J., concurring, in affirmance of the judgment in *Dennis v. United States*, 341 U.S. 494 (1951), excerpt in ibid., 966.

lichkeitsrecht (personality right), that is, one's fundamental right to the free development of his or her personality.[160] Depending on the concrete circumstances of the case, the court will attempt to strike a balance between the different basic rights and interests involved. Also the French courts, when dealing with freedom of the press cases, will try to find a reasonable balance between opposing interests, such as protection of public order, respect for the liberty of others, and preservation of the pluralistic character of the media.[161]

Weighing competing fundamental rights does not imply that the courts, that is, the European Courts (the ECJ, CFI, and ECtHR) and the various Member State courts, would not follow guidelines that they themselves have developed in earlier case law, often in interaction with one another. To give just one example, in a 1993 judgment the German Federal Court, the Bundesgerichtshof, attempted to strike a balance between the *Persönlichkeitsrecht* of the president of a large company and the freedom of expression of the environmental organization Greenpeace. The organization had launched a vehement attack on the president for having issued a press release concerning the impact of the company's products on the ozone layer, which Greenpeace considered a "swindle by misdescription." In its judgment, the court set forth a number of principles enshrined in earlier decisions. Summing up these principles, it held:

> Where the person expressing the opinion is not pursuing objectives of self-interest, but rather contributing to the public debate on a question of substantive concern to the public, then there is a presumption that the expression of opinion is permissible; an interpretation of the laws restricting freedom of opinion which makes excessively high demands as regards the permissibility of public criticism is not compatible with Art. 5 (1) Basic Law [on freedom of expression]. . . . The position is different if the statement is no longer predominantly aimed towards public discussion but rather towards the humiliation of the person; then, and only then, the statement, even if it concerns a question of substantive concern to the public, being in the nature of a libel, must yield to the rights of personality of the person affected.[162]

Applying these principles to the concrete case, the court dismissed the president's action. The ruling shows that, in balancing fundamental rights, courts do not rely on intuition, but make rational choices on the basis of guidelines derived from earlier decisions.

[160] Koopmans, n. 147 above, 197–98, with reference to BVerfGE 34, no. 25, *Princess Soraya*, 1973.

[161] Ibid., 198–99. This is in stark contrast, Koopmans adds, with the "frank and libertarian, but also very individualistic, tone of the US Supreme Court" (197).

[162] BGH, October 12, 1993, *NJW* 1994, 124, translated into English by N. Sims and reproduced in van Gerven, Lever, and Larouche, *Cases, Materials and Text on National, Supranational and International Tort Law* (Oxford: Hart Publishing, 2000), 149–51.

V. CONCLUSIONS

In this chapter, it has been examined to what extent open government is part of the EU's management culture. The following components of open government were taken into account: civic responsibility, free access to documents, civil society and citizen participation, a vibrant public opinion, and a free press.

Starting with the republican virtue of feeling responsible—not antagonistic to liberalism but complementary to it—five conceptions of responsibility were briefly examined: the hierarchical (Weberian), personal, social, professional, and civic conceptions. The last of these is the one most consistent with democracy, focusing as it does on civic values such as democratic control, loyalty to an elected parliament, and loyalty to the public cause. Controversial behavior of civil servants, and particularly whistle-blowing, civil disloyalty, or even disobedience, should be assessed in light of that conception. It follows from the analysis that the Union's attitude still draws too little inspiration from the civic conception. The Commission rules on whistle-blowing, put in place after the resignation of the Santer Commission in 1999, indeed do not give sufficient guidance to potential whistle-blowers, as they do not contain any indication as to the grounds of justification a whistle-blower may rely on. Nor do they set out the standards of care a whistle-blower should comply with. They do not provide civil servants with the possibility of seeking independent external advice.

Free access to public documents, for which the Swedish example serves as a model, is a keystone of open government. The difference between the Swedish and European attitudes became apparent in the case of the Swedish Journalists Association. In that case, Swedish journalists asked for access to the same twenty Europol documents from the EU Council in Brussels and from the Swedish administration in Stockholm. Access to only four documents was granted in Brussels under the European rules, while the Swedish administration granted access to eighteen of the twenty documents. Transparency in the Union has since improved significantly, not the least as a result of joint efforts of the European Parliament, the European Ombudsman, and the Court of First Instance, and because of the persistence of a number of transparency-minded Member States, mainly the Nordic states and the Netherlands. These efforts resulted, after difficult negotiations between the Commission, Council, and Parliament (following the Solana incident in the summer of 2000), in the enactment of Regulation 1049/2001. Although the regulation is broad in purpose, scope, and beneficiaries, it contains a long list of exceptions—not unlike the exceptions in the U.S. Freedom of Information Act. To be sure, transparency in the Union has outgrown the stage of an international organization, but it is not yet an overarching principle of law, apt to be fully enforced before the ECJ and CFI.

"Civil" society—consisting of organizations that are concerned with public interest goals but remain autonomous from the state—*and* "civic" society—composed of voluntary associations generating social capital, that is, creating connections and networks of relations among citizens—are the grass roots of any political system that wants to develop into an increasingly liberal and responsible democratic order. Together with political parties and elections, they are essential for the involvement of citizens in the political process, and the building of trust in the political system. To some extent, they may be capable of making up for the low turnout in elections, which is as common in many democratic states, including the United States, as it is in the European Union.

Regarding political parties, as long as Euro-parties are not getting involved in the designation of the European executive, in contrast to their national counterparts' involvement in the parliamentary regimes of the Member States, they will not be in a position to properly fulfill their role as mediators between the citizens and their institutions. As long as this does not happen, interest groups will remain the most important actors influencing the Union's legislative and executive process, now that Parliament and the Commission have made it a top priority to consult with all "stakeholders" in the preparation of executive and legislative acts. Unfortunately, these interest groups do not always act in an unbiased way, as is the case with the many lobbying groups operating in Brussels.

The involvement of interest groups in the political process has been enhanced with the use of new modes of governance, as exemplified by the use of the open method of coordination in the anti-poverty project set up by the Union, jointly with the Member States and NGOs, to fight social exclusion. Such involvement has its drawbacks, however, as it creates fluid boundaries between governmental and non-governmental actors, and it may lead to "governmentalization" and "bureaucratization" of private actors whose role it is in the first place to remain autonomous from state intervention in the pursuit of "citizen" goals.

It is often said that public opinion does not exist at the European level. That is only so if one looks at public opinion as a monolithic opinion related to the European integration as a global project. But it is clearly not true when public opinion is measured at the level of each Member State, and with regard to specific European policies. An analysis of the Eurobarometer surveys (which the Commission has conducted since the 1970s) shows that, indeed, from the very outset of the European construction, public opinion has contributed substantially to define preferences in the Member States, and has guided the respective governments in a significant way. That obviously applies to major integration policies, such as the internal market policies, but also to environmental policy and to such "hard-core" policies as foreign policy, internal and external policy, and defense policy. As could be expected, Eurobarometer surveys show that the European integration experiment meets most resistance whenever it impinges on the substratum of cultural and national identification that is built over hundreds of years—if not a millennium (as in the case of France and England).

Freedom of the press is a major contributor to the formation of public opinion. Investigative reporting, since Watergate popular around the world, is a strong weapon for fighting maladministration. More importantly, a responsible and pluralistic press is a crucial actor in democratic society, as it informs the public and offers a public space for the exchange of ideas and opinions—provided that it focuses on general interest issues and is not driven by commercial profit in the first place. In both the United States and Europe, the freedom of expression and of the press is strongly supported and guaranteed in constitutional texts and by supreme courts. Nevertheless, approaches vary considerably, European States being more inclined to balance freedom of the press with other competing values and interests. This practice is confirmed in Article 10 (2) of the European Convention of Human Rights, which enumerates a large number of compelling interests that can be taken into account by states when enacting legislation that may be restrictive of freedom of expression and the press. To balance competing fundamental values, European courts will invariably use the principle of proportionality. In the United States such a balancing act is perhaps less likely to occur because of the absence, in the First Amendment, of a similar list of potential restrictions.

CHAPTER SIX

Making a Constitution for Europe

On December 15, 2001, the European Council of Heads of State or Government met in Laeken to issue the Declaration on the Future of the European Union and to convene a Convention. The Convention was modeled on the one that drew up the EU Charter of Fundamental Rights proclaimed on December 8, 2000, at Nice, and was to be chaired by the former French president Valéry Giscard d'Estaing[1] and composed of representatives of the Member States' governments, the European Commission, the European Parliament, and the national parliaments. The Declaration charged the Convention with drafting a document that would answer basic questions about the Union's future and raised the issue of a constitution with a notable degree of caution. The document was to be ready by the end of June 2003 and was meant to provide a starting point for discussions between the Member States, in anticipation of the Intergovernmental Conference (IGC) to be held in Rome during the second half of 2003.

[1] For a brief overview of the composition and the working methods of the Convention, see A.A., editorial, "From Opinion 2/94 to the Future of Europe," 27 *ELRev.*, 2002, 1–2, and editorial comments, "What Is Going on in the European Convention?" 39 *CMLRev.*, 2002, 677–81. At Laeken, the leaders of the fifteen Member States decided that thirteen candidate Member States would be involved: the ten Member States that were scheduled to join (and did join) in May 2004, as well as Bulgaria, Romania, and even Turkey, which had not yet begun to negotiate membership. The only restriction on the candidate countries was that they were not entitled to block any consensus that might emerge among the current fifteen Member States. All in all, the Convention was composed of 105 members and 102 alternates. See further Peter Norman, *The Accidental Constitution: The Story of the European Convention* (Brussels: EuroComment, 2003), 38–39.

I. CONSTITUTION MAKING IN THE
EUROPEAN UNION

The Convention, which became known as the European Convention, met to resolve the following major issues: 1) how to create a clear and precise division of competences between the Union and the Member States; 2) how to enforce the principle of subsidiarity, with particular attention to whether national parliaments should be empowered to block proposed Community legislation under certain conditions; 3) whether the Charter of Fundamental Rights should be made binding on the Member States and become part of the Constitution; 4) how to simplify the Union's instruments and decision-making procedures; 5) how to reorganize the legislative and executive branches of the Union to enhance the Union's democratic legitimacy; and 6) how to increase the role of national parliaments in the European architecture. In the end, the issue of legitimacy gave rise to several more questions, one of them being whether the Union should have a presidency that would be a permanent office rather than an office that would continue to rotate between the Member States every six months.

a) The proceedings of the Convention
The European Convention got off to a slow start after its launch in February 2002.[2] The Convention being composed primarily of elected politicians, the understanding from the outset was that, if all parties were able to agree on a final text, the legitimacy of the text would be such that it would be difficult for the IGC to reject the document.[3] For that reason, Chairman Valéry Giscard d'Estaing was anxious that the discussions involve the entire Convention and not be divided into various forums. Nevertheless, for practical reasons, eleven working groups had to be created.[4] All working documents of these groups, and those of the Convention as a whole, have been made available to the gen-

---

[2] The inaugural session was held on February 28, but the first plenary session was not held until March 21–22. For a detailed overview of what happened during the whole period from February 2002 to July 2003, see Norman, n. 1 above.

[3] Editorial comments, *CMLRev.*, n. 1 above.

[4] The eleven groups addressed the following subjects: 1) subsidiarity, 2) the inclusion of the EU Charter of Fundamental Rights, 3) the legal personality of the Union, 4) the role of national parliaments, 5) complementary competences, 6) economic governance, 7) external action, 8) defense, 9) simplification, 10) liberty, security, and justice, and 11) a social Europe. For details, with references to the reports of each of these groups, see Norman, n. 1 above, 61–62.

eral public in an effort to make the activities of the Convention as transparent as possible.[5]

June 2003 saw the formal end of the Convention. After two busy weeks of negotiations during which last-minute compromises were reached on a few remaining questions, an overwhelming majority of the Convention approved the official Draft Treaty Establishing a Constitution for Europe, on Friday, June 13, 2003.[6] A week later, on Friday, June 20th, Convention chairman Giscard d'Estaing submitted the draft treaty to the heads of state or government of the existing and candidate Member States, which were assembled in Thessaloniki (or Salonica) under the Union's Greek presidency.[7] The assembly approved the draft as a valid basis of discussion, but it allowed the Convention some extra time to organize a few additional sessions of "technical drafting." During those drafting sessions, held on July 4 and July 9–10, 2003, a limited number of amendments were taken into consideration, and some were accepted.[8] At its last session, the Convention also adopted a proposal to "consti-

---

[5] See Jürgen Schwarze, "Guest Editorial: The Convention's Draft Treaty Establishing a Constitution for Europe," 40 *CMLRev.*, 2003, 1037–45, at 1042–43, where it is noted that citizens have been able to follow all the debates via the Internet and discuss several proposals in special forums, and that both academics and politicians have contributed to the debate by designing their own constitutional texts (some mentioned in nn. 2 and 5 of the guest editorial). For a full account, with references to Web sites that will remain accessible for some time, see Peter Norman, n. 1 above, xi–xiii.

[6] Only a small group of nine Euro-sceptics, led by MEP Jens-Peter Bonde and U.K. MP David Heathcoat-Amory, presented a minority report.

[7] The Conclusions of the European Council of Copenhagen, published in December 2002, had already made it clear that "the new Member States will participate fully in the next Intergovernmental Conference" and that "the new treaty will be signed after accession" (para. 8 of the Presidency Conclusions).

[8] See, for details, Norman, n. 1 above, 306–9. Two important changes to Part III of the draft Constitution were accepted. As a result of strong lobbying from the German government, a national veto over the access of immigrants to the labor market was maintained. At the insistence of the French government a national veto with regard to the "cultural exception" in external trade (to protect national music and cinema) was retained at the last minute. Of the ten article amendments proposed by the parliamentary delegations, only three were agreed upon: 1) the establishment of one joint service to assist the Union minister of foreign affairs (see below, p. 300); 2) the recognition de facto, rather than in name, of an open method of coordination on behalf of the Commission in the areas of public health, industry, social policy, and employment, with a view to promoting, encouraging, and facilitating Member State cooperation in those areas (see chapter 4, p. 169); and 3) the addition of structured cooperation under the Union's common foreign and defense policy to the areas of enhanced cooperation. See the EU Constitution Project Newsletter, volume 1, no. 4, July 2003, an initiative launched by The Federal Trust for Education and Research.

tutionalize" the already existing symbols of the Union: a flag, anthem, motto, and Europe Day.[9]

On July 18, 2003, Chairman Valéry Giscard d'Estaing handed the final text of the Constitutional Treaty to the (then) Italian presidency of the Union, which immediately communicated the text to the twenty-five States for scrutiny in anticipation of final decision making at the IGC. The IGC was launched on October 4, 2003, with negotiations expected to run for six months—ready for the treaty to be signed by the twenty-five Member States of the enlarged Union in May 2004. Because of the failure of the December 2003 IGC meeting (see below), it has not been able to respect that schedule. Once adopted by the IGC, probably with some amendments, the draft Constitutional Treaty will still need to be ratified by all Member States in accordance with their individual constitutions.[10]

b) Name and contents of the draft Constitution

The draft is named "A Treaty Establishing a Constitution" and, indeed, it is exactly that. On the one hand, the adoption and implementation of the draft document will depend upon the mutual agreement of the Member States, like an international treaty; on the other hand, the draft is intended to establish a basic legal order, as does a constitution.[11] Once ratified and entered into force,

---

[9] The EU's flag is defined as "a circle of twelve golden stars on a blue background;" its anthem is "based on the Ode to Joy from the Ninth Symphony by Ludwig van Beethoven;" and its motto is "United in Diversity." Europe Day is the 9th of May, the day in 1950 when Robert Schuman started the process of European integration with his proposal for a European Coal and Steel Community. Thus Article IV-1 [now Article I-8] of the Draft Constitution.

[10] See Article IV-8 [now Article IV-447] of the draft Constitution. Taking into account these ratifications, the treaty establishing the Constitution was expected to come into effect at the beginning of 2006. See, in that context, the third declaration attached to the draft (see n. 14 below), providing that: "If two years after the signature of the Treaty . . . , four fifths of the Member states have ratified it and one or more Member States have encountered difficulties in proceeding with ratification, the matter will be referred [for further consideration] to the European Council." If ratification by all Member States finally occurs, the treaty will lead to substantial institutional changes, the most controversial of which, such as those relating to the reduction of the number of Commission members and to the calculation of a qualified majority in the Council, are only set to enter into effect at a later date. Actually, as shown in this chapter, pp. 289–90, and in the Epilogue, pp. 375 and 379ff, with regard to both these issues, the initial text of the draft Constitution has been amended pursuant to the meeting of Heads of State or Government held in Brussels on June 17–18, 2004. For an overview of the most important amendments to the draft Constitution agreed at the June 2004 meeting, see editorial comments, "A Constitution for Europe" 41 *CMLRev.*, 2004, 899–907.

[11] Schwarze, n. 5 above, 1043.

the treaty would take the place of the earlier European Community (EC) Treaty and the Treaty on the European Union (EU), and their amending acts and treaties (Article IV-2 [now Article IV-437]).[12]

The draft Constitution does not have the outlook of a normal constitution. It consists of four parts, the longest of which is Part III, which is entitled "The Policies and Functioning of the Union." This part consists of 342 articles (Articles III-1 through III-342 [now 322 articles (Article III-115 through III-346)] and unites, revises, and rearranges the provisions of the three pillars currently contained in the EC and EU Treaties. Parts I, II, and IV are much shorter and more constitutional in outlook. Part I (untitled) contains fifty-nine articles (Articles I-1 through I-59) [now sixty articles (Articles I-1 through I-60)] and is divided into nine sections: 1) the definition and objectives of the Union, 2) the fundamental rights and citizenship of the Union, 3) the Union competences, 4) the Union's institutions, 5) the exercise of Union competence, 6) the democratic life of the Union, 7) the Union's finances, 8) the Union and its immediate environment, and 9) Union membership. Part II is entitled "The Charter of Fundamental Rights of the Union" and contains fifty-four articles (Articles II-1 through II-54 [now Articles II-61 through II-114]), incorporating the text of the existing EU Charter of Fundamental Rights. Part IV is entitled "General and Final Provisions" and contains ten articles (Articles IV-1 through IV-10 [now twelve articles (Articles IV-437 through IV-448)]. Altogether, the draft Constitution has 465 [now 448] articles, all of which have the same constitutional status, even though the constitutional content of Parts I, II, and IV and the provisions in Title II of Part III on non-discrimination is clearly higher than that of most other provisions in Part III. Their equal status was confirmed by the fact that Article IV-7 [now Article IV-443] subjects the revision of *any* provision of the draft Treaty to the same complex procedure.[13] In addition to the text of the

---

[12] The Euratom Treaty establishing the European Atomic Energy Community will remain in effect as amended by the draft Constitution: see Protocol Amending the Euratom Treaty in Annex to the Draft Constitution (see n. 14 below). To revise that treaty substantially would have led to delicate discussions mainly with the Green parties on the use of nuclear power. See Norman, n. 1 above, 309.

[13] See K. Lenaerts, J.-M. Binon, and P. Van Nuffel, "L'Union européenne en quête d'une Constitution: Bilan des travaux de la Constitution sur l'avenir de l'Europe," *JTDE*, 2003, 289–99, at 289. Before and during the Convention suggestions have been heard from different quarters for providing a less complex revision procedure for some provisions in Part III, but, unfortunately, they have not succeeded. For an overview, see Bruno de Witte, "Entry into Force and Revision," in *Ten Reflections on the Constitutional Treaty for Europe*, ed. Bruno de Witte (Florence: European University Institute, 2003), 207–23, at 212–17. However, after the Convention, an amendment to the draft Constitution was agreed by the Heads of State or Government at their June 17–

draft Constitution itself, five protocols and three declarations [now many more of each] were attached to the draft.[14]

As Convention chairman Giscard d'Estaing said in his final address when the draft was approved by the Convention on June 13, 2003, "The result is not perfect, but it is unhoped-for."[15] After many earlier attempts to write a constitution for Europe, the result was indeed unhoped-for. Putting the undertaking in historical perspective, German constitutionalist Jürgen Schwarze observed:

> The search for a European constitution is not a new phenomenon. When the Prussian King Friedrich II "the Great" had a look at the "Project for Eternal Peace in Europe" developed by the French Abbé de Saint Pierre, he commented to Voltaire, his partner in many philosophical dialogues: "The idea is very useful, except for the fact that the consent of the European princes (Fürsten) is lacking, and some other trifle issues."[16]

More recently, within the context of European integration, the European Parliament, under the guidance of Altiero Spinelli, promoted plans for constitutional reform but failed to deliver it.[17] Even as the Convention met, many believed that it would not be able to finalize a draft constitution. The result is not perfect either: the draft is at best "a promising and pragmatic reform concept"[18]—one, however, that makes progress possible, as we will see hereinafter.[19]

c) Recent developments

As mentioned, the early discussions in the IGC were not successful. Negotiations broke down in mid-December 2003, while the Union was still under

---

18, 2004 meeting in Brussels. See Article IV-7b [now Article IV-445] of the revised draft Constitution and this chapter, p. 305, n. 145.

[14] The protocols are on: 1) the role of national parliaments; 2) the application of the principles of subsidiarity and proportionality; 3) the representation of citizens in the European Parliament and the weighting of votes in the European Council and the Council of Ministers; 4) the Euro group; and 5) the amending of the Euratom Treaty. The three declarations are on: 1) the representation of citizens in the European Parliament and the weighting of votes (attached to the aforementioned protocol with the same name); 2) the creation of a European external action service; and 3) the final act of signature of the draft Constitution.

[15] Quoted by Norman, n. 1 above, 299.

[16] Schwarze, n. 5 above, 1037. The author adds, "This time it was the European Council consisting of the Heads of State or Government—the princes of our time . . . who proposed the idea of constitutional reform."

[17] See S. Douglas-Scott, *Constitutional Law of the European Union* (Harlow, England: Longman, 2002), 10.

[18] Ibid., 1042.

[19] For a brief discussion of the draft, see Schwarze, n. 5 above; for an extensive analysis, see Lenaerts, Binon, and Van Nuffel, n. 13 above.

the Italian presidency of Prime Minister Berlusconi. This breakdown was the result of Spain and Poland's refusal to give up their disproportionate number of votes in the Council of Ministers, which was granted to them by the 2000 Nice Treaty.[20] The summit meeting ended without any decision being made as to what happens next.[21] However, it was predictable at the time that not much would happen before the Spanish election in March 2004, or even before the June 2004 European Parliament elections. Moreover, as pointed out by Stanley Crossick, director of the European Policy Centre in Brussels, there was no intrinsic urgency: "The new treaty was expected to come into force at the beginning of 2006; it still need not be delayed beyond 2006 and many of the key provisions, including the one which sabotaged the summit, would not come into effect until 2009. A 6–9 months' delay does not, therefore, present any serious practical problems."[22]

That may be true. However, in six or nine months the situation would be even more complicated because of the coming close of the 2006 negotiations on the Union's multiannual budget. Immediately after the breakdown of the negotiations on the draft Constitution, a letter was, indeed, made public in which the leaders of the six chief contributors to the EU's budget (France, Germany, the U.K., the Netherlands, Sweden, and Austria) called on the president of the Commission to cap the Union's budget at 1 percent of gross national income. Given that the main victims of the budgetary cut would be Spain and Poland, the move was seen by many as "retaliation" by Germany and France.[23] Another factor that may have an impact on the constitutional negotiations is the well-known intention of a number of Member States (again, led by France and Germany) to start enhanced cooperation, within or outside the Union, if negotiations fail.[24] These factors, together with the nega-

[20] See Stanley Crossick, "Failed Summit Unfortunate, but Not Disastrous," *European Voice*, December 18, 2003–January 14, 2004, 7, which expresses the differences between the positions of Spain and Poland and those of France and Germany in concrete figures. Crossick observes, "The difference has little objective significance, bearing in mind that the Council rarely votes."

[21] The Convention has yielded some benefits, though, mainly by reaching an agreement in Naples on November 28 concerning enhanced cooperation in matters of defense between those Member States who wanted to join military forces. The agreement was brokered by Tony Blair and garnered the later consent of NATO. See *The Economist* of December 6, 2003, 25.

[22] Crossick, n. 20 above, 7.

[23] Dana Spinant, "Verheugen: Germany Will Link Cash and Constitution," *European Voice*, December 18, 2003–January 14, 2004, 1.

[24] For a positive view, see Brandon Mitchener, "Europe Scales Back Unified Agenda," *Wall Street Journal Europe*, December 19–21, 2003, A1, who concludes, "It

tive impact of Sweden's recent refusal to join the euro-zone, and the disagreement between the larger and smaller euro-zone countries over the Stability and Growth Pact, clouded the atmosphere surrounding the oncoming enlargement, suggesting that a bumpy flight might be ahead.

In the following sections I will discuss some of the answers that the framers of the draft Constitution gave to the questions on which the European Convention was asked to make proposals. I will first, in Section II, discuss competences and legislative procedures. Then, in Section III, I will deal with institutions, focusing on a few key controversial issues as they have been resolved in the draft Constitution. Finally, in Section IV, some questions that were left unresolved by the draft will be discussed.

II. COMPETENCES AND PROCEDURES IN THE DRAFT CONSTITUTION

Since the beginning of the European construction, the allocation of competences and the definition of decision-making procedures have been at the center of the integration process, and an indication of the progress or failure of integration. Competences and procedures have indeed been a permanent bone of contention between integrationists and intergovernmentalists.

The Union on a Continuum between Intergovernmentalism and Supranationalism

Political scientists view European integration as the outcome of three factors: 1) a political process determined by the interests, motives, and actions of political actors (such as elites, bureaucrats, voters, political parties, and interest groups); 2) institutions, both those of the Union and those of the Member States; and 3) political structures, such as decision-making procedures and social norms.[25] Since the beginning of European integration in the 1950s, several

---

wouldn't be the first time cooperation-minded EU member-states had plowed on ahead in hopes that others would follow. In fact, Europe already works at multiple speeds—a situation the new constitution wouldn't change. Switzerland, Norway and Iceland aren't EU members at all, for example, but they often live by its rules. Only 12 of the union's members use the euro as their currency" (A8). On this phenomenon of spillover of EU legislation and policy *beyond* the borders of the Union, which gives rise to a special form of differentiation, see chapter 1, p. 29, n. 87.

[25] For an overview, see Simon Hix, *The Political System of the European Union*, 2d ed. (London: Palgrave, due out in January 2005), 9–12 of the manuscript at http://personal.lse.ac.uk/HIX/Working Papers.HTM).

political theories have been presented to explain the dynamics of the integration process. The first grand theory was "neo-functionalism," which sees integration "as a process based on spill-over from one initially non-controversial, technical sector [coal and steel] to other [first economic, then also non-economic] sectors of possible greater political salience, involving a gradual reduction in the power of national government and a commensurate increase in the ability of the centre to deal with sensitive, politically charged issues."[26] Neo-functionalists believe that the driving forces behind this "spill-over" process are non-state actors, such as business associations, trade unions, and political parties.[27] A second and starkly opposing grand theory is known as "intergovernmentalism," which, faced with neo-functionalism's failure to explain the slowdown of European integration in the 1960s, argues that European integration is driven by the interests and actions of the European nation-states, whose main aim is to protect their geopolitical interests, such as national security and national sovereignty.[28]

Subsequent generations of political scientists have developed new theoretical constructs against the background of these two grand theories.[29] They were applied to the renewed dynamism and deepening of the integration process in the 1980s and the early 1990s, leading to the signing of the Maastricht European Union Treaty, and concentrated as much on examining the nature of the political entity that exists, and how it is governed, as on seeking to explain the dynamics of the integration process.[30]

Whatever the merit of these theories, it is clear that a simple characterization of the Union as either "intergovernmental" or "supranational" will not do: "The brute fact is that integration has proceeded unevenly, and theories of integration have failed to explain this unevenness."[31] The most appropriate

[26] Thus J. Lodge, *The European Community and the Challenge of the Future* (London: Pinter, 1993), quoted by P. Craig and G. de Búrca, *EU Law, Text, Cases, and Materials*, 3d ed. (Oxford: Oxford University Press, 2003), 5. In Craig and de Búrca, one finds an excellent brief overview of analyses of integration (5–7).

[27] Hix, n. 25 above, 14.

[28] Ibid., 14–15.

[29] They are: "liberal-intergovernmentalism," "supranational governance," and "rational choice institutionalism": see Hix, n. 25 above, 15–18, where these theories are further defined.

[30] Thus Craig and de Búrca, n. 26 above, 6, with references to an abundant literature.

[31] Alec Stone Sweet and Wayne Sandholtz, "Integration, Supranational Governance, and the Institutionalization of the European Policy," in *European Integration and Supranational Governance*, ed. Wayne Sandholtz and Alec Stone Sweet (Oxford: Oxford University Press, 1998), 1–26, at 7–8.

way to discuss the Union is to propose a continuum that stretches between two ideal-typical modes of governance: the *intergovernmental* pole, where the central players are "the national executives of the member states, who bargain with each other to produce common policies," and the *supranational* pole, where centralized governmental structures possess jurisdiction at the supranational level over specific domains within the Member States' territories, enabling them to constrain "the behavior of all actors, including member states, within those domains."[32] In principle, this continuum is able to accommodate all international regime forms. It is specifically able to accommodate the European Union, despite its peculiar construction. That construction gives it differing degrees of competence across a diverse range of policy areas. It has therefore been recommended to disaggregate the EU governing processes by policy sector, and to use the continuum as an instrument to examine European integration sector by sector, rather than applying it to the integration process as a whole. Thus, "we will be able to learn more about the nature of European integration than we can by working to characterize, in a blank fashion, the [EU] as an 'intergovernmental' or 'supranational' regime."[33]

With these insights from political science, we are better placed to assess the European constitution-making process and its outcomes. Both the actors represented at the European Convention and external groups that have expressed their views on integration have contributed to the end result. That result can be assessed by viewing where the winners and losers in the process are located along the continuum. Some actors are situated at the intergovernmental pole, such as the Member State governments and parliaments and the Council of Ministers,[34] while others are situated at the supranational pole, such as the European Commission,[35] the European Parliament,[36] those supporting the

[32] Ibid., 8.

[33] Ibid., 9. See, for a similar analysis regarding the role of public opinion as a societal actor, the contribution of Russell J. Dalton and Richard C. Eichenberg in the same book, discussed in chapter 5, p. 240.

[34] In the Council, national interests are represented by Member State ministers who look at the Community through national spectacles. That does not necessarily mean that national interests prevail over Community interests, if only because the interests of Member States often conflict with each other. What it does mean is that compromises are struck and "package deals" are arranged among Member States. Moreover, when vital national interests are at stake and no consensus can be reached on issues for which progress is absolutely needed, the matter is referred to the European Council of Heads of State or Government, the members of which, on the occasion of regular summit meetings, often force a political breakthrough at dinnertime in the relaxed atmosphere of beautiful castles and historic places.

[35] The Commission is, no doubt, the most "integration-driven" European institu-

views of the European Court of Justice, and parts of civil society that favor European integration, such as business associations and academics. Some actors, like the Presidium of the European Convention, the European Council, the political parties, and the trade unions, are more difficult to situate; whether they belong at one or the other pole depends very much on the specific issue. But that is true for all actors. In addition, there are, obviously, Member States that favor European integration more than others, again depending, however, on the issue involved.

That Member States differ in their views about integration should not come as a surprise because of the very different backgrounds of the now twenty-five Member States. The most important differences can be organized into the following categories: those between large, medium, and smaller states; those between the original founding states and the states that became members in recent decades or years; those between northern and southern Member States; those between more and less agricultural states (the latter contributing more to the Community budget than the former); those between more and less "welfare"-minded states; those between states with a strong capitalist past and those with a communist past or influence; and those between states with a strong military tradition and those without (either by choice or by force).

The differences between the large states and the smaller ones remain particularly substantial, mainly for geopolitical reasons. Indeed, in spite of European integration, the larger States continue to see themselves as important international players and continue their attempts to carve out a special sphere of influence for themselves in the global arena. This dynamic is exemplified by the United Kingdom's relationship with the Commonwealth countries and the United States; by Germany's post-unification position as the largest European nation and a model for the neighboring Central European Member States making the transition from communist to free market states; by Spain's privileged relations with South America; and by France's desire to benefit from its relationships with Africa and the Arab countries.[37]

---

tion, even though its members are essentially appointed by the Member States for renewable five-year periods. However, under Article 213 (2) EC Treaty, commissioners are required to act in the general interest of the Community and with complete independence, that is, without taking instructions from any national government or from any other body.

[36] The European Parliament is a strong supporter of European integration for reasons of its own, for example, in order to emphasize its autonomy as compared with the national parliaments. Being elected by universal suffrage, for the first time in 1979, the EP is the EU institution with the highest degree of democratic legitimacy.

[37] Only Italy is difficult to place among the "old" large Member States, no doubt

In the following pages, I will try to use the insights above to explain how some parts of the draft Constitution came about. I will concentrate on the rules relating to competences, institutions, and decision-making procedures, trying to find out which actor gained or lost in the process, and focusing on which direction the constitution, if adopted, would move European integration on the scale between intergovernmentalism and supranationalism.

Distribution of Power in the Draft Constitution

The adoption of the draft Constitution will mark the end of the three-pillar system. This is the result of both the constitutional structure laid out in Part I and, more conspicuously, the stated purpose of Part III, which is to turn the EC and EU Treaties into one coherent text. These founding treaties, and the acts and treaties that have supplemented and amended them, will therefore be repealed on the date the draft Constitution enters into force.[38] This will require a rearrangement of the present treaties and yet another renumbering of the articles. "Depillarization" does not mean, however, that matters previously falling under the second and third pillars will be regulated in the same way under the draft Constitution as matters previously falling under the first pillar.[39] On the contrary, large differences will remain in the scope of the Union's competences and decision-making abilities with regard to common foreign and security policy, and, to a lesser extent, with regard to police and judicial cooperation in criminal matters.[40]

---

because it has never seen itself as a closely united nation-state. On the tumultuous emergence of the Italian state, see Mark Kesselman et al., *European Politics in Transition*, 3d ed. (Boston: Houghton Mifflin Company, 1997), 341–42, where the authors also describe the making of the modern British, French, and German states, as well as the making of East-Central Europe, in a context of European integration.

[38] Article IV-1 [now Article IV-437] of the draft Constitution.

[39] Nevertheless, as a result of the merging of the three pillars into one, several essentially first-pillar doctrines would be transformed into doctrines that, if the draft Constitution is adopted, would apply equally to matters now falling under the second and third pillars. See Michael Dougan, "The Convention's Draft Constitutional Treaty: Bringing Europe Closer to Its Lawyers?" 28 *ELRev.*, 2003, 763–93, who cites two examples at 764: first, according to Article I-39 (3) [now Article I-40 (3)], the Union would be empowered to adopt decisions that Article I-32 (1) [now Article I-33 (1)] declares "binding in [their] entirety" (see below, p. 278); and, secondly, according to Article I-10 (1) [now Article I-6], Union law shall have primacy over national laws (see below, p. 269). However, the latter statement reflects case law of the ECJ, which has not had the opportunity so far to rule on primacy of Union law over national laws under the second and third pillars: editorial comments, n. 10 above, at 900.

[40] Particularly in the field of a common foreign and security policy, Member States will continue to play a predominant role either individually or through their repre-

a) Principles governing the exercise of competences

Naturally, the division of competences[41] between the federation and its component entities is a matter of great concern in the Union, as it is in any federal structure.[42] It is not surprising, therefore, that the draft Constitution gives a prominent place to "the Union's competences" in Title III of Part I, largely following the example of the German Basic Law.[43] Title III begins with Article I-9 (1)'s enumeration of three fundamental principles of Union competency: conferral, subsidiarity, and proportionality, which together limit the enjoyment and use of Union competences. As we saw in chapter 3,[44] these principles are already overarching principles of Union law, and will continue to be so, as the draft Constitution envisages no substantial changes.

The principle of *conferral* remains the most important principle of these three, as it limits the competences that the Union possesses to those conferred upon it in the Constitution (Article I-9 [2]; now Article I-11 [2]). In addition, the draft Constitution specifies two concomitant principles that can already be derived from case law of the Court of Justice but are now explicitly mentioned. The first, laid down in same paragraph, is that "competences not conferred upon the Union by the Constitution remain with the Member States."[45]

---

sentatives in the European Council and the Council of Ministers. As for the present situation, see chapter 1, pp. 22–25, and for the situation after entry into force of the Constitutional Treaty, see Lenaerts, Binon, and Van Nuffel, n. 13 above. The role of the Community courts would remain limited as well; for the present situation, see chapter 3, pp. 118–21.

[41] In Union law powers are consistently called "competences."

[42] EU discussions traditionally avoid the word "federal" to describe the nature of the Union. In an earlier version of the draft Constitution the term was incorporated in the first article, which said that the Union "shall administer certain common competences on a federal basis." As a result of strong opposition from the U.K. representative to the Convention, the present version of Article I-1 no longer uses the term, but that does not prevent the Union from having a de facto federal structure. See also Kalypso Nicolaides, "Future of Europe Talks Should be FUN!" *European Voice*, March 20–26, 2003, 13.

[43] The German Basic Law contains a number of detailed provisions; see Articles 70–75, including Article 74a. They relate, respectively, to "legislative jurisdiction of the Federation and the *Länder*," "exclusive legislation of the Federation," "concurrent legislation of the Federation," "areas of exclusive legislation," "areas of concurrent legislation," "[further] concurrent legislation," and "areas of federal framework legislation."

[44] See above, pp. 138–41.

[45] Although the principle of conferral will not, in itself, be subject to change, Part III of the draft Constitution does contain some redistributions of powers in favor of the Union: for an enumeration, see Dougan, n. 39 above, 765–66.

The second, set out in Article I-10 (1) [now Article I-6], is that laws adopted by the Union within the scope of its powers "shall have primacy over the laws of the Member States." The principle is not new, as it was laid down in case law of the ECJ as early as 1964.[46]

As explained previously,[47] the other two principles, subsidiarity and proportionality, are currently understood to restrict the *use* that the Union can make of the competences it has.[48] The draft Constitution understands the *subsidiarity* principle in the same way, providing in Article I-9 (3) [now Article I-11 (3)] that the Union may *only* use its powers, with the exception of those granted on an exclusive basis (see below), "if and insofar as the objectives of the intended action cannot be sufficiently achieved by the Member States, either at central level or at regional and local level, but can rather, by reason of the scale or effects of the proposed action, be better achieved at Union level." However, the draft Constitution would take the subsidiarity principle one step forward—a step that was hailed by the defenders of the powers of national and regional parliaments as "innovative and bold."[49] Indeed, the draft provides in the second paragraph of Article I-9 (3) [now Article I-11 (3)] that "National Parliaments shall ensure compliance with that principle in accordance with the procedure set out in the Protocol [on the application of the principles of subsidiarity and proportionality]."

Paragraph 5 of this protocol authorizes any national parliament, or any chamber of a national parliament of a Member State, to send a reasoned opinion "within six weeks from the date of transmission of the Commission's legislative proposal . . . to the Presidents of the European Parliament, the Council of Ministers and the Commission . . . stating why it considers the proposal in question does not comply with the principle of subsidiarity." The protocol further specifies, in paragraph 6, that where reasoned opinions of non-compliance represent (as a general rule) at least one-third of all votes allocated to the Member States' national parliaments, the Commission "shall review its proposal," and may, after review, "decide to maintain, amend or withdraw its proposal, . . . giv[ing] reasons for its decision."[50] When the Com-

[46] For the first instance, see the judgment of the ECJ in Case 6/64, *Costa v. ENEL*, [1964] ECR 585.

[47] See pp. 138ff above.

[48] The application of the principle of subsidiarity (and of proportionality) is currently further circumscribed in a protocol attached to the Treaty of Amsterdam.

[49] See Norman, n. 1 above, 96.

[50] See paras. 5 and 6 of the Protocol on the Application of the Principles of Subsidiarity and Proportionality, attached to the draft Constitution (that protocol would replace the one mentioned in n. 48 above). The "early warning" procedure, as it is

mission maintains or amends the proposal, and the proposal is then adopted by the Union legislature, the Court of Justice is given explicit (ex post) jurisdiction in paragraph 7 "to hear actions on grounds of infringement of the principle of subsidiarity." Such actions may be brought by Member States on behalf of themselves or of their national parliament.

This complicated "early warning" procedure[51] will also apply when the Commission intends to use the so-called "flexibility clause" of Article I-17 [now Article I-18] of the draft Constitution, which would replace the present (and controversial) Article 308 EC Treaty.[52] The *flexibility clause* empowers the Council, acting unanimously with the consent of Parliament, to take measures that are necessary to attain one of the objectives set by the Constitution for which the Constitution has not provided the Council with the necessary powers. To prevent the Union institutions from making excessive use of this general supplementary power, the Commission would be obliged to apply the "early warning" procedure, giving the national parliaments notice of the proposals for which it intends to use the "flexibility clause." As a further protection, it is specified that the Commission proposals may not entail the harmonization of national laws "in cases where the Constitution excludes such harmonisation."

In parallel with the subsidiarity principle, the principle of *proportionality*, currently inscribed in EC Article 5, will continue to restrict the use of Union powers. Contrary to the subsidiarity principle, however, the proportionality principle circumscribes *all* Union powers, whether exclusive or not. It requires any Union action, in scope and form, not to go any further than "what is necessary to achieve the objectives of the Constitution" (Article I-9 [4]; now Arti-

---

called, has given rise to conflicting views within the Convention, with some asking that it be compulsory for the Commission to withdraw its proposal when a one-third or a two-thirds majority issues an opinion of non-compliance. Others have asked, on the contrary, for the whole procedure to be abolished. The majority finally decided to maintain the proposed system: see *European Voice*, March 20–26, 2003, 6.

[51] The procedure leaves a number of questions unanswered. See Dougan, n. 39 above, 767–768.

[52] The flexibility clause, comparable to the "necessary and proper" clause in Article I, section 8 [18] of the U.S. Constitution, would replace and limit the use of the present Article 308 EC Treaty. That article has been the object of severe criticism on the part of Member States, particularly on the part of some subdivisions of Member States such as the German Länder, which fear an erosion of their own powers if Article 308 were to be too frequently used. This fear was reflected in the Laeken Declaration and in the Maastricht judgment of the German Constitutional Court (BVerfGE 89, 155; see above, pp. 41–42). For a (brief) discussion of the issue, see Stephen Weatherill, "Competence," in *Ten Reflections on the Constitutional Treaty for Europe*, n. 13 above, 45–66, at 59–61.

cle I-11 [4]). As pointed out previously,[53] since the 1960s and '70s, the principle of proportionality has played a significant role in the case law of the ECJ. The adoption of the Constitution will both confirm that role and flesh it out in the attached protocol on subsidiarity and proportionality. Paragraph 4 of the protocol specifies that the Commission shall justify its legislative proposals, with regard to both these principles, by way of a detailed statement containing "some assessment of the proposal's financial impact and, in the case of a framework law, of its implications for the rules to be put in place by the Member States, including, where necessary, the regional legislation." It further requires that "the Commission shall take account of the need for any burden, whether financial or administrative, falling upon the Union, national governments, regional or local authorities, economic operators and citizens, to be minimised and commensurate with the objective to be achieved." In other words, deregulation is seen as an ingredient of proportionality.

One further principle deserves to be mentioned, that is, the principle of *loyal cooperation* set out in Article I-5 (2) of the draft Constitution, which requires the Union and the Member States to assist each other "in full mutual respect, . . . to carry out the tasks which flow from the Constitution." The principle, currently laid down in Article 10 EC, is an overarching principle in legal orders of Member States with federal structures.[54] It has been at the basis of several judgments of the ECJ, which has made it a cornerstone of its case law, as is discussed in chapter 3.[55]

b) Categories of competences and policies

The aforementioned principles relate to the possession and the use of existing Union competences. Currently, neither the EC nor the EU Treaty enu-

---

[53] See p. 141 above.

[54] For example, the German Constitutional Court uses the principle of Bundestreue (loyalty to the Union) to oblige the Federation and the Länder to cooperate and assist each other in preserving the constitutional order at all levels of the Federation and its component states. In concrete terms, this means that the Federation and the Länder are required, in the exercise of their competences, to take into account the effect their regulations may have on the interests of the other entities, and to refrain from using a competence when those other entities' interests would be unacceptably harmed. See BVerfGE, 4, 111; also BVerfGE, 12, 205, and H. Maurer, *Staatsrecht I*, 3d ed. (Munich: Verlag CHBeck, 2003), 318–21. A similar principle is used in Article 143, §1 of the Belgian Constitution, which requires the federal government, the linguistic communities, and the economic regions to act in the interests of federal loyalty in order to prevent conflicts of interests.

[55] See p. 139 above.

merates or defines those competences.[56] One of the most conspicuous changes introduced by the draft Constitution is the definition and classification of three categories of Union competences to legislate and take other legally binding acts. Those three categories are classified as "exclusive competence," "shared competence," and "supporting, coordinating or complementary action," and are defined in Article I-11 [now Article I-12] of the draft Constitution. First, according to paragraph 1 of Article I-11, when the Constitution confers *exclusive competence* on the Union, "only the Union may legislate"; Member States can only legislate when they are "so empowered by the Union." Those exclusive competences are exhaustively enumerated in Article I-12 (1) and (2) [now Article I-13 (1) and (2)].[57] Second, in certain areas,[58] the Union has *supportive, coordinating, or complementary competences*, which allow it to "carry out actions to support, coordinate or supplement the actions of the Member States . . . without superseding thereby their competence in these areas" (Article I-11 [5]; now Article I-12 [5]). Third, competences that the Union *shares* with the Member States are enumerated in Article I-13 (2), (3), and (4) [now Article I-14 (2), (3), and (4)].[59] This category of competences is a residual one, comprising all competences attributed to the Union that are neither ex-

[56] For a contribution clarifying, from a German viewpoint, the basics of vertical delimitation of competences in the EU—a subject less explored than horizontal delimitation of competences—see Armin von Bogdandy and Jürgen Bast, "The European Union's Vertical Order of Competences: The Current Law and Proposals for Reform," 39 *CMLRev.*, 2002, 227–68.

[57] The Union has exclusive competence to establish competition rules within the internal market as well as in the following areas: monetary policy for the Member States that have adopted the euro, common commercial policy, customs union, and conservation of marine biological resources (Article I-12 [1]; now Article I-13 [1]). Within the scope of competence set out in Article III-225 (1) [now Article III-323 (1)] of the draft Constitution, the Union also has exclusive competence to conclude an international agreement (Article I-12 [2]; now Article I-13 [2]). See Lenaerts, Binon, and Van Nuffel, n. 13 above, 292, no. 23.

[58] Those areas are: industry, protection and improvement of human health, education, vocational training, youth and sports, culture, and civil protection: Article I-16 (2) [now Article I-17, as amended and enlarged].

[59] Article I-13 (2) [now Article I-14 (2), as amended and enlarged] contains a list of the principal areas in which shared competences exist. They are, in the initial text of the Article: the internal market; the areas of freedom, security, and justice; agriculture and fisheries (excluding the conservation of marine biological resources); transport and trans-European networks; energy; certain aspects of social policy; economic and social cohesion; the environment; consumer protection; and common safety concerns in public health matters. Paragraphs 3 and 4 contain special rules for research, technological development, and space, as well as development cooperation and humanitarian aid.

clusive nor supportive competences (Article I-13 [1]; now Article I-14 [1]). Member States may exercise these shared competences to the extent that the Union has not exercised them, or has ceased to do so (Article I-11 [2]; now Article I-12 [2]). In other words, although in the case of supportive, coordinating, and complementary competences the Union cannot preempt Member State competences, it can do so in the case of concurrent competences by exercising its competence first. Moreover, in the case of supportive, coordinating, and complementary competences, the Union is not allowed to adopt legally binding acts that "entail harmonisation of Member States' laws or regulations" (Article I-16 [3]; now Article I-12 [5]).[60]

Apart from the competence to legislate or adopt other legally binding acts, the draft Constitution also provides the Union, in Article I-14 (1) and (3) [now Article I-15 (1) and (3)], with the competence to adopt measures to ensure the coordination of the Member States' *economic* and *employment policies*. The draft does this, in particular, by adopting guidelines for these policies; however, according to paragraph 2 [now paragraph 1], specific provisions of economic policy shall only apply to the Member States that have adopted the euro. Paragraph 4 [now 3] of the same article also provides the Union with the ability to adopt initiatives to ensure the coordination of Member States' individual *social* policies. Furthermore, Article I-15 (1) [now Article I-16 (1)] describes the Union's competence in matters of *common foreign and security policy* as covering "all areas of foreign policy and all questions relating to the Union's security, including the progressive framing of a common defence policy, which might lead to a common defence." According to Article I-15 (2) [now Article I-16 (2)], the Member States are obliged to "actively and unreservedly support the Union's common foreign and security policy in a spirit of loyalty and mutual solidarity and shall comply with the acts adopted by the Union in this area. They shall refrain from action contrary to the Union's interests or likely to undermine its effectiveness."[61]

c) No major changes but some unanswered questions
There is not that much to be said about the changes that the draft Constitution will insert into the current system of distribution of power between the Union and its Member States. If the draft were to be adopted, the principles of conferral, subsidiarity, and proportionality will remain the guiding policies. The three categories of competences that the draft defines also correspond to

[60] Some imperfections of the competence provisions have been noted: see Dougan, n. 39 above, 769–71.
[61] That duty is already laid down in Article 11 (2) EU, which defines the term "'effectiveness' as a cohesive force in international relations."

the current situation, though the categories are better defined and distinguished from one another. The most prominent change is the draft's effort to give teeth to the principle of subsidiarity by involving the national parliaments in an "early warning" procedure, and enabling them, ex post, to bring an action before the Court of Justice through their Member State. It is doubtful though, whether that change will be able to stem the tide, given the large amount of legislation that passes through the EU institutions every year.[62]

However, subsidiarity as a principle is neither the only nor by any means the most important indicator of how competences are divided between the Union and the Member States. First, many of the pieces of legislation adopted by the Community legislature are directives—or framework laws, as they will be called when the draft Constitution is put in place (see below)—that are binding upon the Member States *only* as to the result to be achieved, with the Member States left to choose the form and means of achieving that result.[63] Second, as will be recalled hereafter, the European Council and the Council of Ministers will continue to play a prominent—in certain areas the *most* prominent—role in making Union laws and establishing Union policies.[64] Both of these bodies are composed of Member State representatives and have committees and working parties in which Member States are represented. Third, since the 1990s, with the completion of the internal market and the extension of Union competences to non-economic areas, the list of areas in which the Union can take only supporting, coordinating, or complementary action has become longer and longer. These are areas in which the Union is *not* allowed to adopt binding acts that entail harmonization of Member State laws and regulations. Lastly, the new methods of governance—as described in chapter 4[65]—shift emphasis away from legal action to policy action in which national authorities and civil society actors are as involved, if not more involved, than Community institutions.

The shift to policy making is a phenomenon that EU lawyers and legislators may especially dislike because the focus of their work and interest tends to be on binding legislative and administrative measures and judicial rulings.[66] These instruments were essential in creating and maintaining the internal

---

[62] According to Hix, n. 25 above, 4, more than three hundred pieces of legislation pass through EU institutions per year, on average. Scholarly estimates would indicate that the EU sets 80 percent of the rules governing the production, distribution, and exchange of goods, services, and capital in the member states' markets: ibid.

[63] Article 249 EC.

[64] See chapter 1, p. 22.

[65] See pp. 167–70 above.

[66] Thus Gráinne de Búrca, "The Constitutional Challenge of New Governance in the European Union," 28 *ELRev.*, 2003, 814–39, at 815.

market but are much less instrumental when economic, monetary, or social policies have to be laid out. A similar lack of interest in, or even skepticism toward, policy making was visible in the work of the Convention preparing the draft Constitution: of the eleven working groups, a majority dealt with institutional, structural, and decision-making questions rather than with substantive policy issues or orientations. Only four groups (defense; freedom, security, and justice; economic governance; and social policy) could be said to have examined substantive policy, and even within these groups the focus was less on substantive policy than on instruments and decision-making methods, with the possible exception of the defense group.[67]

As highlighted by Gráinne de Búrca, the shift of focus from legislation to policy inherent in the new methods of governance gives rise to a number of tensions and a number of constitutional issues. Tensions exist: 1) between legally limited competences and ever-expanding policy activities, 2) between the depiction of a clear but static division of powers and a more fluid sharing of powers and responsibilities between Union and national authorities and private actors, 3) between policy segmentation and policy integration, 4) between a human rights conception that imposes negative constraints on government and a conception of human rights as an articulation of values, 5) between the emphasis on representative governmental institutions as the key to legitimacy and the inclusion of a wider array of stakeholders, and 6) between the traditional intergovernmentalism/supranationalism dichotomy and the conception of multilevel governance.[68]

The constitutional issues that these tensions entail are, among others: 1) whether the traditional constitutionalism based on a neo-liberal emphasis of the EU project as a whole must be revised or adjusted so as to mitigate the existing hierarchical relationship between the treaty's entrenched internal market norms and the softer powers in the social field;[69] 2) whether the "rights" approach, prescribing outcomes and setting them in law, must give way to the flexibility of open methods of governance, which are essentially a "process" aimed at satisfactory policy targets that will hopefully emerge over time through information exchange, identification of best practices, reporting, monitoring, and iteration;[70] and 3) whether the commitment of the new gov-

---

[67] Ibid., 821–22.

[68] Ibid., 814–15.

[69] Such an adjustment could be accomplished, for example, by weaving the requirement of consideration of the aim of social protection throughout the Union's other policies and powers, as has been done for gender equality and environmental protection: ibid., 831–32.

[70] Ibid., 833–35.

ernance methods to participation and transparency is genuine, that is, whether those methods' alleged openness to a greater range of non-traditional actors, which varies a great deal in practice from one policy sector to another and from state to state, will not result, as much as the traditional forms of law-making, in a technocratic network of faceless policy-making civil servants and national experts.[71] Sooner or later these issues have to be addressed. Apart from last-minute additions in some provisions of Part III of the draft Constitution, the Presidium of the Convention has chosen not to incorporate the open method of coordination as a general instrument in the draft.[72]

d) Conclusion

In sum, the draft Constitution provisions on distribution of powers do not move the Union on the intergovernmentalism/supranationalism continuum very much. The only novelty is the involvement of national parliaments in as-suring "ex ante" compliance with the principle of subsidiarity. This would seem to have a neutral impact on the continuum. On the one hand, it involves national actors in the Union's legislative process; on the other hand, it strengthens the legitimacy of that legislative process and makes it more ac-ceptable to the Member States. As for the emergence of new methods of gov-ernance, if it proves anything, it is that the extremes of the continuum are no longer extremes because the new process involves all actors, national and su-pranational, public and private, in a new form of governance. The outcome of the process, and specifically whether these new forms of governance based on soft law processes present a valid alternative for the traditional lawmaking methods of governance, is still uncertain though.

Legal Instruments, Legislative Procedures, and Voting Requirements

Legislative procedures granting more or less decision-making power to the European Parliament, and voting requirements that allow the possibility of special (so-called "qualified") majority voting or unanimity voting, are an-other battleground where supranationalist and intergovernmentalist forces face each other. Before explaining the compromises reached by the framers of the draft Constitution with respect to these two subjects, I will first deal with a more mundane subject: legislative instruments.

---

[71] A classic criticism of the new methods is that they exclude the participation of parliament, and that open methods of coordination lack the democratic legitimacy and accountability that traditional constitutionalism highly values: ibid., 835–38.

[72] Ibid., 838. For more details, see Norman, n. 1 above, 213–14 and 311–12.

a) Legal instruments defined

The draft Constitution tries to bring some order to the legal instruments that the Union institutions use to attain their assigned objectives.[73] Currently, the EC and EU Treaties do not contain a list of instruments, and they have not been able to prevent new categories of instruments, especially "soft law" (non-binding) instruments, from being added to the ones mentioned in the treaties. The draft Constitution would change that situation by enumerating and defining, in Article I-32 (1) [now Article I-33 (1)], a series of legal instruments that the Union legislature is permitted to use in all areas covered by the Constitution.[74]

At the top of the hierarchy of legal instruments are "legislative acts," which are, as a rule, adopted by the legislature proper in accordance with the "ordinary legislative procedure."[75] That procedure, outlined in Article I-33 [now Article I-34] of the draft Constitution, is modeled after the current co-decision procedure of Article 251 EC, and provides for joint decision making by the European Parliament and the Council, at the proposal of the Commission (see below). Legislative acts can be either European *laws*, directly applicable in all Member States, or European *framework laws*, binding on Member States only as to the result to be achieved.[76]

---

[73] For a critical assessment of this part of the draft Constitution, see Dougan, n. 39 above, 781–87.

[74] It follows, though, from Article I-39 (3) and (7) [now Article I-40 (3) and (7)] of the draft Constitution, that no legislative acts can be used for the common foreign and security policy. In that sphere, and in the sphere of a common defense policy—see Article I-40 (4) [now Article I-41 (4)]—only "European decisions," which are "non-legislative acts" (see below in the text), can be made. This term is flexible enough to include "common strategies," "joint actions," and "common positions" (see Lenaerts, Binon, and Van Nuffel, n. 13 above, 293, no. 37), which are the instruments currently used for the second pillar: see Article 12 EU.

[75] According to Article I-33 (2) [now Article I-34 (2)], specific cases will remain in which European laws and European framework laws will not be adopted in accordance with the ordinary legislative procedure, but rather in accordance with specific legislative procedures, including a procedure in which the Council acts unanimously after consultation with the European Parliament: see further Lenaerts, Binon, and Van Nuffel, n. 13 above, 293, no. 35, n. 20. See also Article I-7a (2) [now Article I-444 (2)].

[76] Laws would take the place of regulations, and framework laws would take that of directives (both defined in Article 249 EC) when issued jointly by Parliament and the Council in accordance with Article 251 EC. The new typology of legislative acts will apply to areas now covered by the first and third pillars, and will abolish the use of framework decisions and decisions for the third pillar currently provided for in Article 34 (2) under b) EU: see Lenaerts, Binon, and Van Nuffel, n. 13 above, 293, no. 34. The term "legislative acts" is reserved for acts laying down essential elements and basic policy decisions in a specific domain: ibid., no. 36.

In contrast, "non-legislative acts," as they are called in Article I-34 [now Article I-35], are comprised of European *regulations* and European *decisions*. European regulations are acts of general application, while decisions are addressed to specific entities or persons to supplement or implement legislative acts under Articles I-35 and I-36 [now Articles I-36 and I-37] (see below), or on the basis of specific constitutional provisions. European regulations can either be binding in their entirety and directly applicable in all Member States, or only binding with regard to the result to be achieved,[77] while European decisions are binding in their entirety, but only on those to whom they are specifically addressed. Non-legislative acts can be adopted, according to Article 34 (1) [now Article 35 (2), as reworded, however], in one of two instances: first, in the specific cases that the Constitution requires the Council or the Commission to act, or authorizes the European Central Bank to do so,[78] and secondly, in cases that laws or framework laws delegate the power to adopt non-legislative acts to the Commission, or confer implementing powers on the Commission, or, in exceptional circumstances, on the Council.[79]

The aforementioned power of the Commission and the Council to adopt *non-legislative acts* by way of delegation or implementation of laws or framework laws is further regulated in Articles I-35 and I-36 of the draft Constitution. Article I-35 [now Article I-36] deals with *delegated regulations*. The first paragraph of the Article states that certain European laws or framework laws can empower the Commission to enact delegated regulations to supplement or amend certain non-essential elements of the law or framework law, as long as the changes are within the objectives, content, scope, *and* duration defined in the empowering law or framework law. The second paragraph explains that a law or framework law can subject the delegation granted to the Commission to two possible conditions, which are as follows: 1) "the European Parliament or the Council may decide to revoke the delegation" (the so-called "right of call-back"), or 2) "the delegated regulation may enter into force only if no objection has been expressed by the European Parliament or the Council

---

[77] Regulations under the draft would replace the present Regulations and Directives issued by the Commission as implementing acts.

[78] For an enumeration, see Lenaerts, Binon, and Van Nuffel, n. 13 above, 293–94, no. 39, n. 22–24.

[79] In addition to *binding* instruments, Article I-32 (1) [now Article I-33 (1)], last sentence, refers to non-binding instruments such as recommendations and opinions, which can be adopted by any one institution. Other "soft law" instruments like resolutions, conclusions, declarations, etc., may be used as well, but not, according to paragraph 2 of Article I-32 [now Article I-33], with regard to subjects on which legislative acts are proposed: ibid., 294, no. 45.

within a period set by the law or framework law" (the so-called "period of tacit approval").[80]

Article I-36 [now Article I-37] concerns *implementing acts*. It first states, in paragraph (1), that it is the duty of *Member States* to adopt all measures of national law to implement legally binding Union acts. The second paragraph then allows the Commission or the Council, "in specific cases duly justified and in the cases provided for in Article I-39 [now Article I-40],"[81] to issue such implementing Union acts,[82] provided that "uniform conditions . . . are needed" at the *Union* level. Since implementation of binding acts remains in principle the prerogative of the Member States ("executive federalism"), paragraph 3 provides that "European laws shall lay down in advance rules and general principles for the mechanisms for control by Member States of Union implementing acts."[83] The latter provision governs the matter currently regulated in Article 202 EC ("comitology") and will, by reserving the creation of control

[80] In a previous draft of Article I-35 (2) [now Article I-36 (2)], a third possibility was provided, i.e., that "the provisions of the delegated regulation are to lapse after a period set by the law or framework law . . . [unless] extended on a proposal from the Commission, by decision of the European Parliament and of the Council." This "sunset clause" is not explicitly mentioned by the current draft, as it is covered by the possible limits on the duration of the delegation mentioned in (1) of Article I-35 [now Article I-36].

[81] Article I-39 [now Article I-40] empowers the European Council and the Council of Ministers to adopt the necessary European decisions to implement the Union's common foreign and security policy: see paragraphs 3 and 7.

[82] That act may be a law, a framework law, a regulation (including an implementing regulation), or a decision: see Lenaerts, Binon, and Van Nuffel, n. 13 above, 294, no. 42.

[83] No reference is made to the possibility of setting up and conferring regulatory powers to independent agencies, a device that the Commission saw in its 2001 White Paper on European Governance as an alternative for implementation through committees ("comitology"), at least in certain areas. The Commission has further developed this idea in its 2002 Communication on European Regulatory Agencies (see chapter 2, pp. 93–94). The possibility of assigning the task of adopting implementing acts to regulatory authorities came up in Working Group IX on Simplification (Document CONV 424/02 of November 29, 2002), but the group considered the issue to go beyond its terms of reference (p. 12). This is not to say that agencies could no longer be created under the draft Constitution. Currently, the Commission considers the legal basis for regulatory agencies to be found in the specific treaty provisions relating to the policy area for which the agency is set up or, in the absence of such a specific treaty provision, in Article 308 EC: 2002 Communication, p. 7. That position remains valid under the draft Constitution, particularly since the flexibility clause of Article I-17 [now Article I-18], which is the successor clause of Article 308 EC, would give the Member States more assurance that the clause is properly used: n. 52 above.

mechanisms to a law, finally comply with the European Parliament's persistent request to enjoy the same competence as the Council in controlling the Commission's implementation of Community legislation.[84]

b) Legislative procedures

The above rearrangement of legal instruments has been presented as "simplification"[85] as it will, when adopted, make a clear distinction between legislative acts (laws and framework laws) and non-legislative acts (regulations or decisions). As stated above, legislative acts will be passed through the "ordinary legislative procedure," as defined in Article I-33 (1), "on the basis of proposals from the Commission, jointly by the European Parliament and the Council." This reference shows that, in the mind of the drafters of the Constitution, the "simplification" of legal instruments goes hand in hand with the simplification of decision-making procedures.

Currently, several decision-making procedures are in place under the first pillar, some with the involvement of the European Parliament, others without. The latter are a remnant of old times, when Parliament was still an assembly of representatives of Member State parliaments with consultative powers only, in specific instances.[86] Subsequent treaties have gradually strengthened the legislative role of the European Parliament, particularly so by providing for the Parliament's direct election by the Member States' citizens. There are six procedures currently in use: 1) the Commission may act alone; 2) the Council and the Commission may act alone; 3) the Council and the Commission may act after consultation with Parliament; 4) the Council and Commission may act in cooperation with Parliament (as defined in Article 252 EC, which grants Parliament a double reading, that is a right to reconsider the legislative proposal, but no decisive voice); 5) the Council, Commission, and Parliament may act in codecision (Article 251 EC, which gives Parliament a decisive voice, jointly with the Council); and 6) the Council and Commission may act with the "assent" of Parliament.[87]

The co-decision procedure of Article 251 EC, as complicated as it may appear on paper, has worked well in the past, and Article I-33 (1) [now Article I-34 (1)] of the draft Constitution promotes it to become the "ordinary legislative

---

[84] For the "comitology" process, see chapter 1, pp. 17–18.

[85] The revision of legal instruments and decision-making processes was prepared by the Convention's Working Group IX on Simplification: n. 83 above.

[86] See Articles 137–44 and 189 of the original EEC Treaty in conjunction, for instance, with Article 100.

[87] For a description of these six procedures, see Craig and de Búrca, n. 26 above, 139–48.

procedure." Even so, paragraph 2 of Article I-33 provides that, in certain matters, special legislative procedures will be established whereby laws and framework laws "shall be adopted by the European Parliament with the participation of the Council, or by the latter with the participation of the European Parliament."[88] The "ordinary legislative procedure" of Article I-33 (1) [now Article I-34 (1)] is based on the assumption that, after a proposal from the Commission,[89] legislative acts ought to be adopted *jointly* by the two arms of the legislative authority, the Parliament and the Council of Ministers, on the basis of parity between these two arms and with the same transparency for both.[90] This preference for the "ordinary legislative procedure" would result in yet another significant extension of the Parliament's legislative influence, as the new procedure would replace, in a number of instances, the aforementioned cooperation procedure, the mere consultation procedure, and the simple assent procedure.[91] It would even extend to areas where Parliament currently has no formal role, specifically to legislation on border controls, asylum and immigration, and police and judicial cooperation in criminal matters.[92]

c) Qualified majority voting

In matters of decision-making procedures, especially in the case of the legislative co-decision procedure referred to above, voting requirements are of

---

[88] Article I-33 (2) [now Article I-34 (2)]. The latter situation would apply, for instance, to legislation addressing the Union's common foreign and security policy, for which no change of the current decision-making procedure is envisaged. According to Article 23 (1) EU, the current procedure provides, as a general rule, for unanimous voting in the Council (abstentions are not counted, but rather make the decision inapplicable in the Member State concerned: see second sentence). With regard to certain matters, those are: implementing acts and procedural questions, Article 23 (2) and (3) EU provides for qualified or simple majority voting.

[89] In the second sentence of para. 1 of Article I-33 [now Article I-34], the draft makes reference to instances where, in derogation from the Commission's quasi-monopoly right of initiative to propose legislation, a group of Member States would also have the initiative to propose laws and framework laws to the European Parliament and the Council for adoption. That would be so, as mentioned in Article III-165 [now Article III-264] of the draft Constitution, in cases relating to judicial and police cooperation in criminal matters, dealt with in Articles III-171 through III-175 [now Articles III-270–74] and Articles III-176 through III-178 [now Articles III-275–77].

[90] For the transparency of the legislative procedures of the Council and Parliament, see Article I-49 (2) [now Article I-50 (2)], where it is provided that "The European Parliament shall meet in public, as shall the Council of Ministers when examining and adopting a legislative proposal." See also paragraphs 4 and 5 with regard to free access to documents.

[91] See the references to Part III of the draft Constitution in Dougan, n. 39 above, 772.

[92] Ibid.

crucial importance. As such, they are the object of heated debates between the Member States with regard to the exercise of Union competences. The major issue is whether qualified majority voting (QMV) will replace the requirement of unanimity in the Council of Ministers, which would strip any single Member State of its veto right. As for the other two legislative institutions, the Commission and Parliament, the matter is simple—both current Union law and the draft Constitution require the Commission, which has the right of legislative initiative, to make decisions by majority vote (Article 219 EC), while Parliament, save as otherwise provided in the treaty, is required to make decisions by an absolute majority of the votes cast (Article 198 EC).[93]

Voting in the Council of Ministers is a far more complicated matter. Although, in the Council also, decisions are made, as a general rule, by a majority of Council members (there are as many members as there are Member States) (Article 205 [1] EC), there are many instances in which the treaty provides that decisions will have to be made either unanimously or by qualified majority. According to the concept of a qualified majority, the number of votes afforded to each Member State is calculated in accordance with the scale reproduced in Article 205 (2) EC. That scale is based, by and large, on each country's population, with a significant correction made for the smaller Member States. Thus, until the most recent enlargement, effective as of May 1, 2004, a measure proposed to the Council by the Commission (as is normally the case) had to obtain 62 out of the 87 weighted votes (71.31 percent) cast in favor. To use a concrete example, the United Kingdom, Ireland, Denmark, Finland, Sweden, and Luxembourg, with their twenty-five total votes, could thus be outvoted by the rest of the Member States.[94] As a result of enlargement, each state's number of votes was adjusted as of May 1, 2004, a qualified majority now requiring 88 votes out of the 124 weighted votes (70.97 percent). The system will be changed again as of November 1, 2004, to apply the (controversial) Nice rules requiring 232 votes out of a total of 321 weighted votes (72.27 percent)—and, moreover, as of January 1, 2005, a vote must pass a triple threshold for a measure to be adopted: a measure must not only obtain 72.27 percent of the weighted vote, but must also be approved by a simple majority of Member States representing at least 62 percent of the EU population.[95]

[93] The number of representatives, and therefore votes, that each Member State has in Parliament is set out in Article 190 EC. It will be amended for the period 2004–9 in accordance with the Act of Accession, as reflected in the protocol on the representation of citizens annexed to the draft Constitution (n. 14 above).

[94] See further K. Lenaerts and P. Van Nuffel, *Constitutional Law of the European Union*, ed. R. Bray (London: Sweet and Maxwell, 1999), 313ff.

[95] Article 205 (2) EC as amended as a result of a protocol annexed to the Nice Treaty,

From the beginning, qualified majority voting has raised two delicate issues: first, whether the number of instances in which the method is used should be extended, and, second, whether the definition should be changed. Unsurprisingly, therefore, both issues were also at the center of debates in the Convention preparing the draft Constitution.

As to the *first* issue, those who wished to reinforce the supranational (or federal) character of the Union regarded extending QMV as essential, as it implies moving away from a consensual conception of decision making that is inherent in unanimous voting toward a (more) majoritarian conception. So far, the majoritarian conception prevails to a large extent under the first pillar, but not under the second or third pillars, where unanimity in the Council remains the general rule. The draft Constitution would result in a significant extension of the QMV procedure by applying it to new areas of substantive law. It would cover, for example: social security coordination for migrant workers, incentive measures in the field of culture, all competences related to border controls, asylum, and migration, and most of the provisions related to judicial and police cooperation in criminal matters. The requirement of unanimity would nevertheless remain in place for the adoption of measures in the field of general discrimination, and in such sensitive areas as social and environmental policy, judicial cooperation in civil matters concerning family law, and the establishment of a European Public Prosecutor's Office.[96] Due to vociferous campaigning by the U.K. and Ireland, unanimity will be retained also for matters of tax harmonization.[97]

As to the *second* issue, while extending the use of QMV is about reinforcing the supranational character of the Union, the revision of the manner in which a qualified majority is calculated is as much about the comparative importance given to larger and smaller states in the voting process. The debate bears more specifically on how much of the formal parity between sovereign states should be abandoned in favor of taking into account the relative populations of the individual states. In the concrete circumstances of the Union, both questions are often related: accepting less formal parity may indeed be the price that the smaller Member States are willing to pay to make the larger states accept more majoritarian decision making. Smaller states often favor majoritarian decision

---

itself replaced by Article 12 (1) and (2) of the Act of Accession: see, on all this, Lenaerts, Binon, and Van Nuffel, n. 13 above, 297, no. 67, n. 57.

[96] Lists taken from Dougan's article, n. 39 above, 776, where references to the relevant Articles in Part III of the draft Constitution can be found.

[97] Articles III-62 (2) and 63 provide, however, for certain matters to be decided by qualified majority voting, so long as the Council has unanimously agreed to do so in advance. See further the "passerelle" procedure referral in n. 101 below.

making because it is less of a burden for them to abandon their veto right than it is for a larger Member State, whose stakes in sovereignty are normally higher. The draft Constitution constitutes an illustration of this type of bargaining: on the one hand, it increases the number of instances to which QMV is applied and makes, in Article I-33, the co-decision procedure based on QMV in the Council the ordinary legislative procedure; on the other hand, however, it changes, in Article I-24, the method of calculating the existence of a qualified majority in favor of the larger Member States.

Under Article I-24 of the draft Constitution, the aforementioned triple threshold that will apply as of January 1, 2005, under the Nice rules would be replaced by a two-tier system. A qualified majority in the ordinary legislative procedure (as well as for other matters to be decided by the Council of Ministers and the European Council) would henceforth "consist of the majority of Member States, representing at least three fifths of the population of the Union." In other words, if the Constitution were adopted in its initial version, the support of half of the Member States would suffice for a qualified majority, so long as their populations total 60 percent of the Union's total population. The change was brought about by the realization, made explicit during Convention deliberations, that, in a Union of twenty-five states, 74 percent of the people live in six large nations with around 40 million or more inhabitants each, that 19 percent of the people live in eight medium-size nations with 8–16 million inhabitants each, and that the remaining 7 percent of the people live in eleven nations with less than 5 million inhabitants each. These differences make it very difficult to maintain the current weighted vote system, which is still based on some concept of formal equality of Member States and ignores the principle of citizen equality.[98] Given the importance of the issue, it was not unlikely that further changes would be made in the aforementioned formula of 50 percent of the Member States and 60 percent of the people—as indeed happened at the June 2004 IGC in Brussels).[99]

[98] Schwarze, n. 5 above, 1040. It should be noted that Article I-24 would only take effect on November 1, 2009: see para. 3 of Article I-24. Pursuant to an amendment approved by the IGC meeting of June 7–8, 2004, this arrangement has been maintained, but paragraph 3 has been transferred to Article 2 (1) of the Protocol on transitional provisions relating to the Institutions and bodies of the Union, appended to the draft Constitution.

[99] During the December 2003 IGC meeting in Rome, the provisions of Article I-24 were fiercely attacked. The attack was lead by Spain and Poland, which had secured a highly favorable number of weighted votes under the post-enlargement provisions agreed upon at Nice. It led to the failure of the December summit meeting, as reported at the beginning of this section. Following bilateral meetings held under the Irish presi-

d) Conclusion

To some, the issues discussed in this section may appear to be rather theoretical and of interest only to lawyers. This is not so, however, because each of these issues has important implications for the balance of power between the Union and its Member States, between the Member States themselves, and between Union institutions. This is obviously true for the revision of the calculation of QMV majority to the advantage of the larger states, or the extension of QMV to new areas, thus abolishing the veto right of any state and strengthening the power of the Union, and particularly of the European Parliament. But it also holds true for concrete decisions as to *whether* framework laws will be used instead of laws, leaving the implementation of Union rules to the Member States;[100] or *whether* laws or framework laws will delegate regulatory powers to the Commission, and what kinds of restrictive conditions will accompany those delegations under Article I-35; and *which* control mechanisms Parliament and the Council will create in favor of Member States when it is decided to grant implementing powers to the Commission or the Council under Article I-36 (2). All of these matters may affect the subtle balance that exists both horizontally among the institutions and vertically, between the institutions and the Member States.

Taking all this into account, the foregoing discussion shows that the draft Constitution, if adopted, would have the effect, as regards legal procedures and voting requirements, to move the Union on the continuum between intergovernmentalism and supranationalism further into the direction of the latter. This is mainly so because of the drafters' decision to make the co-decision procedure the "ordinary legislative procedure," which enhances the involvement of the European Parliament in lawmaking, as well as because of their decision to ex-

---

dency during the first half of 2004, and after several alternatives had been put forward (see, for example, the alternative reported in *European Voice*, March 11–17, 2004, 3), a compromise was finally found and approved at the June 17–18, 2004 IGC meeting in Brussels. The compromise is based on a double threshold of 55 percent of (at least fifteen) Member States and 65 percent of the population of the Union, and providing for a blocking minority that must include at least four Member States (Article I-24, as amended [now Article I-25 (1)]). See further the Epilogue, pp. 379–80. For the background of this complex formula, see editorial comments, 41 *CMLRev.*, 2004, n. 1 above, 904–5.

[100] In the initial text of the draft, there is an intriguing difference in the definition of a framework law in Article I-32 (1) and the current definition of a directive in Article 249 EC Treaty. Article I-32 states that Member States are "entirely free to choose" the form and means of achieving the result imposed, while Article 249 EC Treaty contains no such language. See further Dougan, n. 39 above, 782. In the text amended at the June 17–18, 2004 IGC meeting, the discrepancy has been eliminated, Article I-31 now providing that national authorities implementing framework laws are left with "the choice of form and methods."

tend the areas subjected to qualified majority voting (rather than unanimity voting), which enhances majoritarian decision making by eliminating the veto right that each Member State possesses in case of unanimity voting.[101] Moreover, the redefinition of QMV and the shift of influence from the smaller to the larger states that it entails reinforces proportional representation and democratic legitimacy by emphasizing the will of a majority of the population over that of the states in the adoption of binding acts.[102]

III. THE INSTITUTIONS' DEMOCRATIC LEGITIMACY

Article I-18 [now Article I-19] of the draft Constitution states that the Union shall be served by a single institutional framework. The framework is made up of five institutions: the European Parliament, the European Council, the Council of Ministers, the European Commission, and the Court of Justice of the European Union. Its aim is to ensure the consistency, effectiveness, and continuity of Union policies and actions, to advance the objectives of the Union, to promote its values, and to serve its interests as well as those of its citizens and Member States.

The Union's Single Institutional Framework

The above enumeration of Union framework institutions differs from the present situation set out in Article 7 EC. The draft Constitution adds the European Council to the framework, whereas the Court of Auditors is relegated to the category of other institutions and bodies. This category of other institutions includes the European Central Bank (Article I-29; now Article I-30), the Court

---

[101] According to Miguel Poiares Maduro, QMV is extended to thirty-two new areas: "The New Form of Majoritarianism in the EU," 28 *ELRev.*, 2003, 900–904, at 901–2. For a detailed account, see Norman, n. 1 above, 249, 315, and 330–31. Moreover, in some of the areas still subject to unanimity, the draft allows a move into majority voting if there is a unanimous decision to do so in the European Council (which, before its decision, must consult the European Parliament and inform the national parliaments). See Article I-24 (4), second sentence. This complicated procedure, called the "passerelle" procedure, is a typical compromise between those supporting and those opposing QMV. The procedure, complicated as it is, has the advantage of avoiding a revision of the Constitutional Treaty when change is agreed on, leaving it to the European Council to opt for QMV. Actually, at the June 17–18, 2004 IGC meeting, it was decided to transfer paragraph 4 of Article I-24 to Article IV-7a (1) [now Article IV-444 (1)] and to refer to it as "Simplified revision procedure."

[102] Maduro, n. 101 above, 902.

of Auditors (Article I-30; now Article I-31), and the Union's advisory bodies, which are the Committee of the Regions and the Economic and Social Committee (Article I-31; now Article I-32). I will first describe the new contemplated framework from a viewpoint of institutional balance, then describe it from a viewpoint of democratic legitimacy and the rule of law.

a) Substantive functions and balance of power

The substantive functions of the five major institutions can be described as follows. The *European Parliament*, jointly with the Council of Ministers, has the power to enact legislation and exercise the budgetary, political control, and consultation functions (Article I-19 [1]; now Article I-20 [1]). The *European Council* is charged with providing the Union with the necessary impetus for its development, and defining its general political directions and priorities. It does not, however, exercise legislative functions (Article I-20 [1]; now Article I-21 [1]). The *Council of Ministers*, jointly with the European Parliament, has the power to enact legislation and exercise the budgetary, policy-making, and co-ordinating functions (Article I-22 [1]; now Article I-23 [1]). The *European Commission* is to promote the general European interest, ensure the application of the Constitution, oversee the application of Union law, execute the budget, and exercise coordinating, executive, and management functions. With the exception of common foreign and security policy, which falls under the jurisdiction of the European Council chair and the Union Minister for Foreign Affairs, the Commission is responsible for ensuring the Union's external representation and initiating the Union's annual and multiannual programming. As a general rule, Union legislative acts can be adopted only on the basis of a Commission proposal (Article 25 [1] and [2]; now Article I-26 [1] and [2]). The *EU Court of Justice* is to ensure respect for the law in the interpretation and application of the Constitution (Article 28 [1]; now Article I-29 [1]). Each of the institutions can only act within the limits of the powers conferred on it by the Constitution and must practice full mutual cooperation (Article I-18 [3]; now Article I-19 [1]).

The preceding description presents the following picture of balance of power in the Union under the draft Constitution:

i. The legislative function will continue to be shared by three institutions: the Commission, which initiates the legislative process through its quasi-monopolistic right of initiative, and the European Parliament and the Council, which under the ordinary legislative procedure act jointly and on an equal footing.

ii. The budgetary function will be exercised by the European Parliament and the Council of Ministers, while the Commission executes the budget.

iii. The European Council will provide the Union with the necessary political impetus and define its general political directions and priorities, but it shall not exercise any legislative function.

iv. The Council of Ministers will carry out policy-making and coordinating functions where the Constitution so provides.

v. The Commission, apart from initiating the legislative process and guarding the rule of law (under the control of the Court of Justice), will manage the Union in the fullest sense of the word, including executing its budget and initiating its annual and multiannual programming.

vi. The Court of Justice of the European Union, which includes the Court of Justice (acting as Supreme Court), the High Court (as the CFI would be renamed), and specialized courts, will exercise the judicial function at Union level and ensure respect for the law.

vii. The European Council, through its president and with the assistance of the Union's foreign minister, will ensure the external representation of the Union in matters of the Union's common foreign and security policy, while the Commission will represent the Union on other issues, mainly through the Union's foreign minister (who will be one of the Commission's vice presidents under Article I-27 [3]; now Article I-28 [4]).

b) Democratic legitimacy and the rule of law

From the viewpoint of *democratic legitimacy*, the following general picture emerges from the draft Constitution. A European Parliament will represent the citizens of the Union at Union level. The members of Parliament are elected for a term of five years by direct universal suffrage of European citizens. The Parliament will elect its own president and officers. It will also elect the president of the European Commission (Article I-19 [1], [2], and [3]; now Article I-20 [1], [2], [3], and [4]), who, however, must first be nominated by the European Council, deciding by qualified majority. If the Council's nominee does not receive the required majority support in Parliament, the European Council will have one month to put forward a new candidate. In proposing a candidate to the Parliament, the European Council is required to take into account the elections to the European Parliament, and to carry out appropriate consultations (Article I-26 [1]; now Article I-27 [1]). The Parliament can also censure the Commission by an open vote, forcing the whole Commission to resign if carried by a two-thirds majority of votes cast, representing a majority of European Parliament members (Articles I-25 [5] and III-243; now Articles I-26 [8] and III-340).

Whereas citizens are directly represented at Union level by the European Parliament, Member States are represented in the European Council of Heads of State or Government and in the Council of Ministers by their governments (Article I-45 [2]; now Article I-46 [2]), which are themselves accountable to popularly elected national parliaments.[103] Like the European Parliament, the Council of Ministers will meet in public; it will do so, however, only when examining and adopting a legislative proposal. Like the other institutions, bodies, or agencies, the European Council and the Council of Ministers will provide access to public documents in accordance with both a European law and their own rules of procedure (Article I-49 [2] and [5]; now Article I-50 [2] and [4]). The draft Constitution does not envisage political responsibility for these councils at Union level, nor does any explicit provision require the two councils to "act" in the interest of the Union. All Union institutions, including the European Council and the Council of Ministers, are obliged to devote equal attention to Union citizens, to give citizens and representative associations the opportunity to announce and publicly exchange their views on all areas of Union action, and to maintain an open, transparent, and regular dialogue with such associations and civil society (Articles I-44 and 46 [1] and [2]; now Articles I-45 and 47 [1] and [2]).

As for the European Commission, it shall, as now, "promote the general European interest and take appropriate initiatives to that end" (Article I-25 [1]; now Article I-26 [1]). It will, for all practical purposes, be the Union's executive, with the exception of matters related to common foreign and security policy. Under the initial text of Article I-25 (3), the Commission would have consisted of a body comprising its president, the Union minister for foreign affairs, and thirteen European commissioners selected on the basis of a system of equal rotation between the Member States.[104] In addition to these thirteen European commissioners, the Commission president-elect would have appointed non-voting commissioners from the other Member States on the basis of the same criteria (Article I-25 [3]). From the beginning, the creation of these two categories of commissioners has been controversial, and the system has not survived the June 2004 IGC, which has amended the initial text of Article I-25 (as will be explained in the text below and discussed in the Epilogue). Under the new Article I-26, as Article I-25 is renumbered, the prin-

---

[103] That is insofar as heads of state (monarchs or presidents) or of government (prime ministers or chancellors) are not politically immune according to their Member State constitution. There would seem to be large differences across the Union: see Dina Spinant, *European Voice*, January 22–28, 2004, 19.

[104] The rotation system will be such that "Member States are treated on a strictly equal footing as regards determination of the sequence of, and the time spent by, their nationals as members of the College; consequently, the difference between the total number of terms of office held by nationals of any pair of Member States may never be more than one" (Article I-25 [3] [a]). The system implies that large Member States would not always have a European commissioner.

ciple of one commissioner per state will be maintained until at least November 1, 2014.[105]

The candidate for president of the Commission will be put forward by the European Council, deciding by qualified majority, and elected by the European Parliament by a majority of its members (Article I-26 [1]; now Article I-27 [1]). The Union minister for foreign affairs, acting as one of the Commission vice-presidents, will be appointed by the European Council, acting by qualified majority, with the agreement of the Commission-president-elect (Article I-27 [1]; now Article I-28 [1]). Under the initial text of Article I-26 (2), the aforementioned thirteen European commissioners would have been chosen by the Commission president-elect from lists of three persons, in which both genders are represented, which each Member State designated by the rotating system submits. They would have been selected by the president-elect "for their competence, European commitment, and guaranteed independence" (Article I-26 [2]). Article I-26 (4), as amended by the June 2004 IGC, now provides that all members of the Commission (proposed, as currently, by the Member State governments) shall be chosen on the basis of "their general competence and European commitment and their independence shall be beyond doubt."

Once all Commission members have been designated, the whole Commission will be submitted collectively to a vote of approval by the European Parliament for a term of office of five years (Article I-26 [2]; now Article I-27 [2]). As already pointed out, while in office, the European Parliament can force the whole Commission to resign by a motion of censure. It cannot censure individual members of the Commission, but the Commission president can request the resignation of any member without having to obtain the prior approval of the other Commission members (as he or she needs now) (Article I-26 [3]; now Article I-27 [3]). Moreover, the Commission president "shall be responsible to the European Parliament for the activities of the Commissioners" (Article I-25 [5]; now Article I-26 [8]).

To make the picture complete, in Title VI on the democratic life of the Union, the draft Constitution seeks to flesh out the principle of representative and participatory democracy. With regard to *representative democracy*, every citizen shall have the right to participate in the democratic life of the Union. In addition, the draft Constitution mandates that decision making be done as openly as possible and as closely as possible to the citizen, and it requires political par-

---

[105] Already at the Convention, the incumbent Commission had indicated that it opposed the distinction between (voting) European commissioners and (non-voting) commissioners and had a strong preference for the "one member per Member State" formula: for more detail, see Norman, n. 1 above, 266–67.

ties at the European level to both contribute to forming European political awareness and to express the will of Union citizens (Article I-45 [3] and [4]; now Article I-46 [3] and [4]). Under the principle of *participatory democracy*, the draft Constitution requires that Union institutions shall make it possible for citizens and representative associations to publicly exchange views. The draft also mandates that the institutions maintain an open, transparent, and regular dialogue with civil society, and carry out broad consultations (Article I-46 [1], [2], and [3]; now Article I-47 [1], [2], and [3]). Though the draft stops short of organizing referenda, it does provide that one million citizens coming from a significant number of Member States may invite the Commission to submit any appropriate proposal on matters where citizens believe that a Union act is required to implement the Constitution (Article I-46 [4]; now Article I-47 [4]). The draft Constitution advocates other devices to promote dialogue and transparency, including the facilitation of dialogue between social partners, the investigation of maladministration by the Office of the European Ombudsman, the promotion of transparency of Union proceedings, and the provision of access to public documents, protection of personal data, and dialogue with churches and non-confessional organizations (Articles I-47 to 51; now Articles I-48–52). Most of these devices, if not all, are already in place now.

Finally, with regard to the *rule of law*, the draft Constitution would continue to exclude jurisdiction of the Community courts over the common foreign and security policy, with the exceptions currently in effect.[106] However, the draft would completely remove the current restrictions on the Community courts' jurisdiction, embodied in Article 68 (1) and (2) EC, over preliminary references and review of measures concerning intra-Community border controls in matters of visa, asylum, and immigration policy.[107] Moreover, the draft would abolish some limitations on jurisdiction over police and judicial cooperation in criminal matters, more specifically those currently provided in Article 35 (2) and (3) EU with regard to the preliminary ruling procedure.[108] The draft would, however, leave in place the restriction in Article 35 (5) EU, which prevents the Court from reviewing the validity or proportionality of operations carried out by the police or other law enforcement services of a Member State, or the exercise of Member State responsibilities with regard to the maintenance of law and the safeguarding of internal security, as long as, according to Article III-283 [now Article III-377], "such action is a matter of

---

[106] See chapter 3, pp. 119–20. For some qualifications, however, see Dougan, n. 39 above, 791.

[107] Ibid., 792.

[108] Ibid.

national law."[109] In addition to the foregoing, Article III-267 [now Article III-362] of the draft Constitution would facilitate enforcement actions against Member States by simplifying the imposition of financial penalties on Member States and, most importantly, Article III-270 (4) [now Article III-365 (4)] would broaden an individual's right to bring an action for annulment of "a regulatory act which is of direct concern to him or her and does not entail implementing measures."[110]

c) Conclusion

The preceding overview indicates that the draft Constitution would not change the current institutional balance: the Commission would retain its quasi-monopoly on legislative initiative, Parliament and Council would continue to act as co-legislators, and the jurisdiction of the Court of Justice would be unaffected. The only important change would be the recognition of the European Council as an institution, which already exists, for all practical purposes. The role of all institutions would certainly be better defined, and the democratic legitimacy of the Union as a whole would be strengthened. The respect for the rule of law would be enhanced thanks to a (limited) extension of the Court of Justice's jurisdiction over border control and criminal matters.

There are some changes in the draft that could have an impact on the balance of power between institutions. One such change relates to the position of president of the European Council, which became a permanent position, the president being elected by the Council for a term of two and a half years, renewable once. Other changes concern the relationship between the Commission and Parliament, which would make it more similar to the relation between the executive and the legislature in a parliamentary system. I will return to these points below, and in the following chapter.

Some Controversial Solutions

Some controversial issues in the draft Constitution need to be highlighted, namely the dual presidency, the organization of the Council of Ministers, and the appointment of a "double-hatted" foreign minister for the Union. Before addressing these issues, however, I will return for a moment to the most controversial issue of all, which, as already mentioned, is the drastic change that Article I-25 (3) of the draft intended to make in the composition of the Commission.

---

[109] Ibid., 792, the author observing that the proposed drafting seems deliberately ambiguous. In the amended text of Article III-283 [now Article III-377], the words in quotes have been deleted.

[110] The undefined term "regulatory act" would seem to refer to "non-legislative acts" as defined in Article I-32 [now Article I-33] of the draft.

Initially, the five large Member States—France, Germany, Italy, Spain, and the United Kingdom—had two commissioners each, whereas the others had only one commissioner. With the entry into effect of the Nice Treaty, it was agreed that, following the latest enlargement and as of November 1, 2004, when a new Commission would take over, the large Member States would abandon their second commissioner, leaving all Member States only one commissioner.[111] Under the draft Constitution prepared by the Convention, that situation was to be changed drastically. As pointed out above, the draft created two categories of commissioners: thirteen European commissioners with voting rights, selected on the basis of a system of equal rotation between the Member States, large, medium, and small, and an additional number of commissioners without voting rights from the Member States that would not have a European commissioner.

Soon after the Convention, it became clear that the proposal was not going to meet the approval of all Member States, particularly of the large ones, and that the principle of one commissioner per state was going to be maintained for at least a transitional period. The principle has, indeed, advantages, one of them being that the lack of voting commissioners from a large number of Member States might affect the credibility of the Commission in those Member States, but it also has disadvantages. One argument in favor of a system that is *not* based on the principle of one commissioner per state is that the principle supports the idea that commissioners should be seen, not as state representatives, but rather as independent officials owing allegiance only to the Union's general interest. Another argument is that, with a steadily increasing number of Member States, it becomes more and more inefficient to have a Commission with a national from each Member State.

As is not unusual in the Union, the solution chosen has been the creation of a transitional system. Under the new text of Article I-25 (6) [now Article I-26 (6), as amended by the 2004 IGC], the membership of the Commission will be restricted to two thirds of the number of the Member States—each of them taking turns on the basis of a system of equal rotation—beginning, however, only with the second Commission set up after the entry into force of the Constitution, which will be in 2014 at best.[112]

I will now address the other controversial solutions mentioned above.

---

[111] Article 4 (1) of the Protocol on Enlargement attached to the Nice Treaty.

[112] See the editorial comments, 41 *CMLRev.*, 2004, n. 1 above, 904 where it is observed that "for those who fear that a composition based on one national per Member State could lead to a weakening of the Commission transformed into an intergovernmental body, it would seem that, if their forecast is correct, it will be difficult for the Commission to regain its lost authority ten years hence." Under the new text of what is now Article I-25 (6), the equal rotation system between Member States would remain subject to

a) A dual presidency

A much-debated question at the Convention concerned the presidency of the European Council. Before the Convention embarked upon the task of writing the first draft texts in the early months of 2003, French president Jacques Chirac and German chancellor Gerhard Schröder had given new life to the Franco-German partnership, which led in January 2003 to the publication of joint proposals on the future of the Union's institutions. The joint proposals set the tone for the rest of the Convention.[113] They contained a plan for a long-term and full-time president of the European Council (a French concern), who would be elected by the European Council. The plan would do away with the present system of rotating the presidencies of the European Council and the Council of Ministers between the Member States every six months. The proposals also contained a plan for the president of the Commission to be elected by the European Parliament (a German concern), which would replace the current system in which the president is designated by the Member States in the European Council, and then approved by Parliament. The joint French-German paper was badly received by the smaller countries, which feared that a full-time European Council president would encroach on the powers of the Commission president.[114] It was, however, by and large endorsed in a U.K.-Spanish paper published on the last day of February 2003.[115]

The discussion about the presidency culminated on the afternoon of April 22, 2003, when Convention chairman Valéry Giscard d'Estaing unveiled his own proposals, on which he had worked privately with the help of Sir John Kerr, the Convention's secretary-general. According to the text, the European Council would become the highest authority of the Union and would have a long-term president supported by a small board, which would act as a powerful cabinet.

---

the same principles, to be defined by unanimous decision from the European Council, as set out in the initial text of Article I-25 (3). See n. 104 above. On the new text, see also further the Epilogue, pp. 377–79.

[113] On this episode, see Norman, n. 1 above, 174–79. The partnership between France and Germany began as early as the 1960s, with the signing of the Elysée Treaty of January 1963 by the French president Charles de Gaulle and the German chancellor Konrad Adenauer. The treaty established a special relationship between the two countries. Since then the Franco-German cooperation, cemented by regular meetings of heads of state, has historically been a motor for the Union. See Norman Davies, *Europe: A History* (London: Pimlico, 1997), 1073.

[114] Norman, n. 1 above, 179–81.

[115] Ibid., 182–83. The consensus between the four large countries came about notwithstanding the growing differences between them over Iraq. To quote U.K. Representative Peter Hain, the war in Iraq had "little to negligible impact . . . on the person to person negotiations, the meetings in the Convention and the outcome for the UK" (185).

The role of the Commission, which as a body would be responsible to both the European Council and the European Parliament, was hardly defined.[116] The short paper, composed of fifteen articles, provoked much anger and was responsible for an institutional imbroglio within the Convention and its Presidium. It was drastically revised in the days thereafter. These revisions finally led to the institutional setup described in the preceding subsection, with a much reduced (and mainly political) role for the European Council, which nevertheless would become a Union institution (as it already is de facto), second only to the European Parliament. As compared with the initial proposal, the revisions also upgraded the role of the Commission (and its president), which was expressly charged with promoting the Union's general interest (as it currently is: Article 213 [2] EC).

In the end, the draft Constitution's system retains two presidents, one of the European Council and one of the European Commission, with neither elected by universal suffrage. The European Council president will be elected, full-time, for a term of two-and-a-half years, renewable once, by qualified majority of the European Council. The European Council may elect any person for president; the only restriction is that he or she may not hold a *national* mandate (Article I-21 [3]; now Article I-22 [3]). The Commission president will be elected, full-time, for a term of five years, by a two-tier procedure. First, the European Council, taking into account the elections to the European Parliament and after making appropriate consultations, will choose a candidate by qualified majority to propose to the Parliament. Then, the Parliament will either elect the candidate by a majority of its members or, if the candidate does not receive such majority support, ask the European Council to put forward a new candidate (Article I-26 [1]; now Article I-27 [1]). Since the Parliament can also refuse the new candidate, or any candidate subsequently proposed by the European Council, this procedure implies that, in the end, a majority in Parliament could impose its own candidate.

Each of the two presidents has his or her own task. The president of the European Council is to 1) "chair and drive forward" the work of the Council, 2) "ensure its proper preparation and continuity in cooperation with the President of the Commission, and on the basis of the work of the General Affairs Council," 3) "facilitate cohesion and consensus within the European Council," and 4) "present a report to the European Parliament after each of its meetings." Moreover, the European Council president is to "ensure the external representation of the Union on issues concerning its common foreign and security policy, without prejudice to the responsibilities of the Union Minister for Foreign Af-

[116] Ibid., 224–28.

fairs" (Article I-21 [2]; now Article I-22 [2]). It is for the European Council to define the Union's general political directions and priorities, but the Council cannot exercise legislative functions (Article I-20 [1]; now Article I-21 [1]). Given this limitation, it is clear that the European Council's chair is not intended to evolve into a fully fledged presidency of the Union. However, the phrase "drive forward [the European Council's] work" in Article 1–21 (2) [now Article I-22 (2)] indicates that the Council's chair will not be a merely ceremonial or parliamentary president either.[117]

The president of the Commission has a quite different task than that of the president of the European Council. He or she is the president of the main body of the European Union, which has large executive and legislative competences in very diverse areas, including acting as external representation in those areas, either alone or in cooperation with the Member States.[118] As mentioned above, that would not change with the adoption of the draft Constitution. However, with the adoption of the draft Constitution, the Commission president's democratic legitimacy would be upgraded, as he would be selected by the European Council "taking into account the elections to the European Parliament" (Article 26 [1]; now Article 27 [1]). This change would make the Commission president's designation similar to that of a prime minister or chancellor in a parliamentary system, in which the head of state directs the leader of the political party that has won the parliamentary elections to form a government that can obtain a political majority in the newly elected parliament.[119]

The resemblance between the Commission president and the prime minister or chancellor of a parliamentary state is even more conspicuous, since Article I-26 (3) [now Article 27 (3)] of the draft Constitution gives the Commission president the ability to 1) lay down guidelines within which the Commission is to work, 2) decide the Commission's internal organization, including the allocation, and reallocation, of portfolios, and 3) appoint vice presidents from

---

[117] See further chapter 7, pp. 366–68.

[118] Depending on whether the Commission competence is exclusive or shared with the Member States: see chapter 1, pp. 10–11. But see Article I-27 (2) [now Article I-28 (2)] of the draft Constitution, which provides that it is for the minister of foreign affairs, who is also one of the vice presidents of the Commission, to conduct the Commission's external relations in those areas of Commission competence. See below, pp. 299–300.

[119] The European People Party (EPP-ED), which is currently the largest parliamentary party (Epilogue, p. 381), had already insisted to the EP before the June 2004 elections that the next Commission president should come from its ranks—even though the party's position as the largest group was threatened by a possible breakaway of MEPs who expressed discontent with the heterogeneous character of the party. See *European Voice*, February 12–18, 2004, 1.

among the members of the Commission. It also gives the president the right to ask a commissioner to resign. All of these are typical prerogatives that a prime minister or chancellor enjoys in a parliamentary system. Moreover, like the government in a parliamentary system, the Commission president, together with the other members of the Commission, shall be responsible to Parliament (Article I-25 [5]; now Article 26 [8]), of which they need the support to be elected to and to stay in office.[120]

Obviously, much will depend upon the personality of the persons who are elected to be president of the Council and of the Commission, how their relationship develops, and how the president of the European Council will give, and be allowed to give, content to his or her function.

b) The composition of the Council of Ministers

Article I-23 [now Article 24] of the draft Constitution mentions the different formations in which the Council of Ministers can meet, in an attempt to put some order to the undefined manner that currently characterizes the holding of Council meetings. The Article singles out two formations specifically. In the initial text of the draft Constitution, the first of these formations, named the Legislative and General Affairs, fulfilled two functions: when it acts in its general affairs function, it prepares, in liaison with the Commission, the meetings of the European Council and ensures the follow-up; when it acts in its legislative function, it discusses laws and framework laws proposed by the Commission, and enacts them jointly with the European Parliament. The second of the formations mentioned in Article I-23 is the Foreign Affairs Council, which, as formulated in paragraph 2 of the article, "shall, on the basis of strategic guidelines laid down by the European Council, flesh out the Union's external policies, and ensure that its actions are consistent." Paragraph 3 states that the European Council has the ability to establish other Council formations.

Under the draft Constitution, the chair of the Foreign Affairs Council is assigned to a specific person, the Union's foreign minister, who is appointed to that position for the term of his appointment (which is five years, as for the

[120] The European Parliament will not have the last word, however, in appointing the president and members of the Commission. In that regard, it is interesting to note that, under the initial text of the draft Constitution, the names of the commissioners (both voting and non-voting), along with the names of the president and the minister for foreign affairs, had to be submitted collectively to a vote of approval by Parliament, and no longer to a QMV of the Council, as is the case currently: see Article I-26 (2) of the draft Constitution as compared with Article 214 (2) EC. This omission has been corrected, however, in the new text of Article I-26 (2), as amended by the June 2004, IGC, which now provides that it is for the European Council, rather than the Council of Ministers, to appoint the Commission upon the Parliament's vote of approval.

other commissioners). The chairs of the other formations will be held by Member State ministers for periods, in the initial text of the draft Constitution, of at least a year (instead of the current six months), on the basis of equal rotation in accordance with a decision of the European Council (Article I-23 [4]). This arrangement is important for what it does not say: it fails to mention either the president of the European Council or the Commission president as the potential chair of any formation of the Council of Ministers, though the vice president of the Commission (the Union foreign minister) will chair one. Nevertheless, some Convention delegates have expressed concern that the president of the European Council might form, with the presidents of the Council formations, a presidential board team that could act as a countervailing power to the Commission. This would imply, however, that the European Council president could overstep his power, which is strictly limited to the prerogatives of that Council.[121]

The merging of general affairs and legislative affairs into one Council formation, as provided in the initial text of the draft Constitution, was regrettable, as it combined legislative and executive functions, and involved the risk that the Council members, when they met to approve legislative texts, would do so in the margin of their dealings with general affairs. Moreover, it made it difficult for the Council to meet in public when dealing with legislative matters. Fortunately, the arrangement has not survived the discussions of the draft Constitution in the following IGC, and has been amended accordingly.[122]

c) The Union's foreign minister

Currently, two officeholders are responsible for the Union's external affairs: the member of the European Commission responsible for external affairs, and the secretary general of the Council and high representative for foreign and security affairs, a post created in 1999.[123] Since the creation of this post, the two officials, Chris Patten and Javier Solana, although belonging to two different EU institutions, have cooperated well, but the risk of turf wars does of course exist.[124]

---

[121] Lenaerts, Binon, and van Nuffel, n. 13 above, 297, no. 66.

[122] Following the June 2004 IGC meeting, Article I-23 [now Article I-24] has been amended in various respects, notably in transforming the Legislative and General Affairs Council into the General Affairs Council and providing that all Council meetings "shall be divided in two parts, dealing respectively with deliberations on Union legislative acts and non-legislative activities" (new Article I-24). When the Council deliberates and votes on a draft legislative act, it shall meet in public (ibid.).

[123] The task of the secretary general/high representative is described in Article 26 EU.

[124] Norman, n. 1 above, 140, who notes that the representative's post is a low-budget, fast-moving operation, while the commissioner can rely on a well-endowed but lumbering external affairs directorate.

The Laeken Declaration already raised the question of whether the synergy between the two offices could be strengthened, a concern echoed by many members in the Convention who would like the Union to articulate a more effective foreign and defense policy commensurate with its status as an important economic and trading power.

There were, however, conflicting ideas as to where the position of Union foreign minister should be located: the European Commission believed that the high representative should be gradually integrated into the Commission, while others believed that the special relationship between the high representative and the Council should be preserved because not all issues in foreign policy could be attributed to the Commission. This matter was taken up in the Convention by the external action working group. The group outlined four options, favoring the "double-hatted" option finally accepted by the Convention, though recognizing its potential weaknesses. This option provided a "European external representative" who would be a member of the Commission, preferably with the rank of vice president. Despite being a member of the Commission, the external representative would have a separate mandate from, and be accountable to, the Council of Ministers' formation for the common foreign and security policy.[125] Because of its obvious weakness, the compromise solution drew much criticism from various quarters.[126]

Nevertheless, Article I-27 [now Article I-28] of the draft Constitution incorporates the compromise, calling the function "the Union Minister for Foreign Affairs." The European Council will appoint the minister by qualified majority, with the agreement of the president of the Commission.[127] He or she will be both one of the vice presidents of the *Commission* and the chair of the *Council of Ministers* when it sits as the Foreign Affairs Council (Article I-23 [2]; now Article I-28 [3]). As vice president of the Commission, the foreign minister will be responsible for handling "external relations and for coordinating other aspects of the Union's external action." In his or her position with the Commission, the foreign minister "shall be bound by Commission procedures" (Article I-27 [3]; now Article I-28 [4]).[128] In the capacity as foreign minister proper, he or she "shall conduct the Union's common foreign and security policy" and "contribute by his proposals to the development of the common foreign policy which he shall carry out as mandated by the Council [of Ministers]," and the

---

[125] See further Norman, n. 1 above, 141–42.

[126] Ibid., 175–76.

[127] Article I-27 (1), which specifies that the minister's tenure may end in accordance with the same procedure.

[128] In other words, for his activities outside the Commission he or she does not need prior approval from the College of Commissioners.

same "shall apply to the common security and defence policy" (Article I-27 [1] and [2]; now Article I-28 [2]). Moreover, in the capacity as foreign minister, and as chair of the Foreign Affairs Council of Ministers, he or she will play a pivotal role among the Member States foreign affairs ministers who sit on the Foreign Affairs Formation of the Council in fleshing out the Union's external policies and ensuring that its actions are consistent (Article I-23 [2] quoted under b) above; now Article I-24 [3]).

As if that is not enough, the foreign minister will also take part in the work of the European Council, though he or she will not be a member of it. Accordingly, he or she will fulfill a function in three Union institutions: the Commission, the Council of Ministers, and the European Council, thus having in fact a "triple-hatted" function. To fulfill these tasks, the foreign minister will have the Joint European External Action Service at his or her disposal.[129] That service will be composed of officials from the general secretariat of the Council of Ministers and of the Commission and of staff seconded from Member State diplomatic services.[130]

If this arrangement is finally adopted, it will not take effect until November 1, 2009, which leaves time to reflect further on whether the idea of a double- or triple-hatted minister of foreign affairs is workable. Few seem happy with a post that blurs interinstitutional boundaries: intergovernmentalists dislike the involvement of a Commission member in the work of the Council; integrationists see it as a half-hearted compromise. Still others fear that the function concentrates too much power in the hands of a single individual whose position is sufficiently elusive that he or she is not accountable to anyone, and that the position of Commission president will be weakened.[131] Here also, much will depend on the personalities of the foreign minister, the Commission president, and the president of the European Council.

IV. ISSUES STILL IN NEED OF A SATISFACTORY SOLUTION

When asked in an interview[132] how permanent the draft Constitution would be after adoption, Jean-Luc Dehaene, one of the two vice presidents of the Convention, mentioned some issues that might need revision as soon as 2006. Two

---

[129] Article III-197 (3) [now Article III-256 (3)].
[130] Thus the Declaration on the Creation of a European External Action Service attached to the draft Constitution.
[131] Dougan, n. 39 above, 780.
[132] *European Voice*, July 3–9, 2003, 1 and 2.

of the issues were the funding of the Union and the constitutional revision procedure.

The Union's Finances

The funding of the Union is currently achieved through a complex system of revenues ("own resources"), which consists primarily of agricultural levies and duties and common customs tariffs on imports from third countries, a percentage of VAT revenues from Member States, and contributions from national budgets linked to each state's gross domestic product (GDP). In the 1980s, when Margaret Thatcher successfully battled to reduce the U.K.'s net contributions to the Union, the Union's budget was the cause of epic struggles among the Member States. Thanks to agreements between the main institutions on budget discipline and the introduction of a multiyear financial perspective, much of the political heat has been taken out of the annual determination of the Union's revenues and expenditures.[133] Even so, this has not prevented significant disagreements over the years, mainly between the European Commission and the European Court of Auditors over the management of the annual budget.[134]

The issues that drew the attention of the Convention were, however, more prosaic: improving the complex budget approval procedures put in place in the 1970s,[135] and determining the proper role of the European Parliament. To be sure, Parliament currently has significant budgetary powers. Although the Commission draws up the Union's budget and implements it, it is Parliament that adopts the budget for the following year, jointly exercises control with the Council over its implementation, and grants the Commission annual discharge on the use of the budget. However, Parliament has no control over revenues, and it has no control either over the so-called "compulsory" expenditures, including those for the Union's agricultural policy, which amounts to approximately 55 percent of the budget. Thus, it has control over only half the budgeted expenditures, the so-called "non-compulsory" spending items that relate to

[133] See Craig and de Búrca, n. 26 above, 17–19.

[134] See Douglas-Scott, n. 17 above, 98–99. One of those disagreements led, in 1998, to the refusal of the European Parliament to give discharge to the Commission in respect of the implementation of the budget, which finally resulted in the resignation of the Santer Commission: chapter 2, pp. 81ff.

[135] On the budget procedures and the size and allocation of the Union budget, see Carol Harlow, *Accountability in the European Union* (Oxford: Oxford University Press, 2002), 115–30. The author reports that in 1999 the EU's general budget amounted to 86.7 billion euros: 117. This compares to an amount of 100 billion euros currently; see editorial, *European Voice*, February 12–18, 2004, 9.

such items as social and regional policy, research and humanitarian aid, and refugee programs.[136]

The Convention's working group on simplification, chaired by Giuliano Amato, proposed a procedure for setting expenditures similar to the ordinary co-decision legislative procedure. Under this procedure, the Commission would submit a preliminary draft budget for approval by the Parliament and the Council, with the Council approving the draft by qualified majority, and with special provisions to prevent a stalemate. In order to further increase Parliament's influence, the group also proposed to abolish the distinction between compulsory and non-compulsory spending and to include the multiyear budgetary perspective in the Constitution, so as to give it constitutional status. The revenue side of the budget was an even more controversial matter. Some Convention members tabled proposals that would have enabled the Union to raise its own taxes and to abolish the current "own resources" system. The idea was not to grant the Union a source of greater income, but instead to ensure the Union a more transparent revenue stream, so that Europe's citizens would know how much they were contributing to the Union. Obviously, the proposals went much too far: the Convention could only agree with the working group's proposal to list the main budgetary principles in the Constitution, but could not agree with the other proposals.[137]

The issue was finally resolved in Articles I-52 to 55 [now Articles I-53 to 56] of the draft Constitution, which relate to the Union's finances.[138] Article I-53 [now Article I-54] concerns the Union's *resources*. Its first two cryptic paragraphs state that "the Union shall provide itself with the means necessary to attain its objectives and carry out its policies," and that "without prejudice to other revenue, the Union's budget shall be financed wholly from its own resources." The third paragraph adds, however, that "a Union law of the Council of Ministers shall lay down the limit of the Union's resources and may establish

---

[136] Douglas-Scott, n. 17 above, 91.

[137] On all this, see Norman, n. 1 above, 106–7. See also *European Voice*, March 20–26, 2003, 6.

[138] Article I-52 [now Article I-53] sets out the budgetary and financial principles of the Union, providing in (3) that the expenditure shown in the budget shall be authorized in accordance with the European law referred to in Article III-318 [now Article I-412]. Article I-53 [now Article I-54] concerns the Union's resources (quoted in text above), Article I-54 [now Article I-55] provides for a multiannual financial framework (also quoted), and Article I-55 [now Article I-56] states that the adoption of the Union's budget by the European Parliament and the Council of Ministers must be preceded by a proposal from the Commission, in accordance with the arrangements laid down in Article III-310 [now Article III-404].

new categories of resources or abolish an existing category." To enact that law the Council of Ministers "shall act unanimously after consulting the European Parliament" (which therefore has no co-decisional legislative power). Moreover, "that law shall not enter into force until it is approved by the Member States in accordance with their respective constitutional requirements." Furthermore, according to the fourth paragraph, the modalities relating to the Union's resources shall be laid down in a law of the Council of Ministers after obtaining the consent of the European Parliament. In simple terms, the "own resources" system continues to exist, and can only be changed by unanimous decision of the Member States' representatives in the Council. Moreover, to enter into effect, a new system would require the approval of all Member States in accordance with the most cumbersome of procedures, that is, in accordance with Member States' constitutional requirements.

For its part, Article I-54 [now Article I-55] provides a multiannual financial framework that is intended to "ensure that Union *expenditure* develops in an orderly manner and within the own resources limits."[139] That framework shall be established by a European law of the Council of Ministers, which shall act after obtaining the consent of a majority of members of the European Parliament (Article I-54 [2]; now Article I-55 [2]).[140] The Council must act unanimously in adopting the first multiannual framework after the Constitution enters into force (Article I-54 [4] but see now Article I-55 [4], as amended).[141] In other words the Member States have the final say on this topic as well, with each having a veto right during the negotiations for the first multiannual financial framework. These negotiations are due to take place in 2006 between the twenty-five Member States, so long as the Constitution has been adopted by then. If these negotiations become deadlocked, the question of changing the constitutional budgetary provisions will be raised again. As mentioned previously, the chief net contributors to the Union budget have already given an

---

[139] The provision goes on to say that the framework "shall determine the amounts of the annual ceilings for commitment appropriations by category of expenditure in accordance with the provisions of Article III-308 [now Article I-402]." See following footnote.

[140] For details, see Article III-308 [now Article I-402] of the draft Constitution, which states, for example, in paragraph 1, that the framework must be for at least five years and, in paragraph 4, that "where no European law establishing a new financial framework has been adopted by the end of the previous financial framework, the ceilings and other provisions corresponding to the last year of that framework shall be extended until such time as that law is adopted."

[141] The unanimity requirement was added during the last weeks of the Convention, and was "construed by some as giving Spain an arm-lock over regional fund negotiations well into the future": Norman, n. 1 above, 288.

early warning by asking the Commission to cap the budget at 1 percent of the EU's gross national income. In the meantime, the Commission has announced its budget proposals for the period 2007–13, envisaging total expenditure during that seven-year period corresponding to 1.14 percent of the EU's gross national income.[142]

The Procedure for Amending the Constitutional Treaty

A related question concerns the revision of the Constitution, a matter regulated in the fourth and final part of the draft Constitution. According to Article IV-7 [now Article IV-443], all amendments to provisions in the preceding parts, and in Part IV itself, are subjected to the same revision procedure. Under that procedure, any Member State, the European Parliament, or the Commission may submit proposals for amendment to the Council. The national parliaments of the Member States shall be notified of these proposals. After consultation with the European Parliament and the Commission, the European Council will decide, by a simple majority, whether the proposal will be examined and whether a convention will be convened. Such a convention would consist of representatives of the national parliaments, the Member State governments, the European Parliament, and the Commission. If that convention, after examination, adopts a recommendation to the Conference of Member State Governments by consensus, that IGC will determine the amendments to be made by common accord. Those amendments shall enter into force after ratification by all Member States in accordance with their respective constitutional requirements.

Obviously, this is a very cumbersome procedure. Indeed, in the Convention preparing the draft Constitution, proposals have been made that would not only obviate the consensus required in the Convention to make a recommendation to the IGC, but that would also, more importantly, differentiate between revision procedures. One differentiation could be to provide a more cumbersome procedure for amendments to Part I, which contains the constitutional structure of the Union, and to Part II, which sets forth the Charter of Fundamental Rights, and a lighter procedure for amendments to (the much longer) Part III, which relates to the policies and functioning of the Union.[143] The lighter

---

[142] See editorial, "Member States Must 'Get Real' about EU Budget Needs," *European Voice*, February 12–18, 2004, 9. The Commission proposals envisage over the seven-year period a rise from 124.6 billion to 143.1 billion euros per year. These figures compare to the current annual budget of around 100 billion euros. Of the total amount of 928.7 billion euros proposed by the Commission for the period 2007–13, spending on agricultural aid would still amount to 301 billion in total, or 43 billion each year.

[143] See further de Witte, n. 13 above, 220–23.

revision procedure could, for example, provide that 1) the Convention, when convened by the European Council, could make its recommendation to the IGC by a majority of two-thirds of its members, and that 2) the recommended amendment could be adopted by means of a decision made by the representatives of the Member State governments at the IGC acting by a majority of three-fourths of the Member State governments, so long as those states represent at least three-fourths of the total population of the Union. Such a requirement would alleviate the need for any further ratification by the Member States.[144]

Unfortunately, none of the proposals has carried the day—although they may have prepared the ground for later concessions[145]—not even one that the three largest political parties in the European Parliament submitted to the Convention. That proposal related to amendments of Part III and tended to introduce a five-sixths majority of Member States where an amendment would not result in a shift of competences.[146] The only concession that was finally agreed on in the draft is the statement in Article IV-7 (2) [now Article IV-443 (2)] that the European Council, acting by a simple majority, may decide in favor of examining the proposed amendments without convening a Convention when the extent of the proposed amendments does not justify such a cumbersome procedure. In that case, the European Council would itself define the terms of reference for the IGC.

V. CONCLUSIONS

Whatever the outcome of the constitutional process will be, the fact that men and women from twenty-eight European States were able to draft a coherent constitutional text and approve it by an overwhelming majority is in itself an unexpected achievement. In the words of a privileged observer, "Never before had the European Union been subject to such intense scrutiny from such a diverse group of people . . . representatives of an area stretching from Finnish Lapland, north of the Arctic Circle, to the toe of Italy in the south, and from the Portuguese Azores islands far to the west of the European mainland to Turkey's

[144] Ibid., 222.

[145] At the June 2004 IGC, a new article IV-7b [now Article IV-445] was agreed to, providing a simplified procedure concerning internal Union policies dealt with in Title III of Part III of the draft Constitution. The article authorizes the European Council, acting by unanimity after consulting Parliament and the Commission, to approve amendments concerning internal policies. However, to come into force, the European Council decision must still be approved by the Member States in accordance with their constitutional requirements.

[146] Norman, n. 1 above, 81 and 332.

eastern frontier with Iraq, close to the cradle of civilisation."[147] Until the very end, the Convention was a tale of the unexpected, which was made possible by a variety of factors, not the least of which were pressure from the triumvirate at the top (Convention president Valéry Giscard d'Estaing and his two vice presidents, Jean-Luc Dehaene and Giuliano Amato, assisted by the Convention's secretary general, John Kerr) and the unrelenting pressure from impatient rank-and-file members of the Convention who wanted to get the job done properly.[148] The stepping stones to the unexpected were numerous: the "invasion of foreign ministers" who wanted to be part of the Convention,[149] the revival of the Franco-German partnership inside and outside the Convention room,[150] the U.K.-Spanish entente and the U.K.'s struggle to keep within the mainstream,[151] the determination of the Benelux countries to preserve the Community method,[152] the alliance of the smaller countries at decisive moments,[153] the role played by groups of like-minded European parliamentarians, national parliamentarians, and transnational political parties, and, finally, the idealism of a large number of individual members of the Convention.[154] One player that was regrettably absent in the negotiations was the European Commission, which managed to marginalize itself after the December 2002 publication of a working document, code-named "Penelope."[155]

Although the crisis in Iraq overshadowed the Convention, it came nowhere near destroying it. To some extent the war over Iraq offered the opportunity to government-appointed representatives from Member States on both sides of the fence to go out of their way to chat civilly with each other. Naturally, the Iraq crisis did have an impact on the Convention, as it exposed the weakness of the Union's common foreign and security policy and the lack of solidarity between the Member States on the international scene. It gave new impetus to an

[147] Ibid., 3.

[148] Ibid., 319.

[149] Ibid., 155–60.

[150] Ibid., 160–61.

[151] Ibid., 198. Tony Blair is reported to have said to Peter Hain, upon his appointment as British representative, that this "was more important than Iraq": ibid.

[152] Ibid., 170.

[153] Ibid., 183–85.

[154] Ibid., 321–26.

[155] Ibid., 322 and 165–71. After the Commission had published its official position, which hid its radical proposals in circumlocution, a more radical paper, the "Penelope" paper (which, in the words of Peter Norman, was "blunt to the point of brutality"), was revealed at the initiative of Commission president Romano Prodi. This second paper came as a shock to most of the other commissioners, who had not been involved in the drafting.

idea that had barely surfaced in the Convention's previous discussions, that of "enhanced cooperation" between members who were ready to push ahead of others with policies of greater cooperation. The idea led to some tension with the United States, as well as between Member States, when it was taken up at a "defense mini summit" of Belgium, France, Germany, and Luxembourg in Brussels on April 29, 2003. The summit announced plans for a military planning center in Tervuren, a suburb of Brussels, that would be independent of NATO. But those tensions proved not to be lasting: by September the U.K. was in discussions with Germany and France to find common ground.[156] The discussions led to an agreement negotiated during the IGC meeting in Naples in November 2003.[157]

Seen from a viewpoint of the continuum between intergovernmentalism and supranationalism, the constitution making at the Convention, with respect to both the process and the results achieved, is an illustration of how Member State governments and parliaments, Community institutions and individual members (mainly from the European parliament), and civil society (which exerted its influence through political parties, NGOs and other organizations, and academics) interacted over a period of almost one-and-a-half years, striking bargains that resulted in concrete texts. As seen by an unbiased observer, journalist Peter Norman, the Convention has been an unmitigated success as a process of interaction, and it has shown that the will is present, even among the post–World War II generations, to carry the integration project further. It may well be that the text of the draft Constitution will not be approved in its present form, but it will not be for lack of interest, but instead because of the uninspiring machinations of states engaged in power politics of the past. Even in that respect, the Member State governments "cannot neglect their own past conduct,"[158] nor can they ignore the active involvement of their national parliaments representing their peoples. To be sure, the draft Constitution remains a product of the elite,[159] and it is not the kind of document that will excite the people and inspire them to rally around the concept of a united Europe, but neither can it be ignored. For the less willing among the Member States, the fi-

---

[156] On all of this and more, see ibid., 185–88.

[157] Above, at n. 21.

[158] Norman, n. 1 above, 328.

[159] Ibid., 327. The author notes, "Although it operated more transparently than any IGC, the Convention failed to generate the public interest that its organisers hoped. True, its website had an average of 47,000 visits a month, rising to 100,000 in June 2003. But a Eurobarometer poll of 25,000 citizens in the 25 member and accession countries just after the June Thessaloniki summit found that only 45 per cent had heard of the Convention."

nal question is: which of them will finally take the responsibility of turning the constitution-making endeavor into a failure, and risk that other Member States will leave them behind?

That said, the merits of the draft Constitution are far from negligible: if adopted, the draft would mark the end of the three pillars, would clarify Union and state competences, would put order into the Union's legal instruments and legislative procedures, and would reform the qualified majority voting formula. All of these reforms would once more move the Union, in a significant manner, in the direction of a supranational political entity. The draft also strengthens the Union's constitutional framework by institutionalizing and fleshing out the function and role of the European Council, and enhances the democratic legitimacy of both the European Commission and the Commission president by emphasizing their political responsibility to the European Parliament. It seeks to flesh out the principles of representative and participatory democracy, and to promote dialogue with the citizens and the social partners. The draft also makes some progress in reinforcing the rule of law in matters of asylum and police cooperation.

The failure of the Heads of State or Government to reach agreement on the draft Constitution at their meeting in Rome in December 2003 was a serious setback, but that failure was rapidly erased in the first half of 2004 under the Irish presidency. Already before the meeting of the Heads of State or Government on 17–18 June 2004 in Brussels, the foreign ministers of the Member States had succeeded in finding acceptable compromises for most of the controversial issues, thus leaving only a small number of questions open for the Heads of State or Government. For all these questions the June 2004 IGC has been able to find solutions, including issues as delicate as the discussion whether the Christian origin of Europe was to be mentioned in the preamble to the Constitution, or issues as controversial as the composition of the Commission and qualified majority voting.[160] To be sure, some issues have perhaps not been resolved in a satisfactory way, such as, for example, the triple allegiance of the European foreign minister, and some have not been resolved at all, such as the funding of the Union and the revision procedure of the Constitution—issues that, if the draft Constitution is adopted, may soon enough prove to be problematic. That, however, should not be a reason for rejecting what has been agreed on, but rather a challenge for going ahead.

[160] For an overview of the main outstanding issues on which agreement was reached after the Convention, see editorial comments, 41 *CMLRev.*, 2004, n. 1 above, 899–907. See also the Epilogue, pp. 376–81.

CHAPTER SEVEN

Which Form of Government for Europe?

In this chapter, I will first, in Section I, describe the two traditional forms of democratic government, the parliamentary and presidential forms. I will use the United Kingdom and Germany as examples of parliamentary government, and the United States and France as examples of presidential government. Then, in Section II, I will examine the merits and disadvantages of both forms of government, and their variants. In Section III, I will discuss bicameralism and the role of political parties in a parliamentary system. Lastly, in Section IV, I use the findings of the previous sections to discuss which form of government is most appropriate for the European Union.

I. FORMS OF GOVERNMENT: A COMPARATIVE OVERVIEW

The American constitutional system shares common threads with the French and the German constitutional systems, though in different ways. Both the American and the French systems have a president elected by universal suffrage, which bestows legitimacy on the elected leader and prevents Congress or Parliament from forcing him or her to resign. Both the American and the German constitutions establish a federal state, thus dividing powers between the federal government and the states. And both systems have a constitutional court that is charged with deciding cases in which conflicts of power arise between the federal and the state levels.

At first glance, the American system has little in common with the British system. This is not surprising given that the American Constitution was ordained in reaction to the British Parliament and monarchy. The British system is a parliamentary regime; it is a unitary (rather than federal) state with a monarch at the top. It has no written constitution, nor a constitutional court. As we will see, the British system differs from both the French and German systems as well on most of these points.

If one looks at political realities, though, the American and the British systems share one characteristic that the American, French, and German systems do not have: they are (basically) two-party political systems.[1] The two-party system provides the prime minister of the United Kingdom, as the effective leader of the winning political party in the most recent election, with essentially the same lasting political support enjoyed by the American president.[2] By contrast, in countries with a multiparty system, like Germany or Italy, even the largest party will normally need the support of at least one other party to form a coalition government, which will be less stable than a one-party government.

Hereinafter, I will compare the British parliamentary system with the American presidential system, and then compare the French semi-presidential system with the German (and British) parliamentary system(s).

The British Parliamentary and American Presidential Systems

In the words of the British author Ian McLeod, "the details and the origins of [the English] parliament are shrouded in a good deal of historical uncertainty."[3] "What is clear," he writes,

> is that the departure of King James II in 1688 caused a fundamental break in the legitimacy of constitutional power. In that year an informal group of peers, former members of the House of Commons (which had not met since 1685) and leading citizens of the City of London, invited William of Orange to summon a

---

[1] To call the British system (or the American system, for that matter) a two-party system is somewhat deceptive since, in the postwar period, a variety of parties other than the two predominant parties have participated in elections and won approximately (in the U.K.) one-fifth of electoral support: Joel Krieger, in Mark Kesselman and Joel Krieger, *European Politics in Transition*, 3d ed. (Boston: Houghton Mifflin, 1997), 107–8. On the origin of the two-party system, which developed in England during the second half of the seventeenth century along with the lower house of Parliament around the issue of royal prerogatives, and developed in the United States around the issue of federal versus state power, see Hartmut Maurer, *Staatsrecht I*, 3d ed. (Munich: Verlag C. H. Beck, 2003), 336. The author observes that a two-party system failed to take root on the European continent because of the existence there of many societal differences and the resulting lack of a polarizing and simplifying issue.

[2] As pointed out in chapter 2, p. 67, however, the job security of the British prime minister during his or her tenure in office may be weaker than that of the American president, particularly in times of war.

[3] Ian McLeod, *Legal Method*, 3d ed. (Basingstoke: MacMillan, 1999), 58.

Convention . . . the Convention passed the Crown and Parliament Act 1689, declaring itself to be a properly constituted Parliament, and it then enacted the Bill of Rights 1689."[4]

Nevertheless, "it was not until the passing of the Great Reform Act in 1832 that the House of Commons started to become genuinely representative."[5]

As a result of a long evolution, sovereign powers were finally transferred to a parliament elected by the people. After this transfer, the monarchs kept only limited powers, and executive powers were attributed to ministers who were made accountable to Parliament. Two important elements characterize sovereign powers Parliament currently enjoys. First, despite the transfer of power to Parliament, power remained concentrated in the hands of one entity, that is, "by slowly transforming the King-as-ruler into the King-in-Parliament . . . the absolute and central powers of the King [passed] into the hands of Parliament—first of the English, later of the British Parliament. Parliament inherited the King's position."[6] The essence of the doctrine of the sovereignty of Parliament, therefore, is that Parliament can, as a legislative body, do exactly what the King could have done in the sixteenth and early seventeenth centuries, that is, act as he pleased. In Dicey's words, the doctrine means that Parliament "has the right to make and unmake any law whatever; . . . no person or body is recognized by the law of England as having the rights to override or set aside the legislation of Parliament."[7]

Second, and just as importantly, the doctrine of the sovereignty of Parliament has only survived because it has been given democratic credentials as a part of the gradual democratization of Parliament. This democratization took place over time as voting rights were extended to new groups of voters in the early nineteenth century, and the granting of universal suffrage and the establishment of cabinet government took place in the twentieth century. This series of events has given the relationship between the electorate, the House of Commons, and the government its present form.[8]

---

[4] Ibid., 60–61.

[5] Ibid., 62. For a fuller account of the formation of the United Kingdom, see Krieger, n. 1 above, 50–52.

[6] Tim Koopmans, *Courts and Political Institutions: A Comparative View* (Cambridge: Cambridge University Press, 2003), 19.

[7] Ibid., 19 and 16. In the following pages, Koopmans describes how that position is singularly inapt to define Britain's relationship with the European integration process, with the recurrent use of referenda in recent times, and with the phenomenon of devolution granting elected assemblies in Scotland and Wales the power to pass regional legislation (30–34).

[8] Ibid., 18, with reference to A. W. Bradley, "The Sovereignty of Parliament," in

In 1776, thirteen English colonies signed the American Declaration of Independence. By 1781, hostilities with England had substantially ceased after the Yorktown campaign, and the American Revolution was formally completed with the signing of a final peace treaty with England. In February of 1781, the thirteen colonies ratified the Articles of Confederation, under which they lived for seven years. The American Constitution was written in 1787 "to form a more perfect Union," and was ratified in 1788. Two years later the Bill of Rights was added.[9] More than any other constitution, the American Constitution is characterized by the principle of separation of powers. Not unlike Montesquieu, Madison thought that

> in framing a government which is to be administered by men over men, the great difficulty lies in this: you must first enable the government to control the governed; and in the next place oblige it to control itself. A dependence on the people is, no doubt, the primary control on the government; but experience has taught mankind the necessity of auxiliary precautions.

According to Madison, those precautions can only be taken "by so contriving the interior structure of the government as that its several constituent parts may, by their mutual relations, be the means of keeping each other in their proper places."[10]

In the American Constitution those grand ideas about separation of powers were given a much more concrete form than Montesquieu could have dreamed.[11] Article I, Section 1 provides that all *legislative* powers "shall be vested in a Congress which shall consist of a Senate and House of Representatives."[12] Article II, Section 1 (1) provides that the *executive* power "shall be vested in a President of the United States of America" elected (together with

---

The Changing Constitution, 4th ed., ed. Jeffrey Jowell and Dawn Oliver (Oxford: Oxford University Press, 2000), chapter 2. See also Krieger, n. 1 above, 55–56.

[9] See further Geoffrey R. Stone et al., *Constitutional Law*, 3d ed. (Aspen Law and Business, 1996), 1–2.

[10] The Federalist no. 51, reproduced in Stone, et al., n. 9 above, 15–17.

[11] The constitutional text itself, though implying the notion of distinct branches, did not invoke the separation of power as a principle: see Gerhard Casper, *Separating Power: Essays on the Founding Period* (Cambridge, Mass.: Harvard University Press, 1997), 12–22, at 18. The Constitution has only seven articles. Besides those mentioned in the text, Article IV contains the "full faith and credit" clause that requires states to enforce judgments and laws of the other states. Article V concerns the power of Congress to propose amendments to the Constitution, and Articles VI and VII concern the implementation and ratification of the Constitution.

[12] But see Section 7 (2) with regard to the veto power of the president, which authorizes him to ask Congress to reconsider a law presented for his signature.

the vice president) for a term of four years.[13] Article III, Section 1 provides that the *judicial* power "shall be vested in one supreme Court, and in such inferior Courts as Congress may from time to time establish." The Constitution further lays out a federal structure that divides powers between the union and the states. The framers regarded this federal structure, together with the separation of powers within the federal government, as an essential component of a system of checks and balances, which was and is necessary to protect the liberty of citizens against abuse of power.[14] As already mentioned in chapter 3, the Supreme Court, in its 1803 judgment *Marbury v. Madison*, gave full content to this constitutional theory by providing that acts of Congress that violate the Constitution are subject to judicial review.[15]

The constitutional situation in the United Kingdom is entirely different. As mentioned earlier, the U.K. has no written constitution, no (official) federal structure,[16] no elected president, and no judiciary with the power to judge the constitutionality of acts of Parliament. Moreover, as McLeod points out, contrary to Montesquieu's ideas, "the strict doctrine of the separation of powers does not characterize the British Constitution, nor has it ever done so. For instance, the members of the executive form part of the legislature. Further-

---

[13] The president and vice president, after being nominated as candidates by their party's convention, are elected on a ticket by electors designated in accordance with Article II, section 1 (2) through (4) of the Constitution and Amendment XII (1804). Each state appoints electors, who then vote for the candidate who obtains the most votes in their state ("winner takes all"). The election of the president therefore comes very close to a direct election by universal suffrage.

[14] Article I, Section 8 (1) through (17) enumerates the powers attributed to Congress, which includes the implied powers to take action that is necessary and proper for the execution of its enumerated powers; see also in Section 10 a list of powers prohibited to the states. According to the Tenth Amendment [1791], "the powers not delegated to the United States by the Constitution, nor prohibited by it to the States, are reserved to the States respectively, or to the people." This compromise between the Federalists (led by Alexander Hamilton) and the Anti-Federalists (led by Thomas Jefferson) has been the source of tension since the ratification of the Constitution: see further K. Lenaerts, *Le Juge et la Constitution aux États Unis d'Amérique et dans l'ordre juridique Européen* (Brussels: Bruylant, 1988), 118ff.

[15] See chapter 3, pp. 105–6. The judgment was given in a very controversial case of litigation, as described and discussed in Stone et al., n. 9 above, 31–37; also Lenaerts, n. 14 above, 10–26.

[16] But see, on the regionalization of the U.K. ("devolution"), N. MacCormick, *Questioning Sovereignty: Law, State and Nation in the European Commonwealth* (Oxford: Oxford University Press, 1999), 193ff. In spite of the officially unitary structure of the U.K., law, courts, and institutions differ greatly in Scotland and Wales.

more . . . the courts have substantial practical power to develop the law through the doctrine of precedent."[17]

As regards the executive power, some important differences between the British and American systems must be highlighted.

First, in the U.K. the Queen appoints the leader of the political party that won a majority in the House of Commons in the most recent elections as prime minister. The new prime minister, in turn, chooses his or her cabinet and the other (junior) ministers from the members of the parliamentary majority. The prime minister also has the power to dismiss the members of his or her cabinet. The cabinet is collectively accountable to Parliament, as are its individual ministers, whose confidence they need in order to remain in office. In the United States, the president (and the vice president) are chosen by the people for a fixed term in office and so, except for the penal procedure of impeachment, cannot be sent home by Congress. The president appoints and dismisses the cabinet members who are not part of Congress and not accountable to it.

A second and even more important difference is the guidance the cabinet of ministers gives to Parliament in the U.K., through the cabinet minister who is the leader of the House of Commons, as to how Parliament should organize its activities. Similarly, in the U.K., the chief whip is charged with maintaining party discipline within the majority of the House. As a result, the executive and legislative functions of government are merged within the parliamentary majority, which, in the House of Commons, faces, literally and figuratively, the members of the parliamentary opposition. The opposition is organized along the same lines as the majority, with "shadow ministers" who sit on the "opposition front bench" and a leader, a potential successor to the incumbent prime minister, who is involved in or at least informed about the state of public affairs.[18] Clearly, these arrangements fly directly in the face of the principle of separation of powers, as applied in the United States. In the words of Tim Koopmans: "Members of the American Congress, particularly senators, are very independent personalities, who would not submit to being directed or admonished by a cabinet minister or a party whip. If a new President has a legislative program of his own, he will have to cajole Congressmen or senators into proposing the necessary bills."[19]

[17] McLeod, n. 3 above, 64.

[18] For a lively description of the British cabinet government, see Krieger, n. 1 above, 85–88. See also T. Koopmans, n. 6 above, 162–63; L. Favoreu et al., *Droit constitutionnel,* 4th ed. (Paris: Dalloz, 2001), 348–50.

[19] T. Koopmans, n. 6 above, 168.

The French and German Variants of Presidential and Parliamentary Systems

Although Montesquieu's theory of separation of power is neatly reflected in the American Constitution of 1787, it was not as well received in France. At least, it is not as well reflected in the present constitution of the Fifth Republic, which dates from October 4, 1958. That constitution was written after the Algerian drama and the May 1958 coup against the Republic by senior French officers.[20] This series of events prompted General Charles de Gaulle's return to power, and caused the new constitution to be written in accordance with de Gaulle's role as the first president of the Fifth Republic.[21] The constitution that emerged transformed the weak parliamentary system—during the twelve years of the Fourth Republic twenty-four successive governments had been in power for an average of six months each—into a strong presidential system, but also a hybrid presidential system that has little resemblance to that of the United States.

Initially, the French president was elected by a limited number of "electors." This changed in 1962, when General de Gaulle called for a constitutional referendum. As a result, the 1958 Constitution was subsequently amended to require that the president be elected by popular vote.[22] Obviously, this gave even greater authority to a president who already enjoyed important autonomous powers. Most important among these powers are the abilities to appoint

[20] The coup took place on May 13, 1958, and resulted in the institution of the Comite de salut public, which was largely dominated by the military and which asked General de Gaulle to take power. In the following days, a large political majority called for his return to power, which was confirmed by President René Coty, who nominated de Gaulle for president on May 30, 1958. A large majority (329 of the 553 votes) in the Assemblée nationale approved de Gaulle's nomination. See Favoreu et al., n. 18 above, 477.

[21] The first task of the new government headed by de Gaulle was to prepare a new constitution. To enable the incoming government to do that, the change of regime—from a straightforward parliamentary regime into one fitting the new presidential situation—first had to be made legal, which happened by Constitutional Law of June 3, 1958: ibid.

[22] The amendment, approved by a referendum in accordance with Article 11 of the Constitution, was promulgated by constitutional law of November 6, 1962, amending Article 7 of the Constitution: see Favoreu et al., n. 18 above, 558. By granting popular legitimacy to the presidency, the amendment changed the physiognomy of the Constitution significantly. Many other revisions of the Constitution have been effected since, though in accordance with the regular procedure of Article 89 of the Constitution: ibid., 655–57. As a result of the 1962 amendment, the president is now directly elected by the people, in two rounds, for renewable periods of five years.

the prime minister and his or her cabinet ministers, to preside over the cabinet, to act as chief of the Army, and to call a referendum. The power to preside over the cabinet, far from being merely ceremonial, is of crucial significance, particularly in periods of so-called "non-cohabitation," when the president and the dominant fraction in Parliament were elected by the same or affiliated political parties.[23] In such a situation, the president can designate a prime minister who belongs to the same political majority as him- or herself, which allows the president to weigh heavily on governmental policy. By contrast, in periods of "cohabitation," when the president and the parliamentary majority have been elected by disparate political majorities, the president will be obliged to designate a prime minister from a different political majority in order to obtain Parliament's approval of his candidate.[24] Even then, though, the president still has a great deal of influence, particularly over matters of national defense and foreign affairs, which are the so-called "privileged" powers of the president.

In addition to strengthening the president's position, the 1958/1962 Constitution weakened the position of Parliament, to the benefit of the cabinet of ministers (and thus often to the benefit of the president as well). The Constitution accomplished this in two ways. First, it reduces Parliament's legislative powers to a limited list of matters that must yet be decided by law, leaving powers that are not delegated to the Parliament within the remit of the executive. Secondly, it places significant restrictions on Parliament's political power to dismiss the government. Parliament's powers are further restricted by the president's power to dismiss the National Assembly, the more powerful of the two parliamentary houses; such a dismissal requires that new parliamentary elections be held. Though the president can only use that power once a year, it allows him or her to impose his or her choice of a prime minister on Parliament and thus avoid a situation of "cohabitation," provided that the new elec-

---

[23] For a description of how the French system came into existence and how it evolved in the years thereafter, see Ezra N. Suleiman, "Presidentialism and Political Stability in France," in *The Failure of Presidential Democracy*, ed. Juan J. Linz and Arturo Venezuela (Baltimore, Md.: Johns Hopkins University Press, 1994), 136–63. See also Alfred Stepan and Cindy Skach, "Constitutional Frameworks and Democratic Consolidation: Parliamentarism versus Presidentialism," 46 *World Politics*, 1993, 2.

[24] Although Article 8 (1) of the 1958 Constitution provides that the president has the (sole) right to appoint (and dismiss) the prime minister, he will need the de facto approval of the National Assembly, to which the prime minister is politically accountable: see Article 20 (3). See also Favoreu et al., n. 18 above, 564–65. On the presidential powers and the relationship between the president and the prime minister in times of cohabitation and of non-cohabitation, see ibid., 580–84.

tions result in a Parliament with a political majority from the same political parties that elected the president.[25]

The German political system is a variant of the Westminster parliamentary model and has little in common with the French system. Moreover, in contrast to both the British and the French systems, Germany is a federal state. The constitution of the Federal Republic of Germany is laid down in the Basic Law (Grundgesetz) of May 23, 1949. Established in the immediate aftermath of World War II, it emphasizes the overarching importance of human dignity as well as the democratic and social nature of the state and its federal structure, none of which can be changed by constitutional amendment.[26] In addition, the Basic Law contains a full list of basic rights that are binding upon the legislature, the executive, and the judiciary as directly enforceable law. Finally, and most important in the context of European constitution making, the Basic Law deals with the difficult problem of delineating federal and national legislative and executive powers, and installs a constitutional court empowered both to adjudicate disputes concerning the interpretation or application of constitutional provisions and to protect the basic rights of individuals.[27]

Although the Federal Republic of Germany has a federal chancellor (Bundeskanzler) rather than a prime minister, the German constitutional structure strongly resembles the British parliamentary system. Both the British prime minister and the German chancellor are the leader, in name or in fact, of the political party that won the elections, and so have the ability to choose their cabinet, mainly from fellow members of Parliament. They also set general policy with the help of their cabinet and are, with their cabinet, accountable and politically responsible for governmental conduct toward Parliament. Both need the support of a majority in Parliament. In the United Kingdom,

[25] See Suleiman, n. 23 above, 149. President François Mitterrand dissolved the National Assembly twice, first in 1981 and then in 1988, which enabled him each time to avoid "cohabitation." Ibid.

[26] On the German Constitution, see chapter 3, p. 108. The Constitution is called the "Basic Law" (Grundgesetz), allegedly because the drafters did not wish to use the term "constitution" as long as East and West Germany were not united. See Christopher S. Allen in Kesselman and Krieger, n. 1 above, 287. Yet after unification in 1990, the term "Basic Law" has been retained because it associates the country with its longest and most successful experience of democracy: ibid., 303, n. 3.

[27] The German Basic law has been amended frequently. For an (unofficial) English translation of the consolidated text, up to and including the 50th Amendment of 2002, see Axel Tschentscher, *The Basic Law (Grundgesetz)*, Studien zu Jurisprudenz und Philosophie 3.1 (Würzburg: Jurisprudentia Verlag, 2002). It can be found on the Web at www.jurisprudentia.de.

this majority is made up of members who belong to the prime minister's own political party; in Germany, the majority is made up of members of Parliament who belong to political parties with which the chancellor's party has formed a coalition. If their government were, notwithstanding this party affiliation, to lose the confidence of Parliament, either of these heads of government and their cabinets would have to step down. More frequently, they would step down voluntarily in anticipation of a censure by Parliament.

An important difference between the British and the German parliamentary regimes—apart from the former having a one-party government, the latter a multiparty government—is the existence in the German regime of a so-called "constructive vote of no confidence." According to that system, as described in Article 67 of the German Basic Law, the Bundestag, the more powerful of the two houses of Parliament, may express its lack of confidence in the chancellor only by electing a successor with the majority of its members and requesting the president to dismiss the incumbent. The president must comply with the request and appoint the person elected by Parliament. If no majority for such a constructive vote of no confidence can be found, the president may, upon the proposal of the incumbent chancellor, dissolve the Bundestag within twenty-one days. However, as soon as the Bundestag elects another chancellor, it can no longer be dissolved.[28] Obviously, the system reinforces the chancellor's position considerably—thus reducing the weakness characteristic of a chief executive in a multiparty system—as it is more difficult, particularly in such a system, to bring together a positive majority to agree on the new chancellor than to assemble a negative majority to oust the government.[29]

II. PURE AND MIXED FORMS OF PRESIDENTIAL AND PARLIAMENTARY GOVERNMENT: AN ASSESSMENT

The foregoing section described the distinctive features of four constitutional regimes as they operate in practice. In this section, I will examine which variant of a presidential or a parliamentary system is generally most appropriate.

---

[28] Article 68 (1) of the Basic Law.

[29] See further Giovanni Sartori, *Comparative Constitutional Engineering: An Inquiry into Structures, Incentives and Outcomes*, 2d ed. (London: MacMillan, 1997), 106–7, where the British premiership system and the German *Kanzlerdemokratie* are further compared, at 104–8. The Federal Republic of Germany has had a history of generally strong chancellors: Konrad Adenauer, Willy Brandt, Helmut Schmidt, and Helmut Kohl, to name the most prominent ones. See further Allen in Kesselman and Krieger, n. 1 above, 290–93.

The issue is part of a larger debate concerning majoritarian versus consensus democracies.

Presidentialism versus Parliamentarism

The American presidential system has been widely recognized as a successful form of government for the United States, and indeed it cannot be denied that it has served the nation well. As noted by political scientists Alfred Stepan and Cindy Skach, the system has been emulated by many countries: "In the 1980s and 1990s, all the new aspirant democracies in Latin America and Asia (Korea and the Philippines) have chosen pure presidentialism. And to date, of the approximately twenty-five countries that now constitute Eastern Europe and the former Soviet Union, only three . . . have chosen pure parliamentarism."[30] Nevertheless, as another political scientist, Juan L. Linz has pointed out, "with the outstanding exception of the United States, most of the stable democracies of Europe and the commonwealth have been parliamentary regimes and a few semi-presidential and semi-parliamentary, while most of the countries with presidential constitutions have been unstable democracies or authoritarian regimes."[31]

And, indeed, in the words of Stepan and Skach, "numerous different sources of data . . . point in the direction of a much stronger correlation between democratic consolidation and pure parliamentarism than between consolidation and pure presidentialism."[32] In conclusion, Stepan and Skach state that parliamentarism has a more supportive constitutional framework because of its "greater propensity for governments to have majorities to implement their programs, and its greater ability to rule in a multiparty setting," because of its "lower propensity for executives to rule at the edge of the constitution and its greater facility at removing a chief executive who does so, and its lower susceptibility to military coup," and because of its "greater tendency to provide long party or government careers, which add loyalty and experience to political society."[33]

[30] Alfred Stepan and Cindy Skach, "Presidentialism and Parliamentarism in Comparative Perspective," in *The Failure of Presidential Democracy*, n. 23 above, 119–36, at 120.
[31] Juan J. Linz, "Presidential or Parliamentary Democracy: Does It Make a Difference?" in *The Failure of Presidential Democracy*, n. 23 above, 3–87, at 4.
[32] Stepan and Skach, n. 30 above, 120.
[33] Ibid., 132. Not everyone has criticized presidential government as the weaker of the two systems, and opponents of presidentialism such as Linz have been accused of generalizing too broadly from the Latin American experience: see Eugene D. Mazo, "Russia's 'Russian Roulette,'" 41 *Stan.J.Int'l L* (Winter 2005), 10, with reference to

a) "The Failure of Presidential Democracy"[34]

The foregoing conclusion requires some explanation as to the way in which presidential and parliamentary regimes are characterized.[35] The presidential system is a system of "dual democratic legitimacy," since both the president and the legislature are elected by the people. Both are elected for a fixed term during which the survival of one is independent of that of the other: this leads to "rigidity" and "mutual independence." In a parliamentary system, only the legislature is elected by the people, as the chief executive must be supported by a majority in the legislature. The chief executive can fall if he or she receives a vote of no confidence from the parliament, while the head of government has the capacity, normally in conjunction with the head of state, to dissolve the legislature and call for elections. As a result, a parliamentary system is characterized by having "single democratic legitimacy," "less rigidity," and "mutual dependence."[36]

The *drawbacks* of the presidential regime follow from the above characteristics. "Dual legitimacy" implies that a president elected by a majority, or sometimes only a plurality,[37] enjoys the same democratic authority as elected legislators, even though the latter represent a variety of political choices that were presented to the electorate as alternatives by the political parties to which they belong; they are therefore better qualified to represent the people as a whole.[38] Most importantly, when a conflict between these two equally legitimate actors is at loggerheads, there are in a presidential system no deadlock-breaking devices because of the actors' mutual independence. In unstable democracies this "rigidity" may lead to a propensity for military coups.

Another and related drawback of the presidential system is its "ambiguity," in that the elected president acts as a head of state (and not just as a head of government) and is therefore expected to represent the whole people, internally and externally. However, in situations of crisis or war, or when controversial decisions are to be made, presidential action may alienate large numbers of citizens who cannot identify themselves with what they see as "imperial" action taken in a partisan way and often driven by electoral consid-

---

Donald Horowitz, "Comparing Democratic Systems," 1 *Journal of Democracy*, 1990, 74. See also n. 46 below.

[34] This is the title of the book referred to in n. 23 and elsewhere above.

[35] The terms quoted in the following sentences are from Linz's chapter, n. 31 above.

[36] Linz, n. 31 above, 6. See also Stepan and Skach, n. 30 above, 120.

[37] Majority refers to an absolute majority (at least 50.01 percent); plurality refers to a relative majority, that is, the largest vote in the case of a race consisting of more than two persons.

[38] Linz, n. 31 above, 7.

erations.[39] During the president's time in office, those citizens have no political recourse, either directly or indirectly (through their elected representatives). In a parliamentary regime, that ambiguity does not arise in the same manner because the two functions, head of state and head of government, are not exercised by the same person.[40] While the head of government, whether prime minister or chancellor, represents the partisan view of the incumbent government (and can be forced to resign), the head of state, president or monarch, incarnates the nation in a non-partisan way—a role that allows the latter to give discrete counseling to the former with a view to moderating extreme positions, but can also take a more decisive form in exceptional circumstances.[41]

By contrast, one of the presumed *advantages* of "mutual independence" inherent in a presidential system is that it assures the stability of the executive, as compared with the alleged instability of a parliamentary regime. This weakness of parliamentary regimes, however, can easily be overcome by providing for a "constructive vote of no confidence," according to which, as seen above,[42] a head of government cannot be removed unless parliament simultaneously elects a new head of government (usually from the opposition parties). More-

---

[39] In his book *The Imperial Presidency* (Boston: Houghton Mifflin Company, 1973), Arthur Schlesinger maintains that, over time, the power of the U.S president grew tremendously, especially in matters of foreign policy. The evolution culminated with, and was exposed by, Richard Nixon and the Watergate affair. See the excerpt from Schlesinger's book in *The Lanahan Readings in the American Polity*, 3d ed., ed. Ann G. Serow and Everett C. Ladd (Baltimore, Md.: Lanahan Publishers, 2003), 221–28. Schlesinger's viewpoint is certainly not contradicted by the action of the incumbent president, George W. Bush, as regards the war in Iraq and the postwar reconstruction of the country.

[40] See further Linz, n. 31 above, 24–26; also 46–47.

[41] But that does not make it less effective, particularly in multicultural or multiethnic states, where the head of state is often seen as the protector of minorities and weaker citizen groups. Moreover, in exceptional circumstances a head of state may be empowered to refuse the signing of a controversial act advocated by the head of government, as happened recently when the Italian president Carlo Azeglio Ciampi refused to sign into law a bill that would reinforce the overwhelming dominance of Prime Minister Berlusconi's mighty media empire. See *The Economist*, January 17–23, 2004, 41.

[42] See above, p. 318. The device was first applied in the Federal Republic of Germany in reaction to the short-lived governments under the Weimar Republic (on the instability of that republic, which lasted from 1918 to 1933, see Allen in Kesselman and Krieger, n. 1 above, 251–53). Moreover, as Linz remarks, n. 31 above, 9, the apparent instability of a parliamentary system is often offset by the continuity of the political parties in power as well as through stability-producing devices, such as the reshuffling of cabinet members, the continuation of a coalition under the same prime minister, and the frequent continuity of ministers in key ministries in spite of cabinet crises.

over, in a presidential system, the price for more stability is a higher degree of "rigidity" and "unaccountability": a leader who has lost the confidence of his own party or constituency cannot be replaced by someone better able to deal with the situation, or more attractive to those who have lost confidence. In the same way, such a leader cannot be held to account—especially when he cannot be reelected at the end of his term.[43]

Another presumed advantage of a presidential system is that the voter knows the person he or she is voting for. However, that knowledge, and the voters' preference for one presidential candidate or another, may be very superficial, as it will often be the result of "videopolitics," or based upon good looks and sound bites.[44] Moreover, even in a parliamentary system the voter will usually know for whom he or she is voting as, most of the time, it will be the leader of the party winning the election who will become prime minister. More importantly, in a parliamentary regime the voter may know the candidate less well but will better know the political program for which he or she is voting, and leaves the choice as to who will implement the program to the party he or she has voted for.[45]

To be sure, the preceding arguments against presidentialism may be based too much on broad distinctions to be true for all purposes, but they have not generally been refuted.[46] The question remains, however, of whether a system of "mixed" presidentialism, as in effect in France under the 1958 Constitution, can be seen as an improvement over "pure" presidentialism.[47]

[43] Linz, n. 31 above, 9–10, and, on the implications of no reelection, 16–18.

[44] See Giovanni Sartori, "Neither Presidentialism nor Parliamentarism," in *The Failure of Presidential Democracy*, n. 23 above, 106–18.

[45] Linz, n. 31 above, 10–11. The difference has been characterized by Yale professor Bruce Ackerman in the following terms: "the cult of presidential personality goes against the grain of republican self-government. It is downright embarrassing for a constitution to ask free and equal citizens to place so much trust in the personal integrity and ideals of a single human being. Far better for the constitution to encourage citizens to engage in a politics of principle—debating which of the existing political parties best expresses their collective ideals": Bruce Ackerman, "The New Separation of Powers," 113 *Harvard Law Review*, 2000, 633, at 663.

[46] For a staunch defender of American presidentialism, see Steven G. Calabresi, "An Agenda for Constitutional Reform," in *Constitutional Stupidities, Constitutional Tragedies*, ed. William N. Eskridge, Jr., and Sanford Levinson, quoted by Bruce Ackerman, n. 45 above, who strongly disagrees with what he calls "triumphalism" (633) and himself favors a form of "constrained parliamentarism."

[47] France, Brazil, and Russia are the three major countries having a semi-presidential system. On the conflictual relationship between the president and parliament in the Russian federation during the period 1993–2002, see Mazo, n. 33 above. For a thorough analysis of semi-presidential systems in Europe, see Robert Elgie, ed., *Semi-*

In an article pointedly titled "Neither Presidentialism nor Parliamentarism,"[48] political scientist Giovanni Sartori defines "pure" presidentialism by three criteria: 1) it is characterized by a popularly elected chief executive; 2) the chief executive can only be discharged under very special circumstances; and 3) the chief executive is both head of government and head of state. The first two criteria apply to a mixed form of presidentialism, but the last criterion does not. Thus, under the French system, the president, who is head of the Republic, is popularly elected and cannot be removed from office, except for reasons of high treason.[49] However, the president is not head of government as well, the top executive being the prime minister, who is designated by the president with the approval of one of the houses of Parliament, the National Assembly.[50]

As pointed out previously, depending on the circumstances, the French system can be more or less presidential. In circumstances of "non-cohabitation," that is, when the president and the prime minister are supported by the same political majority, the president dominates the political scene, and the system is therefore more presidential. By contrast, the system is less presidential in the case of "cohabitation," that is, when the president and the prime minister are supported by disparate political majorities. In such a situation the prime minister can rely on a majority in Parliament that supports him or her but that does not support the president. In this situation the system has more in common with a parliamentary system.[51] As we have seen,[52] this ambiguous system was established in 1958 under the pressure of a major crisis, the Algerian war and its aftermath. As such, it constitutes "a delicate instrument that should be emulated only with extreme caution by more divided countries."[53]

Presidentialism in Europe (Oxford: Oxford University Press, 1999). The book does not aim to demonstrate which form of government—presidentialism, semi-presidentialism, or parliamentarism—is better, but is concerned with the need to reconsider the assumptions underlying the debate (282).

[48] Sartori, n. 44 above.

[49] Favoreu et al., n. 18 above, 562–63.

[50] See n. 24 above.

[51] See further Suleiman, n. 23 above, 136–63.

[52] See p. 315 above.

[53] Suleiman, n. 23 above, 160. Suleiman notes that the two major side effects of the system have been, on the one hand, the necessity for the (until then) weak political parties to organize themselves in a more disciplined way and to make alliances with other parties on the right or the left in order to win the presidential election and, on the other hand, the polarization and politicization of the administration, the consequence of the presidential system being that only political loyalists will be rewarded during the tenure of the president (146–48 and 152–54).

It follows from the foregoing that a semi-presidential system has some of the characteristics and drawbacks of a presidential system. These are: dual legitimacy and independence of the presidency from the elected legislature (even in a situation of "cohabitation") and rigidity in the sense that there are no mechanisms for breaking the deadlock when dual legitimacy leads to a lasting conflict between the presidency and parliament. The one notable exception to this rigidity is that the president may, once a year, dissolve parliament and call new parliamentary elections that may avoid "cohabitation" if the elections are won by the political party to which the president belongs.[54] Precisely because of this exception, the president in the French system, as in a pure presidential system, will be seen as a partisan head of state.

In addition to this drawback that the French system shares with pure presidential systems, there is another reason for others not to emulate the French system: the system consists of a series of overlapping relationships not only between the president, the prime minister, and the parliamentary majority, but also between the executive and wider state structures, such as between the judiciary and independent administrative regulatory agencies, between the political elite and the people, and between France and Europe.[55] As has been noted, "to describe France as having a dual executive, as many do, obscures the power of the bureaucracy, a third key element within the executive apparatus."[56]

b) *The transformation of "pure" parliamentarism into a*
mixed form of government
Parliamentarism in its *purest* form is a system that lost its appeal with the French Third (1870–1940) and Fourth (1946–58) Republics and the German Weimar Republic (1918–33).[57] It refers to a system in which the executive is prevented from governing the country by a parliament that is unwilling or unable to give political backing to the executive. In other words, it is a system that is *too* parliamentarian, in that parliament does not limit itself to controlling government, and if necessary eventually ousting it, but instead makes im-

---

[54] See p. 316 above.
[55] Elgie, n. 47 above, 67–85, who observes, at 83, that in recent years all of these relationships have been subjected to considerable changes that have "challenged the basic authority of the French executive."
[56] Kesselman in Kesselman and Krieger, n. 1 above, 180, where the triple executive is accurately described at 180–92.
[57] Between 1879 and 1914 French governments had to step down about fifteen times: Favoreu, n. 18 above, 473. Between 1946 and 1958 governments lasted approximately six months on average: ibid., 476. On the Weimar Republic (1918–33), see Allen in Kesselman and Krieger, n. 1 above, 251–53.

portant decisions itself. As such, the system is too "assembly centered" and totally unfit to govern a modern state.[58] To be sure, most often the situation comes about not because parliament is too strong and the executive power too weak,[59] but rather because parliament is too divided as a result of party proliferation.[60] When there are too many political parties, many of them lacking sufficient cohesion to give lasting support to a "coalition government," the executive will not be in a position to make decisions and will be forced either to resign or to ask the head of state to dissolve parliament and call new elections. If these elections are inconclusive, this may lead to even more instability, as happened in the last months of the Weimar Republic, during which no fewer than six elections were held, all resulting in minority governments.[61]

"Pure" parliamentarism is therefore a form of government that must be avoided and is currently neglected in favor of one form or another of "mixed" parliamentarism. In that respect, Giovanni Sartori makes a distinction between three different kinds of parliamentarism hinging on the strength of the position of the prime minister or chancellor. A prime minister may be a *primus solus*, that is, a "first above unequals"; this is most often the case when the prime minister is the party leader of a one-party government. In such a situation the prime minister has a free hand in picking and dismissing subordinate ministers and, as party leader, cannot be easily removed by a parliament that is dominated by the party he or she leads. At the other extreme, a prime minister may be a *primus inter pares*, that is, a "first among equals," and not the leader of the ruling political party. Such a prime minister is on a par

---

[58] Sartori, n. 29 above, 110.

[59] In most modern parliamentary systems the complaint is rather that power has shifted away from parliamentary assemblies to the executive. For an analysis (unfortunately not in English) of the reasons for this shift of power from the legislature to the executive, see Tim Koopmans, "De rol van de wetgever" [The role of the legislator], in *Honderd Jaar Rechtsleven: de Nederlandse Juristenvereniging 1870–1970* (Zwolle: Tjeenk Willink, 1970), 221–35.

[60] On party proliferation and the ways to avoid it through electoral laws, see text accompanying nn. 173 and 174; see also nn. 80 and 82.

[61] Allen in Kesselman and Krieger, n. 1 above, 252, notes that the last several months of the Republic (1932–33) witnessed no fewer than six elections, all resulting in minority governments. According to Sartori's writings in the mid-1990s, most post-communist parliamentary regimes would have had such an "assembly-centred" system: n. 29 above, 111. This is contradicted by David Ost, who wrote in 1997 that "executive authority—the power to carry out decisions—is strong throughout East-Central Europe, as befits a region undergoing rapid transformations where decisions need to be made fast and there is general agreement on the move to a market economy": in Kesselman and Krieger, n. 1 above, 516.

with the other cabinet ministers (often in a coalition cabinet) and heavily dependent on party secretaries and faction leaders who, when governmental crises occur, work out compromises or, failing that, agree to elections. As a consequence, the prime minister falls with the cabinet when parliament (that is, the political majority of parties in parliament) withdraws its confidence.[62] In between, a prime minister may be "first among unequals," meaning that he or she cannot be unseated by a mere parliamentary vote of no confidence but can unseat fellow ministers without being expected to leave office him- or herself.[63]

Though the distinction is not always clear in practice, it should be clear that the British prime minister is an example of a "first above unequals," while the German chancellor is an example of a "first among unequals." It may become more difficult, however, to give an example of a prime minister who is a "first among equals." This is so because since the early 1990s many parliamentary systems that were cited as examples of this category, such as the Belgian and the Italian systems, have amended their systems to make their prime minister resemble a "first among unequals" rather than a "first among equals."[64] These changes were needed because "a prime minister who cannot control his ministers . . . cannot be expected to be really in charge," with the result that the only "power-sharing formulas that hold 'governing promise' are . . . first above unequals, and . . . first among unequals."[65]

Majoritarian versus Consensus Democracies; Plurality versus Proportional Electoral Systems

Sartori's threefold distinction—between "first above unequals," "first among unequals," and "first among equals," each of them related to a different degree of strength of the top executive—runs parallel to a distinction between majoritarian and consensus democracies described by political scientist

[62] See Stephen Hellman describing the Italian system in Kesselman and Krieger, n. 1 above, 401.

[63] See Sartori, n. 29 above, 109–10.

[64] The Belgian Constitution was amended in 1993 to provide for a constructive vote of no confidence (Article 96). Since 1994 the Italian electoral system has been based on a (complex) mix of plurality and proportional representation that has reshaped the multipolar party system into a bipolar party coalition system binding fragmented parties together in the interelectoral period, and thus making the incumbent government less dependent on individual parties. For a brief description, see Hellman, n. 62 above, 418–19.

[65] See Sartori, n. 44 above, 110.

Arend Lijphart.[66] In a majoritarian democracy "the majority of the people" decide what is good for them, while under a consensus model "as many people as possible" make those decisions.[67] In other words, while the majoritarian model concentrates power in the hands of a bare majority, the consensus model tries to share, disperse, and limit power in a variety of ways. Lijphart's distinction outlines, in Sartori's words, "a scale of power-sharing that cuts across, and undercuts, the presidential-parliamentary dichotomy."[68]

a) Majoritarian versus consensus democracies

To determine whether a democracy is majoritarian or consensus, Lijphart proposes the use of two clusters of five characteristics each. The first cluster of interrelated characteristics, called the "executives-parties" dimension, concerns the arrangement of executive power, the party, and electoral systems and interest groups. The second cluster of equally interrelated characteristics, called the "federal-unitary" dimension, concerns the contrast between federalist and unitary governments.

The characteristics in the first cluster that define a government as majoritarian or consensus are:

1. A concentration of executive power in a single-party majority cabinet versus a shared executive power in broad multiparty coalitions

2. The dominance of executive power in the executive-legislative relationship versus a balance of power between the executive and the legislature

3. A two-party system versus a multiparty system

4. A majoritarian and disproportionate ("winner takes all") electoral system versus an electoral system with proportional representation

5. Competitive and clashing interest groups versus interest groups that aim at working in concert and compromise.

---

[66] In *Patterns of Democracy: Government Forms and Performance in Thirty-Six Countries* (hereinafter *Patterns*) (New Haven, Conn.: Yale University Press, 1999), Arend Lijphart examines different forms of government and their performance in thirty-six democratic countries. To decide whether a country qualifies as a democracy, the author uses the ratings for all countries in the world established by Freedom House since 1972 (50–51). Lijphart developed his theory in an earlier work in which he examined twenty-one democracies: *Democracies: Patterns of Majoritarian and Consensus Governments in Twenty-One Countries* (hereinafter *Democracies*) (New Haven, Conn.: Yale University Press, 1984).

[67] *Patterns*, n. 66 above, 1–2.

[68] Sartori, n. 44 above, 110. Sartori adds. "For one the scale indicates that an English prime minister can govern far more effectively than an American president." But see Lijphart's opinion further down in the text.

The characteristics in the second cluster that define a government as majoritarian or consensus are:

1. A unitary centralized government versus a federal, decentralized government

2. The concentration of legislative power in a unicameral legislature versus a division of legislative power among two equally strong but differently constituted houses

3. A flexible constitution that can be amended by simple majorities versus rigid constitutions that can only be changed by extraordinary majorities

4. A legislature with the final word on the constitutionality of its own legislation versus a supreme or constitutional court with the last word on constitutionality

5. A central bank that is dependent on the executive versus an independent bank.

In his work Lijphart uses the distinctive characteristics of both clusters to qualify the thirty-six countries under scrutiny as more or less majoritarian democracies or as more or less consensus democracies.[69] For example, the British parliamentary system is qualified as clearly majoritarian,[70] whereas the

---

[69] Lijphart combines both clusters because, although they do not necessarily occur together in the real world, they are logically connected: *Patterns*, n. 66 above, 2–3. Indeed, majoritarian features in the second cluster (unitary government, a unicameral legislature, a constitution amendable by simple majority, a legislature that reviews the constitutionality of its own legislation, and a central bank dependent on the executive) are clearly not "consensus minded," whereas the corresponding consensus features (divided government, bicameralism, a constitutional court, and an independent central bank) are not inductive to "single" majoritarian decision making.

[70] That the United Kingdom is, under both clusters, the prototype of a majoritarian country is obvious, given Lijphart's variables. It has a strong cabinet composed of members of the same party, which is in a dominant position due to a disciplined party system, even though its existence is ultimately dependent on a majority in Parliament. British politics is dominated by two large parties, and members of the House of Commons are elected through a majoritarian and disproportional electoral system. Except for devolution (see below), the U.K. is probably the most centralized system of Western Europe, and has a nearly unicameral system (the House of Commons being able to override the objections of the House of Lords under certain circumstances). It also has an unwritten constitution, and it is for Parliament itself to decide whether its legislation is constitutional. In recent times, however, the United Kingdom has become less majoritarian, partly as a result of devolution for Scotland and Wales in 1997, and partly as a result of the U.K.'s membership in the European Union. As a result of the latter, the election of British representatives in the European Parliament takes place, as in other EU Member States, in accordance with a system of proportional representa-

systems in Switzerland and Belgium (and the European Union) are described as consensus models.[71] In contrast, the governments of both the United States and Germany are qualified as intermediate forms.[72]

For lawyers who are used to treating unitary (or centralized) states and federal (or decentralized) states as totally different organizations, it is rather confusing to see how the American presidential system is qualified as less majoritarian than the British parliamentary system mainly because of the second cluster, that is, because the United Kingdom is a unitary state and the United States is a federal state. However, Lijphart's classification makes clear that it is not sufficient for a state to have a parliamentary system in order to be a consensus democracy—even though, as Lijphart acknowledges elsewhere,[73] a presidential system has of itself a "strong inclination toward majoritarian de-

---

tion—a system that is now also used for the election of the regional assemblies in Scotland and Wales: *Patterns*, n. 66 above, 16. On the complicated workings of devolution in a U.K. consisting of four units (England—by far the most predominant, having nine-elevenths of the U.K.'s population—Scotland, Wales, and Northern Ireland), see MacCormick, n. 16 above, 193–204.

[71] Within the European Union, Belgium has the most pronounced form of consensual government. It has a system characterized by power sharing and by broad coalition cabinets. These coalitions are largely uncohesive because of their multilingual composition. Belgium also has a multiparty system divided along several lines: socioeconomic, religious, and cultural-linguistic. It also has an electoral system of proportional representation. In 1993 it became a federal state with a bicameral parliament at the federal level and separate parliaments at the regional level. It has a rigid constitution that governs the relations between the economic regions and the cultural communities and a strong constitutional court. *Patterns*, n. 66 above, 34–41.

[72] *Democracies*, n. 66 above, 32–36. The United States is the prototype of a mixed majoritarian-consensual form of democracy. It is majoritarian in its concentration of executive power in the hands of the president, but consensual because of its strict separation of power, which results in a kind of power sharing between the president and the congressional leaders. It is majoritarian in its two-party system, but consensual in its balanced form of bicameralism. It is largely majoritarian in its "winner takes all" electoral methods, but consensual in its political parties that are heterogeneous, but have not led to sharp socioeconomic differences. It is a strong federal state with a written constitution and a powerful constitutional court. For Germany, see Table 13.2 in ibid., 216: like the United States, Germany is classified as a majoritarian-federal system. See also n. 76 below.

[73] See Lijphart, "Presidentialism and Majoritarian Democracy: Theoretical Observations," in *The Failure of Presidentialism*, n. 23 above, 91–105. As confusing as it may be at first sight, to describe the American presidential system as less majoritarian than British parliamentarism, it is equally confusing to liken the latter to General de Gaulle's (semi-presidential) Fifth Republic, called by Lijphart "the most Anglo-Saxon of any of the continental European democracies": *Patterns*, n. 66 above, 250–51.

mocracy." A parliamentary system with a strong head of government may indeed be as majoritarian as a presidential system—which is why, in Lijphart's classification, Germany and the United States, both federal states, fall within the same category of majoritarianism.

Lijphart's widely respected analysis does not stop there. In an effort to compare the merits of majoritarian and consensus democracies, whether presidential or parliamentary, he propounds the view that conventional wisdom has it wrong supposing that majoritarian ("one-party") governments are more decisive or effective policy makers than consensus ("multiparty") governments. He shows, on the basis of objective research, that neither is superior to the other in that regard. By contrast, conventional wisdom has it right when it maintains that, because of the overall capacity of consensus democracy to engage as many people as possible in the decision-making process, consensus democracies are better than majoritarian democracies at representing particular minority groups and minority interests.[74]

Consensus democracies also tend to make democracy "kinder and gentler." To make that point Lijphart examines the impact of several measures relating to the quality of democracy, namely women's representation, political equality, electoral participation, satisfaction with democracy, government-voter proximity, accountability and corruption, and more faithful adherence to the majority principle.[75] He also examines the impact of consensus democracy on social welfare, protection of the environment, criminal justice, and foreign aid. His conclusion is that, in all these respects, consensus democracy does make a difference for the better.

b) Plurality versus proportional electoral systems

Lijphart's conclusion is not contradicted, but rather supplemented, by Sartori, who concedes that a strong executive, as in the United Kingdom[76]

---

[74] *Patterns*, n. 66 above, chapters 15 and 16. Lijphart maintains his view notwithstanding strong objections from other political scientists to the first limb of his analysis (concerning efficiency of the decision-making process): see Arend Lijphart, "Double-Checking the Evidence," in *The Global Resurgence of Democracy*, 2d ed., ed. Larry Diamond and Marc F. Platter (Baltimore, Md.: Johns Hopkins University Press, 1996), 187–93.

[75] *Patterns*, n. 66 above, 280–93.

[76] See n. 71 above. In contrast, Germany, which is an example of the "first among unequals" system, displays less majoritarian characteristics than the U.K. system: it has a proportional electoral system and a multiparty system, but is still a sufficiently strong parliamentary democracy for having a system with strong party discipline and an executive power that is concentrated in the hands of the chancellor. Moreover, as a result of the "constructive vote of no confidence" instrument, and of a 5 percent

(characterizing, in Lijphart's terminology, a strong majoritarian democracy), "is inadvisable when a polity is polarized or characterized by a heterogeneous political culture."[77] Sartori adds the following new dimension to the problem, however: "Indeed, without proportional representation (and coalition governments) the integration of . . . parties of a century ago—mainly Socialist and Catholic parties—into a liberal democratic state, would have been hazardous. Proportional representation and coalitions are thus essential devices for 'difficult' societies."

The importance of electoral systems in shaping a political system as a more or less "consensus democracy," and in particular the importance of a proportional representation system to adapt the system to a polarized political culture, is also highlighted by Arend Lijphart. He compares three basic types of democracy: presidential-plurality systems (as in the United States), parliamentary-plurality systems (as in the U.K.), and parliamentary-proportional systems (as in most of Western Europe).[78] Plurality and proportionality refer to the electoral system: in a *plurality* system, the voting occurs in constituencies in which the winner (person or party) that obtains a plurality (or relative majority), that is, the highest vote, "takes all" (the so-called first-past-the-post system) and is elected; by contrast, in a system of *proportional* representation (PR), the voting occurs in constituencies in which two or more winners, elected on a "highest votes" basis, take the seats in some proportion to the votes obtained.[79] According to Lijphart, the comparative study of democracies has shown

> that countries that use the plurality method of election . . . are likely to have two-party systems, one-party governments, and executives that are dominant in relation to their legislatures. These are the main characteristics of the Westminster or *majoritarian* model of democracy, in which power is concentrated in the hands of the majority party. Conversely, PR is likely to be associated with multiparty systems, coalition governments (including in many cases broad and inclusive coalitions), and more equal executive-legislative power relations. These latter characteristics typify the *consensus* model of democracy, which, instead of relying on pure and concentrated majority rule, tries to limit, divide, separate, and share power in a variety of ways.[80]

---

minimum threshold for a party to gain representation in Parliament, Germany qualifies as a stable form of government. See Sartori, n. 29 above, 105–7.

[77] Ibid., 110–11.

[78] Arend Lijphart, "Constitutional Choices for New Democracies," in *The Global Resurgence of Democracy*, n. 74 above, 162–74. Because of the difficulty of finding reliable data, Lijphart leaves out a fourth group of countries, the Latin American democracies, which have a presidential plurality system.

[79] Sartori, n. 29 above, 3–4.

[80] Lijphart, n. 78 above, 162–63. Plurality methods are known to favor two-party

As pointed out previously,[81] according to Lijphart, parliamentary-proportional democracies are better equipped than plurality systems, whether presidential or parliamentary, to involve minority groups in the political process.[82] Moreover, they would have a slight edge in economic policy making as well. His conclusion in that respect is that the widespread skepticism about those systems' economic capability stems from confusing governmental strength with effectiveness. In the long run, economic policies supported by a broad consensus are more likely to be successfully carried out and to remain on course than policies imposed by a "strong" government against the wishes of important (public or private) interest groups.[83]

III. TWO SPECIFIC ISSUES: BICAMERALISM AND POLITICAL PARTIES

These two issues are unrelated to each other, but they are both important elements of a democracy "under construction," as the European Union is.

The Significance of Bicameralism

A bicameral system is one with two houses (or chambers) of parliament. While it is controversial whether bicameralism is necessary in a unitary state,[84] bicameralism is unavoidable in a federal state, where there is a need for one

---

systems because electors and politicians realize that their votes or chances are wasted if they are to give their vote to, or run for, a third party. Indeed, in a plurality or majority system all but the two strongest parties are underrepresented because they tend to lose in each district: ibid., 165. This theory was first developed by the French constitutionalist Maurice Duverger in *Political Parties: Their Organization and Activity in the Modern State*, 3d ed. (London: Methuen, 1964).

[81] See p. 330 above.

[82] This is particularly true for moderate, rather than extreme, proportionality: a moderate system tries to limit the influence of minor parties through such means "as applying PR in small districts instead of large districts or nationwide balloting, and requiring parties to receive a minimum percentage of the vote in order to gain representation": Lijphart, n. 78 above, 163.

[83] Ibid., 173.

[84] There are many unicameral unitary states, for example Denmark, Finland, Sweden, Greece, and Luxembourg: see Sartori, n. 29 above, 183, where a short overview of bicameralism and its problems in parliamentary systems is given at 183–89. The reason for upholding bicameralism in a unitary state is that two houses "are a safety valve, and that the concentration of all legislative power in just one body is not only dangerous but also unwise: for two eyes are better than one, and prudence requires any decision-making process to be controlled and assisted by brakes": ibid., 184–85.

house to represent the people and another to represent the component states. Accordingly, in the European Union, which assembles both states and peoples, bicameralism is an important issue as well.

Before addressing the issue, it may be recalled that the constitutional systems described in the first section of this chapter, those of the United States, France, Germany, and the United Kingdom, all have a parliament with two houses. In the latter three countries, the people directly elect the members of only one house, which, as the representative of the people, is the house with power to make the government resign.[85] In France that institution is known as the Assemblée nationale, in Germany, the Bundestag, and in the United Kingdom, the House of Commons. In each of these countries, the "other" house, called the Sénat, the Bundesrat, and the House of Lords, respectively, plays a less influential political role than the "people's" houses. Hereinafter, I will deal only with the situation in Germany, because, among the three European countries mentioned, it is the only one that is a federal state.[86]

a) Bicameralism from a European Union perspective

The relation in a federal system between the house representing the people and the one representing the component states is crucial in a European context. One view, which I will call the "federalist" view, sees the relation as an elementary piece of the future institutional structure of the Union. Those espousing this view favor the role of Parliament and advocate for a reduction in the currently predominant role of the Council of Ministers, which, as pointed out previously, acts under the first pillar as the Community's legislative branch together, in a growing number of matters, with the European Parliament. Under the second and third pillars, where the European Parliament and the European Commission play a less prominent role than they do under the first pillar, the Council of Ministers is by far the most prominent law- and policy-making institution. In the "federalist" vision that situation should, at least in the long run and for the three pillars, be transformed into a bicameral

[85] In the United States each state is represented in the Senate by two senators. Though they represent their state, they are directly elected by the people of the state they represent: Seventeenth Amendment [1913]. Bicameralism in the United States is bicameralism in the fullest sense of the word, as both houses possess equal powers, which is not the case of the Bundestag and the Bundesrat, as we will see below. For that reason, it remains controversial among German writers whether the Bundesrat is a second chamber (or house): see Maurer, n. 1 above, 533.

[86] For an in-depth discussion of bicameralism in Germany, see Allen in Kesselman and Krieger, n. 1 above, 305–10; in France, see Kesselman, ibid., 199–206; and in the U.K., see Krieger, ibid., 101–7.

system in which the directly elected Parliament would become the more influential parliamentary house and the Council of Ministers the less influential house, as the non–directly elected house often is in a federal state.

The federalist vision is not to the liking of most, if not all, of the Member States, as they want to preserve, if not enhance, the Council's importance. Moreover, in the view of moderate "federalists," of which I am one, such a drastic change, if at all politically attainable, would not be desirable, at least not for many years to come. This is because the change would reduce the Member States' influence to a point that, rather than enhancing the Union's legitimacy *in* the Member States, would diminish Member State support for the Union by concentrating too much power in the hands of the European Parliament and the European Commission. Furthermore, and by implication, it would also reduce the role of the national parliaments that are charged with controlling their government's representatives in the Council (even though they do not fulfil that function as well as they should, as will be pointed out later).

b) Bicameralism in a federal state: Germany

That said, and leaving theoretical considerations aside, it is noteworthy that the European system, as it presently operates under the first pillar, has many similarities with the current system in the Federal Republic of Germany. As mentioned, the German Parliament consists of two houses—the Bundestag, which represents the people, and the Bundesrat, which represents the Länder.

Article 38 (1) of the Basic Law states that members of the Bundestag "shall be elected in general, direct, free, equal and secret elections. They shall be representatives of the whole people; they shall not be bound by any instructions, only by their conscience." As for the Bundesrat, Article 50 of the Basic Law states that through it, the Länder "shall participate in the legislative process and administration of the Federation and in matters concerning the European Union." Article 51 (1) states that its members "shall consist of members of the Land governments which appoint and recall them." Other members of the Land governments "may serve as alternates." Because members of the Bundesrat are representatives of the Land governments, they change along with the outcome of elections in each Land; such changes may alter the political majority in the Bundesrat.

Each Land in the Bundesrat has between three and six votes, depending on the size of its population. Each Land may delegate as many members as it has votes, but Article 51 (2) and (3) requires that the votes of each Land "may be cast only as a block vote." This reflects the principle that it is the Länder themselves that are members of the Bundesrat rather than their individual (and changing) government representatives. Individual members do have special participatory rights, though, including the rights to participate in the meetings, to take the floor, and to put questions forward. In exercising their rights, however, they have the duty to act on behalf of their Land and their government, and to undertake action (*agieren*) on its behalf.[87]

On each of these points, the Bundesrat bears a striking resemblance to the Council of Ministers when it legislates under the first pillar of the European Union. The Council of Ministers is similarly composed of alternating representatives of the Member State governments, which change with the elections in each state. As in the Bundesrat, votes in the Council of Ministers are roughly weighted in accordance with the size of each state's population, with a minimum for the smaller states. Votes in the Council of Ministers are also required to be cast as a block vote. Members of the Council of Ministers will, like the representatives of the Länder in the Bundesrat, defend the position of their state in the Council.

The functioning of the Bundesrat and the Council of Ministers is very similar as well. The work of the Bundesrat takes place in committees in which all Länder are represented and in which government ministers are normally represented by members of their administrations. These committees prepare the decisions for vote by the full Bundesrat, however, with the notable exception of the committee that deals with matters concerning the European Union (*Europakammer*), which may make final decisions on behalf of the Bundesrat for reasons of urgency.[88] As pointed out in chapter 1, in the European Union committees and working groups function no differently in preparing the legislative work of the Council of Ministers. The members of the Bundesrat elect their president for one year, not unlike the Council of Ministers, where the mandate of the president lasts for six months.[89] Decisions in the Bundesrat are made with at least the majority of votes, as is generally required in the Council of Ministers.[90]

Most importantly, Article 50 of the Basic Law empowers the Bundesrat to participate in the legislative process of the federation on behalf of the Länder. First, like the federal government and members of the Bundestag, the Bundes-

---

[87] Maurer, n. 1 above, 515. All of the specific points that have been mentioned in the above paragraph are discussed there at 510–17. At 516 there is a brief but instructive comparison of the situation of members of the Bundesrat with that of members of the Bundestag.

[88] Article 52 (3a) Basic Law.

[89] Article 203, second para., EC.

[90] Article 205 (1) EC.

rat has the right of initiative in legislative matters.[91] Second, in many instances[92] the Basic Law authorizes the Bundesrat to take part in the decisional
process. Bills adopted by the Bundestag must be transmitted to the Bundesrat.
In matters where the consent of the Bundesrat is required for a bill to become
law, and no agreement is reached by that body, either the Bundesrat, the
Bundestag, or the federal government may demand for the bill to be referred
to a committee composed of members of the Bundestag and members of the
Bundesrat.[93] This committee may propose an amendment on which the
Bundestag must vote a second time. Although the consent of the Bundesrat is
not required for a bill to become law, it may nevertheless raise an objection to
the bill, which can be overruled by a majority vote of the Bundestag.[94] All in
all, the legislative powers of the Bundesrat are far from insignificant, but they
must always be exercised jointly with the Bundestag. That is not so for the
Bundestag, which in matters for which the consent of the Bundesrat is not required may act alone.

The legislative process in the European Union is not so different from that
in Germany. The most frequent decision-making procedure under the first
pillar is the co-decision procedure between the Parliament and the Council of
Ministers. Under this procedure, when no agreement can readily be reached a
conciliation committee composed of an equal number of representatives from
both legislative branches is convened to reach an agreement on a joint text.[95]
What differentiates the Union from the German Republic (and from other
federal Member States), apart from the Commission's *sole* right of initiative,[96]
is that the Council of Ministers (the equivalent of the Bundesrat), *not* the Parliament (the equivalent of the Bundestag), decides matters for which the co-
decision procedure does not apply. This is still the case for matters as crucial
as fiscal and social matters, and for second- and third-pillar matters, for which
the European Parliament may only provide the Council with advice, or non-

[91] Article 76 (1) Basic Law.

[92] Too many instances, according to some, and indeed constitutional reforms are
underway to reduce the Bundesrat's interference with federal matters but, at the same
time and by way of compensation, to increase the autonomy of the Länder: see *The
Economist*, November 8–14, 2003, 27–28.

[93] Article 77 (2) Basic Law.

[94] Article 77 (3) and (4) Basic Law. The Bundesrat also has significant powers with
regard to executive matters: see Maurer, n. 1 above, 522.

[95] Article 251 (3) and (4) EC.

[96] Parliament and the Council may urge but not force the Commission to use its
rights of proposal on matters for which they feel legislative action is needed: see Article
192, second paragraph, EC and Article 208 EC.

decisive cooperation in certain instances.[97] To be sure, if the draft Constitution were adopted the number of instances where co-decision is required would be further increased,[98] but, even so, the Council of Ministers would retain a larger say than the European Parliament in many important matters.

Summing up, the relation between the two legislative branches in the European Union, the Parliament and the Council of Ministers, bears a striking resemblance to the relation between the two legislative branches in the Federal Republic of Germany, the Bundestag and the Bundesrat. However, in the European Union's version of bicameralism, the body representing the states rather than the body representing the citizens is the most prominent part of the legislative branch. This will remain the situation for the foreseeable future, indicating that the Union does not constitute a genuine federal entity.

The Importance of Political Parties

I will now focus on the role that political parties play in the Union and compare it to the role political parties play in a parliamentary (or, for that matter, in a semi-presidential) regime, as exists in the Member States. As we have seen, a parliamentary regime requires that the executive government must have the support of a political majority in parliament; without this support, it cannot survive. This support is supplied by the members of parliament, who belong to the political parties that uphold the government. This means that those parties must be able to actually deliver the vote of "their" members of parliament. In turn, this means that they must have the capacity to impose voting guidelines on their members. Party discipline is therefore essential for a party that wishes to participate in government: the stronger a party's discipline, the more reliable that party is as a "coalition partner." Though discipline can be imposed, it is preferably spontaneous as a result of a party's internal cohesion. A party can best achieve this by organizing itself around ideological or political convictions that are widely shared by a large group of citizens. The creation of sufficiently cohesive political parties is essential for parliamentary democracies to work.[99]

---

[97] As explained previously (chapter 6, p. 280), there are currently some six legislative procedures in the first pillar of the European Union, the most common procedure being the co-decision procedure of Article 251 EC. Under the other procedures, Parliament has no role or only a limited role to play.

[98] See chapter 6, p. 281.

[99] On party discipline, see Sartori, n. 29 above, 190–91. Party discipline has its limits, though, as Tony Blair experienced in early 2004 when he only narrowly prevailed in the House of Commons with a close vote, 316 to 311, in favor of his proposal on the reform of the British university system: see *The Economist*, January 31–February 6, 2004, 57.

Obviously, political parties play a different role in a pure presidential system, as in the United States, in which the directly elected president does not need the support of a majority in Congress to survive. He does need that support, however, to carry out his political program, to have Congress adopt legislation that he has recommended,[100] and to provide him with the budgetary means to implement that legislation. In that respect, he will be better off if he can rely on members in Congress who belong to his own political party. To be sure, though, the president can face complicated negotiations with Congress even when his party has a majority in both Houses, as the U.S. Congress is known for its independence, and its members are known for demonstrating less party discipline than their counterparts in a parliamentary system.[101]

a) The Role of political parties in the Member States

Despite the constitutional importance of political parties in a parliamentary system, that importance has rarely been formally recognized or defined.[102] The German Basic Law of 1949 is one constitution that does discuss political parties: Article 21 states that the task of political parties is to "help form the political will of the people." In legal doctrine, this language is described as commanding the parties to select and promote candidates for elections at the federal and national levels, as well as at the level of the European Union. It

---

[100] According to Article II, sec. 3 and Article I, sec. 7, cl. 2 of the U.S. Constitution, respectively, the president has the right to recommend legislation to Congress but remains dependent on Congress to vote on the bill. Moreover, he cannot prevent Congress from passing legislation, even though he has the right to veto any bill that it passes, remanding it to Congress for reconsideration.

[101] Differences may occur not only between the White House and Congress, but also between the two houses of Congress, even when the same party has a majority in both houses, as demonstrated recently with respect to President Bush's tax cut program. These differences were finally settled in a House-Senate conference committee: *New York Times*, May 23, 2003, 1. Clashes between the two houses of Congress occur, even with one-party control, because of vast differences in the way that the House and Senate operate, mainly because the House applies rules that severely restrain the power of the opposition, which gives the majority leaders "iron-fisted control to ram through" legislation they favor; in the Senate, any member can raise procedural obstacles to a piece of legislation on the floor. See Carl Hulse, "Congressional Memo," *New York Times*, May 12, 2003, A18.

[102] For an attempt to define the role of political parties and party systems, see Alan Ware, *Political Parties and Party Systems* (Oxford: Oxford University Press, 1996), who proposes to define a party as "an institution that (a) seeks influence in a state, often by attempting to occupy positions in government, and (b) usually consists of more than a single interest in the society and so to some degree attempts to 'aggregate interests'" (5).

further implies that, in between elections, parties must record, collect, and represent the political opinions and interests close to the people, and develop political programs containing concrete proposals for political action and viable alternatives to current government policies. In doing so, political parties should operate as a link between the state and the people, and encourage the participation of the citizens in public life.[103]

Under the German Basic Law, political parties have rights and duties: they have the right to establish themselves, without public interference, as an association of citizens; and they have the concomitant duty to grant citizens the possibility to become members of the party, or to resign from it. Political parties enjoy the fundamental rights guaranteed by the constitution and are entitled to equal treatment with other political parties. However, to enjoy these rights, Article 21 (1) states that their internal organization "shall conform to democratic principles."[104] This means that decision making within the party must take place from the bottom up, and that the party leadership must be democratically elected.[105] For its part, Article 21 (2) imposes an important restriction: "Parties which by reason of their aims or the conduct of their adherents seek to impair or do away with the free democratic basic order or threaten the existence of the Federal Republic of Germany shall be unconstitutional." It is for the Constitutional Court to rule on the question of the unconstitutionality of a party.[106]

The most crucial role of political parties is to recruit party members and party representatives to stand as candidates in the many local, regional, national, and European public elections, and to take part in the formation of governments at each of these levels (with the exception of the European level). More specifically, at the national level, party leaders will de facto select the prime minister, approve his or her choice of cabinet ministers, and maintain his or her position, and that of the cabinet, in office. This is so because it is normally the leader of the political party that prevailed in the last parliamentary election who will be asked by the head of state to form a new government, and who will often become the prime minister, if he or she succeeds in forming a government.[107] Because not even the largest political party will normally

<hr />

[103] Maurer, n. 1 above, 343.

[104] Article 21 (1) Basic Law. It further requires that the parties "shall publicly account for the sources and use of their funds and for their assets": ibid. On all this, see Maurer, n. 1 above, 353–60.

[105] Ibid.

[106] See further, ibid., 790–97, with references to case law of the constitutional and other courts at 797.

[107] The role of political parties in the formation of a new government is rarely de-

have enough seats to secure a majority in parliament in a multiparty political system (as countries with a proportional electoral system mostly have), the party leader asked to form the government will need the support of other political parties. Securing that support sometimes requires difficult negotiations with the leaders of these other parties, each of them ensuring that the political opinions of his or her party are sufficiently taken into account in the drafting of the new government's political program. That program is to become the new government's "road map." Once it is agreed upon, discussions between the party leaders on the allocation of portfolios between the coalition parties, and on the names of the persons that each party proposes as cabinet ministers, will begin.

If the negotiations do not succeed, the head of state will call on the leader of another political party, normally the second largest party, to start new negotiations with the same or other parties. When a government is finally formed and sworn in, the role of the coalition parties will consist of following up on the political situation, and specifically watching whether the government advocates the points that each of them contributed to the "coalition agreement." If they are disappointed in the government's actions, each of the coalition parties can, at any time, withdraw its support and, if no other party is found ready to take its place as a member of the coalition, make the government step down.

While a government is in office, it will continuously be confronted by fierce opposition from the MPs who represent the political parties in opposition. Those parties will not only criticize the incumbent government but will also present the electorate with alternative solutions that will be incorporated into a coherent political platform with which the opposition parties will try to defeat the former coalition parties at the next parliamentary elections.

The foregoing must be anathema to readers who have been brought up in an American context. In a presidential system, as the one functioning in the United States, political parties are mainly instruments used by presidential candidates to collect huge amounts of funds, which are necessary to conduct a strongly "candidate-personalized" and excessively "mediatized" campaign. In other words, political parties are necessary to win the elections. In between elections, however, political parties keep a relatively low profile: they do not continuously monitor their elected leaders' performance, nor do they design a coherent alternative political program to use against the incumbent govern-

---

scribed. For some indications, see Kesselman and Krieger, n. 1 above, 85–86 (U.K.), 187 (France), and 290–291 (Germany).

ment at the next election.[108] If alternatives are presented, they are proposed by presidential candidates who, even when they belong to the same party, aggressively compete with each other on the basis of sometimes diametrically opposed political viewpoints. The media then turn these differences into important bones of contention.

The result is that the two political parties in the United States do not succeed in creating a nationwide coherent program with which to oppose the opponent party in the elections. Robert B. Reich, a former U.S. secretary of labor and professor of social and economic policy, describes this failure, particularly of the Democratic Party, as follows:

> Every four years party loyalists throw themselves behind a presidential candidate who they believe will deliver them from the rising conservative tide. After the elections, they go back to whatever they were doing before. Other Democrats have involved themselves in single issue politics—the environment, campaign finance, the war in Iraq and so on—but these battles have failed to build a political movement. Issues rise and fall, depending on which interests are threatened and when. They can even divide Democrats, as each advocacy group scrambles after the same set of liberal donors and competes for the limited attention of the news media.[109]

c) Political parties in the European Union

Currently there are five main Euro-parties, which are "federations of national parties that have a formal legal and organizational existence at the supranational level."[110] These are the European People's Party (EPP-DE, grouping Christian democrats and European democrats), the Party of European Socialists (PES, grouping social democrats), the European Liberal, Democrat, and Reform Party (ELDR, grouping liberal democrats), the European Federation of Greens (grouping environmental parties), and the democratic Party of the Peoples of Europe/European Free Alliance (grouping nationalist and ethno-regionalist parties).[111] These parties have been in existence since the

---

[108] Even during the Iraq war the Democrats did not formulate a coherent political viewpoint, though a large number of Americans were against war. There were also other reasons for that: early on, in October 2002, the Democrats in Congress had voted with the Republicans to authorize the president to start a war, when appropriate; moreover, once the war had started, it would have been political suicide for the Democrats to give the impression that they did not support the troops.

[109] "The Dead Center," *New York Times*, January 29, 2004, A27.

[110] Stephen Day and Jo Shaw, "The Evolution of Europe's Transnational Political Parties in the Era of European Citizenship," in *The State of the European Union*, ed. Tanja A. Börzel and Rachel A. Cichowski (Oxford: Oxford University Press, 2003), 149–69, at 149.

[111] Ibid. More information can be found at http://www.europarl.eu.int/presentation/default_en.htm.

1970s, but developed mainly in the 1990s in a rather hidden way. They have been widely confused and conflated with the existing party groups in the European Parliament to which they are linked. Indeed, for a long time Euro-parties remained dependent upon subsidies from the EP groups, and thus upon the budget of Parliament, which financed their staff, logistical costs, conferences, workshops, and other expenses.[112]

As this situation verged on the misappropriation of the Union's budgetary means, the Commission was asked to draw up a proposal for a measure granting the Euro-parties their own statute. The Commission proposal "Statute and Financing of European Political Parties" was submitted to Parliament in 2000 but failed to command the (then) required unanimous vote in the Council.[113] It was only after the entry into force of the Treaty of Nice in February 2003, amending Article 191 EC and allowing a qualified majority in the Council, that Regulation (EC) No. 2004/2003 concerning political parties at European level and their funding was adopted on November 4, 2003, by the European Parliament and the Council, acting jointly.[114]

Underlying the whole discussion on Euro-parties are questions of identity and aims. Currently, the Euro-parties are still conglomerates or alliances of national parties, meeting at the European level and presenting some form of common manifesto or common positions at the elections for the European Parliament. In between elections, these groupings try to have an impact on the preparation of legislation in the European Parliament. According to the new 2003 Regulation, the main conditions that must be satisfied by a political party or alliance of political parties to be considered as a political party at European level, are 1) representation in at least one-fourth of Member States, either by members of the European Parliament or of national or regional parliaments, or by at least 3 percent of votes cast in one-fourth of Member States at the most recent European Parliament election; and 2) the observance, in the party or party alliance's program and activities, of the principles on which the EU is founded (as set out in Article 6 EU).

---

[112] Day and Shaw, n. 110 above, 157.

[113] For the Commission proposal as it was amended after being discussed in Parliament, see COM (2001) 343, OJ C270 E/103.

[114] Regulation (EC) No. 2004/2003 of the European Parliament and the Council of November 4, 2003, on the regulations governing political parties and the rules regarding their funding, (2003) OJ L297/2. The regulation contains definitions and conditions to be satisfied by political parties to be regarded as political parties at the European level, as well as rules on applications for, and obligations linked to, funding. It also lays down certain funding prohibitions and rules on the nature of expenditures.

Obviously, and understandably, it is not required that the component groups of a Euro-party agree to "pursue increasing levels of integration" or subscribe to a "federalist vision of the EU."[115] A Euro-party should, of course, be permitted to challenge the pursuit of European integration, and to campaign against integration. This is not where the problem is; it lies rather with the wording of Article 191 EC, which defines "political parties at European level . . . as a factor for integration" and requires them to "contribute to forming a European awareness." However, this wording has not prevented the existing Euro-parties, which, by and large, are in favor of integration, to welcome into their midst national parties that like to contain integration within limits.[116] An illustration thereof is the deal recently struck between the EPP and the British conservatives allowing the latter to promote their own agenda of an EU of nation-states without being bound by federalist EPP aspirations.[117] The desire of Euro-parties (like that of national parties) to become larger and to enhance their power in Parliament has even been responsible for the inclusion in Euro-party alliances of components that belong only marginally to the core of the party's original convictions, as was illustrated by the earlier inclusion of Berlusconi's Forza Italia in the EPP (initially a center party of Christian democrats, including trade unions). It is not certain whether the arrival of ten new Member States with their own political party structures will bring about a further dilution of the Euro-party identities.[118]

---

[115] Day and Shaw, n. 110 above, 161.

[116] Ibid. As a matter of fact, in Article I-45 (4) [now I-46 (4)] of the draft Constitution, Euro-parties are no longer defined as "a factor for integration within the Union." That said, Euro-sceptics do not have a large impact in Union politics, as exemplified by their role in the Convention preparing the draft Constitution. Only eight members of the Convention finally signed a minority report, which did not prevent them in the end from signing the Convention text: P. Norman, *The Accidental Constitution* (Brussels: Eurocomment, 2003), 325–26.

[117] The deal, renewing the already existing alliance of the U.K. conservative MEPs with the EPP parliamentary group, was approved on March 31, 2004, by a majority of the 232-strong MEPs from the EPP: *European Voice*, April 1–14, 2004, 2. Ultimately, the deal resulted in the breakaway from the EPP of a group of MEPs joining the Liberal Democratic and Reform Party (ELDR,) which, after the June 2004 elections for the European Parliament, changed its name to Alliance of Liberals and Democrats for Europe (ALDE). See http://en.wikipedia.org/wiki/European_Parliament_election_2004.

[118] By contrast, it may also lead to renewed soul-searching on the part of Euro-parties and act as a magnet to regroup political forces, more particularly around the "more or less European integration" divide. See in that respect, Giovanni Grevi's contribution to *European Voice*, June 17–23, 2004, 17, titled "Time For a 'Progressive' Group to Inject EP with New Blood." On this desirable evolution, see below, at pp. 356ff.

The problem with this evolution is the lack of cohesion on the part of the existing parties, and the consequence that this may have on the involvement of citizens in the political process, more particularly in the formation of European government. I will return to that question below.

IV. A DEMOCRATIC FORM OF GOVERNMENT FOR THE EUROPEAN UNION

In this section I will examine, in light of the foregoing analysis, which governmental structure the Union should adopt to enhance its polity's democratic character in the future; not the near future however, as the issue has not been debated at the Convention preparing the draft Constitution, and therefore has not been the subject of explicit provisions in the draft.

Not a Presidential but a Strong Parliamentary System

a) Neither a pure nor a semi-presidential system

It is clear from the outset that the Union's decision-making process is unlikely to result in a presidential system for the Union. First, only one of the twenty-five Member States, Cyprus, has a pure presidential system. Second, the present political system of the Union already has more parliamentary features than presidential ones, and the draft Constitution would add some more. Third, the foregoing discussion has not shown that a presidential system is superior to a parliamentary system. I will hereinafter briefly deal with each of these elements.

Of the fifteen old EU members, ten states have either no president or only a parliamentary president who is not popularly elected, two states have a popularly elected president who functions, however, as a parliamentary president, two have a semi-presidential system, and one has had a semi-presidential system for a few years but has changed it into a parliamentary presidency.[119]

[119] Belgium, Denmark, Luxembourg, the Netherlands, Spain, Sweden, and the United Kingdom are monarchies, whereas Germany, Greece, and Italy have a parliamentarily elected president. Austria and Ireland have a popularly elected president but function as parliamentary systems. Finland and France are semi-presidential systems; however, since President Kekkonen's resignation in 1981, Finland has evolved into a more parliamentary system: see David Arter's country report in Elgie, n. 47 above, 48–66. Portugal was a semi-presidential system until the constitution was substantially revised in 1982 and again in 1989, and the constitutional powers of the president were reduced to little more than those of a parliamentary president. See Sartori, n. 29 above, 125–31. For a description of the semi-presidential systems in Austria, Finland, France, and Ireland, see Elgie, n. 47 above.

Among the ten new EU members, six have a system without a popularly elected president, three have a semi-presidential system, and (as mentioned) one has a pure presidential system.[120]

The present political system of the Union is more parliamentary than presidential. The European Commission is currently the Union's executive under the first pillar and is accountable to the European Parliament, which has the power to make it resign using a motion of censure made by a special majority.[121] The Commission works under the political guidance of its president, who allocates responsibilities between the members of the Commission and can ask a member to resign. The Commission president and members are appointed by the Member States with the approval of Parliament.[122] All of these elements point in the direction of a parliamentary regime. Moreover, if the draft Constitution is adopted in its present form, the Commission president shall be proposed to Parliament by the European Council, "taking into account the elections to the European Parliament," and shall "be elected by the European Parliament by a majority of its members" (and then only be appointed by the European Council)—both of which point even more in the direction of a parliamentary regime.[123] To be sure, the European Council, which consists of the Member States' heads of state or government, shall be chaired by a president who is elected by the Council for two-and-a-half years (renewable once). His or her powers will, however, not resemble those enjoyed by a president in a semi-presidential system, let alone a president in a pure presidential system or a monarch in a parliamentary state, albeit that, in the political field, his or her powers will be (much) more than purely ceremonial.[124]

I will not repeat the reasons why a parliamentary system is preferable to a presidential system, as I have examined the question in the preceding section. Let me only mention that if a pure presidential system were chosen as a form of government for the Union, it would require a fundamental reshuffling of

---

[120] Cyprus has a genuine presidential system, while Lithuania, Poland, and Slovenia have a semi-presidential system. The Czech Republic, Estonia, Hungary, Latvia, Malta, and Slovakia have parliamentary systems. Of the three semi-presidential systems mentioned, Slovenia has a figurehead presidency like Austria and Ireland, and Lithuania and Poland have a presidency that is still in flux, sometimes more presidential, sometimes more parliamentary, depending on the personality of the incumbent president. See the country reports in Elgie, n. 47 above.

[121] Chapter 2, pp. 83–84.

[122] Ibid.

[123] Article I-26 (1) [now I-27 (2)] of the draft Constitution (which further provides that, if the candidate does not obtain the required majority, the European Council shall put forward a new candidate); see also chapter 6, pp. 289–90 and p. 295.

[124] See chapter 6, p. 296.

the present institutional balance. As we saw in chapter 1, that institutional balance is characterized by a complex and delicate system of power sharing between the institutions, and between the Union and the Member States, and not at all by a neat separation of power. Such adjustments to the Union would be too drastic, especially given that the system would still have to prove its value in surroundings that are completely different from those prevailing in the United States. Though the presidential system certainly works well in the United States, it is a system that is difficult to define, let alone to imitate.[125] And, when it has been emulated, as it has been in Latin America and Eastern Europe, it has not proven successful, as most of the countries that have attempted to do so have unstable or authoritarian governments.[126]

Neither should the Union adopt a semi-presidential system modeled on the French example. As pointed out previously, the popularly elected French president shares the executive power with a prime minister, who is designated by the president but approved by Parliament.[127] If such a system were transposed to the European Union, it would imply that the president of the European Council would be deeply involved in both the Union's executive powers and its legislative powers. This would mean that the Commission president, as the head of the European executive, would exercise his or her powers in the shadow of a directly elected president who would have his or her own, far stronger legitimacy. It would also imply a serious curtailment in the powers of the European Parliament, which would increase the Union's so-called "democratic deficit."[128] Both these features make the French system unsuitable to a system like that of the European Union, which needs a strong executive to effectuate its integration project, and a strong parliament to enhance its democratic legitimacy.

b) A consensus democracy with a strong executive

In *Patterns of Democracy*, Lijphart defines the European Union from a political science point of view as a consensus democracy with the following dis-

---

[125] See, for example, Richard Neustadt's book *Presidential Power and the Modern Presidents* (Simon and Schuster, 1990), in which it is argued that the president's real power comes neither from the Constitution nor from formal authority, but rather from the authority to persuade others, and also the book of Arthur Schlesinger, *The Imperial Presidency*, n. 39 above, who argues that the power of the presidency has grown tremendously over the years, and that Americans must remain on guard in the future, even although the "imperial presidency" was exposed with Richard Nixon. For excerpts, see *American Polity*, n. 39 above, 217–28.

[126] Linz, n. 31 above, 4.

[127] See p. 316 above.

[128] Ibid.

tinctive characteristics: 1) its executive, the Commission, which is comparable to a cabinet, constitutes a broad internation and interparty coalition; 2) with regard to the executive-legislative balance of power, the Commission is an equal partner in the relationship between the three EU institutions (Commission, Parliament, and Council) rather than subordinate to the European Parliament; 3) the Union has a multiparty system with a large number of political parties represented in Parliament and several parties represented in the Council of Ministers; and 4) the European legislature consists of two legislative bodies, Parliament and the Council, with the first representing the people and the second representing the states. Moreover, the Union as a whole has a "con-federal" and decentralized structure.[129] Not only is defining the Union as a consensus democracy correct, but it is also desirable that the Union be one. Given the large cultural, linguistic, political, and sociological differences that exist in a Union of now twenty-five Member States (with more to come), a consensus democracy is the only suitable system. It is the only system that is capable of involving very different segments of the population in the decision-making process; a majoritarian democracy, whether presidential or parliamentary, is therefore not to be recommended as a form of government for the Union.

The fact that the Union takes the form of a consensus democracy should not prevent it from having a strong executive. As pointed out previously,[130] consensus democracies have not been proven to be less decisive policy makers than majoritarian democracies. Currently, the Union already has a strong government in the European Commission, at least under the first pillar, where the Commission takes part in each of the three basic functions of government. Through its (quasi-) monopoly on legislative initiative, it participates in the Community's legislative process; it exercises much of the Community's executive power, autonomously or by delegation; and it exercises an important supervisory role through its power to institute proceedings in the European Court of Justice against any Member State that has failed its Community obligations.[131] This polyvalent position has made the Commission the driving force behind the Community's economic and social policies—a role that it has fulfilled for half a century with great skill and dedication. The draft Constitution maintains the Commission's stronghold.[132]

The Union has also, under the first pillar, a strong head of government in

---

[129] *Patterns*, n.66 above, 42–45.
[130] Pp. 330 and 332 above.
[131] See, generally, chapter 1, pp. 14–18.
[132] See chapter 6, pp. 287–88.

the Commission president. He or she is not just, in Sartori's terms, a *primus inter pares*, that is, a "first among equals," but a "first among unequals."[133] Many elements prove this point: 1) members of the Commission cannot be appointed without the accord of the president; 2) the president decides on the internal organization of the Commission, allocates responsibilities among its members and, with the approval of his or her colleagues, appoints vice presidents; 3) the president gives political guidance to the work of the Commission and participates in the meetings of the European Council; and 4) he or she may ask a Member of the Commission to resign.[134] In the draft Constitution these prerogatives are confirmed and extended to areas now belonging to the second or third pillar—though the president's position would be somewhat affected by the appointment of a foreign affairs minister, who would become a vice president of the Commission as well as the conductor, on behalf of the European Council, of the Union's common foreign and security policy.[135] But that is the price to be paid for a larger involvement of the Commission in the Union's foreign policy.

It is essential for the Union's further development that both these characteristics, a consensus democracy and a strong head of government, be maintained. The first characteristic secures the involvement of all Member State governments, of several political and civil society actors, and, through elections to the European Parliament, of all Member State citizens in the Union's legislative and executive functions; the second allows the executive to give strong and coherent leadership to the Union. Since the Commission is the institution that, more than any other, is responsible for developing the Union's laws and policies and is the guardian of the Union's general interests,[136] any reform to make the Commission politically responsible to Parliament must go hand in hand with safeguards for the strong and independent leadership of the Commission and its president. Reconciling the Commission's accountability to Parliament with a sufficient degree of independence from Member States and the other Union institutions, including Parliament, is undoubtedly the greatest challenge of a parliamentarian democracy for the Union.

c) The Union's democratic deficit

As has been mentioned several times, the institutional structure of the European Union results in a hybrid form of government. Under the first and

---

[133] For the distinction, see above, pp. 325–26.
[134] Articles 214 and 217 EC and Article 4 EU.
[135] Article I-27 [now I-28]. See above, pp. 299–300.
[136] Article 213 (2) EC.

most integrated pillar, the legislative, budgetary, and executive powers are divided between the three political institutions: the Commission, Parliament, and the Council. With the draft Constitution, that situation would not fundamentally change, except that the present structure would be basically extended to the area of police and judicial cooperation in criminal matters that now falls under the third pillar.[137]

This hybrid form of government presents major problems from a viewpoint of political accountability. As pointed out previously,[138] of the three political institutions involved, only the European Parliament is directly elected by popular vote. The Council of Ministers is not politically accountable to any Community or state institution, though its individual members are accountable, in a distant way, to a parliament in their own Member State.[139] The Commission's members are de facto nominated by the Member States, and are collectively politically responsible to the European Parliament, but can only be compelled to resign under procedurally restrictive conditions.[140] From a viewpoint of accountability and political responsibility, the adoption of the draft Constitution would not significantly change this picture.

In the following subsections, I will try to answer the question of how the Union's institutional system could be transformed, with time, into a more accountable (parliamentary) regime.

Improving the Commission's Accountability

Let me first recapitulate the present situation. Currently, commissioners are not democratically elected. Each commissioner is proposed by his or her Member State in accordance with varying (and often untransparent) procedures: most frequently, Member State governments propose acting or former politicians, after which the list of commissioners is adopted by the Council of Ministers in accord with the nominee for president and then subjected to a vote of approval by Parliament.[141] Since 1994, before giving its approval, Parliament has required nominees to appear before a parliamentary committee

---

[137] See chapter 6, pp. 280–81.

[138] See chapter 2, pp. 83–85.

[139] This is obviously also the case of the European Council of Heads of State or Government, which over the years has emerged as the Union's epicenter of political decision making at the highest level. See Helen Wallace, "Designing Institutions for an Enlarging EU," in *Ten Reflections on the Constitutional Treaty for Europe*, ed. Bruno de Witte (Florence: European University Institute, 2003), 90.

[140] See Article 201 EC.

[141] Article 214 (2) EC.

and to answer long questionnaires.[142] Moreover, as mentioned previously, Article 201 EC gives Parliament the ability to make the full Commission resign by passing a motion of censure carried by a two-thirds majority of votes cast in open session, representing a majority of the members of the European Parliament. As yet, this procedure has never led to the Commission's resignation, not even in 1999, when the Commission chose to resign voluntarily rather than face a motion of censure.[143] This does not mean that the procedure is not a useful instrument, as it makes the Commission *feel* responsible for its actions toward Parliament and, through Parliament, toward the community of citizens.

To enhance its democratic legitimacy, the Union should increase Parliament's involvement in the appointment of a European government to make its role comparable to that of national parliaments in the appointment of Member State governments.[144] This would mean that, after the elections to the European Parliament, the president of the European Council[145] would first invite the leader of the largest political party to initiate negotiations with other party leaders to form a Commission. If that leader does not find enough support to secure a majority of votes in Parliament, the president would ask another party leader to try a second time.[146] Once a majority has been found and

---

[142] S. Douglas-Scott, *Constitutional Law of the European Union* (Harlow, England: Longman, 2002), 56–57.

[143] See chapter 2, pp. 81–82. The procedure almost succeeded, though, in January 1999, when a censure motion was narrowly defeated, with 232 MEPs in favor of the censure and 293 opposed. After the report of the Committee of Independent Experts was published in March 1999, Pauline Green, the leader of the Party of European Socialists (PES), then the largest party group in Parliament, informed the president of the Commission, Jacques Santer, that the majority of her group would be voting for censure: Simon Hix, *The Political System of the European Union*, 2d ed.(London: Palgrave, forthcoming), http://personal.lse.ac.uk/HIX/WorkingPapers.HTM, 30.

[144] See above, pp. 339–40.

[145] The European Council, to be distinguished from the Council of Ministers, brings together the heads of state or government of the Member States and the president of the Commission: Article 4 EU. The chair of that Council is held by the head of state of the country that holds the presidency of the Council of Ministers, a position that currently rotates every six months among the Member States. See above, pp. 13–14 and 22.

[146] In the unlikely situation that no party leader succeeds in forming a new Commission within a period of, for instance, four months—during which the incumbent Commission remains in office, as foreseen in Article 201 EC—the European Council presidency should be given the power to call new parliamentary elections. The mere existence of that possibility would normally persuade political parties to reach an agreement.

agreement has been reached between the political parties involved on policies that the coalition will pursue, the leaders of the coalition are to agree on the allocation of portfolios, and on which persons will be appointed Commission president (often the political leader who has made the coalition possible) and Commission members. For reasons of democratic legitimacy, those persons should preferably be politicians who have been elected in European *or* Member State parliamentary elections. They could also be "non-parliamentarians" if they have the support of a majority in Parliament. Moreover, the Commission should be composed so that it reflects "satisfactorily the demographic and geographical range of all Member States of the Union."[147] Any newly formed Commission would be submitted for approval by Parliament, which would be required to approve the Commission acting by an absolute majority of votes cast.[148]

The involvement of Euro-party leaders in the formation of a new Commission in accordance with the Member States' parliamentary traditions would be a substantial change. Commissioners would be approved by Parliament on the proposal of political parties represented in Parliament rather than on the proposal made by Member State governments.[149] There is no reason to believe that the new procedure would be less capable than the current procedure of selecting competent and independent persons as required by Article 213 (1) EC. To the contrary, with the involvement of political parties representing civil society, the procedure would at least be more transparent than the current procedure, under which Member State governments nominate the

---

[147] Thus Article I-25 (3) (b) [now I-26 (6) (b)] of the draft Constitution. This would require the cooperation of Member State governments: for example, each government should provide non-binding three-candidate lists, in which both genders are represented, of persons holding elected office at the European, national, or regional level, or otherwise chosen on the basis of preferences expressed by the Member States' national parliaments. Compare Article I-26 (2) of the initial draft Constitution (see chapter 6, p. 290). Since state governments will not all belong to the same political configuration as the party leader in charge of the formation of the Commission and the parties with which he or she will make an alliance, this would mean that the leader in charge has the possibility of including in his or her team of proposed commissioners persons of a political affiliation other than that of the coalition partners, thus allowing him or her to incorporate into the Commission a certain degree of ideological diversity.

[148] As provided in Article I-26 (2) [now, in amended form, I-27 (2)] of the draft Constitution.

[149] The current situation is already evolving in that direction as shown by the insistence of the EPP, on the eve of the June 2004 European Parliament elections, that, if it emerges as the largest political party, the next Commission president should be chosen from its ranks. See also nn. 117 and 118 above.

members of the Commission on the basis of personal preferences. Of course, the current practice of advance screening of candidate commissioners by multipartisan parliamentary committees in the European Parliament should be maintained.[150]

Involving Euro-parties in the formation of European government should encourage voters to participate in the European elections, as it should make them realize that, through the parties for which they vote, they have a say in the selection of the president and members of the European executive.[151] The involvement of citizens could be enhanced further by revising the way in which party lists for the European Parliament are constituted, as I will discuss below.

Adapting the Role of Euro-Parties

The new procedure of appointing commissioners—in combination with the existing procedure of censuring commissioners[152]—can only work adequately if the political parties operating at the European level (so-called "Euro-parties") are reorganized accordingly. In that respect, it is not enough for Article 191 EC to provide that these parties "are important as a factor for the integration within the Union" and should "contribute to forming a European awareness and to expressing the political will of the citizens of the Union."[153] The existing parties must also change their own attitudes with a view to playing a decisive role in forming the Union's executive government, and supporting it while it is in office, and, even more importantly, with a view to enhancing the role of registered voters in establishing transnational party lists.

[150] That practice could even be extended by requiring multipartisan parliamentary committees in the Member States' *national* parliaments to screen the candidates on the three-person lists that the Member State governments would propose: see n. 147 above.

[151] For a similar argument: Dana Spinant, "How to Make the Elections Sexy: Give Voters a Say over Europe's Top Jobs," *European Voice*, February 5–11, 2004, 12.

[152] The procedure to vote a motion of censure on the Commission, currently laid down in Article 201 EC, should be revised in line with the procedure proposed for appointing commissioners. Both procedures should provide for the same voting conditions, i.e., an absolute majority of votes cast. At the same time, the censuring procedure could be extended to include the possibility for Parliament to withdraw its confidence in individual commissioners. Moreover, and more importantly, in order to promote the stability of the Commission, it would be advisable to introduce the device of "constructive vote of no confidence," as applied in Germany and a number of other Member States, when a motion of censure is tabled against the Commission as a whole, or against its president.

[153] On European parties, see Day and Shaw, n. 110 above; also Douglas-Scott, n. 142 above, 87. As mentioned, n. 113 above, in Article I-45 (4) of the draft Constitution, the reference to Euro-parties "as a factor for integration within the Union" has been deleted.

a) Involving citizens

Currently, the parliamentary Euro-party groups play a role mainly within the European Parliament in the preparation of Community legislation. Except for screening candidates proposed by the Member States, they are not actively involved in the political process leading to the formation of a European government, nor are they involved in the formulation of citizen goals to be pursued by that government. Moreover, while in office, the president and the other members of the Commission are not allowed to proclaim an affiliation with any political party, nor may they consider themselves to be bound by a specific political program. This implies that, conceptually, they have no political ties with any of the political groups in the European or Member State parliaments, and therefore no political ties with European citizens.

This would change if Euro-parties and their leaders were to become involved in the formation of a European government and the formulation of a European program. This would imply that Euro-parties would fulfill the tasks that political parties fulfill in parliamentary democracies. These tasks consist primarily of explaining the impact of political decision making on the citizens' personal life and well-being,[154] offering citizens alternative programs and appropriate candidates for elected office and championing popular issues and proposals.[155] Most importantly, it would require political parties, or coalitions of political parties, to campaign in the name of their candidates for the top positions in European government. The way to achieve this would be for the Euro-parties to present partly transnational lists to constituencies in the Member State, on which candidate MEPs are presented whom the European public knows for their achievement on the European or international scene, along with candidates known for their achievements on the national scene.[156]

Moreover, Euro-parties should enhance the democratic legitimacy of this electoral process by organizing advance primaries among their registered voters to designate the transnational candidates on their lists. On the basis of the outcome of these primaries, the parties would then announce the names of the candidates whom they propose for the presidency and membership of the European Commission, if, after the elections, they were involved in negotiations on the formation of the Commission.[157] Obviously, the actual number of

---

[154] According to Simon Hix, n. 143 above, 4, scholars have estimated that the EU sets over 80 percent of rules governing the production, distribution, and exchange of goods, services, and capital in the Member States' markets. Moreover, EU policies cover virtually all areas of public policy.

[155] Kesselman and Krieger, n. 1 above, 17.

[156] See also, in the same sense, Day and Shaw, n. 110 above, 167.

[157] On the idea of breathing life into European elections by organizing primaries,

votes that these "pan-European" candidates would have assembled behind their names in the national constituencies would have an impact on the party's final decision as to whom they would put forward as a candidate for the Commission presidency and membership.

b) Strengthening party identities

To take on these tasks, and to assemble citizens and involve them in the electoral process, the existing Euro-parties will need to associate themselves with clear issues that appeal to actual citizen preferences.

According to Arend Lijphart, seven traditional "issue" dimensions can be identified.[158] These are the socio-economic dimension (left versus right), the religious dimension, the cultural-ethnic/linguistic dimension, the urban-rural dimension, the dimension of regime support (parties opposing the democratic or the capitalistic regime), the foreign policy dimension (pro- or anti-NATO, pro- or anti-EU), and the materialist versus post-materialist dimension (for example, anti- or pro-environment).[159] Each of these dimensions may be responsible for the emergence of an independent party: a labor or socialist party, a Catholic or Christian party, a nationalist party, a farmer's party, a communist party, a pro-European party, a Green party. Belgium is an extreme example: it has liberal, social democratic, Christian democratic, nationalistic and Green parties on both sides of the linguistic border, making ten parties.

Obviously, the impact of these *identity* dimensions varies with the transitions in society.[160] In the postwar period, those transitions were responsible for an important transformation of political parties on the European scene: although parties had previously demonstrated organizational and ideological

---

see Tom Spencer in *European Voice*, April 22–28, 2004, 9. The idea would certainly help to encourage the media to pay more attention to the European elections. In today's heavily mediatized society, newspapers and broadcasters in the Member States have indeed an important role to play: see Dana Spinant, n. 151 above.

[158] See *Democracies*, n. 66 above, 127–49. See also Alan Ware, n. 102 above, 17, who distinguishes two approaches to party ideologies in most liberal societies, one that tends to reflect a single "left-right" spatial dimension with four broad types of party families on the spectrum—"communist," "socialist," "centrist," and "conservative"—and another approach that adds to the "left-right" confrontation the view that the behavior of political parties may also be governed by much older beliefs and values that the party had at its founding. In the second view, one centered on the European liberal democracies, nine *"familles spirituelles"* can be identified: liberal and radical, conservative, socialist and social democrat, Christian democrat, communist, agrarian, regional and ethnic, right-wing extremist, and ecology movement: ibid., 17–24.

[159] *Democracies*, n. 66 above, 127–49.

[160] For a detailed description of transitions in European politics, see Kesselman and Krieger, n. 1 above, 18–37.

links to the working classes or had been linked to the interests of the economic elites, in the 1980s parties emerged on both the left and the right that sought to generate broad-based electoral support.[161] Simultaneously, a broad shift occurred in expectations about the role of the state in economic management. In the new vision the state surely continues to play an important role, but, henceforth, that role consists of activity to bolster rather than to curtail the operation of markets.[162] The disappearance of class-based identities does not signify that the opposition between right and left is no longer important: many of the concerns championed by the right, notably the need for removing restrictions on market forces, have gained popular support; at the same time, however, leftist themes, including the need to limit private enterprise in order to protect the environment and workers' health and safety, also enjoy high levels of support.[163] Moreover, in the 1980s and 1990s political leaders such as the French socialist president François Mitterrand and the German Christian democrat chancellor Helmut Kohl, as well as prominent business executives, cast their lot with a strengthened European Union. The shift in power toward the EU limited the capacity of the Member States to regulate their own economies and societies considerably, making it impossible to tell the story of the domestic politics of Western European countries without paying close attention to the EU.[164]

These transformations have not prevented the socioeconomic dimension from being the most important divide, even though the emphasis has shifted from differences based merely on class to broader left-right issues. The divide still predominates in any democratic society, so much so that it is the only divide that determines the political landscape in two-party systems such as the United States.[165] However, because of these transformations, other traditional dimensions became less divisive in recent years. This is the case of the religious dimension, which has lost much of its attraction, at least in the old EU Member States, with the growing secularization of society; of the urban-rural dimension, which has lost importance with the reduction of the number of

[161] Ibid., 23–24.
[162] Ibid., 32.
[163] Ibid., 33.
[164] Ibid., 34.
[165] Ibid., 127. See also Alan Ware, n. 102 above, who regards the United States as an "unusual case" for having produced two liberal parties, both practicing "bourgeois, business-oriented politics typical of European liberalism." However, in competing against each other, they have developed rather different variants of liberalism, and the Republicans have taken on some socially conservative values that would fall well outside the mainstream of European liberalism (25–26).

farmers; and of the dimension of regime support, which has been decimated with the disappearance of communism. Other dimensions, however—mainly the cultural/ethnic dimension—have become more divisive as a result of large waves of immigration, first from the former colonies, and now fomented by instability and insecurity in large parts of the world.

While the identity of political parties turns around divisive issues, the *number* of political parties is affected by other factors, not the least a political regime's institutional and electoral system.[166] Countries with a presidential regime, such as the United States, are best off with a two-party system and a "winner take all" majority electoral system. Countries with a parliamentary regime will have a small number of political parties when they have chosen for a "first-past-the-post" plurality electoral system, as in the United Kingdom, whereas parliamentary regimes with a proportional representation system will normally have a multiparty system.[167] Whether a country chooses a majoritarian/plurality or a proportional representation electoral system will often be determined by its past. As pointed out previously,[168] experience and political analysis show, however, that heterogeneous countries with large ethnic or cultural differences are better off with a system in which a large number of groups are allowed to participate in government (whether at the national, regional, or municipal level). These countries will normally belong to the group of consensus-type democracies with (sometimes too-large) coalition governments in which a variety of political parties take part.

c) Changing the focus of Euro-parties

Given these characteristics, it was foreseeable that the European Union would have a (relatively) large number of political parties—as befits a heterogeneous society that requires the involvement of a large variety of groups in political decision making through an electoral system of proportional representation.[169] It was also foreseeable that these European political parties would

---

[166] The importance of electoral systems has long been downplayed. For a brief but illuminating analysis, see chapters 3 and 4 in Sartori's *Comparative Constitutional Engineering*, n. 29 above, 27–52 and 53–79.

[167] For the terminology, see the text accompanying nn. 78 and 79 above.

[168] See pp. 330–32 above.

[169] According to Article 190 (4) EC, Parliament "shall draw up a proposal for elections by direct universal suffrage in accordance with a uniform procedure in all Member States or in accordance with principles common to all Member States." Parliament approved a draft proposal on July 15, 1998, [1998] OJ C292/66, which provides for proportional representation in Article 1. The draft has not yet been adopted, but a system of proportional representation was already imposed upon the Member States by Council Decision of September 20, 1976, concerning the elections of the Members of

reflect the issues that divide and characterize European societies. These issues relate to socioeconomic concerns embodied in the social democrat PES and the liberal ELDR, to religious concerns in conjunction with socioeconomic concerns found in the Christian democrat and conservative EPP-ED, and to post-material concerns such as those embodied by the environmental Green Party. Surprisingly enough, though, the issue of more or less European integration is not clearly reflected in the political party divide, the Euro-sceptics having a small representation only in the European Parliament.

However, today these distinctions say more about each party's national-level components than about their own transnational identity. Moreover, because of their desire to become as influential as possible in Parliament, some Euro-parties have accepted into their midst groups that represent ideologies falling outside their core beliefs. The crucial question, then, is how to make Euro-parties identify themselves with an ideology that is strong enough to secure the party both internal cohesion and a clear identity in the eyes of the electorate. A clear identity is needed to attract a large group of loyal and faithful voters; internal cohesion is needed to ensure trust between political parties so that, when they have decided to form a coalition government, they can rely on their partners to form a stable and politically determined government.

Ways must be found to encourage Euro-parties to reinforce their ideological identity. Legislation concerning the public funding of parties may certainly help by establishing conditions that require Euro-parties to present candidates on transnational lists and draw up party manifestos and political platforms focusing on European issues.[170] Obviously, adopting transnational lists requires that European elections be conducted in all Member States on the same date

---

the EP by direct universal suffrage, [1976] OJ L278/5, with amendments in [2002] OJ L283/1.

[170] Regulation 2004/2003 of November 4, 2003 (see n. 114 above) requires, as a condition for funding, a certain degree of transnational representativity, i.e., the election of parliamentary representatives in at least one-fourth of Member States, or the receipt of at least three percent of the votes cast in one-fourth of Member States at the most recent European Parliament elections (see the paragraph in the text following n. 114 above). Furthermore, the regulation requires as a condition for funding "a political programme setting out the objectives" of the political party concerned. See also the following note. For a full overview of how Regulation 2004/2003 came about and has been implemented since, see Stephen Day and Jo Shaw, "Political Parties in the European Union: Towards a European Party Statute?" forthcoming. The funding scheme provided in the regulation came into effect in July 2004 at the first session of the newly elected Parliament: see "Multi-Euromillion Allocation Approved for Larger Parties," *European Voice*, October 14–20, 2004, 3.

or within the same three- or four-day period, as they already are. But that will not suffice to strengthen the parties' ideological identity to the point that they will be capable of assembling voters around European issues with which they can be clearly identified in the eyes of a transnational European electorate. Further analysis will be needed to find out how this can be achieved and how the Internet can be put to use, not only in promoting European "e-voting" and "e-democracy," but also in giving Euro-parties a stronger political profile by making their political program and their internal organization more transparent and more accessible to a transnational electorate,[171] and in the process improving turnout figures.[172]

Apart from strengthening Euro-parties' identity, measures must also be taken to avoid party fragmentation that would undermine the stability of the system. To be sure, in themselves, clear-cut ideologies on the part of the major Euro-parties should enable these parties to attract the vast majority of citizens, thus avoiding extreme party fragmentation by eliminating parties that do not appeal to large numbers of citizens. But that may not be enough.[173] Obviously, the most efficient way to achieve that is to establish thresholds for admission to representation (often 5 percent).[174]

d) Taking the risk of enhanced democratic legitimacy

In conclusion, for the purposes of involving political parties and citizens in the selection of a European government, it is essential to create a "greater citizen linkage" with the European public sphere.[175] More concretely, this means that members of the European executive government (the president and members of the Commission) are selected on the basis of elections at the

---

[171] The presentation of a common manifesto, the potential of the Internet to promote e-democracy and e-voting, and the introduction of transnational party lists in time for the 2009 European Parliament elections are themes that are on the agenda of the major Euro-parties: see Day and Shaw, n. 110 above, 160–62. For the 2004 elections, most parties have presented a manifesto.

[172] Since direct elections for the European Parliament started in 1979 the overall voter turnout has fallen steadily, in some countries dramatically (the Netherlands and Germany), in others with ups and downs (France and Greece). For figures since the 1979 elections and including the 2004 elections: http://www.euractiv.com/Article?tcmuri=tcm:29-117482-16&type=LinksDocuments.

[173] According to Sartori, n. 29 above, 8–9, providing large constituencies in terms of the number of representatives that each district elects helps to reduce party fragmentation since it favors larger parties. Indeed, "the smaller the constituency is, the greater the waste of votes," because in small constituencies more votes cannot be used to meet the electoral quotient needed to win a seat.

[174] Ibid., 10.

[175] Day and Shaw, n. 110 above, 167.

European level and that the political options for which they stand reflect preferences submitted to the European electorate. That will only be possible if voters can identify each political party with a clear stance on divisive issues within policy areas that appeal to the electorate. One such policy area is surely socioeconomic issues, which includes the role of the "state," the size of the public sector, the "social face" of the European construction, and the role that the European legislature should play in welfare policies. Another policy area is European integration itself, which raises a variety of questions concerning integration and intergovernmentalism in different sectors. Other policy issues include cultural diversity, the Union's openness toward third countries, and environmental issues.

Only when Euro-parties are willing to focus on such divisive issues[176] and and not to allow national components to join the transnational party unless those components are committed to that party's mainstream position on these issues, will Euro-parties have the external identity necessary to persuade citizens to give their vote to the parties' political leaders and have the internal cohesion needed to support, in a coalition government, a clear action plan for European governance.

Having said that, the crucial question is whether the European elites that have been responsible for a steadily expanding European integration over the last fifty years are ready to leave the future of European integration in the hands of the people. This entails the risk that the integration process could be slowed down, if not arrested or even turned back, by an electorate that is indifferent to the European cause. This is a risk, however, that I believe must be taken in the years to come, for several reasons. First and foremost, it is not possible to claim democratic legitimacy for the European construction and, at the same time, not to allow the European citizens to decide on the future course of action. Second, and more pragmatically, given that the Member States' economies and societies have become so intertwined (and those of the new Member States will soon become so), turning the clock back in a sub-

---

[176] I would assume that this would lead to the creation of center-left and center-right parties—both committed to (moderate) European integration, and each with a (somewhat, i.e., not totally) different emphasis on social versus market orientation—*and* to the creation of a number of smaller parties, such as a conservative party strongly committed to the nation-state and to cultural (including religious) identity, a leftist party committed to anti-globalism, and a Green party committed to broad environmental issues with a strong emphasis on citizen participation. Both the center-left and center-right parties would be able to form coalitions, if not with each other, then the former with the leftist and, presumably, the Green parties, and the latter with the conservative and, possibly, the Green parties.

stantial manner is no longer a viable alternative, particularly because the institutions at the Union (and Member State) level have developed their own momentum toward integration. This applies not only to the European Parliament, the European Commission, and the European Court of Justice, but also to the European Council and the Council of Ministers, as well as the administrations of all these institutions and the numerous committees of civil servants and experts working under or with them.

Moreover, as we saw in chapter 5,[177] public opinion on European issues has already, in each of the Member States, had a powerful impact on the attitudes of the Member State governments. Should the European Commission consist of politicians selected by political parties, and thus on the basis of popular elections, the role of the people would simply be increased—but in a more direct and transparent way, that is through general elections. Finally, the risk that the course of European integration may be slowed down as a result of citizen involvement in European decision making through political parties is certainly smaller than in the case of referenda concerning the approval of European Treaty amendments. This is readily exemplified by the Treaty Establishing a Constitution for Europe, in respect of which many Member States currently envisage organizing referenda for approval of this treaty, even in cases where a referendum is not required by their national constitution.

Constructing Accountability in the Council of Ministers?

The Council of Ministers is, as a body, not politically accountable at the European level. Neither are its individual members, though they are politically accountable to their own national or regional parliament even for actions performed in their capacities as members of the EU Council.[178] As a result, national parliaments judge the actions or inactions of individual Council members from a purely national or even regional perspective and, because the Council's composition changes depending on its agenda, often from a purely sectoral perspective. In other words, no one judges the performance of the Council as a body or of its individual members from a global European Union or Community perspective. If the draft Constitution is adopted, the situation will be no different.

This lack of accountability of the Council of Ministers would not be a problem in itself if its members were directly elected, as are the members of the European Parliament.[179] However, EU Council members are, at the state

[177] See pp. 260–62, above.
[178] See above, p. 349.
[179] The fact that MEPs are directly elected, and thus enjoy democratic legitimacy,

level, ministers of the national or regional government who are mandated to sit on the Council to represent their Member State. The question, then, is whether these ministers must be made accountable, at the Union level, for actions or inactions in their capacities as members of the EU Council, and if so how. To put the problem in perspective, it is useful to review the status of the upper house of a bicameral parliament in a federal state.

a) The Council: One of two parliamentary houses (or chambers)?

In a bicameral parliamentary regime it is often the case that one of the parliamentary houses is not, or not fully, elected directly by the people.[180] Federal states in which this is the case convincingly justify the phenomenon: because the lower house represents the people, it should be directly elected, while the upper house represents the component states, and should therefore be composed of representatives appointed by the member state governments. In the Federal Republic of Germany, for example, the members of the Bundesrat are appointed by the Länder governments and so represent the interests of their Länder rather than those of the federation, when, in matters affecting the Länder, they exercise the legislative power of the Bundesrat, which it shares with the Bundestag. The same holds true for the members of the EU Council when that Council exercises its legislative powers jointly with the European Parliament under the first pillar. As we saw previously,[181] there are many more similarities between the operations of the Bundesrat and the EU Council. One that I should emphasize in the present context is that neither the Bundesrat nor the Council of Ministers has the power to unseat the executive, which, as

---

does not mean that they should not comply with the highest standards of integrity in public life. Gaining legitimacy through elections is one thing, earning credibility another. This issue came to the fore as a result of Parliament's expense policy, which, until recently, accorded MEPs a lump sum to cover their expenses without requiring proof of expenditure. The system was invented to compensate MEPs, to some extent, for the large salary differences between them (MEPs of the different Member States receive the same salary as members of their state's national parliament). Obviously, the system was open to abuse and severely affected Parliament's public profile. Nevertheless, it took twenty-five years for the system to be changed. In December 2003, the deputies approved a new salary and expense package providing a uniform salary for all MEPs. This salary is taxable in the Member States (at different rates), with reimbursement of expenses on the basis of receipts: *European Voice*, December 18, 2003–January 14, 2004, 2. Parliament's proposal was still to be approved by the Council of Ministers, some countries finding the harmonized salary too high: *European Voice*, January 22–28, 2004, 9, and January 29–February 4, 2004, 5.

[180] This is different in the United States, where, since the adoption of the Seventeenth Amendment (1913), the people of each state directly elect their senators.

[181] See above, pp. 334–37.

is usual in bicameral parliamentary systems, is a prerogative that belongs only to the house that represents the people. These similarities thus show that, under the first pillar, the Council of Ministers acts de facto as one of two arms of the Union legislature, and it resembles the upper house that represents the component states in a federal State.

There is, however, a fundamental difference between the EU and the Federal Republic of Germany in terms of how legislative powers are allocated between the upper and lower houses of the legislature. In the Union the Council of Ministers currently has full legislative powers, whereas those of the European Parliament are limited. It is only under the legislative co-decision procedure of Article 251 EC, which applies to the first pillar, that Parliament operates on a par with the Council of Ministers as a legislature in a number of steadily increasing instances. In other instances, Parliament has no, or only limited, decisional powers under the first pillar, and no legislative powers under the second and third pillars.[182] Consequently, in the Union, the Council representing the states takes precedence over Parliament in all instances in which it acts alone, or has the last and decisive word. This means that in the EU the situation is exactly opposite to the situation in the Federal Republic of Germany, where the Bundestag representing the people has legislative powers in all instances, whereas the Bundesrat representing the component states has legislative powers only in matters that affect the Länder, and even then shares power with the Bundestag.[183]

The relationship between the federal and state levels of government belongs in a federal (as opposed to a unitary) state to the very essence of the statal structure. In a bicameral system, which a federal state normally has, it means that the house that is elected by the people, and which therefore has more democratic legitimacy than the other, is generally the more prominent part of the legislature—as is the case of the Bundestag in the Federal Republic of Germany, or the Assemblée nationale in France. In the Union, by contrast, the Council of Ministers, that is, the institution with a lesser amount of democratic legitimacy, is the more prominent part of the legislature—which shows that the Union is not a federation but only a confederation of states. This defining difference leads to the following observation. Because of the prominence that the lower house representing the people has in a federal state,

---

[182] When the draft Constitution is adopted that will only change to the extent that Parliament will reach a par with the Council in a larger number of instances now falling under the first and third pillars. See chapter 6, pp. 280–81.

[183] See above, pp. 335–37. For an additional account of the relationship between Bundestag and Bundesrat, see Allen in Kesselman and Krieger, n. 1 above, 306–10.

the state representatives in the upper house can be permitted to fully represent their state's interests. This is so because the federal interest will in any case be adequately safeguarded by the lower house, whose authority takes precedence over that of the upper house. In the Union, by contrast, Parliament can play this corrective role only in instances when it is on a par with the Council, which makes it necessary to preserve the "federal," or rather the "supranational," interest in the Union through other means, as we will now see.

b) Striking balances in the common interest

The need to protect the "supranational" interest was a major concern for the framers of the (then) EEC Treaty, of which they took heed by according the Commission the right of legislative initiative. That right ensures that, under the first pillar, no legislation can be passed if the Commission has not proposed it first. It implies, moreover, that the Commission dominates the ensuing legislative process because, according to Article 250 EC, the Council can only amend a Commission proposal by unanimity, which means that in the Council any one Member State can veto an amendment to the Commission proposal, whereas the Commission can alter its proposal at any time during the legislative procedure.[184]

Another device to protect the "supranational" interest is the obligation for Member States and their representatives to respect the principle of loyal cooperation with the Union (and vice versa)—a principle that the Union has in common with federal states.[185] The principle, laid down in Article 10 EC, has been fleshed out by case law of the ECJ to the effect that any one Member State 1) may not paralyze the Union's decision-making process through individual action (as France did under de Gaulle in the early years of the Community),[186] 2) must have respect for the vital interests of other Member States, 3) must do its utmost to take the general interest of the Union into account, and 4) must try to reach conclusions by consensus.[187]

---

[184] See further K. Lenaerts and P. Van Nuffel, *Constitutional Law of the European Union*, ed. Bray (London: Sweet and Maxwell, 1999), 434–39.

[185] See chapter 6, p. 271. For Germany, see Maurer, n. 1 above, at 321.

[186] From July 1, 1965, France boycotted the Community's decision-making process by remaining absent (the so-called "empty chair" strategy). The ensuing institutional crisis was settled in January 1966 by the Luxembourg Accords: see Douglas-Scott, n. 142 above, 17–18.

[187] It is standing practice in the Council that when Member States representing twenty-three to twenty-five votes indicate that they do not agree with a proposal, the chair will take the initiative to facilitate consensus with the help of the Commission and members of the Council. This practice, known as the "Ioannina Compromise,"

However theoretical the principle of loyal cooperation may seem to be, it functions well in daily practice, mainly because of two bodies: the Committee of Permanent Representatives of the Member States (COREPER) and the Council's General Secretariat. The Member States' permanent representatives, along with their deputies and "working parties," reside in Brussels, where they meet frequently to prepare legislation and common policies and to reach common positions on pending issues. The Council's General Secretariat has a key role in the drafting of texts, working out their content and shaping compromises that make the texts acceptable to all relevant constituents.[188] As a result of these efforts, the Council produces decisions that reconcile the interests of both the Union and the Member States. Paradoxically enough, although this decision-making process is conducted by Member State representatives and the Council of Ministers' own General Secretariat, it generally operates in the interest of integration and at the expense of national sovereignty. This led an expert commentator looking for an explanation for this paradox to say, as early as 1958, "if parties to a conference enjoy specific and well-articulated ends of participation, if they identify themselves completely with procedures and codes within which their decisions are made, they consider themselves completely 'engaged' by the results even if they do not fully concur with them."[189]

c) Securing accountability

It follows from the foregoing that it is not exceptional in a federal structure that the component entities pursue their interest at the federal level through one of the legislative chambers at that level, provided that the "federal" interest is adequately preserved. It is therefore consistent with democratic legitimacy that, in the Union, which is not a (genuine) federal entity, the Member States are pursuing their own interests in the Council of Ministers, given the fact that the supranational interest is sufficiently preserved though other means (as described above).This does not mean, however, that the question should not be asked as to how to make the Council, as an un-elected institution of the Union, more accountable toward the citizens. Actually, the more impact the Council has as a result of the steady extension of the EU's jurisdiction in economic and monetary as well as non-economic areas, the more acute the question becomes.

---

was adopted in the beginning of 1998: see "Editorial Comments: The Ioannina Compromise—Towards a Wider and Weaker European Union?" 34 *CMLRev.*, 1994, 453–57.

[188] On COREPER and the Council's General Secretariat, see Article 207 (1) and (2) EC, and chapter 1, p. 20.

[189] E. Haas, *The Uniting of Europe* (Stanford, Calif.: Stanford University Press, 1958), 522, quoted by Douglas-Scott, n. 142 above, 81.

I see four possibilities for increasing the Council's accountability, two of which are self-evident. The first is to insist on full transparency of Council procedures, by making access to Council documents as broad as possible, and requiring the Council to meet in public whenever it acts "in its legislative capacity."[190] This will allow public opinion and the media to follow Council action as closely as it follows the activities of Parliament. A second way is to foster the mutual accountability of the two legislative branches by increasing the instances in which they must consult and report to one another, which should give each branch proper insight into what the other intends to do, and actually does.

A third possibility is to draft a code of ethics that outlines the individual ministers' duties and responsibilities as members of a Union institution. Such a code should make the principle of loyal cooperation as concrete as possible. A more far-reaching proposal would be to subject acting members of the Council to a (quasi-) disciplinary procedure before the ECJ in cases where they are accused of serious misconduct in the performance of their Council duties. Implementing this proposal would require extending the procedure currently applicable to members of the Commission under Article 216 EC to ministers sitting on the Council. I do not think, though, that this is a workable solution, as it would oblige the court to deal with the core of political decision making.

A fourth option is to increase the involvement of national parliaments in the supervision of the Council of Ministers' work. This could be achieved by entrusting the (existing) Conference of European Affairs Committees (COSAC) with the monitoring of the performance of national ministers when they act in their capacity as Council members. That committee, which is composed of representatives who are in charge of European affairs in the national parliaments,[191] could set up an internal board to operate as a standing cross-

[190] See Article 207 (3) EC and Article I-49 (2) [now I-50 (2)] of the draft Constitution. According to European Ombudsman Jacob Söderman, the Council is still very "old-fashioned" in its approach to transparency compared with the other main EU institutions: *European Voice*, March 27–April 2, 2003, 4.

[191] See point 4 of the Protocol on the Role of National Parliaments in the European Union, attached to the Amsterdam Treaty. The role played by such European affairs committees in the Member States' national parliaments differs greatly from one country to another. See the overview by Carol Harlow, *Accountability in the European Union* (Oxford: Oxford University Press, 2002), 85–92. Although one of the working groups of the Convention has, in a paper on the role of national parliaments in the European Union, recommended that national parliaments facilitate scrutiny of their own governments in matters relating to Union activities (document CONV 579/03 of February 27, 2003, 14), the Convention does not seem to really have tackled the issue of Council accountability.

national parliamentary committee,[192] which would be responsible for monitoring the way that the Council deals with difficult cases. By subjecting the Council, as a Union institution, to a parliamentary committee composed of national MPs, but operating at the European level, we move as close to political accountability as we possibly can. It is not clear, however, which political sanction the committee would be able to impose when it judged some behavior of the Council to be inappropriate. The most COSAC could probably do in a case where it suspects a serious malfunctioning is to publicly ask the Council presidency that the Council reconsider its position.

Which Future for the European Council?

As we saw in chapter 6, Article I-21 [now I-22] of the draft Constitution provides for the appointment of a full-time European Council president, who would be elected by the Council for a term of two-and-a-half years, renewable once. The president would chair the meetings of the Council, which, according to Article I-20 (2) [now I-21 (2)], assembles the heads of state or government with the president of the European Council and the president of the Commission. The Council presidency would basically have the power (as it already has currently) to drive the work of the European Council forward, to facilitate cohesion and consensus within the Council, and to ensure the external representation of the Union on issues concerning the Union's common foreign and security policy. The presidency would have no legislative or executive powers.[193]

The solution proposed by the framers of the draft is a modest one: the creation of a president who chairs the European Council and is elected by that Council. In making this proposal, the framers rejected two other proposed solutions: the creation of a popularly elected president of the European Union, and making the president of the Commission the president of the European Council as well. The first solution would have transformed the Union's institutional system into a semi-presidential system, French style, a solution that I rejected earlier in this chapter. The second solution would have made the Commission president, in Sartorian terms, not only, as head of government, "a first among unequals," that is, above the other commissioners,[194] but also, as president of the Council assembling the heads of state or government,

---

[192] But see on the practical difficulties of cooperation between national parliaments in COSAC, Harlow, n. 191 above, 103–5.

[193] See the enumeration of powers of the European Council president in Article I-21 (2) [now I-22 (2)] of the draft Constitution, and the definition of powers of the European Council itself in Article I-20 (1) [now I-21 (1)].

[194] See above, p. 325.

a "first among equals" among the Member State heads of state or government. Such a concentration of power in the hands of one person would necessarily lead to the conclusion that the Commission president must be elected by the people for reasons of democratic legitimacy. None of these solutions would be consistent with the choice of a parliamentary system as advocated herein.

The presidential office envisaged by the framers of the Constitution resembles in some way the office of a president in a parliamentary state. In Germany for example,[195] the federal president (*Bundespresident*) is not elected by the people nor by the federal Parliament, but is elected for a renewable five-year term by a majority of a convention consisting of an equal number of members of the Bundestag and members elected by the parliaments of the Länder.[196] His or her function consists primarily in representing the federation in its international relations and concluding treaties with foreign states with the approval of the appropriate legislative body.[197] He or she has other, mostly ceremonial, functions as well.[198]

What the office of president of the European Council will look like when it is created after the adoption of the draft Constitution will depend very much on the personality of the first incumbent. Although the office was initially, in the heading above Article I-21, called "the European Council Chair" in a rather diminutive fashion [later amended to read "the European Council President," now above Article I-22], the text of Article I-21 (2) [now I-22 (2)] was (and still is) flexible enough for the president to make his or her position a significant one. The rotating presidency of the European Council already currently benefits from the prestige that the Council has bestowed upon itself, and takes a

[195] The German type of presidency is not the only presidential model that is compatible with a parliamentary system. For example, both Ireland and Austria have a president who is elected by the people but lacks the powers that directly elected presidents normally have. See Sartori, n. 29 above, 83 and 126. In addition, the president of Poland is elected by the people to represent the state in foreign affairs, serve as the supreme commander of the armed forces, exercise a right of legislative initiative, and sign or refuse to sign bills. On paper the Polish presidency is closer to a semi-presidential system, similar to the French system, but it seems it will evolve over the years into a presidency with limited powers, as the Finnish presidency has done. See Ania Van Der Meer-Paszkowska, in Elgie, n. 47 above, 170–92.

[196] Article 54 of the German Basic Law.

[197] Article 59 of the German Basic Law.

[198] In the *New York Times* of March 5, 2004, the function of a parliamentary president is correctly described by Richard Bernstein as "a largely ceremonial post but one that is seen in this country [Germany] to have a great deal of moral authority to influence the nature of public discourse" (A4).

prominent role at summit meetings, where all important political decisions have been made during the last two or three decades. It is more than likely that, when the president of the European Council is appointed for a longer term, he or she will not only take over that role, but will also be able to develop it further and give it more visibility. However, this would not turn the Union into a semi-presidential system, as in France, where the popularly elected president clearly holds the supreme political office, particularly during periods of "non-cohabitation."

V. CONCLUSIONS

In this chapter we have examined which form of government would be the most appropriate for the European Union. Though this is not a question for the immediate future, it may nevertheless help to have a blueprint in mind for how the Union might or should develop.

The chapter began with a brief comparison of four different forms of government. First, I compared the British parliamentary system to the American presidential system. Though they both have a one-party executive government, they have little else in common. The British system is a unitary system and a monarchy, and it has no written constitution and no constitutional court. The American system, on the other hand, is a federal republic, and it has a constitution and a powerful Supreme Court. The American system is characterized by its separation of powers, while the British system is characterized by the sovereignty of Parliament. Typical for a parliamentary system, the British prime minister and his or her cabinet are collectively and individually accountable to Parliament, and can be forced by Parliament to resign. In the United States, the popularly elected president and his or her appointed cabinet are not dependent on Congress for remaining in power.

Next I compared the German variant of parliamentary democracy to the French variant of presidential democracy. The French 1958 Constitution of the Fifth Republic, written after the May 1958 "coup" of the weak Fourth Republic, installed a form of semi-presidentialism. The 1958 Constitution was written to suit General de Gaulle, whom the military called to power. At first the Constitution provided for the president to be elected by a limited number of electors, but amendments in 1962 provided for the president to be directly elected by the people. The new constitution also reduced Parliament's legislative powers and placed significant restrictions on its power to dismiss the government, as this power was the source of the weakness of the governments of the Third and Fourth Republics. The resulting system is semi-presidential: it is presidential in that it confers far-reaching powers on the elected president, who cannot be ousted by Parliament, but it is only semi-presidential in that it also entails a prime minister who acts with the approval of Parliament. Under such a system, when a majority of MPs belong to political parties that do not support the president, the prime minister takes de facto precedence over the president, except in some matters that the Constitution delegates to the president, such as foreign policy and national defense.

In contrast, the 1949 German Basic Law installed a parliamentary regime with a chancellor who leads his cabinet in much the same way as the British prime minister. Like the British prime minister, the chancellor must have the confidence of Parliament to continue in office, as Parliament can ask the chancellor and his or her cabinet to resign. There are, however, important differences between the German and British parliamentary regimes. First, Parliament can only oust the German chancellor if it immediately selects a successor. This device, called a "constructive vote of no confidence," strengthens the chancellor's position considerably, as it is more difficult for a majority in Parliament to agree on a new chancellor than it is to simply agree that the old chancellor must withdraw. Secondly, the German system is basically a multiparty government, which makes it dependent on good relationships between the parties supporting the government, but which also makes it more difficult for a majority in Parliament to agree on a new chancellor in case of a constructive vote of no confidence.

After this survey of constitutional systems, I then examined them from a viewpoint of comparative political science. In that respect, the British and French systems are strongly majoritarian, whereas the German and American systems are less majoritarian and more consensus-minded. A system is majoritarian, in Arend Lijphart's terms, when "the majority of people" decide what is good for them, whereas it is consensual when "as many people as possible" make those decisions. Lijphart's classification of the United States as less majoritarian than Britain is somewhat confusing. Presidential systems are, by nature, more majoritarian than parliamentary because they concentrate a great deal of power in the hands of a president who is not dependent on a parliament (or is less so than an executive in a parliamentary system). This is only so, however, when the only characteristics taken into account are those that relate to the arrangement of executive power. Lijphart's classification takes into account another cluster of characteristics as well, which relates to the arrangement of power between the federal and state levels. Since the U.K. is a highly centralized state (because of devolution, now less than before) and the United States is a federal state, the U.K. ranks highly as a majoritarian system under both clusters of characteristics, while the United States only ranks highly as a majoritarian system under the first cluster. Even in this first cluster, the United States ranks lower than the U.K. because of the power sharing between the president and Congress *and* between the two houses of Congress.

Lijphart uses his classification of thirty-six democratic countries to test the conventional wisdom, according to which majoritarian democracies are more prone to decision making than consensual democracies, while consensual democracies are more responsive to minority groups and minority interests. In his analysis, based on quantifiable data, he finds that the conventional wisdom is wrong as to the first proposition, but is correct as to the second. In other words, the decisional power of one-party (majoritarian) governments is not superior to that of multiparty (consensus) governments, but consensus democracies are more responsive democracies in that they engage more segments of the population in the decision-making process.

In some ways Lijphart's analysis runs parallel to an analysis of presidentialism versus parliamentarism carried out by Giovanni Sartori. Taking into account the position of the prime minister in a parliamentary system, Sartori distinguishes between three forms of parliamentarism. These are systems where the prime minister is a "first above unequals," as in the Westminster system; systems where the head of government is a "first among unequals," as in the German system; and systems where the prime minister is a "first among equals." Heads of government of the first kind are strong, particularly when they serve in a one-party government, because they are also the leader of the party that supports the government and holds the majority in parliament. This gives such a leader a free hand in picking and firing cabinet ministers, but this leader cannot easily be removed by a parliament that is dominated by his or her own party. In the second kind of parliamentary system, which normally occurs with a multiparty government, the head of government is less able to unseat fellow ministers but can only be removed him- or herself by a "constructive vote of no confidence," when the parties in government succeed in agreeing on the name of a successor. In the third kind of parliamentary system, the head of government who is not the head of the dominant political party and his or her cabinet both fall when the party leaders of the coalition no longer agree to support the government, with the result that those parties' representatives in parliament withdraw their support by a mere vote of no confidence. The distinction is not always clear in practice, but it allows us to make a choice in theory. That choice is between the two former types, as the third type entails too much instability (as experiences in France with the Third and Fourth Republics and in Germany with the Weimar Republic have shown). As for these two types, the second one is preferable in a polity characterized by a heterogeneous political culture, which needs a consensus-based democracy and, therefore, a system of proportional representation to involve several political parties in government.

These analyses lead to the questions of 1) whether a presidential form of government is more appropriate than a parliamentary one, and 2) whether pure presidentialism (that is, a system in which the president is both head of state and head of government, as in the United States) is better than semi-presidentialism (that is, a system in which these two functions are largely separated, as in France), and 3) whether mixed forms of parliamentarism of the first and second "Sartorian" kind are better forms of government than pure parliamentarism (that is, party- and assembly-driven parliamentarism) or mixed parliamentarism of the third "Sartorian" kind.

In the analysis of leading political scientists, pure presidentialism has only been successful in the United States, and it has failed in most countries that have emulated the American model, including those in Latin America and Eastern Europe. Several reasons are given to explain this proposition. First, the "dual legitimacy" that characterizes a presidential system contains no "dead-lock-breaking" devices when a conflict between the two elected actors, president and parliament, comes to loggerheads. Second, the price a presidential system pays for stability is "rigidity" and "unaccountability": a leader who has lost the confidence of his or her own party or constituency cannot be replaced by someone better qualified, and cannot be held to account, especially when he or she is in the last term of his or her mandate and therefore cannot be reelected. Third, a presidential system is ambiguous in that it combines the function of head of state and head of government in one person. This dichotomy is of a nature to alienate a large number of citizens when a president makes controversial decisions or is seen to act in a partisan way. According to some political scientists, such as Giovanni Sartori, these drawbacks can be reduced, if not eliminated, by adopting a semi-presidential system like the French system. Others believe, however, correctly in my view, that the French system is far too delicate to be emulated in more divided countries.

As for parliamentarian systems, "mixed" systems are certainly better than pure parliamentarian systems for reasons of stability, as mentioned above. However, among the "mixed" parliamentary systems, the less majoritarian, more consensual types are better adapted to govern heterogeneous societies because they are more capable of engaging diverse groups of the population in the political decision-making process. Typical for consensual democracies is an electoral system in which proportional representation prevails, leading to a multiparty system that should be kept within limits, though, in order to avoid a rampant proliferation of political parties. Such a proliferation would make the formation of a stable government a great deal more difficult than necessary. For these reasons also, a "first among unequals" form of parliamentarism should be preferred above a "first among equals" form.

In light of the foregoing, it should be clear that the European Union, which is a highly heterogeneous polity, is best served by a "consensus" system with a strong executive. Thus, a non-majoritarian, multiparty parliamentarian system of the second Sartorian type with an electoral system of proportional representation would be appropriate; to avoid proliferation, however, it should not be proportional in the extreme. In concrete terms, this is a system in which the head of the Union is not popularly elected (or, if the head were popularly elected, as for example in Ireland, then he or she would have no real powers), and in which the head of the executive is accountable to an elected parliament that can remove him or her, but only by a constructive vote of no confidence.

Before explaining how such a system can be put in place in the Union, I examined two specific issues, namely the significance of bicameralism and the role of political parties. Bicameralism is essential in a system such as that of the European Union, which is a union of both Member States *and* peoples and therefore needs a system in which both the states and the people can be represented in an upper and lower house, respectively. Setting aside the delicate discussion of whether the Council of Ministers is already one of two legislative houses, one is struck by the resemblance, in both organization and operation, between the EU Council of Ministers and, for instance, the German Bundesrat. The Council is currently an assembly of ministers from the twenty-five Member States, while the Bundesrat is an assembly in which, since unification of East and West Germany, sixteen Länder are represented. There is a major difference between the two assemblies, however. The Council of Ministers is the most prominent part of the Union's legislative branch with full legislative powers, whereas the directly elected European Parliament has only limited legislative powers under the first pillar and almost no powers under the second and third pillars. In the Federal Republic of Germany the reverse is true: the Bundestag, which is directly elected by the people, has full legislative powers, whereas the Bundesrat participates in the legislative process at the federal level only when legislation that directly affects the interests of the component states is passed. The difference is essential as it means that, in the Union, the legislative process is still very much under the control of the Member States, which want their interests to be represented. The system could be detrimental to the interests of the Union as a whole, were it not that, under the first (and still most important) pillar, the legislative process is steered by the Commission because of that institution's (monopoly) right of legislative proposal, and is subject to an obligation of loyalty on behalf of all institutions and Member States.

Political parties are another important issue, especially if the Union system were to be transformed into a parliamentarian type of democracy, such as those operating currently in most of the Member States. In those states political parties play a crucial role in the selection of political leaders, as well as in the formation of a new government after parliamentary elections have been held and the formulation of citizen goals for the new government to pursue. Political parties operating at the European level, the so-called "Euro-parties," do not yet play that role. Moreover, these Euro-parties currently act as conglomerates of national parties with insufficient party identity and little party autonomy. In order to achieve these goals, these political parties must identify themselves with distinctive, and divisive, issues around which large citizen groups can be assembled. The most prominent of these issues at the European level are the "socioeconomic" dimension, the "integration versus intergovernmental" dimension, the "cultural-ethnic/linguistic" dimension, and the "pro-environment and basic citizen participation" dimension. At the level of the Member States, but also at the European level, these dimensions are responsible for the emergence of larger or smaller political parties. In the Member States, these parties derive their power, and electoral attraction, from their involvement in the formation of governments, the selection of political leaders, and the formulation of political options that will guide the new government's actions once it has been formed by political parties representing a majority in parliament. If that system were transplanted to the Union, it would most likely lead to an enhanced European awareness among voters of issues that affect the Union, and to a larger involvement of citizens in the European political process.

In conclusion, a European democratic government would encompass the following elements: 1) an elected parliament, as exists already, with steadily increasing legislative powers exercised on a par with the Council of Ministers, and with political parties involved in the selection of the Commission president and Commission members; 2) a multiparty "consensus" government, relying upon the Commission—with a strong head of government, the Commission president—which, as now, would retain a right of legislative initiative to preserve the Union interest in the Union's decisional process; 3) a Commission that is fully accountable to Parliament, which would control the Commission's appointment and operational activities, and would be able to make it resign with a constructive vote of no confidence; 4) a Council of Ministers that is held accountable to the Union citizens (and residents) by increasing the transparency of its legislative action, and is possibly made accountable to the national parliaments by extending the supervisory powers of the existing Conference of European Affairs Committees (COSAC); and 5) a European Council that remains the driving force behind the political process of European integration, with a president elected by the Council but not directly by the people.

If adopted, the draft Constitution would constitute a further step in this process of "parliamentarization" of the Union's political structure, but it would not yet be the final stage in transforming the Union into a fully democratic polity of states and peoples, as it does not address all of the aforementioned elements.

Epilogue

At the Intergovernmental Conference (IGC) meeting held in Brussels on June 17 and 18, 2004, the heads of state or government of the twenty-five Member States gave their assent to the text of the draft Treaty Establishing a Constitution for Europe. The draft then approved by the Member State representatives resembles by and large the draft prepared by the European Convention,[1] but it nevertheless contains, besides a large number of textual improvements, several substantive amendments, some of which relate to important institutional issues discussed in the previous chapters and mentioned below. After the June 2004 IGC, legal and linguistic experts started work on the amended text with a view to making it legally accurate and internally consistent, and translating it correctly in all the official languages of the European Union. As a result, a consolidated text was published on October 13, 2004,[2] that, under the Dutch presidency, was solemnly signed by the heads of state or government assembled in Rome on October 29, 2004. This final text has now been submitted to the Member States for ratification in accordance with their respective constitutional requirements (parliamentary approval or referenda). In addition to the

[1] According to the President of the Convention, Valéry Giscard d'Estaing, more than 90 percent of the Convention draft ended up in the final draft Constitution: "Vive la Constitution, vive l'Europe," *Le Monde* of July 10, 2004, as reported (and put in proper perspective) in the Editorial Comments, "A Constitution for Europe," 41 *CMLRev.*, 2004, 899–907, 899.

[2] Document CIG 87/1/04, REV 1. See also Introduction, n. 4. The consolidated draft can be consulted at http://www.europa.eu.int/constitution/constitution_en.htm. As pointed out in the Introduction, p. 5, the text of the four parts of the draft Constitutional Treaty has been continuously renumbered (retaining, however, the roman numerals referring to the four parts alongside the arabic article numbers) from Article I-1 to Article IV-448.

states that are legally bound under their national constitutions to do so, several other Member States have voiced their intention to hold referenda on the adoption of the treaty. If all goes well, the ratification procedure will be completed in the course of 2006 and the treaty will enter into effect in 2006/2007.

With the approval of an amended version of the draft Treaty on June 18, 2004, and the signing of the consolidated text on October 29, 2004, the Member States have overcome the third hurdle for the entry into force of the Constitution. The first hurdle consisted of the drawing up of a draft Treaty by the European Convention, which achieved a broad consensus at the Convention's plenary session on June 13, 2003. The second hurdle was surmounted on June 20, 2003, when the Member States' heads of state or government assembled in Thessaloniki solemnly accepted the Convention draft as a valid basis for discussion by the Member States. As noted in chapter 6,[3] that discussion started in October 2003, but it came to an abrupt end at the IGC meeting of December 12, 2003, in Rome. The constitutional process might have been stopped in its tracks, if the Irish presidency had not been able during the first half of 2004 to reach acceptable compromises on all pending matters, either before or at the June 18, 2004 IGC meeting—thus making it possible for the Treaty Establishing a Constitution for Europe to be signed in Rome, under Dutch presidency, on October 29, 2004.[4] The third hurdle now having been overcome, the fourth and most formidable hurdle remains: the ratification of the Constitutional Treaty by all twenty-five Member States.

Substantive Changes

Compromises come at a price. They have led to a number of amendments of the initial draft of the constitution, some of which are of particular importance within the context of this book, namely the changes made to Articles I-25 [now Article I-26] and I-26 [now Article I-27] relating to the European Commission and its president and those made to Article I-24 [new Article I-25] relating to the definition of qualified majority voting (QMV).

a) Composition of the Commission and appointment of its president
As to the composition of the Commission, the Member States were quick to agree that Article I-25 [now Article I-26] had to be amended. The article

---

[3] At pp. 261–62 and 308.
[4] On the reasons for the breakdown of the December 2003 meeting in Rome under the Italian presidency, see the editorial comments in *CMLRev.*, 2004, 1–4. On the last-minute efforts of the Irish presidency to achieve a blueprint for agreement for the June 2004 meeting in Brussels, see David Cronin and Martin Banks, "Irish Plan to Pave Way for Constitution," *European Voice*, June 17–23, 2004, 3.

provided for the appointment, for a term of five years, of thirteen so-called "European commissioners" (in addition to the president and the minister for foreign affairs), the Member States not having a European commissioner to be represented by non-voting commissioners. Under the amended version of Article I-25 (5) and (6) [now Article I-26 (5) and (6)], the Commission will again, as it currently does, consist of one commissioner per Member State (including the president and the foreign affairs minister). However, from the end of the term of the first Commission appointed after the entry into force of the Constitution, "the Commission shall consist of a number of members . . . corresponding to two thirds of the number of Member States, unless the European Council, acting unanimously, decides to alter this figure." These commissioners "shall be selected among the nationals of the Member States on the basis of a system of equal rotation between the Member States."[5]

The change implies not only that the controversial distinction between European voting commissioners and non-voting commissioners has been definitively set aside, but also that, as is currently the case (Article 214 (2) EC), each commissioner will again be proposed by the Member State entitled to have a commissioner (see Article I-26 [2] [now I-27 (2)] of the draft Constitution, as amended). By contrast, under the initial text of Article I-26 (2) as prepared by the Convention, each Member State entitled to have a commissioner would establish a list of three persons from whom the president-elect would choose one.[6]

Article I-26 [now Article I-27] on the appointment of the president of the Commission also underwent an important change. In fact, for the appointment of the president and the appointment, subsequently, of the other commissioners, three formulas have been used or considered. According to the first, currently retained in Article 214 EC, the Council, composed of heads of state or government and acting by a qualified majority, nominates the person it intends to appoint as president and submits the nomination to the approval of the European Parliament. When this approval is obtained, the Council, acting by a qualified majority and by common accord with the nominee for president, *adopts* the list of the other persons whom it intends to appoint as

---

[5] The new system will, at best, enter into effect on November 1, 2014. See p. 290. The amendment does not prevent larger Member States, once the transitional period expires, from not having a national on the incumbent Commission. But see in that context a new declaration concerning Article I-25 [now Article I-26] that emphasizes the need for the Commission to "liaise closely" with all Member States and take into account the "political, social and economic realities in all Member States, including those which have no national serving as Member of the Commission," and states that the position of the latter should be "addressed by appropriate organisational arrangements."

[6] See, on all these points, chapter 6, pp. 289–90 and 293.

commissioners, drawn up *in accordance with* the proposals made by each
Member State. The full list of president and commissioners is then submitted
to the approval of the Parliament. If approval of the Commission as a body is
obtained, the president and the other commissioners will be appointed by the
Council acting again through a qualified majority. It is already current practice, under the formula as it is now applied, that, after his or her approval by
Parliament, the nominated (but not yet appointed) Commission president
will allocate portfolios among the nominated (but not yet appointed) commissioners, and that Parliament, before deciding to approve or reject the full
Commission, will screen the proposed commissioners in relation to the portfolio suggested for each of them by the nominated president.

Under the second formula, as proposed in Article I-26 of the initial draft
Constitution, the European Council of heads of state or government, deciding
by qualified majority and taking into account the elections to the European
Parliament, "shall put to the Parliament its proposed candidate for the presidency of the Commission." If Parliament does not elect this candidate by a
majority of its members, the Council shall within one month put forward a
new candidate. When the candidate is elected by Parliament, the president-
elect shall then *select* the other commissioners (thirteen under the initial draft;
see above) from the lists of *three* persons established by each Member State.
The full list of nominees, including the president-elect, shall then "be submitted collectively to a vote of approval by the European Parliament." Under
the initial draft, it was not provided, probably inadvertently, that after the approval by Parliament the full Commission would be appointed by the European Council. That said, under this formula, as under the first, it will be the
responsibility of the president-elect to allocate the portfolios to the commissioners selected by him or her, and for the Parliament to screen the candidate
commissioners.

Under the third formula, retained in Article I-26 [now Article I-27] of the
draft Constitution as amended by the June 2004 IGC, the second formula is
modified, and brought in line with the currently applicable (first) formula, on
two important points: 1) it would be the responsibility of the European Council, by common accord with the president-elect, to *adopt* the list of the other
commissioners, on the basis, again, of the suggestions made by Member States
entitled to have a commissioner; and 2) after the approval of the full list by the
European Parliament, the Commission (including its president and the minister for foreign affairs) will be appointed by the European Council, acting by a
qualified majority. As a result of these changes, the Member States will remain
fully involved, as they currently are, in the selection and appointment of all

members of the Commission.[7] That is not a fortunate development, as we will see below.

b) Redefining qualified majority voting, and some other changes

Another important change agreed at the June 2004 IGC meeting concerns the redefinition of qualified majority voting in Article I-24 [now Article I-25]. As was already mentioned,[8] under the amended version of the draft Constitution a qualified majority shall be defined (as of November 1, 2009) "as at least 55% of the members of the Council, comprising at least fifteen of them and representing Member States comprising at least 65% of the population of the Union." Moreover, "[a] blocking minority must include at least four Council members, failing which the qualified majority shall be deemed attained" (Article I-24 [1], as amended; now Article I-25 [1]). By derogation, "when the Council is not acting on a proposal from the Commission [as it is normally required to do] or from the Union Minister for Foreign Affairs," a qualified majority will be even more difficult to attain: "at least 72% of the members of the Council, representing Member States comprising at least 65% of the population of the Union" is then required (Article I-24 [2], now Article I-25 [2]).[9] The effect of the blocking minority requirement under paragraph 1 of Article I-24 [now Article 25]—no such requirement applies under paragraph 2—is that three of the six largest countries in terms of population, representing more than 35 percent of the Union's population, cannot block a decision to be made by QMV without the help of at least one other (large, medium, or small) Member State.[10]

---

[7] On a less important point: the amended version of Article I-26 [now Article I-27] clarifies that the Commission president's power, under paragraph 3 of that article, to ask an individual commissioner to resign encompasses the minister for foreign affairs. If the president requests the minister's resignation as a member (and vice president) of the Commission, the minister shall resign "in accordance with the procedure set out in Article I-27 (1) [now Article I-28 (1)]." Under that article, the European Council, acting by qualified majority, may "end [the minister's] tenure." The clarification is important, as it highlights the possibility for the Commission president to put an end to a conflict between him or her and the minister for foreign affairs. On the delicate position of the foreign minister, see chapter 6, pp. 299–300.

[8] Chapter 6, p. 284, n. 99.

[9] This is mainly the case in Justice and Home Affairs when the Council acts on an initiative from the Member States, or in the field of Common Foreign and Security Policy matters when the Council acts on its own initiative.

[10] Currently the Union's population totals 451 million. The six largest Member States in terms of population are Germany (82.5 million), the U.K. (60.5 million), France (60.4 million), Italy (58.2 million), Spain (41.1 million) and Poland (38.2 million).

The effect of the rule will, however, be mitigated by a mechanism reminiscent of the 1994 Ioannina compromise. If members of the Council representing at least three-quarters of the population or the number of States needed to constitute a blocking minority "indicate their opposition to the Council adopting an act by qualified majority," the Council shall do all it can, "within a reasonable time and without prejudicing obligatory time limits laid down by Union law," to reach a wider measure of agreement. The mechanism is set out in an IGC declaration, but is to be embodied in a legally binding European decision adopted by the Council on the day the Constitution enters into effect.[11]

Apart from the above, many other changes have been made in form or substance, several of which pertain to institutional matters discussed in this book. With respect to substance, for example, Article I-19 [now Article I-20] increases the maximum number of members of the European Parliament from 736 to 750 and raises the minimum threshold per Member State from four to six members. The amendment to this provision also introduces a ceiling of ninety-six seats for the largest Member State (Germany). Furthermore, as was mentioned in chapter 6, in Article I-23 [now Article I-24], the controversial configuration of the Legislative and General Affairs Council of Ministers is abolished[12] and replaced by a more elegant arrangement under which each Council meeting, in whatever configuration, will be divided into two parts, one for legislative acts, another for non-legislative activities. A change in form that is worth mentioning concerns the heading of Article I-21 relating to the president of the European Council. This president is no longer named "European Council Chair" but rather "European Council President."[13]

It would take too long to discuss all the additional changes; it may suffice to warn the reader that many textual improvements have been made in the amended IGC draft, some of which affect the wording of provisions of the initial Convention draft that have been quoted in this book. Moreover, as mentioned in the Introduction,[14] in the final draft solemnly signed in Rome on October 29, 2004, by the Heads of State or Government, the articles as amended at the June

---

[11] On this point see A.A., Editorial "Ireland's qualified success" 29 *ELRev,* 2004, 581–82. The editorial contains a very useful overview of the successive qualified majority formulas in effect before November 1, 2004, and to be in effect after that date until November 1, 2009, and thereafter. The three formulas are compared from a viewpoint of the ease or difficulty of mustering a qualified majority. On the 1994 Ioannina compromise, see Editorial Comments, 31 *CMLRev,* 1994, 453–57.

[12] See chapter 6, p. 298.

[13] A name corresponding better to the function, as mentioned in chapter 6, p. 296.

[14] See Introduction, p. 5.

18, 2004, IGC meeting have been numbered continuously over the four parts, but with, for each part, the roman numerals alongside the arabic article numbers. To make it easier for the reader to locate the articles quoted in this book in the renumbered final version of the constitutional treaty, the new numbers have been added between square brackets throughout the book.

The Search for a New President of the Commission and the Appointment of a New Commission.

The agreement on the amended draft Constitution at the June 18, 2004, IGC meeting was overshadowed by the acrimony surrounding the appointment of a new president of the Commission, just as the signing of the final text of the Constitution in Rome on October 29, 2004, was overshadowed by the no less acrimonious clash between the new president and a majority in Parliament concerning the appointment of the new Commission. I will briefly describe these events.

Starting November 1, 2004, the new Commission president had to succeed the former president, Romano Prodi, for a period of five years. In this context, substantial disagreement came to light between the French and German political leaders, President Jacques Chirac and Chancellor Gerhard Schröder, and the British prime minister Tony Blair. The former favored the candidacy of the Belgian prime minister Guy Verhofstadt, while the latter opposed the appointment of Mr. Verhofstadt, considering him, if not too much in favor of European integration, then at least to have been too much against the Anglo-American policy in Iraq. Moreover, the center-right EPP-ED party, which before and after the June 2004 parliamentary elections was and remains the largest political party in the European Parliament, insisted upon the appointment of a Commission president from its own ranks. This would have caused no difficulties if the Luxembourg prime minister Jean-Claude Juncker, a member of the EPP-ED who had the support of all his colleagues, had not refused to accept the job in spite of intense behind-the-scenes pressure. Finally, unanimous agreement was reached on the appointment of José Manuel Barroso, the Portuguese prime minister, also a member of EPP-ED, whose nomination was confirmed by the heads of state or government on June 30, 2004, and later approved by the European Parliament in conformity with Article 214 (2) EC.[15]

[15] On the developments leading to the proposal of Mr. Barroso's candidacy, see Dana Spinant, "High-profile 'Withdrawals' Leave President's Post Open," *European Voice*, June 24–30, 2004, 16. José Manuel Barroso was not well known outside Portugal, except for the fact that he organized a meeting before the Iraq war with President George W. Bush and his European allies in the Azores. This factor was responsible for

The approval of José Barroso's nomination by Parliament remained an uncertainty until the last minute as, for a long time, he could rely only on the support of the EPP-ED, having 276 seats in the newly elected Parliament. The next two largest parties, the socialists and the liberals, had refused to commit themselves as a group and invited Mr. Barroso to appear before them in the week before Parliament's vote, which was scheduled to take place on July 22, 2004. On that date and after the parliamentary hearing, Mr. Barroso obtained a comfortable majority of 413 votes in favor, 251 MEPs voting against, 44 members abstaining. The EPP-ED, with 267 members present, voted *en bloc* for Barroso, the remaining 146 votes coming from other political parties. As a result, and in conformity with Article 214 (2) EC, José Manuel Barroso was called upon to proceed with the composition of the Commission, that is, with the allocation of portfolios to the persons proposed by each of the Member States, and confirmed by the Council, as members of the new Commission.

Allocating portfolios among persons proposed by Member States is always a delicate transaction, particularly so because the large Member States expect their candidate to obtain an influential position within the new Commission, and therefore to be allotted an important portfolio. The selection process became extremely difficult, however, because the candidate proposed by the Italian prime minister Berlusconi, Rocco Buttiglione, a devout Catholic, had during the parliamentary hearing outraged a majority in the assembly with controversial comments on homosexuality and women. The problem was exacerbated by the fact that Mr. Barosso had assigned to Mr. Buttiglione, before the latter's unfortunate statements, the portfolio of justice, freedom, and security. In these circumstances, it was clear that a majority in parliament, consisting mainly of the same parties that had opposed Mr. Barosso's own election, was going to refuse approval of the full commission—in the absence of a provision in the treaty that would allow Parliament to reject one individual candidate commissioner.

The problem could have been avoided in several ways: Rocco Buttiglione could have withdrawn his candidacy; prime minister Silvio Berlusconi could have designated a new candidate, asking Mr. Buttiglione to withdraw; and president-designate Barroso could have allotted another portfolio to Buttiglione. None of this happened, Mr. Barroso offering only to set up a committee to monitor civil rights, apparently confident this would suffice to persuade Parliament to approve his Commission as a whole. That was clearly a miscalculation, as he had to concede the morning of the vote scheduled for October

considerable uncertainty as to whether his designation would be endorsed, as required, by a simple majority of votes cast in the European Parliament.

27, when he asked Parliament to postpone its decision.[16] The following day, Rocco Buttiglione withdrew his candidacy and, within a week, the Italian prime minister had put forward the name of a new candidate: his foreign minister, Franco Frattini. That, however, was not the end of the story, since other commissioners had also been criticized at the parliamentary hearings, mainly for reasons of insufficient expertise or conflict of interest. This finally resulted in the replacement of one more commissioner and some reshuffling in the allotment of portfolios.[17] In the end, the revised version of Barroso's Commission was approved by Parliament on November 18, 2004, 449 members voting in favor, 149 against, and 134 abstaining or remaining absent.

The nomination of the new Commission president and the composition of the new Commission bring us back to the point discussed in chapter 7, namely, whether it would not be appropriate to reform the selection procedure by putting the responsibility of the formation of the new Commission and its president in the hands of political parties, as is the case in parliamentary democracies (which most EU Member States are), rather than in the hands of the Member States in Council. As pointed out in chapter 7,[18] this would imply that the European Council, when putting forth its proposed candidate for the presidency of the Commission, should take "into account the elections to the European Parliament," as is prescribed in Article I-26 (1) [now Article I-27 (1)] of the draft Constitution (in its original *and* amended versions). It would mean, in effect, that the president of the European Council asks the leader of the largest political party (either its president or the leader of that party's delegation in the European Parliament) to form a new Commission that has the support of a majority in Parliament. After the June 2004 elections, none of the political parties represented in Parliament would be able to obtain such a majority (requiring 367 out of 732 seats) without the support of one or more of the other parties.[19]

The result attained would not be that different from the present situation.

---

[16] For an assessment of the whole episode, see "The European Commission. A Knight in Tarnished Armour," *The Economist*, October 30–November 5, 2004, 35–36.

[17] See further Martin Banks and David Cronin, *European Voice*, October 28–November 3, 1, and Martin Banks, *European Voice*, November 18–24, 2.

[18] At pp. 350ff.

[19] On the distribution of the 732 seats among the Euro-parties represented in the Parliament, elected in June 2004, see the European Parliament's site http://www.europarl. eu.int/facts/1_3_1_en.htm. The political leader asked to form the new Commission should seek to compose the Commission so as "to reflect satisfactorily the demographic and geographical range of all the Member States of the Union": thus Article I-25 [now I-26] (6) (b)] of the amended (July 2004 IGC) draft Constitution, corresponding to Article I-25 (3) (b) of the original version. See further chapter 7, p. 351, n. 147.

The Commission already operates de facto as a multiparty executive, as the commissioners other than the president are proposed by the individual Member State governments and therefore reflect different political perspectives. One notable difference, however, would be that, under the new political party–driven system, the political parties that are not part of the parliamentary majority supporting the incumbent Commission would not be represented on the Commission (unless the political leader forming the Commission would, of his or her own initiative, include some representatives from these parties in the Commission).[20] But that would not prevent these "non-coalition" parties—depending on the outcome of the national elections in the twenty-five Member States—from being represented on the Council of (national) Ministers that is currently, and undoubtedly for a long time to come, the most prominent part of the Union's legislative and policy-making branch. Furthermore, the adoption of such a new political party–driven system would probably make alliances between the existing political parties have a larger impact on the designation of the European executive. It might also lead to a regrouping of the existing political parties around divisive pan-European issues, which would give them a more distinctive image and make them more attractive to large segments of the electorate.[21]

Yet the crucial advantage of the "new" system would be that it is far more democratically legitimated than the current one, as it would involve the electorate, through transnational political parties, in choosing the Commission president and the other commissioners and influencing the policies that the Union's executive government, that is, the Commission, would pursue during its term in office.[22] Moreover, it would bring to an end the secretive and tangled way in which the head of the EU executive is currently appointed.[23] This un-

[20] So as to make the Commission reflect the ideological range of all Member States as well. If repeated by later political leaders, the initiative could become a constitutional tradition.

[21] See chapter 7, pp. 342–43 and 354ff. This would not necessarily result in less European awareness, all of the major Euro-parties being, on the whole, rather integration-minded. Indeed, in the newly elected European Parliament the group of Euro-sceptics called Independence and Democracy have no more than thirty-one seats. The alliance is more a marriage of convenience than a real group; it consists mainly of twelve U.K. Independence Party members and ten members of the pro-life Polish Catholic League of Families. See "Eurosceptics: 'We Will Be the Trojan Horse against Constitution,'" *European Voice*, July 1–7, 2004, 6.

[22] See further chapter 7, pp. 353–54. See also John Wyles, "Time to Admit That the European Commission *Is* a Political Animal," *European Voice*, June 24–30, 2004, 12.

[23] See Dana Spinant, "No Defence for Secretive Way of Choosing Commission Chief," *European Voice*, June 17–23, 2004, 12.

satisfactory situation results from the fact that the two institutions instrumental in the appointment of the president and the members of the new Commission, Council and Parliament, are currently focused too much on their own political position: the Council wants to retain its strong involvement in the designation of the Commission and to have the last word; Parliament wants to reinforce its present position and not to let pass an occasion to show that it cannot be ignored in the selection process. Considering the disagreements that normally exist in the Council between Member State representatives and in Parliament between political factions, this focus on one's own political position is scarcely the best way to ensure that the best candidates are selected for president and members of the Commission.

Obviously, to involve the electorate in the appointment procedure, and thus to increase the procedure's democratic legitimacy, is not a matter that will be decided in the years (or even decades) to come. In the meantime, other, less radical changes should be envisaged to improve the current procedure. As pointed out by political commentator Dana Spinant, a more civilized way than the current one would be for the heads of state and government to hand over to the Parliament a shortlist of three candidates for president whom the assembly would cross-examine in specialized committees and in plenary and perhaps submit to a "face-off presidential debate" before casting its vote.[24] That solution could be combined with the proposal contained in the initial version of Article I-26 of the draft constitution, according to which each Member State should propose more than one candidate for the post of commissioner (and assure that on its list candidates of both genders would be represented)—a proposal which, unfortunately, has not been retained in Article I-26 [now Article I-27] of the final draft (see above, pp. 378–79). This solution would give more leeway to both the European Council and Parliament to appoint the best candidates for the job of president and commissioners. If the proposal had been in effect, it would probably have obviated the unfortunate circumstances under which the appointment of President Barroso and the members of his Commission was taking place.

The Union in the Wider World

In an earlier draft of this book I had included an additional chapter on the European Union in the wider world. In it I described the external competences that the Union currently enjoys under the present three-pillar structure, and those that it will enjoy when the draft Constitution is adopted. I also

---

[24] Ibid., quoting James Searles, a partner with the Washington law firm Steptoe and Johnson.

attempted to explain and assess some basic differences in attitudes toward international law between the European Union (and Europe as a whole) and the United States (for example, regarding the preemptive use of force in international relations[25] and the protection of human rights in the war on terrorism).[26] To be sure, these (and other) differences already existed before the September 11, 2001, terrorist attacks and the ensuing war in Iraq,[27] but, as a result of these events, their significance has dramatically increased. Given the necessity to keep the book to a manageable length, I reluctantly decided not to include the chapter.

Another international issue facing the EU that I can only briefly mention here concerns the way in which the Union sees its relationship with Eastern

[25] As for the use of force, it is clear that the United States is generally less patient with diplomacy than the EU is prepared to be. The more patient attitude of the EU was clearly demonstrated by the unanimous position taken in February 2003 by the (then fifteen) EU Member States, including the U.K., to grant UN weapons inspectors in Iraq more time than the United States was ready to give. However, that did not prevent the EU from accepting that inspections could not continue indefinitely and that the use of force should be considered as an alternative, but only as a last resort. For a discussion of the conclusions reached by the European Council on February 17, 2003, see A.A., editorial, "War-torn," 28 *ELRev.*, 2003, 301–2.

[26] As a result of well-established case law of the European Court of Human Rights, all EU Member States accept that anti-terrorist measures are subject to judicial scrutiny on the part of an independent court when violations of human rights have allegedly occurred. For an overview of the ECtHR's case law with regard to terrorist acts, see Tim Eicke, "Terrorism and Human Rights," 4 *EJML*, 2003, 449–67. In the United States, the matter of judicial scrutiny of anti-terrorist state action by an independent court arose in the case of the indefinite detention of hundreds of suspected foreign foot soldiers of the Taliban at the naval basis at Guantanamo (and a few American Taliban fighters in U.S. military brigs). For a stark criticism, see Johan Steyn, "Guantanamo Bay: The Legal Hole," 53 *International Comparative Law Quarterly*, 2004, 1–15. Lord Steyn is a Lord of Appeal in Ordinary, that is, a member of the Appellate Committee of the House of Lords. But see the judgments of the U.S. Supreme Court rendered in early July 2004, which granted access to court in the case of the American and some foreign detainees: "The Supreme Court and Enemy Combatants: Too Far Say the Judges," *The Economist*, July 3–9, 2004, 41–42.

[27] As pointed out by Robert Kagan in *Of Paradise and Power: America and Europe in the New World Order* (New York: Alfred A. Knopf, 2003), many differences have arisen in the years since the dismantling of the Soviet regime. These differences were poignantly described by Serge Schemann in his review of Kagan's book in the *New York Times Book Review* of March 30, 2002. They relate to issues such as "the Balkans, the environment, the death penalty, bioengineered food, the ABM treaty, the International [Criminal] Court of Justice, the United Nations or how to handle Saddam Hussein" and, most important, the issue of Israeli politics vis-à-vis Palestine.

Europe, and particularly how far it wants to continue its expansion eastward given the uncertainty about where Europe's borders lie.[28] Clearly Romania, Bulgaria, and probably Turkey (the final decision to start negotiations has to be made in December 2004) are next in line, and, when they are ready for it, the former Yugoslavian countries and Albania are next. Yet further enlargement cannot be excluded: Georgia, for example, may one day have a good case, and perhaps Armenia as well. The basic question is whether the Union, starting with Turkey, which comprises a population approaching 70 million, can permit itself, from a viewpoint of manageability, to grow indefinitely into a Union of more than half a billion of people and an enormous range of cultural, religious, demographic, and economic differences. The only viable alternative, in my view, is for the Union to develop "special relationships" with its eastern neighbors, in the first place Russia. This implies, as formulated in Article I-56 [now Article I-57] of the draft Constitution, that the Union's relations with neighboring States would be based on "a special relationship . . . , aiming to establish an area of prosperity and good neighbourliness, founded on the values of the Union and characterized by close and peaceful relations based on cooperation."[29]

As to Russia, the alternative would be in line with the entry of that country into the World Trade Organization (WTO)—an issue that both the EU and Russia are keen to press ahead with. It has been recalled in that respect that, economically, Russia and the EU "are made for each other."[30] Russia is the Union's fifth largest trading partner, after the United States, Switzerland, China, and Japan, with trade in 2002 worth 18 billion euros, and the EU is Russia's main trading partner, accounting for 40 percent of its total trade, cheap energy and fuels alone accounting for more than half of Russia's exports to the EU. WTO membership would bring additional benefits to both parties. For Russia, it would boost economic growth by acting as a catalyst for competition and liberalization in domestic industry and inward investment. From the EU perspective, WTO membership would subject Russia to a wide number of regulations and trade rules, and might bring the country to tackle the problem, essential for EU investment, of poor protection of property rights.[31]

[28] See chapter 1, n. 147.

[29] This may not exactly correspond to Mikhail S. Gorbachev's vision of "a common European house" (see Mark Kesselman and Joel Krieger, *European Politics in Transition*, 3d ed. [Boston: Houghton Mifflin, 1997], 4), but that vision has certainly been overtaken by the Union's 2004 enlargement with eight former communist countries (and before that with East Germany).

[30] On this, see Peter Chapman, "Benefits for All to Be Enjoyed If Russia Can Tie the Knot with WTO," *European Voice*, May 19–26, 2004, 21.

[31] Ibid.

Obviously, how the political relationship between the Union and Russia will develop in the future is ultimately Russia's decision, the country being faced, according to one scholar, with three policy choices: rebuild U.S.-Russian relations, team up with the EU to constitute a counterweight against the United States, or secure its position as a European great power. Probably, it will pursue all three options at the same time.[32] This assumption may be correct in a polarized Atlantic world in which the relations between the United States and the EU would continue to deteriorate and Russia would have to choose which camp it wants to belong to. More likely, however, and also more desirable, is that, with the growth of new and not always democratic superpowers, the United States and the EU will need to remain close allies, whatever their differences, in order to preserve a political and social system that is based on values that they broadly share.[33] Russia may therefore want to pursue a fourth option, contingent upon its own development as a liberal democratic system, which is to associate with both the United States and the EU to strengthen democratic forces in the global world.[34]

Leuven, December 2, 2004

[32] See Eugene D. Mazo, "Clinton, Bush, and Chechnya: Understanding America's Influence on Russia's Deadly Conflict," Stanford Center on Conflict and Negotiation Working Paper Series (2004), with a further reference to Risto E. J. Pentilla, "Russia Eyes a Key Trans-Atlantic Role," *International Herald Tribune*, March 29–30, 2003, 6.

[33] On the need for Europe and the United States to join forces, see also Robert Kagan in his "post–Iraq war" article, "America's Crisis of Legitimacy," *Foreign Affairs*, March/April 2004, 65–87, where he writes, "There are indeed sound reasons for the United States to seek European approval. . . . Europe matters because it and the United States form the heart of the liberal, democratic world. The United States' liberal democratic sensibilities make it difficult, if not impossible, for Americans to ignore the fears, concerns, interests, and demands of their fellows in liberal democracies. U.S. liberalism will naturally drive U.S. foreign policy to seek greater harmony with Europe" (84).

[34] This does not mean that geopolitical competition and rivalry will no longer have a chance to resurge. See Charles A. Kupchan, *The End of the American Era: U.S. Foreign Policy and the Geopolitics of the Twenty-First Century* (New York: Alfred A. Knopf, 2003). European history of the First and Second World Wars teaches the opposite. For an instructive narrative of how World War I—a war of nations—came about, see Michael Howard, "Europe on the Eve of the First World War," in *The Lessons of History* (Oxford: Clarendon Press, 1991), 113–26. On the Second World War—a war of ideologies—see "1945—End of an Era," ibid., 127–38.

Index